Index to
Black Periodicals

1986

G. K. Hall & Co.
70 Lincoln Street, Boston, Massachusetts 02111

This publication is printed on permanent/durable acid-free paper.

Copyright © 1988 by G.K. Hall & Co.
ISBN 0-8161-0471-9
ISSN 0899-6253

Preface

The *Index to Black Periodicals* is an index to Afro-American periodicals of general and scholarly interest. The 1986 volume covers articles in a total of 32 black American journals.

The *Index* formerly appeared under the titles *Index to Periodical Articles By and About Blacks, Index to Periodical Articles By and About Negroes,* and *Index to Selected Periodicals.* G.K. Hall published a ten-year cumulation of the *Index* covering the years 1950-1959 and began publishing the *Index* on an annual basis in 1961. The volumes from 1961 forward were published in conjunction with The Hallie Q. Brown Memorial Library at Central State University in Wilberforce, Ohio; the New York Public Library's Schomburg Collection of Negro Literature and History also participated during the years 1960-1970.

In mid-1984, because of other demands on the resources of the library at Central State University, the library was unable to continue its work on the *Index.* As a result, G.K. Hall has now assumed editorial responsibility for the *Index.* An Advisory Board, composed of librarians and scholars in the field of Black Studies, is now being formed and will begin its work with the 1988 volume.

Suggestions for additional titles may be directed to the Index to Black Periodicals, G.K. Hall & Co., 70 Lincoln St., Boston, MA 02111.

Notes on Using the Index

ARRANGEMENT: In this index, authors, subjects, and cross-references are interfiled into a single alphabetical arrangement. Headings are alphabetized in a strict letter-by-letter sequence. For example, the heading "Newcastle" appears before the heading "New York," but "New Brunswick" appears before "Newcastle."

SUBJECT POLICY: In general, the authority for subject headings in this index is *Library of Congress Subject Headings*. Owing to the specialized scope of this index, however, the subject "Afro-Americans" and subjects starting with the word "Afro-American" are used infrequently. Instead, users of the index should refer to appropriate subject headings such as "Religion, Afro-American."

PERSONAL NAMES: The term "(About)" following a personal name means that the name is being used as a subject heading. The term is used only for articles that contain substantive information about the individual, and not for incidental or indirect references.

GEOGRAPHIC HEADINGS: Whenever it is possible in choosing headings, specific countries are preferred to broader regions. Headings for specific countries, in turn, are often subdivided by topic: "Nigeria--Poetry." When the subject involved is larger than one specific country, broad geographical areas are sometimes included as the second element in the heading: "Politics--Africa."

CREATIVE WORKS: These are indexed under the author's name. In addition, the headings "Poems" and "Short Stories" are used for works in those categories.

REVIEWS: These are indexed under the name of the author whose work is being reviewed, under the name of the reviewer, and under any appropriate subject headings. The following special headings are also used:

> Book Reviews
> Film Reviews
> Music Reviews
> Record Reviews
> Theater Reviews

Notes on Using the Index

CITATION FORMAT: Each citation in the *Index to Black Periodicals* contains the article's title and author(s), unless there is no author; the journal title, volume and page numbers; and the month and year of publication. When clarification is needed, additional information, such as "Book review" or "Editorial," is also included.

SAMPLE SUBJECT ENTRY:

Academic Achievement

Education in the Post-Integration Era. Russell William Irvine. Journal of Negro Education 55, No. 4 (Fall 1986):508-517

List of Periodicals Indexed

Note:

Black Law Journal has also appeared under the title *National Black Law Journal.*

Black Art changed its name to *International Review of African-American Art,* beginning with Vol. 6, No. 1.

Addresses of Periodicals Indexed

about . . . time
283 Genesee Street
Rochester, NY 14611

Afro-Americans in New York
   Life and History
P.O. Box 1663
Buffalo, NY 14216

Black American Literature
   Forum
Parsons Hall 237
Indiana State University
Terre Haute, IN 47809

The Black Collegian
1240 South Broad Street
New Orleans, LA 70125

Black Enterprise
P.O. Box 3010
Harlan, IA 51593-4101

The Black Law Journal
University of California
   School of Law
405 Hilgard Avenue
Room 2125
Los Angeles, CA 90024

The Black Perspective in Music
Afro-American Creative Arts,
   Inc.
P.O. Box 1
Cambria Heights, NY 11411

The Black Scholar
P.O. Box 2869
Oakland, CA 94609

CAAS Newsletter
University of California
Center for Afro-American Studies
3111 Campbell Hall
Los Angeles, CA 90024

Callaloo
The Johns Hopkins University
   Press
701 West 40th Street
Suite 275
Baltimore, MD 21211

Caribbean Review
P.O. Box 651370
Miami, FL 33265

CLA Journal
Morehouse College
Atlanta, GA 30314

The Crisis
4805 Mount Hope Drive
Baltimore, MD 21215-3297

Ebony
Johnson Publishing Co., Inc.
820 South Michigan Avenue
Chicago, IL 60605

Essence
P.O. Box 53400
Boulder, CO 80322-3400

Howard Law Journal
Howard University School of
 Law
2900 Van Ness Street, NW
Washington, DC 20008

International Review of African-
 American Art
1237 Masselin Avenue
Los Angeles, CA 90019

Interracial Books for Children
 Bulletin
The Council on Interracial
 Books for Children
1841 Broadway
New York, NY 10023

Jet
Johnson Publishing Co., Inc.
820 South Michigan Avenue
Chicago, IL 60605

Journal of African Civilizations
Transaction Books
Rutgers University
New Brunswick, NJ 08903

The Journal of Black
 Psychology
Association of Black
 Psychologists
P.O. Box 55999
Washington, DC 20040-5999

Journal of Black Studies
Sage Publications, Inc.
2111 West Hillcrest Drive
Newbury Park, CA 91320

The Journal of Negro Education
Howard University
Bureau of Educational Research
P.O. Box 311
Washington, DC 20059

Journal of Religious Thought
Howard University Divinity School
1240 Randolph Street, NE
Washington, DC 20017

Negro Educational Review
P.O. Box 2895
General Mail Center
Jacksonville, FL 32203

Phylon
Atlanta University
Atlanta, GA 30314

Race and Class
The Institute of Race Relations
2-6 Leeke Street
King's Cross Road
London WC1X 9HS
England

Research in African
 Literatures
University of Texas Press
P.O. Box 7819
Austin, TX 78712

Review of Black Political
 Economy
Transaction Books
Rutgers University
New Brunswick, NJ 08903

Sage
P.O. Box 42741
Atlanta, GA 30311-0741

The Urban League Review
Transaction Books
Rutgers University
New Brunswick, NJ 08903

Western Journal of Black Studies
Washington State University
Pullman, WA 99164

Enhancing Minority College Students'
Performance on Educational Tests. Henry T.
Frierson. *Journal of Negro Education* 55, No. 1
(Winter 1986):38–45

Making the Grade: The *Essence* Guide to College
Survival. Edited by Janine C. McAdams and
Elaine C. Ray. *Essence* 17, No. 4 (August 1986):67

Accounting Firms

An Accountant and His Finances. Errol T. Louis.
Black Enterprise 17, No. 3 (October 1986):42

Achebe, Chinua (about)

A Reconsideration of Achebe's *No Longer at Ease.*
E. A. Babalola. *Phylon* 47, No. 2 (June
1986):139–147

Achievement

Alabama Super Mom Rears Officers, Gentlemen
and Scholars. *Ebony* 41, No. 6 (April 1986):101

Brothers and Sisters Who Made It to the Top.
Ebony 41, No. 9 (July 1986):74

Acholonu, Catherine Obianuju

Critical Perspectives on Christopher Okigbo.
Book review. *Research in African Literatures* 17,
No. 4 (Winter 1986): 613–614

Acquired Immune Deficiency Syndrome

AIDS...Fact or Fantasy? A Devastating Disease.
Margie Lovett-Scott. *About Time* 14, No. 4 (April
1986):20

AIDS...Fact or Fantasy? Impact on Black
Children/Adults. Henry Duvall. *About Time* 14,
No. 4 (April 1986):20–21

Actors

227—Marla's Masterpiece. Aldore Collier. *Ebony*
42, No. 2 (December 1986):92

Additional Light on S. Morgan Smith. William
Norris. *Black American Literature Forum* 20, Nos.
1–2 (Spring/Summer 1986):75–79

Danny Glover: The Reluctant Movie Star. Aldore
Collier. *Ebony* 41, No. 5 (March 1986):82

Diahann Carroll Tells All: Autobiography Details
Stormy Nine-Year Love Affair with Sidney
Poitier. *Ebony* 41, No. 8 (June 1986):126

Gregory Hines: Dancer Wins Stardom as Chicago
Vice Cop. *Ebony* 41, No. 12 (October 1986):100

Keshia Knight Pulliam: Coping with Success at
Seven. Marilyn Marshall. *Ebony* 42, No. 2
(December 1986):27

Malcolm-Jamal Warner Has His Feet on Solid
Ground. Charles E. Rogers. *Black Collegian* 17,
No. 1 (September/October 1986):17–23

Margaret "Shug" Avery—Beyond "The Color
Purple." Stephanie Stokes Oliver. *Essence* 17, No.
5 (September 1986):118

Meet Laura Carrington. *Black Collegian* 17, No. 1
(September/October 1986):40

The Real-Life Tragedy of Dorothy Dandridge.
Walter Leavy. *Ebony* 41, No. 11 (September
1986):136

Shakespeare in Sable: A History of Black
Shakespearean Actors. By Errol Hill. Reviewed by
Ruth Cowhig. *Research in African Literatures* 17,
No. 2 (Summer 1986): 284–287

TV's Top Mom and Dad: Bill Cosby, Phylicia
Ayers-Allen Are Role Model Parents on
Award-Winning Television Show. Robert E.
Johnson. *Ebony* 41, No. 4 (February 1986):29

Acupuncture

Healing through Acupuncture. Sharon S. Martin.
Black Collegian 16, No. 4 (March/April
1986):90–93

Adamo, David Tuesday

Black-American Heritage? Reviewed by Emma S.
Etuk. *Journal of Religious Thought* 43, No. 1
(Spring-Summer 1986):128

Adams, Joyce Davis

At the Bargaining Table. *Black Enterprise* 17, No.
1 (August 1986):52–54

Corporate Profile: Success among the Suds. *Black
Enterprise* 16, No. 11 (June 1986):242

More Health and Wealth. *Black Enterprise* 16, No.
10 (May 1986):20

NBA Sets Strategies. *Black Enterprise* 16, No. 6
(January 1986):23

Adams, Joyce Davis, and Clayton, Janet

A Tale of Two Franchises. *Black Enterprise* 16,
No. 12 (July 1986):42–46

Addiction—Personal Narratives

Coming to Faith: My Testimony. Loretta A.
Kelly. *Essence* 16, No. 11 (March 1986):56

Administration—Religion

See Church Management

Adolescent Mothers

Black and White Children in America: Key Facts.
Children's Defense Fund. Reviewed by Gayl
Fowler. *Journal of Religious Thought* 43, No. 1
(Spring-Summer 1986):130

Not Your Typical Teen Mother: Chicago Honor
Student Barbara Washington Balances Books and
Her Baby. *Ebony* 41, No. 10 (August 1986):67

Where There's a Will...from Dropout to M. D.
Bebe Moore Campbell. *Essence* 17, No. 6 (October
1986):79

Adoption

One Church/One Child: Chicago Priest's Black
Adoption Campaign Is Smash Success. Lynn
Norment. *Ebony* 41, No. 5 (March 1986):68

Adult Education

Gideonites and Freedmen: Adult Literacy Education at Port Royal, 1862–1865. John R. Rachal. *Journal of Negro Education* 55, No.4 (Fall 1986):453–469

Advertising Agencies

Golden Nuggets. Ken Smikle. *Black Enterprise* 17, No. 3 (October 1986):26

Out-of-Town Campaigns. *Black Enterprise* 16, No. 8 (March 1986):17

Affirmative Action

Affirmative Action Defended: Exploding the Myths of a Slandered Policy. Carter A. Wilson. *Black Scholar* 17, No. 3 (May-June 1986):19–24

Affirmative Action: Evolving Case Law and Shifting Philosophy. William L. Robinson and Stephen L. Spitz. *Urban League Review* 10, No. 2 (Winter 1986–87):84–100

Affirmative Action Strong despite Reagan Opposition. Jan Turner. *About Time* 14, No. 8 (August 1986):27

Affirmative Reaction. Errol T. Louis. *Black Enterprise* 17, No. 3 (October 1986):21

Falling Behind: A Report on How Blacks Have Fared under Reagan. Center on Budget and Policy Priorities. *Journal of Black Studies* 17, No. 2 (December 1986):148–171

The Future of Affirmative Action in Higher Education. Richard P. Thornell. *Howard Law Journal* 29, No. 1 (1986):259–278

Legal Comments. Grover G. Harkins. *Crisis* 93, No. 5 (May 1986):34–35

Remedies for Victim Group Isolation in the Work Place: Court Orders, Problem-Solving and Affirmative Action in the Post-*Stotts* Era. Paul J. Spiegelman. *Howard Law Journal* 29, No. 1 (1986):191–258

Reversing Affirmative Action: A Theoretical Construct. Mfanya Donald Tryman. *Journal of Negro Education* 55, No.2 (Spring 1986):185–199

Same Questions, Different Answers. Robert A. Monroe. *Black Collegian* 17, No. 1 (September/October 1986):66–71

Africa Centre

The Traveling Life. Kris DiLorenzo. *Crisis* 93, No. 4 (April 1986):9

Africa—Cities and Towns

La ville dans le roman africain. By Roger Chemain. Reviewed by S. Ade Ojo. *Research in African Literatures* 17, No. 4 (Winter 1986): 574–576

Africa in Literature

The Black Woman Writer and the Diaspora. Gloria T. Hull. *Black Scholar* 17, No. 2 (March-April 1986):2–4

Joseph Conrad and Africa. By Henryk Zins. Reviewed by Martin Tucker. *Research in African Literatures* 17, No. 3 (Fall 1986): 440–442

Stories from Central and Southern Africa. Paul A. Scanlon, editor. Reviewed by Adrian Roscoe. *Research in African Literatures* 17, No. 3 (Fall 1986): 413–416

African Studies—Dissertations and Theses

Master's Theses in Progress in Selected Colleges and Universities. Mac A. Stewart. *Negro Educational Review* 37, Nos. 3–4 (July-October 1986):106

African Studies Programs

Bibliographies for African Studies, 1980–1983. Yvette Scheven, compiler. Reviewed by Nancy J. Schmidt. *Research in African Literatures* 17, No. 1 (Spring 1986): 145–146

AFSCME

See American Federation of State, County and Municipal Employees

Aged—Care and Hygiene

Health Policy and the Black Aged. Nelson McGhee, Jr., and others. *Urban League Review* 10, No. 2 (Winter 1986–87):63–71

Aged—Health Care

Health Policy and the Black Aged. Wilbur H. Watson and others. *Urban League Review* 10, No. 2 (Winter 1986–87):63–71

Aged—Nutrition

Effects of Food Stamp Program Participation and Other Sociodemographic Characteristics on Food Expenditure Patterns of Elderly Minority Households. Carlton G. Davis and others. *Review of Black Political Economy* 15, No. 1 (Summer 1986):3–25

Aged—Socioeconomic Status

Sitting Location as an Indicator of Status of Older Blacks in the Church: A Comparative Analysis of Protestants and Catholics in the Rural South. Appendix. Wilbur H. Watson. *Phylon* 47, No. 4 (December 1986):264–275

Agriculture—Dissertations and Theses

Master's Theses in Progress in Selected Colleges and Universities. Mac A. Stewart. *Negro Educational Review* 37, Nos. 3–4 (July-October 1986):93–95, 107

Agriculture and State

Estado empresario y lucha politica en Costa Rica. By Ana Sojo. Reviewed by Francisco A. Leguizamon. *Caribbean Review* 15, No. 2 (Spring 1986):45–46

No Free Lunch: Food and Revolution in Cuba Today. By Medea Benjamin, Joseph Collins, and Michael Scott. Reviewed by James E. Austin. *Caribbean Review* 15, No. 2 (Spring 1986):45

Ahadi, Hurumia

The Myth of Black Progress. Book review. *Black Scholar* 17, No. 2 (March-April 1986):50-51

Ai

Blue Suede Shoes. Poem. *Callaloo* 9, No. 1 (Winter 1986):1-5

Sin. Book review. Cyrus Cassells. *Callaloo* 9, No. 1 (Winter 1986):243-247

Aid to Families with Dependent Children

Seeking Realistic Solutions to Welfare. Margaret Simms. *Black Enterprise* 17, No. 1 (August 1986):25

Akello, Grace

Iteso Thought Patterns in Tales. Reviewed by John Lamphear. *Research in African Literatures* 17, No. 2 (Summer 1986): 298-299

Akyem (about)

Interviews with Five Bajan Artists. Illustrated. *International Review of African American Art* 7, No. 1 (1986):45-55

Alabama—Race Relations

Defending Voting Rights in the Alabama Black Belt. Frances M. Beal. *Black Scholar* 17, No. 3 (May-June 1986):34

On Freedom's Road Again. Yvette Moore. *Black Enterprise* 16, No. 11 (June 1986):50

Alavi, Hamza

The Politics of the World Economy. Book review. *Race and Class* 27, No. 4 (Spring 1986):87-90

Alba, Richard D.

Ethnicity and Race in the USA: Toward the Twenty-First Century. Book review. Mary Ellison. *Race and Class* 27, No. 3 (Winter 1986):109-110

Alcoholic Beverages

See also Liqueurs

Alcoholics

Loving a Troubled Man. Janice C. Simpson. *Essence* 17, No. 6 (October 1986):75

Alden, Morris

The Origins of the Civil Rights Movement: Black Communities Organizing for Change. Book review. Diane Pinderhughes. *CAAS Newsletter* 9, No. 2 (1986):14

Alexander, Elizabeth

The Dirt-Eaters. Poem. *Callaloo* 9, No. 1 (Winter 1986):7-8

Letter: Blues. Poem. *Callaloo* 9, No. 1 (Winter 1986):6

Alexander-Thompson, Lessie

Reflections in Black. Poem. *Essence* 17, No. 4 (August 1986):159

Alford, Robert L.(joint author)

See Clark, Vernon L.

Algeria—Literature—French Language

Assia Djebar: Romancière algérienne, cinéaste arabe. By Jean Dejeux. Reviewed by Bernadette Cailler. *Research in African Literatures* 17, No. 4 (Winter 1986): 579-581

Alkalimat, Abdul

Mayor Washington's Bid for Re-Election. *Black Scholar* 17, No. 6 (November-December 1986):2-13

Alladice, Darryl

Wind. Poem. *Essence* 16, No. 11 (March 1986):110

Allen, Joan Marie

The Art of Diplomacy: Bob Brown and Local 435. *About Time* 14, No. 12 (December 1986):9-10

A Call to Action: Community Crusade for Learning. *About Time* 14, No. 11 (November 1986):22-24

The Homeless. *About Time* 14, No. 10 (October 1986):18-20

Preservation Hall Jazz Band. *About Time* 14, No. 12 (December 1986):26-27

Als, Hilton

So You Want to Be a Fashion Model. *Essence* 17, No. 1 (May 1986):25

Alvin Ailey American Dance Theatre

Alvin Ailey American Dance Theatre. Kris DiLorenzo. *Crisis* 93, No. 2 (February 1986):16

Amadi, Elechi (about)

The West African Village Novel with Particular Reference to Elechi Amadi's *The Concubine*. By George Nyamndi. Reviewed by Ernest N. Emenyonu. *Research in African Literatures* 17, No. 4 (Winter 1986): 622-625

Ambassadors

Terence Todman: Top Diplomat Ambassador to Denmark. D. Michael Cheers. *Ebony* 41, No. 4 (February 1986):67

Ambition

"What I Wanted to Be When I Grew Up." Julie Chenault. *Essence* 17, No. 1 (May 1986):80

America—Antiquities

The African Presence in Ancient America: Evidence from Physical Anthropology. Notes. Keith M. Jordon. *Journal of African Civilizations* 8, No. 2 (December 1986):136–151

America—Civilization—African Influences

Africa and the Discovery of America, Volume I. By Leo Wiener. Reviewed by Phillips Barry. *Journal of African Civilizations* 8, No. 2 (December 1986):197–201

African Sea Kings in America? Evidence from Early Maps. Bibliography. Joan Covey. *Journal of African Civilizations* 8, No. 2 (December 1986):152–168

The First Americans. Notes. Legrand H. Clegg II. *Journal of African Civilizations* 8, No. 2 (December 1986):264–273

Leo Wiener—A Plea for Re-Examination. Notes. David J. M. Muffett. *Journal of African Civilizations* 8, No. 2 (December 1986):188–196

Mandinga Voyages across the Atlantic. Notes. Harold G. Lawrence. *Journal of African Civilizations* 8, No. 2 (December 1986):202–247

Men Out of Asia: A Review and Update of the Gladwin Thesis. Notes. By Harold Sterling Gladwin. Reviewed by Runoko Rashidi. *Journal of African Civilizations* 8, No. 2 (December 1986):248–263

Pyramid—American and African: A Comparison. Notes. Beatrice Lumpkin. *Journal of African Civilizations* 8, No. 2 (December 1986):169–187

Ten Years After: An Introduction and Overview. Ivan Van Sertima. *Journal of African Civilizations* 8, No. 2 (December 1986):5–27

Trait-Influences in Meso-America: The African-Asian Connection. Notes. Wayne B. Chandler. *Journal of African Civilizations* 8, No. 2 (December 1986):274–334

Unexpected African Faces in Pre-Columbian America. Alexander Von Wuthenau. *Journal of African Civilizations* 8, No. 2 (December 1986):56–75

American Association of Blacks in Energy

Blacks in Energy Meet. Solomon J. Herbert. *Black Enterprise* 16, No. 11 (June 1986):48

American Black Achievement Awards

American Black Achievement Awards: A Tribute to Black Excellence. *Ebony* 41, No. 3 (January 1986):124

American Cancer Society

Saving Lives through Public Education. Kelly Papa. *About Time* 14, No. 6 (June 1986):21

American Federation of State, County and Municipal Employees (AFSCME)

Room at the Top: The Case of District Council 37 of the American Federation of State, County and Municipal Employees in New York City. Jewel Bellush. *SAGE* 3, No. 1 (Spring 1986):35–40

American Folk Theatre

Theatre. Cecilia Loving-Sloane. *Crisis* 93, No. 4 (April 1986):10–12

American Shared Hospital Services

Entrepreneurial Surgeon: Dr. Ernest Bates Nurses Ailing Firm to Fiscal Health. Mark McNamara. *Ebony* 41, No. 6 (April 1986):84

Ameritech Capital Corporation

The Benefits of Leasing. Lloyd Gite. *Black Enterprise* 17, No. 2 (September 1986):27

Amin, Ruhul, and Mariam, A. G.

Black-White Differences in Housing: An Analysis of Trend and Differentials, United States of America, 1960–1978. *Negro Educational Review* 37, No. 1 (January 1986):27–38

Amuge, Immaculate Mary

The Dilemma of the Contribution of African Women toward and the Benefits They Derive from Economic Development. *Western Journal of Black Studies* 10, No. 4 (Winter 1986):205–210

Anders-Michalski, Judith, and Nohe, Lauran M.

The Liberal Arts Make a Comeback. *Black Collegian* 17, No. 1 (September/October 1986):124–126

Anderson, Bernard E.

Economic Structural Change: A Challenge for Full Employment. *Urban League Review* 10, No. 1 (Summer 1986):41–48

Statement on Dr. Clifton R. Wharton, Jr.—Recipient of the Samuel Z. Westerfield Award. *Review of Black Political Economy* 14, No. 4 (Spring 1986):5–7

Youths and the Changing Job Market. *Black Enterprise* 16, No. 8 (March 1986):25

Anderson, Janice S. (about)

More Health and Wealth. Joyce Davis Adams. *Black Enterprise* 16, No. 10 (May 1986):20

Anderson, Rueben V. (about)

A Mississippi First: Black Judge Serves on State Supreme Court. *Ebony* 41, No. 4 (February 1986):37

Andic, Fuat M.

What Price Equity? A Macroeconomic Evaluation of Government Policies in Costa Rica. Reviewed by Irma T. De Alonso. *Caribbean Review* 15, No. 1 (Winter 1986):44

Ando, Faith H.

An Analysis of the Formation and Failure Rates of Minority-Owned Firms. *Review of Black Political Economy* 15, No. 2 (Fall 1986):51–71

Andrews, William L.

The Slave's Narrative. Book review. *Black American Literature Forum* 20, Nos. 1–2 (Spring/Summer 1986):203–207

Angelou, Maya

The Bridge. Fiction. *Essence* 16, No. 11 (March 1986):66

Save the Mothers. *Ebony* 41, No. 10 (August 1986):38

Singin' and Swingin' and Gettin' Merry Like Christmas. Book review. Liz Fekete. *Race and Class* 27, No. 4 (Spring 1986):106–107

Anna, Timothy E.

Spain and the Loss of America. Reviewed by Joaquin Roy. *Caribbean Review* 15, No. 2 (Spring 1986):48

Anonyms and Pseudonyms

So the Name Has Been Changed: Celebrities Have Various Reasons for Adopting New and Sometimes Strange Monikers. *Ebony* 41, No. 6 (April 1986):46

Anrig, Gregory R., and others

Teacher Competency Testing: Realities of Supply and Demand in This Period of Educational Reform. *Journal of Negro Education* 55, No.3 (Summer 1986):316–325

Anthropological Linguistics

Africa and the Discovery of America, Volume I. By Leo Wiener. Reviewed by Phillips Barry. *Journal of African Civilizations* 8, No. 2 (December 1986):197–201

Anthropologists

African-American Soul Force: Dance, Music and Vera Mae Green. A. Lynn Bolles. *SAGE* 3, No. 2 (Fall 1986):32–34

Death Shall Not Find Us Thinking That We Die. Notes. Ivan Van Sertima. *Journal of African Civilizations* 8, No. 1 (June 1986):7–16

Meeting the Pharoah: Conversations with Cheikh Anta Diop. Interview. Charles S. Finch. *Journal of African Civilizations* 8, No. 1 (June 1986):28–34

Anthropology, Physical

See Physical Anthropology

Anthropology, Structural

Le Roi Nyamwezi, la Droite et la Gauche: Révision Comparative des Classifications Dualistes. By Serge Tcherkezoff. Reviewed by Wyatt MacGarrey. *Research in African Literatures* 17, No. 2 (Summer 1986): 304–306

Antilles—Folktales

La Parole des Femmes: Essais sur des Romancières des Antilles de Langue Française. By Maryse Conde. Reviewed by John William. *Black Scholar* 17, No. 4 (July-August 1986):57

Anti-Semitism

Anti-Semitism: A Modern Perspective. By Caroline Arnold and Herma Silverstein. Reviewed by Albert V. Schwartz. *Interracial Books for Children Bulletin* 17, No. 2 (1986):18–19

Anyahuru, Israel (about)

Conversation with Israel Anyahuru. Joshua Uzoigwe. *Black Perspective in Music* 14, No. 2 (Spring 1986):126–142

Anyidoho, Kofi, and others (editors)

Interdisciplinary Dimensions of African Literature. Reviewed by C. L. Innes. *Research in African Literatures* 17, No. 3 (Fall 1986): 449–451

Apartheid

Apartheid Lives On. Frank Dexter Brown. *Black Enterprise* 16, No. 12 (July 1986):13

Black Students' Perceptions of Factors Related to Academic Performance in a Rural Area of Natal Province, South Africa. Alan Simon. *Journal of Negro Education* 55, No.4 (Fall 1986):535–547

Daughter of Tutu Spreads Appeal to Dismantle Apartheid. Henry Duvall. *About Time* 14, No. 5 (May 1986):18–19

"In Memory of Our Children's Blood": Sisterhood and South African Women. *SAGE* 3, No. 2 (Fall 1986):40–43

Kaffir Boy: The True Story of a Black Youth's Coming of Age in Apartheid South Africa. By Mark Mathabane. Reviewed by Tonya Bolden Davis. *Black Enterprise* 17, No. 5 (December 1986):20

Martin Luther King, Jr.'s "Beloved Community" Ideal and the Apartheid System in South Africa. Lewis V. Baldwin. *Western Journal of Black Studies* 10, No. 4 (Winter 1986):211–222

The NAACP and South Africa. *Crisis* 93, No. 9 (November 1986):35–39

Nadine Gordimer's "A Chip of Glass Ruby": A Commentary on Apartheid Society. Evelyn Schroth. *Journal of Black Studies* 17, No. 1 (September 1986):85–90

The Origins of Forced Labor in the Witwatersrand. Moitsadi Moeti. *Phylon* 47, No. 4 (December 1986):276–284

Remember Soweto. Frank Dexter Brown. *Black Enterprise* 17, No. 2 (September 1986):17

Statement at Hunter College. Martin Luther King, Jr. *Black Collegian* 16, No. 3 (January/February 1986):36–38

Who Can Speak for South Africa? Felicia Kessel. *Crisis* 93, No. 9 (November 1986):28

Apartheid—Anti-Apartheid Organizations

The Sullivan Principles. Linn Washington. *Black Enterprise* 16, No. 6 (January 1986):23

Apartheid—Economic Aspects

Investing with a Conscience. Frank Dexter Brown. *Black Enterprise* 17, No. 3 (October 1986):91

Appalachia—Blacks

Blacks in Appalachia. By William H. Turner and Edward J. Cahill. Reviewed by Tommy W. Rogers. *Black Scholar* 17, No. 3 (May-June 1986):58–59

Appiah, Anthony

Beyond Ethnicity: Consent and Descent in American Culture. Book review. *Black American Literature Forum* 20, Nos. 1–2 (Spring/Summer 1986):209–224

Aptheker, Herbert (compiler and editor)

Newspaper Columns by W. E. B. Du Bois. Reviewed by David F. Dorsey (Jr.) *CLA Journal* 30, No. 2 (December 1986):254–258

Arab Countries

See also Israel-Arab War

Archaeologists

Men Out of Asia: A Review and Update of the Gladwin Thesis. Notes. By Harold Sterling Gladwin. Reviewed by Runoko Rashidi. *Journal of African Civilizations* 8, No. 2 (December 1986):248–263

Archaeology

Trait-Influences in Meso-America: The African-Asian Connection. Notes. Wayne B. Chandler. *Journal of African Civilizations* 8, No. 2 (December 1986):274–334

Archbishop of Canterbury's Commission on Urban Priority Areas

Faith in the City: A Call for Action by Church and Nation. Book review. Paul Grant. *Race and Class* 27, No. 4 (Spring 1986):97–98

Architects

Blacks Who Overcame the Odds. *Ebony* 42, No. 1 (November 1986):148

Aresu, Bernard

Soleil éclate. Book review. *Research in African Literatures* 17, No. 4 (Winter 1986): 588–591

Ariel Capital Management, Inc.

The Young Tycoons. Lloyd Gite. *Black Enterprise* 16, No. 6 (January 1986):44–47

Arkansas—Centennial Celebrations

Persistence of the Spirit: Arkansas Sesquicentennial Celebration Salutes Black Achievement. *Ebony* 41, No. 11 (September 1986):36

Arnez, Nancy L.

Black Public Policy. *Journal of Black Studies* 16, No. 4 (June 1986):397–408

Keeping Track: How Schools Structure Inequality. Book review. *Journal of Negro Education* 55, No.2 (Spring 1986):244–246

Arnold, Caroline, and Silverstein, Herma

Anti-Semitism: A Modern Perspective. Book review. Albert V. Schwartz. *Interracial Books for Children Bulletin* 17, No. 2 (1986):18–19

Arnold, James A.

Modernism and Negritude: The Poetry and Poetics of Aime Cesaire. Book review. Vera M. Kutzinski. *Callaloo* 9, No. 4 (Fall 1986):740–748

Art

Tradition and Conflict: Images of a Turbulent Decade, 1963–1973. *Black Collegian* 16, No. 3 (January/February 1986):48–49

The Visual Arts. Nia Mason. *Crisis* 93, No. 2 (February 1986):50–53

Art, Afro-American

Diagnosis of Art...Hidden Heritage: Afro-American Art, 1800–1950. Illustrated. *About Time* 14, No. 4 (April 1986):24–25

Sterling A. Brown: Building the Black Aesthetic Tradition. By Joanne V. Gabbin. Reviewed by Leonard Green. *Black American Literature Forum* 20, No. 3 (Fall 1986):327–334

Art, Prehistoric

The African Presence in Ancient America: Evidence from Physical Anthropology. Notes. Keith M. Jordon. *Journal of African Civilizations* 8, No. 2 (December 1986):136–151

The Egyptian Presence in South America. Notes. R. A. Jairazbhoy. *Journal of African Civilizations* 8, No. 2 (December 1986):76–135

Trait-Influences in Meso-America: The African-Asian Connection. Notes. Wayne B. Chandler. *Journal of African Civilizations* 8, No. 2 (December 1986):274–334

Unexpected African Faces in Pre-Columbian America. Alexander Von Wuthenau. *Journal of African Civilizations* 8, No. 2 (December 1986):56–75

Art—Exhibitions

Diagnosis of Art...Hidden Heritage: Afro-American Art, 1800–1950. Illustrated. Adolph Dupree. *About Time* 14, No. 4 (April 1986):24–25

An Exhibition for National Peace. Sandra Serrano. *Caribbean Review* 15, No. 1 (Winter 1986):33

Art Galleries

Queen of Arts. Fatima Shaik. *Essence* 17, No. 2 (July 1986):15

Art as an Investment

Collecting Black Art. Tonya Bolden Davis. *Black Enterprise* 17, No. 5 (December 1986):85

Artist Development Group, Inc.

Catch a Rising Star: Savvy Rhode Island Talent Agent Polishes Up New Acts. Carol R. Scott. *Essence* 17, No. 2 (June 1986):18

Artists

Clarence Talley: New Spiritual Art. *Black Collegian* 17, No. 1 (September/October 1986):60–61

A Creative Marriage: Artists Michael and Michelle Nero Singletary Share A Passion for Each Other and Painting. *Ebony* 41, No. 9 (July 1986):96

Fifteen Leading Black Artists. *Ebony* 41, No. 7 (May 1986):46

Interviews with Five Bajan Artists. Illustrated. *International Review of African American Art* 7, No. 1 (1986):45–55

Jacob Lawrence: The Man and His Art. Illustrated. Stephanie Stokes Oliver. *Essence* 17, No. 7 (November 1986):89

Jimmy James Greene. Illustrated. *Black Collegian* 17, No. 2 (November/December 1986):72–73

June Beer: Nicaraguan Artist. Betty LaDuke. *SAGE* 3, No. 2 (Fall 1986):35–39

Karl Broodgagen. Illustrated. David Gall. *International Review of African American Art* 7, No. 1 (1986):56–63

Malcolm Brown Gallery. Illustrated. *Western Journal of Black Studies* 10, No. 2 (Summer 1986):77–78

Tayo Tekovi Quaye's Images of Traditional African Life. Illustrated. *Black Collegian* 16, No. 4 (March/April 1986):48–49

Artists—Cuba

The Mythical Landscapes of a Cuban Painter: Wilfredo Lam's *La Jungla*. Juan A. Martinez. *Caribbean Review* 15, No. 2 (Spring 1986):32–36

Artists—Panama

An Exhibition for National Peace. Sandra Serrano. *Caribbean Review* 15, No. 1 (Winter 1986):33

Searching for Pretto: Politics and Art in Panama. Sandra Serrano. *Caribbean Review* 15, No. 1 (Winter 1986):29–32+

Art—Panama

Searching for Pretto: Politics and Art in Panama. Sandra Serrano. *Caribbean Review* 15, No. 1 (Winter 1986):29–32+

Art in Public Places

Art in Public Places: An African American Perspective. *International Review of African American Art* 7, No. 2 (1986):5

Asante, Molefi K.

Report to the Ford Foundation on Afro-American Studies. Book review. *Journal of Black Studies* 17, No. 2 (December 1986):255–262

Ascher, William

Scheming for the Poor: The Politics of Redistribution in Latin America. Reviewed by John Waterbury. *Caribbean Review* 15, No. 1 (Winter 1986):42–43

Ashford, Evelyn (about)

World's Fastest Mom: On the Track or in the Nursery, Evelyn Ashford Is a Winner. *Ebony* 41, No. 8 (June 1986):155

Asian-American Students

The Asian-American Success Myth. Deborah Wei. *Interracial Books for Children Bulletin* 17, Nos. 3–4 (1986):16–17

Asiegbu, J. U. J.

Nigeria and Its Invaders 1851–1920. Book review. Lai Olurode. *Journal of Black Studies* 16, No. 4 (June 1986):457–460

Assensoh, A. B.

Waiting: The Whites of South Africa. Book review. *Phylon* 47, No. 3 (September 1986):248

Association for the Study of Afro-American Life and History

The Price of History. Gwen McKinney. *Black Enterprise* 16, No. 11 (June 1986):48

Astronauts

A Dream Fulfilled. Blair Walker. *Black Enterprise* 16, No. 9 (April 1986):25

Requiem for a Hero: "Touching the Face of God." D. Michael Cheers. *Ebony* 41, No. 7 (May 1986):82

Ronald Ervin McNair: First and One of a Kind. Adolph Dupree. *About Time* 14, No. 6 (June 1986):12–13

Athletes

The Exploitation of the Black Athlete: Some Alternative Solutions. Editorial. Gary A. Sales *Journal of Negro Education* 55, No.4 (Fall 1986):439–442

NCAA Rule 48: Racism or Reform? Vernon L. Clark, Floyd Horton, and Robert L. Alford. *Journal of Negro Education* 55, No.2 (Spring 1986):162–170

World's Fastest Mom: On the Track or in the Nursery, Evelyn Ashford Is a Winner. *Ebony* 41, No. 8 (June 1986):155

The World's Greatest Woman Athlete: Jackie Joyner Shatters Heptathalon Record Twice in 26 Days. Aldore Collier. *Ebony* 41, No. 12 (October 1986):77

Athletes, Handicapped

Where There's a Will: Bonnie's Story. Bill Rhoden. *Essence* 17, No. 1 (May 1986):82

Athletes—Legal Status

Gladiator Traps: A Primer on the Representation of Black Athletes. Weldon C. Williams III. *Black Law Journal* 9, No. 3 (Winter 1986):263–279

Athletic Clubs

As Gentle As the Wind: The Falcon Trap and Game Club. Adolph Dupree. *About Time* 14, No. 12 (December 1986):20–24

Athletics—Career Opportunities

Is Sports the Great Career It's Cracked Up to Be for Blacks? Norman Riley. *Crisis* 93, No. 8 (October 1986):30–35

Athletics—Management

Tracey at the Bat. Timothy W. Smith. *Black Enterprise* 17, No. 2 (September 1986):52

Athletics—Psychology

The Destruction of the Young Black Male: The Impact of Popular Culture and Organized Sports. John C. Gaston. *Journal of Black Studies* 16, No. 4 (June 1986):369–384

Atlanta—Child Slayings

The Evidence of Things Not Seen. By James Baldwin. Reviewed by Tonya Bolden Davis. *Black Enterprise* 16, No. 11 (June 1986):38

Atlanta—Politics and Government

The Fight for the Fifth. Ann Kimbrough. *Black Enterprise* 17, No. 4 (November 1986):21

Atomic Weapons and Disarmament

Inside the Philippine Resistance. Zoltan Grossman. *Race and Class* 28, No. 2 (August 1986):1–29

Atungaye, Monifa

Lullaby and Sweet Goodnight. Poem. *Black American Literature Forum* 20, No. 3 (Fall 1986):312–313

Aubert, Alvin

All Singing in a Pie. Poem. *Callaloo* 9, No. 1 (Winter 1986):9

A Light Outside. Poem. *Callaloo* 9, No. 1 (Winter 1986):11

Van der Zee Extrapolation #1. Poem. *Callaloo* 9, No. 1 (Winter 1986):10

Auctions, Municipal

Own a Piece of the City. Britt Robson. *Black Enterprise* 17, No. 3 (October 1986):67

Audelco Awards

The 1985 Audelco Awards. A. Peter Bailey. *Black Collegian* 16, No. 3 (January/February 1986):28

Augustine, Saint (about)

From Sinners to Saints: The Confessions of Saint Augustine and Malcolm X. Notes. Winston A. Van Horne. *Journal of Religious Thought* 43, No. 1 (Spring-Summer 1986):76–101

Austen, Jane (about)

Letters to Alice: On First Reading Jane Austen. By Fay Weldon. Reviewed by Louis D. Mitchell. *CLA Journal* 30, No. 1 (September 1986):104–106

The Life of Jane Austen. By John Halperin. Reviewed by Louis D. Mitchell. *CLA Journal* 30, No. 1 (September 1986):104–106

Austin, Diane J.

A Review of Urban Life in Kingston, Jamaica. Reviewed by Bernard D. Headley. *Caribbean Review* 15, No. 1 (Winter 1986):42

Austin, James E.

No Free Lunch: Food and Revolution in Cuba Today. Book review. *Caribbean Review* 15, No. 2 (Spring 1986):45

Australia—Aborigines

The Aboriginal Struggle: An Interview with Helen Boyle. Mike Cole. *Race and Class* 27, No. 4 (Spring 1986):21–33

Australia—Society and Culture

Ethnicity, Class and Gender in Australia. Edited by Gill Bottomley and Marie de Lepervanche. Reviewed by Stephen Castle. *Race and Class* 27, No. 4 (Spring 1986):94–96

Authoritarianism

An Interview with Hugo Spadafora Four Months before His Death. Interview. Beatrix Parga de Bayon. *Caribbean Review* 15, No. 1 (Winter 1986):24–25+

Political Systems as Export Commodities: Democracy and the Role of the US in Central America. Ricardo Arias Calderon. *Caribbean Review* 15, No. 1 (Winter 1986):21–23+

Authors

See Writers

Autobiographies

"My Life as a Supreme." Mary Wilson. *Essence* 17, No. 8 (December 1986):80

Automobile Industry and Trade

Auto Overview: The Autocrats. Jay Koblenz. *Black Enterprise* 16, No. 11 (June 1986):191

A First for Ford. Jay Koblenz. *Black Enterprise* 16, No. 12 (July 1986):16

Bahia—Description and Travel

Sample the Spice of Salvador. Curtia James. *Essence* 16, No. 11 (March 1986):86

Bahia—Religion

Catholicism and Candomble: The Mystical Mix. Harriette Cole. *Essence* 16, No. 11 (March 1986):92

Bailey, A. Peter

The 1985 Audelco Awards. *Black Collegian* 16, No. 3 (January/February 1986):28

Bailey, Lynn B. (joint author)

See Davis, Carlton G.

Bail Reform Act

Focus on the 1984 Bail Reform Act: Pretrial Detention Permitted. Sandra Dickerson. *Black Law Journal* 9, No. 3 (Winter 1986):280–295

Bajan Culture

When Banja Play, Bajan Come. Illustrated. Elton Elombe. *International Review of African American Art* 7, No. 1 (1986):32–40

Baker, Anita (about)

Anita Baker: Soul's New Romantic Singer. Lynn Norment. *Ebony* 42, No. 2 (December 1986):52

Baker, Jeannie

Home in the Sky. Book review. Emily Leinster. *Interracial Books for Children Bulletin* 17, No. 1 (1986):8–9

Baker, Josephine (about)

Josephine Baker: A Lifetime of Struggle and Romance. S. Brandi Barnes. *Black Collegian* 16, No. 3 (January/February 1986):98–102

Baker, Roland C. (about)

The Maestro of Marketing. Jacqueline Moore. *Black Enterprise* 16, No. 12 (July 1986):32

Bakery, Confectionery and Tobacco Workers International Union

At the Bargaining Table. Joyce Davis Adams. *Black Enterprise* 17, No. 1 (August 1986):52–54

Baldwin, James

The Evidence of Things Not Seen. Book review. Joe Johnson. *Crisis* 93, No. 3 (March 1986):14–48

The Evidence of Things Not Seen. Book review. Tonya Bolden Davis. *Black Enterprise* 16, No. 11 (June 1986):38

The Price of a Ticket. Book review. Joe Johnson. *Crisis* 93, No. 2 (February 1986):12

Baldwin, James—Criticism and Interpretation

Black Women in the Fiction of James Baldwin. By Trudier Davis. Reviewed by Ketu H. Katrak. *Black American Literature Forum* 20, No. 4 (Winter 1986):449–458

Baldwin, Joseph A.

African (Black) Psychology: Issues and Synthesis. *Journal of Black Studies* 16, No. 3 (March 1986):235–250

Baldwin, Lewis V.

Martin Luther King, Jr.'s "Beloved Community" Ideal and the Apartheid System in South Africa. *Western Journal of Black Studies* 10, No. 4 (Winter 1986):211–222

Bales, Fred

Television Use and Confidence in Television by Blacks and Whites in Four Selected Years. *Journal of Black Studies* 16, No. 3 (March 1986):283–291

Ball, William

Entrepreneurs, Students of the 80's: Financing Their Educations and Making a Profit. *Black Collegian* 17, No. 1 (September/October 1986):128–132

Ballard, Allen B.

One More Day's Journey. Book review. Beth Brown Utada. *Journal of Black Studies* 16, No. 4 (June 1986):453–456

Ballard, Portia (joint author)

See Kazi-Ferrouillet, Kuumba

Balliett, Whitney

Jelly Roll, Jabbo and Fats: Nineteen Portraits in Jazz. Book review. Beth Brown Utada. *Journal of Black Studies* 16, No. 4 (June 1986):451–453

Bame, Kwabena N.

Come to Laugh: A Study of African Traditional Theatre in Ghana. Reviewed by Alain Ricard. *Research in African Literatures* 17, No. 2 (Summer 1986): 287

Bank Management

NBA Sets Strategies. Joyce Davis Adams. *Black Enterprise* 16, No. 6 (January 1986):23

Bank Mergers

Bank Overview: Merge or Purge? William Bradford. *Black Enterprise* 16, No. 11 (June 1986):143

UNB Merger Announced. Kirk Jackson. *Black Enterprise* 17, No. 5 (December 1986):26

Banks, Samuel L.

The Education of Black Children and Youths: A Framework for Excellence. Reviewed by Sandra Noel Smith. *Journal of Negro Education* 55, No.4 (Fall 1986):551–552

Banks and Banking

In Banks We Trust. Sandra Roberts Bell. *Black Enterprise* 16, No. 12 (July 1986):47

Bank of the Year: Banking on Boston. Gregg Patterson. *Black Enterprise* 16, No. 11 (June 1986):150

The *Black Enterprise* List of Black Banks. *Black Enterprise* 16, No. 11 (June 1986):147

Black Managers: The Case of the Banking Industry. By Edward D. Irons and Gilbert W. Moore. Reviewed by Willene A. Johnson. *Review of Black Political Economy* 14, No. 4 (Spring 1986):103–108

Linkages between Minority Business Characteristics and Minority Banks' Locations. John A. Cole and Lucy J. Reuben. *Review of Black Political Economy* 15, No. 2 (Fall 1986):73–92

NBA Protests Treasury's Banking Policy. David C. Ruffin. *Black Enterprise* 17, No. 1 (August 1986):17

Banks and Banking, International

Minority Business Development: An International Comparison. Gavin M. Chen. *Review of Black Political Economy* 15, No. 2 (Fall 1986):93–111

Bannerman, Charles (about)

Two Business Achievers Die. Sharon Shervington. *Black Enterprise* 17, No. 2 (September 1986):20

Bantu—Language

The Bantu-Speaking Heritage of the United States. By Winifred Kellersberger. Reviewed by Joseph E. Holloway. *Phylon* 47, No. 2 (June 1986):167–168

Baraka, Amiri—Criticism and Intepretation

Amiri Baraka in the 1980's. James A. Miller. *Callaloo* 9, No. 1 (Winter 1986):184–192

Baranco, Gregory (about)

Revving Up for Sales. Nathan McCall. *Black Enterprise* 17, No. 4 (November 1986):44

Baranco Pontiac/GMC Truck Inc.

See Baranco, Gregory

Barbados—Art

Emancipation. Illustrated. *International Review of African American Art* 7, No. 1 (1986):42–45

The Growth of an Artistic Tradition in Barbados. Illustrated. Trevor Marshall. *International Review of African American Art* 7, No. 1 (1986):4–25

Barbados Dance Theatre Company

1627 and All That Sort of Thing. Illustrated. *International Review of African American Art* 7, No. 1 (1986):29–31

Barbados—Description and Travel

Barbados: From Sea to Shining...Ocean. E. D. Smith. *Black Enterprise* 16, No. 10 (May 1986):84

Barbados—Music

The Ruck-a-Tuck International. Illustrated. Wayne Willock. *International Review of African American Art* 7, No. 1 (1986):27

Barbados—Photographs

Bajan Places and Faces. Sid Fridkin. Illustrated. *International Review of African American Art* 7, No. 1 (1986):65–71

Barbanel, Linda

Piggy-Bank Savvy. *Essence* 17, No. 1 (May 1986):16

Barbour, Julia Watson

We Shall Bloom Again. Poem. *Essence* 16, No. 11 (March 1986):122

Barksdale, Marcellus

Civil Rights Organization and the Indigenous Movement in Chapel Hill, N. C., 1960–1965. *Phylon* 47, No. 1 (March 1986):29–42

Barksdale, Richard K.

Castration Symbolism in Recent Black American Fiction. Notes. *CLA Journal* 29, No. 4 (June 1986):400–413

Barley, Nigel

Symbolic Structures: An Exploration of the Culture of the Dowayos. Reviewed by Wyatt MacGaffey. *Research in African Literatures* 17, No. 2 (Summer 1986): 295–296

Barnes, S. Brandi

How to Get in Graduate School. *Black Collegian* 17, No. 2 (November/December 1986):74–78

Josephine Baker: A Lifetime of Struggle and Romance. *Black Collegian* 16, No. 3 (January/February 1986):98–102

Barrax, Gerald

Breaking Camp. Book review. *Callaloo* 9, No. 1 (Winter 1986):265–269

Elegies for Patrice. Book review. *Callaloo* 9, No. 1 (Winter 1986):263–265

Movement in Black: The Collected Poetry of Pat Parker. Book review. *Callaloo* 9, No. 1 (Winter 1986):259–262

Not Often Near Such Water. Poem. *Callaloo* 9, No. 1 (Winter 1986):12–14

Now Is the Thing to Praise. Book review. *Callaloo* 9, No. 1 (Winter 1986):248–254

Songs for My Fathers. Book review. *Callaloo* 9, No. 1 (Winter 1986):255–259

The Watermelon Dress: Portrait of a Woman. Book review. *Callaloo* 9, No. 1 (Winter 1986):265–269

Barrow, Jocelyn (joint author)

See Gibson, Ashton

Barry, E. Jeannie

Share the Wealth: Who Will Teach the Black Children? *Black Collegian* 16, No. 4 (March/April 1986):122

Barry, Marion S. (about)

Washington: District of Commerce. Patricia A. Jones. *Black Enterprise* 16, No. 11 (June 1986):253

Barry, Phillips

Africa and the Discovery of America, Volume I. Book review. *Journal of African Civilizations* 8, No. 2 (December 1986):197–201

Barthelemy, Sidney (about)

Mayor Sidney Barthelemy: New Orleans' Gentle Giant. *Ebony* 41, No. 9 (July 1986):120

Bartsch, Friedemann K.

Brother to Dragons : The Burden of Innocence. Notes. *CLA Journal* 29, No. 3 (March 1986):336–351

Baseball Managers

Tracey at the Bat. Timothy W. Smith. *Black Enterprise* 17, No. 2 (September 1986):52

Baseball Players

Reggie Jackson: More than Just a Baseball Superstar. Walter Leavy. *Ebony* 41, No. 9 (July 1986):104

Basketball Coaches

A Boom in Black Coaches. *Ebony* 41, No. 6 (April 1986):59

Basketball Players

Kareem Abdul-Jabbar: Veteran Cage Star Starts Life Anew after Fire and Break-Up. Norman O. Unger. *Ebony* 41, No. 7 (May 1986):164

Manute Bol: Tallest Man in Pro Sports Outgrows "Tall Jokes." Norman O. Unger. *Ebony* 42, No. 2 (December 1986):59

Patrick Ewing: Can This Man Save the Knicks? Walter Leavy. *Ebony* 41, No. 4 (February 1986):59

Baskin-Robbins Inc.

A Tale of Two Franchises. Joyce Davis Adams and Janet Clayton. *Black Enterprise* 16, No. 12 (July 1986):42–46

Bass Clef

The Traveling Life. Kris DiLorenzo. *Crisis* 93, No. 4 (April 1986):9

Bates, Ernest A. (about)

Entrepreneurial Surgeon: Dr. Ernest Bates Nurses Ailing Firm to Fiscal Health. Mark McNamara. *Ebony* 41, No. 6 (April 1986):84

Bates, Timothy

Characteristics of Minorities Who Are Entering Self-Employment. *Review of Black Political Economy* 15, No. 2 (Fall 1986):31–49

Bates, Timothy (joint author)

See Fusfield, Daniel R.

Bauman, Michael E.

Heresy in Paradise and the Ghosts of Readers Past. Notes. *CLA Journal* 30, No. 1 (September 1986):59–68

Bazin, Nancy Topping

Feminist Perspectives in African Fiction: Bessie Head and Buchi Emecheta. *Black Scholar* 17, No. 2 (March-April 1986):34–40

Beal, Frances M.

Black Gains Tied Directly to Pursuit of Peace. *Black Scholar* 17, No. 1 (January-February 1986):8–11

Defending Voting Rights in the Alabama Black Belt. *Black Scholar* 17, No. 3 (May-June 1986):34

Beal, Frances M. and dePass, Ty

The Historical Black Presence in the Struggle for Peace. *Black Scholar* 17, No. 1 (January-February 1986):2–7

Beard, Linda Susan

Bessie Head in Gaborone, Botswana: An Interview. *SAGE* 3, No. 2 (Fall 1986):44–47

The Black Woman Writer and the Diaspora, October 27-30, 1985. *SAGE* 3, No. 2 (Fall 1986):70–71

Beasley, Robert R. (joint author)

See Smith, Willy Demarcel

Beauchamp, Clarke (about)

The Young Tycoons. Lloyd Gite. *Black Enterprise* 16, No. 6 (January 1986):44–47

Beavers, Herman

I Yam What You Is and You Is What I Yam. *Callaloo* 9, No. 4 (Fall 1986):565–577

Bechet, Sidney (about)

Sidney Bechet. The Complete Blue Note Sidney Bechet. Record review. Lewis Porter. *Black Perspective in Music* 14, No. 3 (Fall 1986):319–321

Beer, June (about)

June Beer: Nicaraguan Artist. Betty LaDuke. *SAGE* 3, No. 2 (Fall 1986):35–39

Beezer, Bruce

Black Teachers' Salaries and the Federal Courts Before *Brown v. Board of Education*: One Beginning for Equity. *Journal of Negro Education* 55, No.2 (Spring 1986):200–213

Behague, Gerard (editor)

Performance Practice: Ethnomusicological Perspective. Book review. Jacqueline Cogdell DjeDje. *Black Perspective in Music* 14, No. 3 (Fall 1986):306–307

Behounde, Ekitike

Dialectique de la ville de la campagne chez Gabrielle Roy et chez Mongo Beti. Reviewed by Mildred Mortimer. *Research in African Literatures* 17, No. 4 (Winter 1986): 572–574

Beifuss, Joan Turner

At the River I Stand: Memphis, the 1968 Strike and Martin Luther King. Reviewed by Cain H. Felder. *Journal of Religious Thought* 43, No. 2 (Fall-Winter 1986–87):93–94

Belford, November

Moving. Poem. *Black American Literature Forum* 20, No. 3 (Fall 1986):265

Spit Mirror. Poem. *Black American Literature Forum* 20, No. 3 (Fall 1986):264

Bell, Sandra Roberts

In Banks We Trust. *Black Enterprise* 16, No. 12 (July 1986):47

Student-Aid. *Black Enterprise* 17, No. 2 (September 1986):59

Bellman, Beryl

The Language of Secrecy. Reviewed by William P. Murphy. *Research in African Literatures* 17, No. 2 (Summer 1986): 296–298

Bell-Scott, Patricia

In the Company of Educated Women: A History of Women and Higher Education in America. Book review. *Journal of Negro Education* 55, No. 1 (Winter 1986):116–117

Bellush, Jewel

Room at the Top: The Case of District Council 37 of the American Federation of State, County and Municipal Employees in New York City. *SAGE* 3, No. 1 (Spring 1986):35–40

Bellville Potato Chip Company

Cashing in on Chips. Lloyd Gite. *Black Enterprise* 16, No. 12 (July 1986):14

Ben-Amos, Dan

Oral-Formulaic Theory and Research: An Introduction and Annotated Bibliography. Book review. *Research in African Literatures* 17, No. 2 (Summer 1986): 309–310

Benjamin, Anne

Winnie Mandela: Part of My Soul Went with Him. Book review. Jeanne M. Woods. *Black Enterprise* 17, No. 5 (December 1986):19

Benjamin, Medea, and others

No Free Lunch: Food and Revolution in Cuba Today. Reviewed by James E. Austin. *Caribbean Review* 15, No. 2 (Spring 1986):45

Bennett, Carolyn L.

Just What is "Racial Pride?" Editorial. *Journal of Negro Education* 55, No. 1 (Winter 1986):1–2

Bennett, Lerone (Jr.)

Great Moments in Black History: The First Black Governor. *Ebony* 42, No. 1 (November 1986):116

The Ten Biggest Myths about the Black Family. *Ebony* 41, No. 10 (August 1986):134

Bennett, Walter Allen

Pleasant Memories. Poem. *Essence* 17, No. 7 (November 1986):151

Bennett, William J.

What Works: Research about Teaching and Learning. Book review. Patricia B. Campbell. *Interracial Books for Children Bulletin* 17, Nos. 3–4 (1986):37

Bennion, John

The Shape of Memory in John Edgar Wideman's *Sent for You Yesterday*. *Black American Literature Forum* 20, Nos. 1–2 (Spring/Summer 1986):143–150

Ben-Tovim, Gideon, and others

The Local Politics of Race. Book review. Lee Bridges. *Race and Class* 28, No. 2 (August 1986):99–102

Berger, Edward (joint author)

See Berger, Morroe

Berger, Morroe, and others

Benny Carter: A Life in American Music. Book review. Eileen Southern. *Black Perspective in Music* 14, No. 2 (Spring 1986):192–194

Berkeley Citizens Mutual Federal Savings and Loan

Savings and Loan of the Year: The Rebirth of Berkley Savings. Gordon Borell. *Black Enterprise* 16, No. 11 (June 1986):166

Berrian, Brenda F., and others

Studies in Caribbean and South American Literature: An Annual Annotated Bibliography, 1985. *Callaloo* 9, No. 4 (Fall 1986):623–672

Berry, Faith

A Question of Publishers and a Question of Audience. *Black Scholar* 17, No. 2 (March-April 1986):41–49

Berry, Jay R.

Countee Cullen. Book review. *CLA Journal* 29, No. 3 (March 1986):372–377

Berry, Mary Frances

Slavery in the Courtroom: An Annotated Bibliography of American Cases. Book review. *Afro-Americans in New York Life and History* 10, No. 2 (July 1986):65

Berry, Mary Frances (about)

Dr. Mary Frances Berry: Educator-Activist Beats Drum for Civil Rights. Henry Duvall. *About Time* 14, No. 11 (November 1986):16–17

Bertoncini, Elena Zubkova

An Annotated Bibliography of Swahili Fiction and Drama Published between 1975 and 1984. Notes. References. *Research in African Literatures* 17, No. 4 (Winter 1986): 525–562

Berube, Dan

The Power of Protesting. *Black Enterprise* 17, No. 3 (October 1986):22

Betancur, Belisario (about)

Betancur's Battles: The Man of Peace Takes Up the Sword. Bernard Diederich. *Caribbean Review* 15, No. 1 (Winter 1986):10–11+

Betsey, Charles L., and others

Youth Employment and Training Programs: The YEDPA Years. Book review. Robert B. Hill. *Review of Black Political Economy* 15, No. 1 (Summer 1986):107–112

Betto, Frei

Fidel y la Religion: Conversaciones con Frei Betto. Interview. Reviewed by Paul E. Sigmund. *Caribbean Review* 15, No. 2 (Spring 1986):30–31

Bevan, John

Nicaragua. Film review. *Race and Class* 27, No. 3 (Winter 1986):99–102

Beverly, Creigs C. and Stanback, Howard J.

The Black Underclass: Theory and Reality. *Black Scholar* 17, No. 5 (September-October 1986):24–32

Bibliographies

See also Children's Literature

Bibliographies—Africa

Bibliographies for African Studies, 1980–1983. Yvette Scheven, compiler. Reviewed by Nancy J. Schmidt. *Research in African Literatures* 17, No. 1 (Spring 1986): 145–146

Littératures africaines à la Bibliotèque Nationale, 1973–1983. Paulette Lordereau, compiler. Reviewed by Hans E. Panofsky. *Research in African Literatures* 17, No. 4 (Winter 1986): 605–606

Bibliographies—Language and Literature

Publications by CLA Members: 1985–86. Bibliography. Robert J. Hudson and Robert P. Smith (Jr.) *CLA Journal* 30, No. 2 (December 1986):241–251

Bibliographies—Latin America

Recent Books on the Region and its Peoples. Bibliography. Compiled by Marian Goslinga. *Caribbean Review* 15, No. 1 (Winter 1986):45–48

Recent Books on the Region and its Peoples. Bibliography. Compiled by Marian Goslinga. *Caribbean Review* 15, No. 2 (Spring 1986):49–52

Biculturalism

Roots...Still Working. Sydney H. Gallwey. *About Time* 14, No. 2 (February 1986):14–17

Biddle, Robert

Masayuke Oda. Illustrated. *International Review of African American Art* 7, No. 2 (1986):52–59

Bierhorst, John

The Mythology of North America. Book review. Jacquelyn M. Dean. *Interracial Books for Children Bulletin* 17, No. 1 (1986):9

Biles, Roger

A Bittersweet Victory: Public School Desegregation in Memphis. *Journal of Negro Education* 55, No.4 (Fall 1986):470–483

Binns, Karen Genevieve

Bondage (South Africa). Poem. *Essence* 17, No. 1 (May 1986):147

Cathexis. Poem. *Essence* 17, No. 1 (May 1986):147

Birth Control

Birth Control at School: Pass or Fail. Lynn Norment. *Ebony* 41, No. 12 (October 1986):37

Bjornson, Richard

A Bibliography of Cameroonian Literature. Bibliography. Notes. *Research in African Literatures* 17, No. 1 (Spring 1986): 85–126

Bjornvig, Thorkild

The Pact: My Friendship with Isak Dinesen. Reviewed by Casey Bjerregaard Black. *Research in African Literatures* 17, No. 1 (Spring 1986): 155–158

Black, Casey Bjerregaard

De uboendige: Om Ibsen—Blixen—hverdagens virkelighed—det ubevidste. Book review. *Research in African Literatures* 17, No. 1 (Spring 1986): 155–158

The Pact: My Friendship with Isak Dinesen. Book review. *Research in African Literatures* 17, No. 1 (Spring 1986): 155–158

Black Agenda Conference

Dust from the Ashes of Canaan: A Black Agenda Conference. Adolph Dupree. *About Time* 14, No. 9 (September 1986):18–22

Black American Literature Forum

The Way We Were, the Way We Are, the Way We Hope to Be. Joe Weixlmann. *Black American Literature Forum* 20, Nos. 1–2 (Spring/Summer 1986):3–7

Black-American Music Symposium

The Black-American Music Symposium. Georgia Ryder. *Black Perspective in Music* 14, No. 1 (Winter 1986):85–86

Concerts of the Symposium. *Black Perspective in Music* 14, No. 1 (Winter 1986):66–84

Huel Perkins. The Symposium on Black American Music: Consultant's Report. *Black Perspective in Music* 14, No. 1 (Winter 1986):87–88

The Keynote Address. William Warfield. *Black Perspective in Music* 14, No. 1 (Winter 1986):7–12

Program of the Symposium. *Black Perspective in Music* 14, No. 1 (Winter 1986):35–65

The Symposium on Black-American Music: Some Comments. Willis Patterson. *Black Perspective in Music* 14, No. 1 (Winter 1986):4–6

Black Book Club of Fanwood, N. J.

Black Books by Mail. Tonya Bolden Davis. *Black Enterprise* 17, No. 3 (October 1986):26

Blackburn, Bob (about)

Bob Blackburn and the Printmaking Workshop. Hildreth York. *Black American Literature Forum* 20, Nos. 1–2 (Spring/Summer 1986):81–95

Blackburn, Douglas (about)

Douglas Blackburn. By Stephen Gray. Reviewed by Michael Chapman. *Research in African Literatures* 17, No. 3 (Fall 1986): 406–408

Blackburn, Laura (about)

Riding Mass Transit. Donna Johnson. *Black Enterprise* 16, No. 7 (February 1986):26

Blackburne, Anna E.

Rights of a Tenant When the Landlord Defaults on the Mortgage. *Howard Law Journal* 29, No. 1 (1986):27–39

Black English

The Black Prole and Whitespeak: Black English from an Orwellian Perspective. Henry J. Grubb. *Race and Class* 27, No. 3 (Winter 1986):67–80

Black Filmmakers Hall of Fame

Coast to Coast Salute to Black Filmmakers: New York Gala Kicks off the Nationwide Drive for Home for This Film Group. *Ebony* 41, No. 12 (October 1986):91

Black History

Black Progress: Reality or Illusion. By Carol C. Collins. Reviewed by Marianne Ilaw. *Black Enterprise* 16, No. 7 (February 1986):19–21

Great Moments in Black History: The First Black Governor. Lerone Bennett, Jr. *Ebony* 42, No. 1 (November 1986):116

History of the Negro Race in America from 1619 to 1880: Negroes as Slaves, as Soldiers, as Citizens. By George Washington Williams. Reviewed by Joe Johnson. *Crisis* 93, No. 4 (April 1986):12–14

The Myth of Black Progress. By Alphonso Pinkney. Reviewed by Marianne Ilaw. *Black Enterprise* 16, No. 7 (February 1986):19–21

The Price of History. Gwen McKinney. *Black Enterprise* 16, No. 11 (June 1986):48

We Must Honor Our Ancestors. Alex Haley. *Ebony* 41, No. 10 (August 1986):134

Black Methodists for Church Renewal

A Pastoral Letter from John P. Carter. John P. Carter. *Journal of Religious Thought* 43, No. 1 (Spring-Summer 1986):120–127

Black Militant Organizations

Selected Correlates of Perceptions of Black Militancy. Richard D. Bucher. *Western Journal of Black Studies* 10, No. 2 (Summer 1986):79–85

Black Muslims

Beyond Black Power: The Contradiction between Capital and Liberty. Anthony J. Lemelle. *Western Journal of Black Studies* 10, No. 2 (Summer 1986):70–76

From Black Muslims to Muslims. By Clifton E. Marsh. Reviewed by Sulayman S. Nyang. *Phylon* 47, No. 2 (June 1986):169–170

From Sinners to Saints: The Confessions of Saint Augustine and Malcolm X. Notes. Winston A. Van Horne. *Journal of Religious Thought* 43, No. 1 (Spring-Summer 1986):76–101

Liberation Theology and Islamic Revivalism. Notes. Mohammad Yadegari. *Journal of Religious Thought* 43, No. 2 (Fall-Winter 1986–87):38–50

Religious Belief and Political Activism in Black America: An Essay. Robert Michael Franklin. *Journal of Religious Thought* 43, No. 2 (Fall-Winter 1986–87):63–72

See also Black Nationalism

Black Nationalism

The African-American Intellectual and the Struggle for Black Empowerment. Charles Green and Basil Wilson. *Western Journal of Black Studies* 10, No. 2 (Summer 1986):59–69

Application of Memmi's Theory of the Colonizer and the Colonized to the Conflicts in Zimbabwe. Dickson A. Mungazi. *Journal of Negro Education* 55, No.4 (Fall 1986):518–534

Frantz Fanon and Black Consciousness in Azania (South Africa). Thomas K. Ranuga. *Phylon* 47, No. 3 (September 1986):182–191

See also Black Muslims

Black Nationalists

Remembering...Marcus Garvey. Julius Garvey. *Essence* 17, No. 7 (November 1986):63

Black Panther Party

Jean Genet and the Black Panther Party. Robert Sandarg. *Journal of Black Studies* 16, No. 3 (March 1986):269–282

The Legacy of the Black Panther Party. JoNina M. Abron. *Black Scholar* 17, No. 6 (November-December 1986):33–38

Blacks in Art

Hogarth's Blacks: Images of Blacks in Eighteenth Century English Art. David Dabydeen. Reviewed by Roslyn Zalin. *Race and Class* 27, No. 4 (Spring 1986):99–100

Blackside, Inc.

Eyes on the Prize: America's Civil Rights Years, 1954–1965. Film review. Shelley Moore. *Crisis* 93, No. 10 (December 1986):12–13

Blacks in Literature

Images of Blacks in Plays by Black Women. Elizabeth Brown-Guillory. *Phylon* 47, No. 3 (September 1986):230–237

Blacks in the Performing Arts

The Media as Opiate: Blacks in the Performing Arts. Robert Staples. *Western Journal of Black Studies* 10, No. 1 (Spring 1986):6–11

Black Studies Programs

Miller Curriculum Development Process Model: A Systematic Approach to Curriculum Development in Black Studies. Howard J. Miller. *Western Journal of Black Studies* 10, No. 1 (Spring 1986):19–28

On Ranking Professional Achievement in Black Studies: A Reply to Carlos Brossard. Gerald A. McWorter. *Journal of Negro Education* 55, No.2 (Spring 1986):229–235

The Sociological Tradition of E. Franklin Frazier: Implications for Black Studies. Clovis E. Semmes. *Journal of Negro Education* 55, No.4 (Fall 1986):484–494

Black Woman Writer and the Diaspora (Conference)

The Black Woman Writer and the Diaspora, October 27–30, 1985. Linda Susan Beard. *SAGE* 3, No. 2 (Fall 1986):70–71

Blair, Dorothy

Senegalese Literature: A Critical History. Reviewed by Mbye B. Cham. *Research in African Literatures* 17, No. 4 (Winter 1986): 567–569

Blakey, Art (about)

Art Blakey: The Big Beat! David H. Rosenthal. *Black Perspective in Music* 14, No. 3 (Fall 1986):267–289

Blamires, Harry (editor)

A Guide to Twentieth Century Literature in English. Reviewed by G. D. Killam. *Research in African Literatures* 17, No. 3 (Fall 1986): 430

Blanchard, Terence (joint artist)

See Harrison, Donald

Blea, Irene I.

Time and Assimilation Clock. *About Time* 14, No. 1 (January 1986):22

Blount, Carolyne S.

Characteristics of the Black Family. *About Time* 14, No. 3 (March 1986):4

Dr. Ann Creighton Zollar: Assessing the Urban Black Family Experience. *About Time* 14, No. 3 (March 1986):10–13

The Multidimensional Role of Nurses. *About Time* 14, No. 4 (April 1986):8–26

New Forms of Leadership. *About Time* 14, No. 2 (February 1986):8–26

Political Update: An Analysis of Election '86. *About Time* 14, No. 10 (October 1986):8–11

The Power Concept of Alpha Kappa Alpha Sorority. *About Time* 14, No. 6 (June 1986):18–19

Setting New Transportation Lanes: E. L. Lawson Trucking Company, Inc. *About Time* 14, No. 8 (August 1986):30–31

Taking Responsibility for Our Health Care. Editorial. *About Time* 14, No. 4 (April 1986):4

Blount, James M.

Education Is a Team Effort. *About Time* 14, No. 11 (November 1986):4

Minority Firms: Growing in Value and Service. *About Time* 14, No. 8 (August 1986):4

Peter McWalters: Acting Superintendent of Rochester Schools. *About Time* 14, No. 5 (May 1986):14–21

The Political Stakes Are High. *About Time* 14, No. 10 (October 1986):4

Blue Angels

The First Black Blue Angel: Lt. Cmdr. Donnie Cochran Makes Naval History as Member of Famed Precision Flying Team. Aldore Collier. *Ebony* 41, No. 8 (June 1986):27

Bodybuilders

Florida Man Sheds 197 Pounds to Become Body-Building Champ. *Ebony* 42, No. 2 (December 1986):86

Boesak, Allan (about)

Who Can Speak for South Africa? Felicia Kessel. *Crisis* 93, No. 9 (November 1986):28

Bol, Manute (about)

Manute Bol: Tallest Man in Pro Sports Outgrows "Tall Jokes." Norman O. Unger. *Ebony* 42, No. 2 (December 1986):59

Bolden, Dorothy (about)

Dorothy Bolden, Organizer of Domestic Workers: She Was Born Poor but She Would Not Bow Down. Imani-Shelia Newsome. *SAGE* 3, No. 1 (Spring 1986):53–55

Boll, Heinrich (about)

Escape from Lethe: "Unforgetting" in H. Boll's *Billiards at Half Past Nine.* Notes. Jerry A. Varsava. *CLA Journal* 29, No. 4 (June 1986):414–423

Bolles, A. Lynn

African-American Soul Force: Dance, Music and Vera Mae Green. *SAGE* 3, No. 2 (Fall 1986):32–34

Bond, Julian (about)

The Fight for the Fifth. Ann Kimbrough. *Black Enterprise* 17, No. 4 (November 1986):21

Bonds

Finding the Best Bets in Bonds. Denise Lamaute. *Black Enterprise* 17, No. 5 (December 1986):39–40

Bone, Robert

Richard Wright and the Chicago Renaissance. *Callaloo* 9, No. 3 (Summer 1986):446–468

Book Clubs

Black Books by Mail. Tonya Bolden Davis. *Black Enterprise* 17, No. 3 (October 1986):26

Book Reviews

Adventurers and Proletarians: The Story of Migrants in Latin America. By Magnus Mörner. Reviewed by Frances Webber. *Race and Class* 28, No. 2 (August 1986):103–105

Africa and the Discovery of America, Volume I. By Leo Wiener. Reviewed by Phillips Barry. *Journal of African Civilizations* 8, No. 2 (December 1986):197–201

African Images: A Look at Animals in Africa. By Dorcas MacClintock. Reviewed by Geraldine L. Wilson. *Interracial Books for Children Bulletin* 17, No. 2 (1986):13–14

Africanity and the Black Family: The Development of a Theoretical Model. By Wade W. Nobles. Reviewed by S. M. Khatib. *Journal of Black Psychology* 13, No. 1 (August 1986):24–26

African Literature Today No. 14: Insiders and Outsiders. Eldred Durosimi Jones, editor. Reviewed by Lemuel A. Johnson. *Research in African Literatures* 17, No. 3 (Fall 1986): 442–444

The African Origin of Civilization: Myth or Reality. Notes. By Cheikh Anta Diop. Reviewed by A. J. Williams-Myers. *Journal of African Civilizations* 8, No. 1 (June 1986):118–126

African Psychology: Towards Its Reclamation, Reascension and Revitalization. By Wade W. Nobles. Reviewed by S. M. Khatib. *Journal of Black Psychology* 13, No. 1 (August 1986):17–19

African Refugees: Reflections on the African Refugee Problem. By Gaim Kibreab. Reviewed by Maurice Herson. *Race and Class* 27, No. 4 (Spring 1986):104–105

African Religions in Western Conceptual Schemes: The Problem of Interpretation. By Ikenga E. Metuh. Reviewed by C. Ejizu. *Journal of Religious Thought* 43, No. 2 (Fall-Winter 1986–87):90

African Short Stories in English: An Anthology. J. de Grandsaigne, editor. Reviewed by Adewale Maja-Pearce. *Research in African Literatures* 17, No. 4 (Winter 1986): 620–622

African Writers at the Microphone. By Lee Nichols. Reviewed by Alex Tetteh-Lartey. *Research in African Literatures* 17, No. 1 (Spring 1986): 153–155

The Afro-American in Books for Children. Reviewed by Patricia Scott. *Black Scholar* 17, No. 5 (September-October 1986):59

All But the Right Folks. By Joan Kane Nichols. Reviewed by Kate Shackford. *Interracial Books for Children Bulletin* 17, No. 2 (1986):14–15

American Reformers. By Alden Whitman. Reviewed by Howard N. Meyer. *Interracial Books for Children Bulletin* 17, No. 1 (1986):10

Anatomy of a War: Vietnam, the United States and the Modern Historical Experience. By Gabriel Kolko. Reviewed by Saul Landau. *Race and Class* 28, No. 1 (Summer 1986):91–93

...And Ladies of the Club. By Helen Hoover Santmyer. Reviewed by Robert F. Fleissner. *CLA Journal* 29, No. 4 (June 1986):486–489

Annual Review of Jazz Studies. Edited by Dan Morgenstern and others. Reviewed by Lewis Porter. *Black Perspective in Music* 14, No. 2 (Spring 1986):195–196

Anti-Semitism: A Modern Perspective. By Caroline Arnold and Herma Silverstein. Reviewed by Albert V. Schwartz. *Interracial Books for Children Bulletin* 17, No. 2 (1986):18–19

Are You Still My Mother? By Gloria Guss Back. Reviewed by Michael E. Grafton. *Interracial Books for Children Bulletin* 17, Nos. 3–4 (1986):38

Assia Djebar: Romancière algérienne, cinéaste arabe. By Jean Dejeux. Reviewed by Bernadette Cailler. *Research in African Literatures* 17, No. 4 (Winter 1986): 579–581

Athol Fugard. By Dennis Walder. Reviewed by Stephen Gray. *Research in African Literatures* 17, No. 2 (Summer 1986): 281–284

At the River I Stand: Memphis, the 1968 Strike and Martin Luther King. By Joan Turner Beifuss. Reviewed by Cain H. Felder. *Journal of Religious Thought* 43, No. 2 (Fall-Winter 1986–87):93–94

Ayahs, Lascars and Princes: Indians in Britain 1700–1947. By Rozina Visram. Reviewed by Angela Sherlock. *Race and Class* 28, No. 2 (August 1986):106–107

Bad Blood: The Tuskegee Syphilis Experiment. By James H. Jones. Reviewed by Ralph Watkins. *Afro-Americans in New York Life and History* 10, No.1 (January 1986):71–72

Banana Bottom. By Claude McKay. Reviewed by Hazel Waters. *Race and Class* 28, No. 2 (August 1986):106–107

The Bantu-Speaking Heritage of the United States. By Winifred Kellersberger. Reviewed by Joseph E. Holloway. *Phylon* 47, No. 2 (June 1986):167–168

Beating Time: Riot 'n' Race 'n' Rock 'n' Roll. By David Widgery. Reviewed by Liz Fekete. *Race and Class* 28, No. 2 (August 1986):91–93

Benny Carter: A Life in American Music. By Edward Berger and others. Reviewed by Eileen Southern. *Black Perspective in Music* 14, No. 2 (Spring 1986):192–194

Betty Friedan: A Voice for Women's Rights. By Milton Meltzer. Reviewed by Carole M. Martin. *Interracial Books for Children Bulletin* 17, No. 2 (1986):19

Between Women: Domestics and Their Employers. By Judith Rollins. Reviewed by Joyce E. Everett. *SAGE* 3, No. 1 (Spring 1986):61

Beyond Ethnicity: Consent and Descent in American Culture. By Werner Sollors. Reviewed by Anthony Appiah. *Black American Literature Forum* 20, Nos. 1–2 (Spring/Summer 1986):209–224

Bibliographie méthodique et critique de la littérature algérienne de langue française, 1945–1977. By Jean Dejeux. Reviewed by Eric Sellin. *Research in African Literatures* 17, No. 4 (Winter 1986): 581

Bibliographies for African Studies, 1980–1983. Yvette Scheven, compiler. Reviewed by Nancy J. Schmidt. *Research in African Literatures* 17, No. 1 (Spring 1986): 145–146

Bibliography of Black Music. Volume 4: Theory, Education, and Related Studies. By Dominique-René de Lerma. Reviewed by Doris E. McGinty. *Black Perspective in Music* 14, No. 2 (Spring 1986):186–187

A Bibliography of Criticism of Southern African Literature in English. Barbara Richter and Sandra Kotze, compilers. Reviewed by G. E. Gorman. *Research in African Literatures* 17, No. 3 (Fall 1986): 419–421

The Black Abolitionists Papers. Volume I: The British Isles, 1830–1865. C. Peter Ripley, editor. Reviewed by Alexa Benson Henderson. *Phylon* 47, No. 2 (June 1986):168–169

The Black Achievers Coloring Book; The Black Achievers Activity Book (2 vols.). By Mary Russell and Charles Russell. Reviewed by Emily Leinster. *Interracial Books for Children Bulletin* 17, No. 2 (1986):17

Black-American Heritage? By David Tuesday Adamo. Reviewed by Emma S. Etuk. *Journal of Religious Thought* 43, No. 1 (Spring-Summer 1986):128

Black American Politics: From the Washington Marches to Jesse Jackson, vol. 1. By Sanford A. Wright. Reviewed by Sanford A. Wright. *Black Scholar* 17, No. 1 (January-February 1986):45–46

A Black Elite. By Daniel C. Thompson. Reviewed by C. J. Wiltz. *Phylon* 47, No. 4 (December 1986):328–329

Black Gospel. An Illustrated History of the Gospel Sound. By Viv Broughton. Reviewed by André Prévos. *Black Perspective in Music* 14, No. 2 (Spring 1986):191–192

Black Journals of the United States. By Walter C. Daniel. Reviewed by Karen Nadeski. *Western Journal of Black Studies* 10, No. 2 (Summer 1986):102

Black Managers: The Case of the Banking Industry. By Edward D. Irons and Gilbert W. Moore. Reviewed by Willene A. Johnson. *Review of Black Political Economy* 14, No. 4 (Spring 1986):103–108

Black Marxism: The Making of the Black Radical Tradition. By Cedric J. Robinson. Reviewed by V. P. Franklin. *Phylon* 47, No. 3 (September 1986):250–251

Black Politics and Urban Crisis in Britain. By Brian D. Jacobs. Reviewed by Lee Bridges. *Race and Class* 28, No. 2 (August 1986):99–102

Black Progress: Reality or Illusion. By Carol C. Collins. Reviewed by Marianne Ilaw. *Black Enterprise* 16, No. 7 (February 1986):19–21

Black and Red—W. E. B. DuBois and the Afro-American Response to the Cold War—1944–1963. By Gerald Horne. Reviewed by Linda Burnham. *Black Scholar* 17, No. 2 (March-April 1986):52–54

Black Religion and Black Radicalism: An Interpretation of the Religious History of Afro-American People. By Gayraud S. Wilmore. Reviewed by Kenneth Leech. *Race and Class* 28, No. 2 (August 1986):97–99

Blacks in Appalachia. By William H. Turner and Edward J. Cahill. Reviewed by Tommy W. Rogers. *Black Scholar* 17, No. 3 (May-June 1986):58–59

Blacks in College. By J. Fleming. Reviewed by Herman Brown. *Journal of Negro Education* 55, No.2 (Spring 1986):237–239

Black Soul, White Artifact: Fanon's Clinical Psychology and Social Theory. By Jack McCulloch. Reviewed by Hal Wylie. *Research in African Literatures* 17, No. 4 (Winter 1986): 599–601

Black Students in Higher Education. By C. Scully Stikes. Reviewed by Roberta N. Morse. *Journal of Negro Education* 55, No. 1 (Winter 1986):118–120

Blacks and Whites: Narrowing the Gap? By Reynolds Farley. Reviewed by Louis Kushnick. *Race and Class* 27, No. 3 (Winter 1986):106–108

Blacks and White T.V.: Afro-Americans in Television since 1948. By J. Fred McDonald. Reviewed by Robert L. Douglas, Sr. *Western Journal of Black Studies* 10, No. 1 (Spring 1986):44–45

Black and White Children in America: Key Facts. Children's Defense Fund. Reviewed by Gayl Fowler. *Journal of Religious Thought* 43, No. 1 (Spring-Summer 1986):130

Black Women in the Fiction of James Baldwin. By Trudier Davis. Reviewed by Ketu H. Katrak. *Black American Literature Forum* 20, No. 4 (Winter 1986):449–458

Black Women Writers at Work. Interviews. By Claudia Tate. Reviewed by Beth Brown. *CLA Journal* 29, No. 3 (March 1986):380–383

Bloods: An Oral History of the Vietnam War by Black Veterans. By Wallace Terry. Reviewed by Joseph P. Reidy. *Afro-Americans in New York Life and History* 10, No.1 (January 1986):76–78

Blues et gospels. By Marguerite Yourcenar. Reviewed by André Prévos. *Black Perspective in Music* 14, No. 2 (Spring 1986):192

Blues off the Record. Thirty Years of Blues Commentary. By Paul Oliver. Reviewed by André Prévos. *Black Perspective in Music* 14, No. 2 (Spring 1986):190

Bold Money. By Melvin Van Peebles. Reviewed by Denise Lamaute. *Black Enterprise* 17, No. 3 (October 1986):88

The Book Trade of the World, IV: Africa. Sigfred Taubert and Peter Weidhaas, editors. Reviewed by Ilse Sternberg. *Research in African Literatures* 17, No. 1 (Spring 1986): 147–149

Breaking Camp. By Jill Witherspoon Boyer. Reviewed by Gerald Barrax. *Callaloo* 9, No. 1 (Winter 1986):265–269

Brothers and Keepers. By John Wideman. Reviewed by Joe Johnson. *Crisis* 93, No. 3 (March 1986):14–48

Bury Me at the Marketplace: Selected Letters of Es'kia Mphahlele, 1943–1980. N. Chabani Manganyi, editor. Reviewed by Brian Worsfold. *Research in African Literatures* 17, No. 3 (Fall 1986): 395–398

Call Me Woman. By Ellen Kuzwayo. Reviewed by Angus Richmond. *Race and Class* 27, No. 4 (Spring 1986):90–92

Causes for Concern: British Criminal Justice on Trial? Edited by Phil Scraton and Paul Gordon. Reviewed by Busi Chaane. *Race and Class* 28, No. 1 (Summer 1986):103–107

The Ceremony of Innocence. By Jamake Highwater. Reviewed by Jamake Highwater. *Interracial Books for Children Bulletin* 17, No. 1 (1986):6

Charlotte Bronte: The Self Conceived. By Helen Moglen. Reviewed by Elizabeth J. Higgins. *CLA Journal* 29, No. 3 (March 1986):368–371

Civilization or Barbarism: The Legacy of Cheikh Anta Diop. By Cheikh Anta Diop. Reviewed by Leonard Jeffries, Jr. *Journal of African Civilizations* 8, No. 1 (June 1986):146–160

Coagulations: New and Selected Poems. By Jayne Cortez. Reviewed by Barbara T. Christian. *Callaloo* 9, No. 1 (Winter 1986):235–239

Come to Laugh: A Study of African Traditional Theatre in Ghana. By Kwabena N. Bame. Reviewed by Alain Ricard. *Research in African Literatures* 17, No. 2 (Summer 1986): 287

The Commonwealth in Canada: Proceedings of the Second Triennial Conference of the Canadian Association for Commonwealth Literature and Language Studies. Ama Parameswaran, editor. Reviewed by Alastair Niven. *Research in African Literatures* 17, No. 3 (Fall 1986): 435–439

Commonwealth Literatur. Jurgen Schafer, editor. Reviewed by Willfried F. Feuser. *Research in African Literatures* 17, No. 3 (Fall 1986): 430–433

In the Company of Educated Women: A History of Women and Higher Education in America. By Barbara Miller Solomon. Reviewed by Patricia Bell-Scott. *Journal of Negro Education* 55, No. 1 (Winter 1986):116–117

Conference on the Acquisition and Bibliography of Commonwealth and Third World Literatures in English. Commonwealth Institute. Reviewed by Nancy J. Schmidt. *Research in African Literatures* 17, No. 3 (Fall 1986): 439–440

Conrad and Imperialism: Ideological Boundaries and Visionary Frontiers. By Benita Parry. Reviewed by Robert D. Hamner. *Research in African Literatures* 17, No. 1 (Spring 1986): 158–162

Contemporary African Literature. Hal Wylie, Eileen Julien, and Russell J. Linnemann, editors. Reviewed by J. I. Okonkwo. *Research in African Literatures* 17, No. 3 (Fall 1986): 445–448

Countee Cullen. By Alan R. Shucard. Reviewed by Jay R. Berry. *CLA Journal* 29, No. 3 (March 1986):372–377

Crazy Quilt. By Jocelyn Riley. Reviewed by Betty Bacon. *Interracial Books for Children Bulletin* 17, No. 1 (1986):6–7

Critical Perspectives on Christopher Okigbo. Donatus Ibe Nwonga, editor. Reviewed by Catherine Obianuju Acholonu. *Research in African Literatures* 17, No. 4 (Winter 1986): 613–614

Critical Perspectives on Ngugi wa Thiong'o. G. D. Killam, editor. Reviewed by D. A. Maughan Brown. *Research in African Literatures* 17, No. 4 (Winter 1986): 614–617

Cuba's Nicolás Guillén: Poetry and Ideology. By Keith Ellis. Reviewed by Chris Searle. *Race and Class* 28, No. 1 (Summer 1986):107-108

The Cultural Unity of Black Africa: The Domains of Patriarchy and of Matriarchy in Classical Antiquity. Bibliography. By Cheikh Anta Diop. Reviewed by Asa G. Hilliard III. *Journal of African Civilizations* 8, No. 1 (June 1986):102-109

A Daughter's Geography. By Ntozake Shange. Reviewed by Beth Brown. *CLA Journal* 29, No. 3 (March 1986):378-380

Dessa Rose. By Sherley Anne Williams. Reviewed by Doris Davenport. *Black American Literature Forum* 20, No. 3 (Fall 1986):335-340

De uboendige: Om Ibsen—Blixen—hverdagens virkelighed—det ubevidste. By Aage Hendriksen. Reviewed by Casey Bjerregaard Black. *Research in African Literatures* 17, No. 1 (Spring 1986): 155-158

The Devil and Dr. Church: A Guide to Hell for Atheists and True Believers. By F. Forrester Church. Reviewed by Kortright Davis. *Journal of Religious Thought* 43, No. 2 (Fall-Winter 1986-87):91

Dialectique de la ville de la campagne chez Gabrielle Roy et chez Mongo Beti. By Ekitike Behounde. Reviewed by Mildred Mortimer. *Research in African Literatures* 17, No. 4 (Winter 1986): 572-574

Don't Be My Valentine. By Joan M. Lexau. Reviewed by Emily Leinster. *Interracial Books for Children Bulletin* 17, No. 1 (1986):6

Doris Lessing. By Lorna Sage. Reviewed by Roberta Rubenstein. *Research in African Literatures* 17, No. 3 (Fall 1986): 411-413

Douglas Blackburn. By Stephen Gray. Reviewed by Michael Chapman. *Research in African Literatures* 17, No. 3 (Fall 1986): 406-408

Drama of the Gods: A Study of Seven African Plays. By Martin Owusu. Reviewed by Mary T. David. *Research in African Literatures* 17, No. 2 (Summer 1986): 276-278

Dreamgirls: My Life as a Supreme. By Mary Wilson. Reviewed by Norman Riley. *Crisis* 93, No. 10 (December 1986):9

Drumbeats, Masks, and Metaphor: Contemporary Afro-American Theatre. By Genevieve Fabre. Reviewed by Errol Hill. *Black American Literature Forum* 20, No. 4 (Winter 1986):459-462

Dyslexia: Understanding Reading Problems. By John Savage. Reviewed by Emily Strauss Watson. *Interracial Books for Children Bulletin* 17, No. 2 (1986):15-16

East African Literature: An Anthology. Arne Zettersten, editor. Reviewed by Peter Nazareth. *Research in African Literatures* 17, No. 1 (Spring 1986): 140-142

The Education of Black Children and Youths: A Framework for Excellence. By Samuel L. Banks. Reviewed by Sandra Noel Smith. *Journal of Negro Education* 55, No.4 (Fall 1986):551-552

Education on Trial: Strategies for the Future. Edited by William L. Johnston. Reviewed by Laurence R. Marcus. *Journal of Negro Education* 55, No.4 (Fall 1986):548-549

Elegies for Patrice. By Kiarri T.-H. Cheatwood. Reviewed by Gerald Barrax. *Callaloo* 9, No. 1 (Winter 1986):263-265

The Elephant Man. By Frederick Drimmer. Reviewed by Emily Strauss Watson. *Interracial Books for Children Bulletin* 17, Nos. 3-4 (1986):33

En defensa de Mexico: pensamiento economico politico. By Jesus Silva Herzog. Reviewed by Jorge Salazar-Carrillo. *Caribbean Review* 15, No. 2 (Spring 1986):46

Endless War: How We Got Involved in Central America—and What Can Be Done About It. By James Chace. Reviewed by Alexander H. McIntire, Jr. *Caribbean Review* 15, No. 1 (Winter 1986):44

Essais d'histoire littéraire africaine. By Albert Gerard. Reviewed by Mohamadou Kane. *Research in African Literatures* 17, No. 4 (Winter 1986): 563-565

Essays on Haitian Literature. By Léon-François Hoffmann. Reviewed by Maurice A. Lubin. *Research in African Literatures* 17, No. 4 (Winter 1986): 593-595

Estado empresario y lucha politica en Costa Rica. By Ana Sojo. Reviewed by Francisco A. Leguizamon. *Caribbean Review* 15, No. 2 (Spring 1986):45-46

Ethics, Education and Administrative Decisions: A Book of Readings. Edited by Peter Andre Sola. Reviewed by Joseph L. DeVitis. *Journal of Negro Education* 55, No.4 (Fall 1986):549-550

Ethnicity, Class and Gender in Australia. Edited by Gill Bottomley and Marie de Lepervanche. Reviewed by Stephen Castle. *Race and Class* 27, No. 4 (Spring 1986):94-96

Ethnicity and Race in the USA: Toward the Twenty-First Century. By Richard D. Alba. Reviewed by Mary Ellison. *Race and Class* 27, No. 3 (Winter 1986):109-110

The Evidence of Things Not Seen. By James Baldwin. Reviewed by Joe Johnson. *Crisis* 93, No. 3 (March 1986):14-48

The Evidence of Things Not Seen. By James Baldwin. Reviewed by Tonya Bolden Davis. *Black Enterprise* 16, No. 11 (June 1986):38

Explorations in the Novel: A Student's Guide to Setworks at South African Universities. C. H. Muller, editor. Reviewed by Martin Trump. *Research in African Literatures* 17, No. 3 (Fall 1986): 419-421

Exploring Buried Buxton: Archeology of an Abandoned Iowa Coal Mining Town with a Large Black Population. By David M. Gradwohl and Nancy M. Osborn. Reviewed by Maria Boynton. *Afro-Americans in New York Life and History* 10, No. 2 (July 1986): 65-68

Faith in the City: A Call for Action by Church and Nation. By Archbishop of Canterbury's Commission on Urban Priority Areas. Reviewed by Paul Grant. *Race and Class* 27, No. 4 (Spring 1986):97–98

Family and Nation. By Daniel Patrick Moynihan. Reviewed by Tonya Bolden Davis. *Black Enterprise* 17, No. 3 (October 1986):17

Fidel y la Religion: Conversaciones con Frei Betto. Interview. Reviewed by Paul E. Sigmund. *Caribbean Review* 15, No. 2 (Spring 1986):30–31

Fire from the Mountain: The Making of a Sandinista. By Omar Cabezas. Reviewed by David E. Lewis. *Black Scholar* 17, No. 1 (January-February 1986):49

First Impressions: Critics Look at the New Literature. Compiled by Forrest D. Colburn. *Caribbean Review* 15, No. 1 (Winter 1986):41–44

First Impressions: Critics Look at the New Literature. Compiled by Forrest D. Colburn. *Caribbean Review* 15, No. 2 (Spring 1986):45–48

First Your Penny. By Donna Hill. Reviewed by Emily Strauss Watson. *Interracial Books for Children Bulletin* 17, No. 2 (1986):17–18

Fools and Other Stories. By Njabulo Ndebele. Reviewed by Gerald D. Kendrick. *Black Scholar* 17, No. 4 (July-August 1986):57–58

Free Coloreds in the Slave Societies of St. Kitts and Grenada, 1763–1833. By Edward L. Cox. Reviewed by Keith C. Simmonds. *Phylon* 47, No. 4 (December 1986):327–328

Freedom Rising. By James North. Reviewed by Mwizenge S. Tembo. *Black Scholar* 17, No. 1 (January-February 1986):47–48

From Black Muslims to Muslims. By Clifton E. Marsh. Reviewed by Sulayman S. Nyang. *Phylon* 47, No. 2 (June 1986):169–170

Getting to Know the General, The Story of an Involvement. By Graham Greene. Reviewed by Neale Pearson. *Caribbean Review* 15, No. 1 (Winter 1986):26–27 +

The Gift of Administration. By Thomas C. Campbell and Gary B. Reierson. Reviewed by James Hammond. *Journal of Religious Thought* 43, No. 1 (Spring-Summer 1986):128–129

Give Us Each Day: The Diary of Alice Dunbar-Nelson. Edited by Gloria T. Hull. Reviewed by Elizabeth Brown-Guillory. *SAGE* 3, No. 2 (Fall 1986):57–59

Gleanings. By Lou Willett Stanek. Reviewed by Christine Jenkins. *Interracial Books for Children Bulletin* 17, No. 1 (1986):8

Gleanings from the Desegregation Research. Essay Review. Marjorie Hanson. *Journal of Negro Education* 55, No.1 (Winter 1986):107–115

Going to the Territory. By Ralph Ellison. Reviewed by Joe Johnson. *Crisis* 93, No. 10 (December 1986):10

The Good Thoughts Series. By Jane Hoober Peifer and Marilyn Peifer Nolt. Reviewed by Ashley Pennington. *Interracial Books for Children Bulletin* 17, No. 2 (1986):16–17

The Gospel Sound. Good News and Bad Times. By Anthony Heilbut. Reviewed by André Prévos. *Black Perspective in Music* 14, No. 2 (Spring 1986):191

Government and Politics in Africa. By William Tordoff. Reviewed by Nancy Murray. *Race and Class* 27, No. 4 (Spring 1986):107–108

Grassroots Development in Latin America and the Caribbean: Oral Histories of Social Change. By Robert Wasserstrom. Reviewed by Linda Miller. *Caribbean Review* 15, No. 1 (Winter 1986):41–42

Grenada: The Hour Will Strike Again. By Jan Carew. Reviewed by Cameron McCarthy. *Race and Class* 28, No. 2 (August 1986):89–91

Groundwork: Charles Hamilton Houston and the Struggle for Civil Rights. By Genna Rae McNeil. Reviewed by Marsha Jones. *About Time* 14, No. 2 (February 1986):18–20

A Guide to Political Censorship in South Africa. By Louise Silver. Reviewed by Neville Choonoo. *Research in African Literatures* 17, No. 3 (Fall 1986): 416–418

A Guide to Twentieth Century Literature in English. Harry Blamires, editor. Reviewed by G. D. Killam. *Research in African Literatures* 17, No. 3 (Fall 1986): 430

A Handbook for Teaching African Literature. By Elizabeth Gunner. Reviewed by Anne Walmsley. *Research in African Literatures* 17, No. 1 (Spring 1986): 149–153

The Happiest Ending. By Yoshiko Uchida. Reviewed by Valerie Ooka Pang. *Interracial Books for Children Bulletin* 17, No. 1 (1986):7

The Harlem Renaissance: A Historical Dictionary for the Era. Edited by Bruce Kellner. Reviewed by Arnold Rampersad. *Callaloo* 9, No. 4 (Fall 1986):749–750

Heart Politics. By Fran Peavey. Reviewed by Tracy Dalton. *Interracial Books for Children Bulletin* 17, Nos. 3–4 (1986):38

Heroes are Grazing in My Garden. By Herbert Padilla. Reviewed by Roland E. Bush. *Caribbean Review* 15, No. 1 (Winter 1986):41

The History and Historiography of Commonwealth Literature. Dieter Riemenschneider, editor. Reviewed by Gareth Griffiths. Book review. *Research in African Literatures* 17, No. 3 (Fall 1986): 433–435

History of the Negro Race in America from 1619 to 1880: Negroes as Slaves, as Soldiers, as Citizens. By George Washington Williams. Reviewed by Joe Johnson. *Crisis* 93, No. 4 (April 1986):12–14

Hogarth's Blacks: Images of Blacks in Eighteenth Century English Art. By David Dabydeen. Reviewed by Roslyn Zalin. *Race and Class* 27, No. 4 (Spring 1986):99–100

Holy Violence: The Revolutionary Thought of Frantz Fanon. By Marie Perinbam. Reviewed by Hal Wylie. *Research in African Literatures* 17, No. 4 (Winter 1986): 597–599

Home and Exile and Other Selections. By Lewis Nkosi. Reviewed by James Booth. *Research in African Literatures* 17, No. 3 (Fall 1986): 398–401

Home in the Sky. By Jeannie Baker. Reviewed by Emily Leinster. *Interracial Books for Children Bulletin* 17, No. 1 (1986):8–9

Horace Bushnell: Sermons. Edited by Conrad Cherry. Reviewed by Kortright Davis. *Journal of Religious Thought* 43, No. 2 (Fall-Winter 1986–87):91–92

The Hornes: An American Family. By Gail Lumet Buckley. Reviewed by Joe Johnson. *Crisis* 93, No. 8 (October 1986):14–16

The Hornes: An American Family. By Gail Lumet Buckley. Reviewed by Tonya Bolden Davis. *Black Enterprise* 17, No. 3 (October 1986):18

The House of Si Abd Allah: The Oral History of a Moroccan Family. Henry Munson, Jr., editor and translator. Reviewed by James A. Miller. *Research in African Literatures* 17, No. 4 (Winter 1986): 582–584

The Ideology of the New Right. Edited Ruth Levitas. Reviewed by Paul Gordon. *Race and Class* 28, No. 1 (Summer 1986):95–97

Igbo Language and Culture II. F. C. Ogbalu and E. N. Emenanjo, editors. Reviewed by Kalu Ogbaa. *Research in African Literatures* 17, No. 2 (Summer 1986): 291–293

Illiterate America. By Jonathan Kozol. Reviewed by Edwin Hamilton. *Journal of Negro Education* 55, No. 1 (Winter 1986):117–118

Illiterate America. By Jonathan Kozol. Reviewed by Sharon Shervington. *Black Enterprise* 17, No. 2 (September 1986):15

Images et mythes d'Haiti. By Daniel-Henry Pageaux. Reviewed by Clarisse Zimra. *Research in African Literatures* 17, No. 4 (Winter 1986): 591–593

The Impact of Cybernation Technology on Black Automotive Workers in the United States. By Samuel D. K. James. Reviewed by Julianne Malveaux. *Review of Black Political Economy* 15, No. 1 (Summer 1986):103–105

Including All of Us: An Early Childhood Curriculum about Disability. By Merle Froschl and others. Reviewed by Emily Strauss Watson. *Interracial Books for Children Bulletin* 17, Nos. 3–4 (1986):37–38

I Never Scream: New and Selected Poems. By Pinkie Gordon Lane. Reviewed by Lillian D. Roland. *Black American Literature Forum* 20, No. 3 (Fall 1986):294–298

Interdisciplinary Dimensions of African Literature. Kofi Anyidoho, Abioseh M. Porter, Daniel Racine, and Janice Spleth, editors. Reviewed by C. L. Innes. *Research in African Literatures* 17, No. 3 (Fall 1986): 449–451

An Introduction to the French Caribbean Novel. By Beverley Ormerod. Reviewed by Suzanne Crosta. *CLA Journal* 29, No. 4 (June 1986):497–500

Issues in American History: The Worker in America. By Jane Claypool. Reviewed by Jan M. Goodman. *Interracial Books for Children Bulletin* 17, No. 2 (1986):13

Iteso Thought Patterns in Tales. By Grace Akello. Reviewed by John Lamphear. *Research in African Literatures* 17, No. 2 (Summer 1986): 298–299

Jamaica's Find. By Juanita Havill. Reviewed by Judy Rogers. *Interracial Books for Children Bulletin* 17, Nos. 3–4 (1986):35

Jazz Styles: History and Analysis. By Mark C. Gridley. Reviewed by George L. Starks, Jr. *Black Perspective in Music* 14, No. 2 (Spring 1986):188–189

Jazz Talk: The Cadence Interviews. By Robert D. Rusch. Reviewed by George L. Starks, Jr. *Black Perspective in Music* 14, No. 2 (Spring 1986):187–188

Jelly Roll, Jabbo and Fats: Nineteen Portraits in Jazz. By Whitney Balliett. Reviewed by Beth Brown Utada. *Journal of Black Studies* 16, No. 4 (June 1986):451–453

The Jesse Jackson Phenomenon: The Crisis of Purpose in Afro-American Politics. By Adolph Reed. Reviewed by Shirley Washington. *Black Scholar* 17, No. 6 (November-December 1986):52–53

Jimmy Lee Did It. By Pat Cummings. Reviewed by Emily Leinster. *Interracial Books for Children Bulletin* 17, No. 1 (1986):8

Joseph Conrad and Africa. By Henryk Zins. Reviewed by Martin Tucker. *Research in African Literatures* 17, No. 3 (Fall 1986): 440–442

Jouer le jeu. L'improviste II. By Jacques Reda. Reviewed by André Prévos. *Black Perspective in Music* 14, No. 2 (Spring 1986):190–191

Journey to Almost There. By JoAnn Bren Guernsey. Reviewed by Betty Bacon. *Interracial Books for Children Bulletin* 17, No. 2 (1986):18

J. P. Clark. By Robert M. Wren. Reviewed by Thomas R. Knipp. *Research in African Literatures* 17, No. 2 (Summer 1986): 278–281

Julie's Daughter. By Colby Rodowsky. Reviewed by Christine Jenkins. *Interracial Books for Children Bulletin* 17, No. 1 (1986):7–8

Junius Over Far. By Virginia Hamilton. Reviewed by Daphne Muse. *Interracial Books for Children Bulletin* 17, Nos. 3–4 (1986):34

Kaffir Boy: The True Story of a Black Youth's Coming of Age in Apartheid South Africa. By Mark Mathabane. Reviewed by Tonya Bolden Davis. *Black Enterprise* 17, No. 5 (December 1986):20

Kaiso! the Trinidad Calypso: A Study of the Calypso as Oral Literature. By Keith Q. Warner. Reviewed by Jacqueline Cogdell DjeDje. *Black Perspective in Music* 14, No. 3 (Fall 1986):309

Kamerunische Marchen: Text und Kontext in ethnosoziologischer und psychologischer Sicht. By Norbert Ndong. Reviewed by Tunde Okanlawon. *Research in African Literatures* 17, No. 2 (Summer 1986): 294

Keeping Track: How Schools Structure Inequality. By J. Oakes. Reviewed by Nancy L. Arnez. *Journal of Negro Education* 55, No.2 (Spring 1986):244–246

Kikuyu People: A Brief Outline of their Customs and Traditions. By E. N. Mugo. Reviewed by Simon Gikandi. *Research in African Literatures* 17, No. 2 (Summer 1986): 299–301

Labor of Love, Labor of Sorrow: Black Women, Work, and the Family from Slavery to the Present. By Jacqueline Jones. Reviewed by Nancy Murray. *Race and Class* 28, No. 2 (August 1986):96–97

Labor of Love, Labor of Sorrow. By Jacqueline Jones. Reviewed by Julianne Malveaux. *Black Scholar* 17, No. 2 (March-April 1986):51–52

The Language of Secrecy. By Beryl Bellman. Reviewed by William P. Murphy. *Research in African Literatures* 17, No. 2 (Summer 1986): 296–298

La nouvelle génération de poètes congolais. By Leopold-Pindy Mamonsono. Reviewed by Daniel Whitman. *Research in African Literatures* 17, No. 4 (Winter 1986): 570–572

La parole des femmes: Essais sur des romancières des Antilles de langue française. By Maryse Conde. Reviewed by John William. *Black Scholar* 17, No. 4 (July-August 1986):57

La rive noire: De Harlem à la Seine. By Michel Fabre. Reviewed by Clarisse Zimra. *Research in African Literatures* 17, No. 4 (Winter 1986): 601–603

La ville dans le roman africain. By Roger Chemain. Reviewed by S. Ade Ojo. *Research in African Literatures* 17, No. 4 (Winter 1986): 574–576

Law and the Political Environment in Guyana. By Randolph W. James and Harold A. Lutchman. Reviewed by Ivelaw L. Griffith. *Black Scholar* 17, No. 3 (May-June 1986):58

Léon-Gontran Dumas: L'homme et l'oeuvre. By Daniel Racine. Reviewed by Martin Steins. *Research in African Literatures* 17, No. 4 (Winter 1986): 587–588

Le Blues authentique. Son histoire et ses thèmes. By Robert Springer. Reviewed by André Prévos. *Black Perspective in Music* 14, No. 2 (Spring 1986):189–190

Legends and History of the Luba. By Harold Womersley. Reviewed by J. Eric Lane. *Research in African Literatures* 17, No. 2 (Summer 1986): 306–308

Le personnage féminin dans le roman maghrébin de langue française des indépendances à 1980: Representations et fonctions. By Anne-Marie Nisbet. Reviewed by Charlotte H. Bruner. *Research in African Literatures* 17, No. 4 (Winter 1986):576–579

Le Roi Nyamwezi, la Droite et la Gauche: Révision Comparative des Classifications Dualistes. By Serge Tcherkezoff. Reviewed by Wyatt MacGarrey. *Research in African Literatures* 17, No. 2 (Summer 1986): 304–306

Lester Young. By Lewis Porter. Reviewed by Eileen Southern. *Black Perspective in Music* 14, No. 2 (Spring 1986):194

Letters to Alice: On First Reading Jane Austen. By Fay Weldon. Reviewed by Louis D. Mitchell. *CLA Journal* 30, No. 1 (September 1986):104–106

The Life of Jane Austen. By John Halperin. Reviewed by Louis D. Mitchell. *CLA Journal* 30, No. 1 (September 1986):104–106

The Life of Langston Hughes: Volume I: 1902–41. By Arnold Rampersad. Reviewed by Joe Johnson. *Crisis* 93, No. 9 (November 1986):12–13

The Limits of Victory, The Ratification of the Panama Canal Treaties. By George D. Moffett III. Reviewed by Neale Pearson. *Caribbean Review* 15, No. 1 (Winter 1986):26–27 +

Linking Our Lives: Chinese American Women of Los Angeles. By the Chinese Historical Society of Southern California. Reviewed by Lillian Yeh. *Interracial Books for Children Bulletin* 17, Nos. 3–4 (1986):34

Literature Africana Literature Necessaria, II—Moçambique, Cabo Verde, Guiné-Bissau, Sao Tomé e Principe. Russell G. Hamilton, translator. Reviewed by Gerald Moser. *Research in African Literature* 17, No. 3 (Fall 1986):422-425

Literature for Children and Young People in Kenya. By Asenath Bole Odaga. Reviewed by Nancy J. Schmidt. *Research in African Literatures* 17, No. 4 (Winter 1986): 609–610

Literature and Imperialism. Bart Moore-Gilbert, editor. Reviewed by Robert D. Hamner. *Research in African Literatures* 17, No. 1 (Spring 1986): 162–165

Littérature et méthodologie. By A. Kone, et al. Reviewed by Mineke Schipper. *Research in African Literatures* 17, No. 4 (Winter 1986): 566–567

Littératures africaines à la Bibliotèque Nationale, 1973–1983. Paulette Lordereau, compiler. Reviewed by Hans E. Panofsky. *Research in African Literatures* 17, No. 4 (Winter 1986): 605–606

Living Room. By June Jordan. Reviewed by Joanne V. Gabbin. *Callaloo* 9, No. 1 (Winter 1986):240–242

Living in Two Worlds. By Maxine Rosenberg. Reviewed by Emily and Sasha Leinster. *Interracial Books for Children Bulletin* 17, Nos. 3–4 (1986):33–34

The Local Politics of Race. By Gideon Ben-Tovim and others. Reviewed by Lee Bridges. *Race and Class* 28, No. 2 (August 1986):99–102

Malagasy Tale Index. By Lee Haring. Reviewed by Daniel J. Crowley. *Research in African Literatures* 17, No. 2 (Summer 1986): 308–309

The Mandinka Balafon: An Introduction with Notation for Teaching. By Lynne Jessup. Reviewed by Jacqueline Cogdell DjeDje. *Black Perspective in Music* 14, No. 3 (Fall 1986):307–308

Man Sharing: Dilemma or Choice. By Audrey B. Chapman. Reviewed by Henry Duvall. *About Time* 14, No. 12 (December 1986):29

Margaret Thatcher: Britain's "Iron Lady." By Doris Faber. Reviewed by Carole M. Martin. *Interracial Books for Children Bulletin* 17, No. 2 (1986):15

Martin Luther King, Jr.: To the Mountaintop. By William Roger Witherspoon. Reviewed by Elaine Gregg. *Black Enterprise* 16, No. 6 (January 1986):18

Martin Luther King, Jr.: To the Mountaintop. By William Roger Witherspoon. Reviewed by Hortense D. Lloyd. *Negro Educational Review* 37, No. 1 (January 1986):46–47

The Marxist Analyses of Manning Marable. By Manning Marable. Reviewed by John Williams. *Phylon* 47, No. 3 (September 1986):248–250

Melvin B. Tolson 1898–1966: Plain Talk and Poetic Prophecy. By Robert M. Farnsworth. Reviewed by Raymond Nelson. *Callaloo* 9, No. 1 (Winter 1986):270–272

Men Out of Asia: A Review and Update of the Gladwin Thesis. Notes. By Harold Sterling Gladwin. Reviewed by Runoko Rashidi. *Journal of African Civilizations* 8, No. 2 (December 1986):248–263

Mexico: A History. By Robert Ryal Miller. Reviewed by Lowell Gudmundson. *Caribbean Review* 15, No. 1 (Winter 1986):43

Modernism and Negritude: The Poetry and Poetics of Aime Cesaire. By James A. Arnold. Reviewed by Vera M. Kutzinski. *Callaloo* 9, No. 4 (Fall 1986):740–748

A Moment's Notice: Portraits of American Jazz Musicians. By Carol Friedman and Gary Giddins. Reviewed by George L. Starks, Jr. *Black Perspective in Music* 14, No. 3 (Fall 1986):312–313

The Motown Story. By Don Waller. Reviewed by Doris E. McGinty. *Black Perspective in Music* 14, No. 3 (Fall 1986):310–311

Movement in Black: The Collected Poetry of Pat Parker. By Pat Parker. Reviewed by Gerald Barrax. *Callaloo* 9, No. 1 (Winter 1986):259–262

The Music of Black Americans: A History. By Eileen Southern. Reviewed by Doris E. McGinty. *Black Perspective in Music* 14, No. 2 (Spring 1986):185–186

Musicmakers of West Africa. By John Collins. Reviewed by Jacqueline Cogdell DjeDje. *Black Perspective in Music* 14, No. 3 (Fall 1986):308–309

The Myth of Black Progress. By Alphonso Pinkney. Reviewed by Hurumia Ahadi. *Black Scholar* 17, No. 2 (March-April 1986):50–51

The Myth of Black Progress. By Alphonso Pinkney. Reviewed by Louis Kushnick. *Race and Class* 27, No. 3 (Winter 1986):106–108

The Myth of Black Progress. By Alphonso Pinkney. Reviewed by Marianne Ilaw. *Black Enterprise* 16, No. 7 (February 1986):19–21

The Mythology of North America. By John Bierhorst. Reviewed by Jacquelyn M. Dean. *Interracial Books for Children Bulletin* 17, No. 1 (1986):9

Myths of Coeducation. By Florence Howe. *Interracial Books for Children Bulletin* 17, No. 1 (1986):10

Nadine Gordimer: Politics and the Order of Art. Reviewed by Sheila Roberts. *Research in African Literatures* 17, No. 3 (Fall 1986): 408–411

Nelson Mandela: The Struggle Is My Life. By Nelson Mandela. Reviewed by Genevieve H. Wilson. *About Time* 14, No. 9 (September 1986):23–25

Newspaper Columns by W. E. B. Du Bois. Compiled and edited by Herbert Aptheker. Reviewed by David F. Dorsey (Jr.) *CLA Journal* 30, No. 2 (December 1986):254–258

Ngambika: Studies of Women in African Literature. Edited by Carole Boyce Davies and Anne Adams Graves. Reviewed by Iely Burkhead Mohamed. *SAGE* 3, No. 2 (Fall 1986):59–60

Nicaragua: Revolution in the Family. By Shirley Christian. Reviewed by Saul Landau. *Race and Class* 27, No. 3 (Winter 1986):95–99

Nicaragua under Siege. Marlene Dixon and Susanne Jonas, editors. Reviewed by John A. Booth. *Caribbean Review* 15, No. 2 (Spring 1986):47

Nigeria and Its Invaders 1851–1920. By J. U. J. Asiegbu. Reviewed by Lai Olurode. *Journal of Black Studies* 16, No. 4 (June 1986):457–460

Night Journey. By Kathryn Lasky. Reviewed by Suzi Wizowaty. *Interracial Books for Children Bulletin* 17, Nos. 3–4 (1986):35–36

No Free Lunch: Food and Revolution in Cuba Today. By Medea Benjamin, Joseph Collins, and Michael Scott. Reviewed by James E. Austin. *Caribbean Review* 15, No. 2 (Spring 1986):45

Nostalgia for the Present: An Anthology of Writings. Edited by Kofi Natambu. Reviewed by Barbara Harlow. *Black American Literature Forum* 20, No. 3 (Fall 1986):317–326

Now Is the Thing to Praise. By Dolores Kendrick. Reviewed by Gerald Barrax. *Callaloo* 9, No. 1 (Winter 1986):248–254

Olive Schreiner and After: Essays on Southern African Literature in Honor of Guy Butler. Malvern van Wyk Smith and Don Maclennan, editors. Reviewed by Dennis Walder. *Research in African Literatures* 17, No. 3 (Fall 1986): 401–404

One More Day's Journey. By Allen B. Ballard. Reviewed by Beth Brown Utada. *Journal of Black Studies* 16, No. 4 (June 1986):453–456

On Fire. By Ouida Sebestyen. Reviewed by Rudine Sims. *Interracial Books for Children Bulletin* 17, Nos. 3–4 (1986):34–35

On Living in an Old Country: The National Past in Contemporary Britain. By Patrick Wright. Reviewed by Nancy Murray. *Race and Class* 28, No. 1 (Summer 1986):93–95

Oral-Formulaic Theory and Research: An Introduction and Annotated Bibliography. By John Miles Foley. Reviewed by Dan Ben-Amos. *Research in African Literatures* 17, No. 2 (Summer 1986): 309–310

Oral Literature of the Maasai. By Naomi Kipury. Reviewed by Clement Abiaziem Okafor. *Research in African Literatures* 17, No. 2 (Summer 1986): 301–304

Oral Poetry from Africa. Jack Mapanje and Landeg White, editors. Reviewed by Oyekan Owomoyela. *Research in African Literatures* 17, No. 1 (Spring 1986): 137–140

The Origin of Faulkner's Art. By Judith L. Sensibar. Reviewed by Elizabeth J. Higgins. *CLA Journal* 29, No. 4 (June 1986):490–492

The Origins of the Civil Rights Movement: Black Communities Organizing for Change. By Alden Morris. Reviewed by Diane Pinderhughes. *CAAS Newsletter* 9, No. 2 (1986):14

Our Dead Behind Us. By Audre Lorde. Reviewed by Joseph A. Brown. *Callaloo* 9, No. 4 (Fall 1986):737–739

Our Nig; Or, Sketches from the Life of a Free Black. Henry Louis Gates, editor. Reviewed by Beth Brown. *CLA Journal* 29, No. 3 (March 1986):383–386

The Oval Amulet. By Lucy Cullyforth Babbitt. Reviewed by Carole M. Martin. *Interracial Books for Children Bulletin* 17, No. 2 (1986):16

The Pact: My Friendship with Isak Dinesen. By Thorkild Bjornvig. Reviewed by Casey Bjerregaard Black. *Research in African Literatures* 17, No. 1 (Spring 1986): 155–158

Palestine and Modern Arab Poetry. By Khalid A. Sulaiman. Reviewed by Barbara Harlow. *Race and Class* 27, No. 3 (Winter 1986):102–103

Panama, Desastre...o Democracia. By Ricardo Arias Calderon. Reviewed by Neale Pearson. *Caribbean Review* 15, No. 1 (Winter 1986):26–27 +

Panama Odyssey. By William J. Jorden. Reviewed by Ambler H. Moss, Jr. *Caribbean Review* 15, No. 1 (Winter 1986):43–44

Panama Odyssey. By William J. Jorden. Reviewed by Neale Pearson. *Caribbean Review* 15, No. 1 (Winter 1986):26–27 +

Passbook Number F.47927: Women and Mau Mau in Kenya. By Muthoni Likimani. Reviewed by Hilary Fisher. *Race and Class* 27, No. 4 (Spring 1986):96–97

Performance Practice: Ethnomusicological Perspective. Edited by Gerard Behague. Reviewed by Jacqueline Cogdell DjeDje. *Black Perspective in Music* 14, No. 3 (Fall 1986):306–307

Phillis Wheatley and Her Writings. By William H. Robinson. Reviewed by Paul Edwards. *Research in African Literatures* 17, No. 1 (Spring 1986): 130–133

Plum Bun: A Novel without a Moral. By Jessie Redmon Fauset. Reviewed by Beth Brown. *Black Scholar* 17, No. 4 (July-August 1986):58–59

The Political Economy of the Urban Ghetto. By Daniel R. Fusfield and Timothy Bates. Reviewed by Barbara A. P. Jones. *Review of Black Political Economy* 14, No. 4 (Spring 1986):99–102

Politics in African Poetry. By Tayo Olafioye. Reviewed by Tanure Ojaide. *Research in African Literatures* 17, No. 4 (Winter 1986): 611–613

The Politics of the World Economy. By Immanuel Wallerstein. Reviewed by Hamza Alavi. *Race and Class* 27, No. 4 (Spring 1986):87–90

Popular Music, 1920–1979; A Revised Cumulation. Edited by Nat Shapiro and Bruce Pollack. Reviewed by Doris E. McGinty. *Black Perspective in Music* 14, No. 3 (Fall 1986):311–312

The Price of a Ticket. By James Baldwin. Reviewed by Joe Johnson. *Crisis* 93, No. 2 (February 1986):12

Private Black Colleges in Texas: 1865–1954. By M. R. Heintze. Reviewed by Antoine Garibaldi. *Journal of Negro Education* 55, No.2 (Spring 1986):239–240

Proceedings of the Symposium on Afro-American and African Poetry and the Teaching of Poetry in Schools. S. W. D. Dube, editor. Reviewed by Ernest Mathabela. *Research in African Literatures* 17, No. 1 (Spring 1986): 133–137

Propos sur la littérature negro-africaine. By Christophe Dailly and Barthelemy Kotchy. Reviewed by Jonathan Ngate. *Research in African Literatures* 17, No. 4 (Winter 1986): 565–566

In Pursuit of Power: Southern Blacks and Electoral Politics, 1965–1982. By Steven F. Lawson. Reviewed by Joe Johnson. *Crisis* 93, No. 7 (August/September 1986):12–13

Sobre Literatura Moçambicana. By Orlando Mendes. Reviewed by Russell G. Hamilton. *Research in African Literatures* 17, No. 3 (Fall 1986): 422–425

A Social History of 20th Century Urban Riots. By James Upton. Reviewed by Earl Smith. *Phylon* 47, No. 1 (March 1986):101–103

Soleil éclate. Jacqueline Leiner, editor. Reviewed by Bernard Aresu. *Research in African Literatures* 17, No. 4 (Winter 1986): 588–591

Sol Plaatje: South African Nationalist, 1876–1932. By Brian Willan. Reviewed by N. Chabani Manganyi. *Research in African Literatures* 17, No. 3 (Fall 1986): 393–395

Song of the Seven Herbs. By Walking Night Bear. Reviewed by Doris Seale. *Interracial Books for Children Bulletin* 17, No. 1 (1986):9

Songs for My Fathers. By Gary Smith. Reviewed by Gerald Barrax. *Callaloo* 9, No. 1 (Winter 1986):255–259

Sorcerer's Apprentice. By Charles Johnson. Reviewed by Joe Johnson. *Crisis* 93, No. 5 (May 1986):12–38

So Spoke the Uncle. By Jean Price-Mars. Reviewed by Michel-Rolph Trouillot. *Research in African Literatures* 17, No. 4 (Winter 1986): 596–597

Spain and the Loss of America. By Timothy E. Anna. Reviewed by Joaquin Roy. *Caribbean Review* 15, No. 2 (Spring 1986):48

Standing Fast: The Autobiography of Roy Wilkins. By Roy Wilkins with Tom Mathews. Reviewed by Donald Culverson. *Western Journal of Black Studies* 10, No. 3 (Fall 1986):159–160

Stay Away from Simon! By Carol Carrick. Reviewed by Emily Strauss Watson. *Interracial Books for Children Bulletin* 17, No. 1 (1986):9

Sterling A. Brown: Building the Black Aesthetic Tradition. By Joanne V. Gabbin. Reviewed by Leonard Green. *Black American Literature Forum* 20, No. 3 (Fall 1986):327–334

Sterling A. Brown: Building the Black Aesthetic Tradition. By Joanne V. Gabbin. Reviewed by Steven C. Tracy. *Callaloo* 9, No. 1 (Winter 1986):273–275

Stories from Central and Southern Africa. Paul A. Scanlon, editor. Reviewed by Adrian Roscoe. *Research in African Literatures* 17, No. 3 (Fall 1986): 413–416

Strangers and Sisters: Women, Race and Immigration. Edited by Selma James. Reviewed by Jenny Bourne. *Race and Class* 27, No. 4 (Spring 1986):100–103

Street Life: Afro-American Culture in Urban Trinidad. By Michael Lieber. Reviewed by Keith Q. Warner. *CLA Journal* 29, No. 4 (June 1986):493–496

Strength for the Fight: A History of Blacks in the Military. By Bernard C. Nalty. Reviewed by William Leyden. *Negro Educational Review* 37, Nos. 3–4 (July-October 1986):155–156

Stride: The Music of Fats Waller. By Paul S. Machlin. Reviewed by Eileen Southern. *Black Perspective in Music* 14, No. 2 (Spring 1986):194

Student Culture and Activism in Black South African Universities. By M. O. Nkomo. Reviewed by Ernest F. Dube. *Journal of Negro Education* 55, No.2 (Spring 1986):240–244

Symbolic Structures: An Exploration of the Culture of the Dowayos. By Nigel Barley. Reviewed by Wyatt MacGaffey. *Research in African Literatures* 17, No. 2 (Summer 1986): 295–296

A Sympathetic History of Jonestown: The Moore Family Involvement in Peoples Temple. By Rebecca Moore. Reviewed by Kortright Davis. *Journal of Religious Thought* 43, No. 2 (Fall-Winter 1986–87):92–93

Tapping Potential: English and Language Arts for the Black Learner. Edited by Charlotte K. Brooks. Reviewed by Hawthorne Faison. *Black Scholar* 17, No. 3 (May-June 1986):60

The Teacher Rebellion. By David Seldon. Reviewed by Kenneth Jennings. *Negro Educational Review* 37, Nos. 3–4 (July-October 1986):154–155

A Teacher's Guide to African Literature. By H. L. B. Moody. Reviewed by Carl Wood. *Research in African Literatures* 17, No. 4 (Winter 1986): 606–609

Teaching Literature in Africa: Principles and Techniques. By Emmanuel Ngara. Reviewed by Florence Stratton. *Research in African Literatures* 17, No. 3 (Fall 1986): 451–453

10 Super Sunday Schools in the Black Community. By Sid Smith. Reviewed by Gayl Fowler. *Journal of Religious Thought* 43, No. 2 (Fall-Winter 1986–87):93

Tessere per un mosaico africano. By Itala Vivan. Reviewed by Jane Wilkinson. *Research in African Literatures* 17, No. 3 (Fall 1986): 425–426

Theater and Cultural Struggle in South Africa. By Robert Mshengu Kavanagh. Reviewed by Ian Steadman. *Research in African Literatures* 17, No. 2 (Summer 1986): 267–271

Theater and Society in Africa. By Mineke Schipper. Reviewed by Olu Obafemi. *Research in African Literatures* 17, No. 2 (Summer 1986): 271–272

Those Preachin' Women: Sermons by Black Women Preachers. Edited by Ella Pearson Mitchell. Reviewed by Gayl Fowler. *Journal of Religious Thought* 43, No. 1 (Spring-Summer 1986):129–130

Those Preachin' Women: Sermons by Black Women Preachers. Edited by Ella Pearson Mitchell. Reviewed by Renita J. Weems. *SAGE* 3, No. 2 (Fall 1986):56–57

Through Foreign Eyes: Western Attitudes toward North Africa. Alf Andrew Heggoy, editor. Reviewed by Aouicha E. Hilliard. *Research in African Literatures* 17, No. 4 (Winter 1986): 584–587

Toad Is the Uncle of Heaven. By Jeanne M. Lee. Reviewed by Valerie Ooka Pang. *Interracial Books for Children Bulletin* 17, No. 1 (1986):9

To Bury Our Fathers: A Novel of Nicaragua. By Sergio Ramirez. Reviewed by Imogen Forster. *Race and Class* 27, No. 4 (Spring 1986):92–93

Tradition afrikanischer Blasorchester und Entstehung des Jazz. By Alfons Michael Dauer. Reviewed by Lewis Porter. *Black Perspective in Music* 14, No. 3 (Fall 1986):314–316

The Transitive Vampire: A Handbook of Grammar for the Innocent, the Eager and the Damned. By Karen Elizabeth Gordon. Reviewed by Elizabeth J. Higgins. *CLA Journal* 30, No. 2 (December 1986):252–253

The Truthful Lie: Essays in a Sociology of African Drama. By Biodun Jeyifo. Reviewed by Elaine Savory Fido. *Research in African Literatures* 17, No. 2 (Summer 1986): 273–275

Un anglo d'Africa: Il Kenya visto dai suoi scrittori. Silvana Bottignole, translator. Reviewed by Jane Wilkinson. *Research in African Literatures* 17, No. 1 (Spring 1986): 142–144

The Unbelonging. By Joan Riley. Reviewed by Jenny Bourne. *Race and Class* 27, No. 3 (Winter 1986):108–109

Understanding the Black Family: A Guide for Scholarship and Research. By Wade W. Nobles and Lawford Goddard. *Journal of Black Psychology* 13, No. 1 (August 1986):20–23

The Unequal Struggle. By Ashton Gibson and Jocelyn Barrow. Reviewed by Paul Okojie. *Race and Class* 28, No. 2 (August 1986):93–95

Unheard Words: Women and Literature in Africa, the Arab World, Asia, the Caribbean and Latin America. Edited by Mineke Schipper. Reviewed by Margaret Marshment. *Race and Class* 28, No. 1 (Summer 1986):97–99

Uwa ndi Igbo: Journal of Igbo Life and Culture I. Chieka Ifemesia, editor. Reviewed by Don Burgess. *Research in African Literatures* 17, No. 2 (Summer 1986): 288–291

Vision in Spring. By William Faulkner. Reviewed by Elizabeth J. Higgins. *CLA Journal* 29, No. 4 (June 1986):490–492

Waiting: The Whites of South Africa. By Vincent Crapanzano. Reviewed by A. B. Assensoh. *Phylon* 47, No. 3 (September 1986):248

Walter Rodney: Poetic Tributes. By Andrew Salkey. Reviewed by Colin Prescod. *Race and Class* 28, No. 2 (August 1986):105–106

The War between the Classes. By Gloria D. Miklowitz. Reviewed by Valerie Ooka Pang. *Interracial Books for Children Bulletin* 17, Nos. 3–4 (1986):33

The Watermelon Dress: Portrait of a Woman. By Paulette Childress White. Reviewed by Gerald Barrax. *Callaloo* 9, No. 1 (Winter 1986):265–269

We Are Your Sisters: Black Women in the Nineteenth Century. By Dorothy Sterling. Reviewed by Beth Brown Utada. *Journal of Black Studies* 16, No. 4 (June 1986):453–456

The West African Village Novel with Particular Reference to Elechi Amadi's *The Concubine*. By George Nyamndi. Reviewed by Ernest N. Emenyonu. *Research in African Literatures* 17, No. 4 (Winter 1986): 622–625

What If They Saw Me Now? By Jean Ure. Reviewed by Michael E. Grafton. *Interracial Books for Children Bulletin* 17, No. 2 (1986):17

What Price Equity? A Macroeconomic Evaluation of Government Policies in Costa Rica. By Fuat M. Andic. Reviewed by Irma T. De Alonso. *Caribbean Review* 15, No. 1 (Winter 1986):44

What Works: Research about Teaching and Learning. By William J. Bennett. Reviewed by Patricia B. Campbell. *Interracial Books for Children Bulletin* 17, Nos. 3–4 (1986):37

When and Where I Enter: The Impact of Black Women on Race and Sex in America. By Paula Giddings. Reviewed by Eleanor Smith. *Western Journal of Black Studies* 10, No. 1 (Spring 1986):45–46

Where Did Our Love Go? The Rise and Fall of the Motown Sound. By Nelson George. Reviewed by Tonya Bolden Davis. *Black Enterprise* 16, No. 11 (June 1986):35–37

Who Speaks for Wolf. By Paula Spencer. Reviewed by Doris Seale. *Interracial Books for Children Bulletin* 17, Nos. 3–4 (1986):36

Why Me? By Ellen Conford. Reviewed by Patricia B. Campbell. *Interracial Books for Children Bulletin* 17, No. 2 (1986):15

Willie and Dwike: An American Profile. By William Zissner. Reviewed by George L. Starks, Jr. *Black Perspective in Music* 14, No. 3 (Fall 1986):313

Winnie Mandela: Part of My Soul Went with Him. Edited by Anne Benjamin. Reviewed by Jeanne M. Woods. *Black Enterprise* 17, No. 5 (December 1986):19

Witness to War: An American Doctor in El Salvador. By Charles Clements, M.D. Reviewed by Neale Pearson. *Caribbean Review* 15, No. 2 (Spring 1986):47–48

Wole Soyinka's *The Road*. By Simon Gikandi. Reviewed by James Gibbs. *Research in African Literatures* 17, No. 4 (Winter 1986): 617–620

Women's Liberation and the Dialectics of Revolution: Reaching for the Future. By Raya Dunayevskaya. Reviewed by Diane Lee. *SAGE* 3, No. 1 (Spring 1986):62–63

The World of Richard Wright. By Michel Fabre. Reviewed by Rudolph Byrd. *Callaloo* 9, No. 4 (Fall 1986):751–752

Worlds Apart: Women under Immigration and Nationality Law. By Women, Immigration and Nationality Group. Reviewed by Busi Chaane. *Race and Class* 28, No. 1 (Summer 1986):103–107

The Worst of Times: An Oral History of the Great Depression in Britain. By Nigel Gray. Reviewed by Graham Murray. *Race and Class* 27, No. 4 (Spring 1986):103–104

Youth Employment and Training Programs: The YEDPA Years. Edited by Charles L. Betsey and others. Reviewed by Robert B. Hill. *Review of Black Political Economy* 15, No. 1 (Summer 1986):107–112

Book Reviews—Poetry

The Poetical Works of Marcus Garvey. Tony Martin. Reviewed by Joanne Veal Gabbin. *Afro-Americans in New York Life and History* 10, No.1 (January 1986):72–74

Booksellers and Bookselling—Africa

The Book Trade of the World, IV: Africa. Sigfred Taubert and Peter Weidhaas, editors. Reviewed by Ilse Sternberg. *Research in African Literatures* 17, No. 1 (Spring 1986): 147–149

Boone, Ashley (about)

Inside Hollywood. Ken Smikle. *Black Enterprise* 17, No. 5 (December 1986):48

Boose, Maryetta Kelsick

The Teenage Strut. Poem. *Black American Literature Forum* 20, No. 3 (Fall 1986):309

Booth, James

Home and Exile and Other Selections. Book review. *Research in African Literatures* 17, No. 3 (Fall 1986): 398–401

Myth, Metaphor, and Syntax in Soyinka's Poetry. Notes. *Research in African Literatures* 17, No. 1 (Spring 1986): 53–72

Booth, John A.

Nicaragua under Siege. Book review. *Caribbean Review* 15, No. 2 (Spring 1986):47

Borders, James

Employment Opportunities in the Defense Industry: The Big Build-Up at the Cutting Edge. *Black Collegian* 16, No. 3 (January/February 1986):140–141

Borrell, Gordon

Harvey Buys Pepsi Plant. *Black Enterprise* 16, No. 11 (June 1986):48

Savings and Loan of the Year: The Rebirth of Berkley Savings. *Black Enterprise* 16, No. 11 (June 1986):166

Boston Bank of Commerce

Bank of the Year: Banking on Boston. Gregg Patterson. *Black Enterprise* 16, No. 11 (June 1986):150

Boswell, Day M.

Coast Guard Offers Opportunity, Responsibility. *Black Collegian* 16, No. 4 (March/April 1986):64–65

Bottignole, Silvana, translator

Un anglo d'Africa: Il Kenya visto dai suoi scrittori. Reviewed by Jane Wilkinson. *Research in African Literatures* 17, No. 1 (Spring 1986): 142–144

Bottomley, Gill, and de Lepervanche, Marie

Ethnicity, Class and Gender in Australia. Book review. Stephen Castle. *Race and Class* 27, No. 4 (Spring 1986):94–96

Bourne, Jenny

Strangers and Sisters: Women, Race and Immigration. Book review. *Race and Class* 27, No. 4 (Spring 1986):100–103

The Unbelonging. Book review. *Race and Class* 27, No. 3 (Winter 1986):108–109

Bowie, John S.

Careers in Technical Writing: Entering a New Era. *Black Collegian* 16, No. 3 (January/February 1986):51–54

Bowling

Bowling for Fame and Fortune. Marilyn Marshall. *Ebony* 41, No. 4 (February 1986):157

Bowman, Philip (joint author)

See Fairchild, Halford H.

Bowman, Timothy and Thomas (about)

Twins in the Ministry: Three Sets from Atlanta. *Ebony* 41, No. 4 (February 1986):99

Boxers

Michael Spinks: The New King of the Ring. Walter Leavy. *Ebony* 41, No. 5 (March 1986):35

Spotlight: Cool-Hand Mark. Joy Duckett-Cain. *Essence* 17, No. 2 (June 1986):76

The Weaver Triplets: Following in the Footsteps of Big Brother Mike. Aldore Collier. *Ebony* 41, No. 9 (July 1986):48

Boycotts

Dearborn Boycott. Margo Walker. *Black Enterprise* 17, No. 1 (August 1986):12

Boyd, Herb

Canada. *Crisis* 93, No. 6 (June/July 1986):47–54

The Color Purple. Film review. *Crisis* 93, No. 2 (February 1986):10

Under the Cherry Moon. Film review. *Crisis* 93, No. 7 (August/September 1986):11

United States Foreign Policy in Southern Africa: Past and Present. *Crisis* 93, No. 9 (November 1986):26–27

Boyer, Jill Witherspoon

Breaking Camp. Book review. Gerald Barrax. *Callaloo* 9, No. 1 (Winter 1986):265–269

Boyle, Helen (about)

The Aboriginal Struggle: An Interview with Helen Boyle. Mike Cole. *Race and Class* 27, No. 4 (Spring 1986):21–33

Boynton, Maria

Exploring Buried Buxton: Archeology of an Abandoned Iowa Coal Mining Town with a Large Black Population. Book review. *Afro-Americans in New York Life and History* 10, No. 2 (July 1986): 65–68

Braden, Anne

Reversing the Tide of Racism. *Interracial Books for Children Bulletin* 17, No. 2 (1986):3–4

Bradford, William

Bank Overview: Merge or Purge? *Black Enterprise* 16, No. 11 (June 1986):143

Bradley, Tom

Vision and Responsibility: The Role of States in Planning for Full Employment. *Urban League Review* 10, No. 1 (Summer 1986):66–70

Brailsford, Karen

Black Toy Makers Make a Play for the Market. *Black Enterprise* 17, No. 5 (December 1986):94

Financial Lessons for After School. *Black Enterprise* 17, No. 3 (October 1986):57

How to Sell Your Boss on Your Ideas. *Black Enterprise* 16, No. 11 (June 1986):284

When Well-Tuned Professionals Talk—People Listen. *Black Enterprise* 16, No. 11 (June 1986):282

Brantley, Daniel

Black Americans as Participants in the Foreign Service. *Crisis* 93, No. 9 (November 1986):31–33

Branton, Wiley (about)

Civil Rights Lawyers Revisited. *Ebony* 42, No. 2 (December 1986):76

Braxton, Charlie R.

The King Uncrowned. Poem. *Black American Literature Forum* 20, No. 3 (Fall 1986):261

Brazil—Description and Travel

Rio Grand! Elaine C. Ray. *Essence* 16, No. 11 (March 1986):31

Brazil—Music

The Life and Works of Nunes-Garcia. Dominique-René de Lerma. *Black Perspective in Music* 14, No. 2 (Spring 1986):93–102

Brazil—Politics and Government

Political Liberalization, Black Consciousness, and Recent Afro-Brazilian Literary Production. James H. Kennedy. *Phylon* 47, No. 3 (September 1986):199–209

Brazil—Race Relations

Brazil and the Blacks of South America. Gloria Calomee. *Crisis* 93, No. 6 (June/July 1986):37

Brazil—Religion

The Feast of Good Death: An Afro-Catholic Emancipation Celebration in Brazil. Sheila S. Walker. *SAGE* 3, No. 2 (Fall 1986):27–31

Brazil—Theater, Black

Black Theater in a "Racial Democracy": The Case of the Brazilian Black Experimental Theater. Notes. Doris J. Turner. *CLA Journal* 30, No. 1 (September 1986):30–45

Bread for the World

How to Shape Policy through Lobbying. David C. Ruffin. *Black Enterprise* 17, No. 5 (December 1986):33

Breasts—Care and Hygiene

Saving Our Breasts. Peggy Ann Taylor. *Essence* 17, No. 2 (June 1986):62

Breland, Mark (about)

Spotlight: Cool-Hand Mark. Joy Duckett-Cain. *Essence* 17, No. 2 (June 1986):76

Brewing Industry

Corporate Profile: Success among the Suds. Joyce Davis Adams. *Black Enterprise* 16, No. 11 (June 1986):242

Bridges, Lee

Beyond Accountability: Labour and Policing after the 1985 Rebellions. *Race and Class* 27, No. 4 (Spring 1986):78–85

Black Politics and Urban Crisis in Britain. Book review. *Race and Class* 28, No. 2 (August 1986):99–102

The Local Politics of Race. Book review. *Race and Class* 28, No. 2 (August 1986):99–102

Brimmer, Andrew F.

Black Income Mirrors Status in Economy. *Black Enterprise* 17, No. 2 (September 1986):33

Blacks Make Moderate Gains in Employment. *Black Enterprise* 17, No. 4 (November 1986):36

Blacks Make Moderate Gains in Labor Market. *Black Enterprise* 16, No. 9 (April 1986):40

Investing and Wealth Accumulation. *Black Enterprise* 17, No. 3 (October 1986):37

Trends, Prospects, and Strategies for Black Economic Progress. *Review of Black Political Economy* 14, No. 4 (Spring 1986):91–97

Trends and Prospects for Black Business. *Black Enterprise* 16, No. 12 (July 1986):29

Brokers

Brokers Go for Growth. Ken Smikle. *Black Enterprise* 16, No. 10 (May 1986):18

Bronte, Charlotte (about)

Charlotte Bronte: The Self Conceived. By Helen Moglen. Reviewed by Elizabeth J. Higgins. *CLA Journal* 29, No. 3 (March 1986):368–371

Broodhagen, Karl (about)

Karl Broodhagen. Illustrated. David Gall. *International Review of African American Art* 7, No. 1 (1986):56–63

Brooklyn African Woolman Benevolent Society

The Brooklyn African Woolman Benevolent Society Rediscovered. Notes. Sandra Shoiock Roff. *Afro-Americans in New York Life and History* 10, No. 2 (July 1986): 55–63

Brooklyn (New York)—History

The Brooklyn African Woolman Benevolent Society Rediscovered. Notes. Sandra Shoiock Roff. *Afro-Americans in New York Life and History* 10, No. 2 (July 1986):55–63

Brooks, Charlotte K. (editor)

Tapping Potential: English and Language Arts for the Black Learner. Book review. Hawthorne Faison. *Black Scholar* 17, No. 3 (May-June 1986):60

Brooks, Tina (about)

The Complete Blue Note Tina Brooks. Record review. Lewis Porter. *Black Perspective in Music* 14, No. 3 (Fall 1986):319–321

Brothers and Sisters

Brothers and Sisters Who Made It to the Top. *Ebony* 41, No. 9 (July 1986):74

Broughton, Viv

Black Gospel. An Illustrated History of the Gospel Sound. Book review. André Prévos. *Black Perspective in Music* 14, No. 2 (Spring 1986):191–192

Brown, Arthur

There Is a Man Moving into My Skin. Poem. *Essence* 17, No. 1 (May 1986):92

Brown, Beth

Black Women Writers at Work. Interviews. Book review. *CLA Journal* 29, No. 3 (March 1986):380–383

A Daughter's Geography. Book review. *CLA Journal* 29, No. 3 (March 1986):378–380

Eulogy for James Weldon Jones. Poem. *Callaloo* 9, No. 1 (Winter 1986):16–17

Father. Poem. *Callaloo* 9, No. 1 (Winter 1986):15

Our Nig; Or, Sketches from the Life of a Free Black. Book review. *CLA Journal* 29, No. 3 (March 1986):383–386

Plum Bun: A Novel without a Moral. Book review. *Black Scholar* 17, No. 4 (July-August 1986):58–59

Brown, Bob (about)

The Art of Diplomacy: Bob Brown and Local 435. Joan Marie Allen. *About Time* 14, No. 12 (December 1986):9–10

Brown, D. A. Maughan

Critical Perspectives on Ngugi wa Thiong'o. Book review. *Research in African Literatures* 17, No. 4 (Winter 1986): 614–617

Brown, Frank Dexter

Apartheid Lives On. *Black Enterprise* 16, No. 12 (July 1986):13

High Court Reviews Civil Rights. *Black Enterprise* 16, No. 6 (January 1986):31

Investing with a Conscience. *Black Enterprise* 17, No. 3 (October 1986):91

Remember Soweto. *Black Enterprise* 17, No. 2 (September 1986):17

Brown, Gerard

Jonin'. Theater review. Cecilia Loving-Sloane. *Crisis* 93, No. 3 (March 1986):11–48

Brown, Herman

Blacks in College. Book review. *Journal of Negro Education* 55, No.2 (Spring 1986):237–239

Brown, James (Jr.) (about)

Tribute to James Brown, Jr., Fighter for Justice. Jerry M. Guess. *Crisis* 93, No. 5 (May 1986):32–33

Brown, Joseph A.

Our Dead Behind Us. Book review. *Callaloo* 9, No. 4 (Fall 1986):737–739

Their Long Scars Touch Ours. *Callaloo* 9, No. 1 (Winter 1986):209–220

Brown, Lorenzo

Why Should Black-Owned Businesses Hire Predominantly Black Labor Forces? *Review of Black Political Economy* 15, No. 2 (Fall 1986):113–121

Brown, Malcolm (about)

Malcolm Brown Gallery. Illustrated. *Western Journal of Black Studies* 10, No. 2 (Summer 1986):77–78

Brown, Maxine Childress

It's In Our Hands! *About Time* 14, No. 7 (July 1986):9

Brown, Tony (about)

The Price of Freedom. Kenneth Maurice Jones. *Black Enterprise* 16, No. 7 (February 1986):28

Brown-Collins, Alice R., and Sussewell, Deborah R.

The Afro-American Woman's Emerging Selves. *Journal of Black Psychology* 13, No. 1 (August 1986):1–11

Brown-Guillory, Elizabeth

Give Us Each Day: The Diary of Alice Dunbar-Nelson. Book review. *SAGE* 3, No. 2 (Fall 1986):57–59

Images of Blacks in Plays by Black Women. *Phylon* 47, No. 3 (September 1986):230–237

Brown University—Fund-Raising

A Sound Investment. *Black Enterprise* 16, No. 7 (February 1986):26

Bruner, Charlotte H.

Le personnage féminin dans le roman maghrébin de langue française des indépendences à 1980: Representations et fonctions. Book review. *Research in African Literatures* 17, No. 4 (Winter 1986): 576–579

Brutus, Dennis

For the Dead South Africans: March, 1986. Poem. *Black Scholar* 17, No. 4 (July-August 1986):51

Remembering the Fort Prison, Johannesburg. Poem. *Black Scholar* 17, No. 4 (July-August 1986):51

Sequence (Part). Poem. *Black Scholar* 17, No. 4 (July-August 1986):51

For W. C. J. B.: Died in Exile: London March 26, '86. Poem. *Black Scholar* 17, No. 4 (July-August 1986):51

Bryan, Louis C.

Modjeska A. Simkins: Profile of a Legend. *SAGE* 3, No. 1 (Spring 1986):56–57

Bryan, Violet Harrington

Frances Joseph-Gaudet: Black Philanthropist. *SAGE* 3, No. 1 (Spring 1986):46–49

Bucher, Richard D.

Selected Correlates of Perceptions of Black Militancy. *Western Journal of Black Studies* 10, No. 2 (Summer 1986):79–85

Buckley, Gail Lumet

The Hornes: An American Family. Book review. Joe Johnson. *Crisis* 93, No. 8 (October 1986):14–16

The Hornes. Book review. Tonya Bolden Davis. *Black Enterprise* 17, No. 3 (October 1986):18

Buddie, James A.

Commonwealth v. Richardson: Voir Dire and the Consent Defense to an Interracial Rape in Pennsylvania—Finding Twelve Not-Too-Angry Men. *Black Law Journal* 9, No. 3 (Winter 1986):300–311

Budget Deficits

Gramm-Rudman and the Politics of Deficit Reduction. Linda F. Williams. *Urban League Review* 10, No. 2 (Winter 1986–87):72–83

Budgets, Personal

Financial Lessons for After School. Karen Brailsford. *Black Enterprise* 17, No. 3 (October 1986):57

Living Well on... Lloyd Gite. *Black Enterprise* 16, No. 10 (May 1986):44

Building and Loan Associations

The *Black Enterprise* List of Black Savings and Loans. *Black Enterprise* 16, No. 11 (June 1986):163

Savings and Loan Overview: Staying Nifty, Thrifty—and Wise. Ann Kimbrough. *Black Enterprise* 16, No. 11 (June 1986):159

Savings and Loan of the Year: The Rebirth of Berkley Savings. Gordon Borell. *Black Enterprise* 16, No. 11 (June 1986):166

Building Trades

Black Hardhats and the Elite Craft Trade Unions. Michael Emerson Howard III. *Crisis* 93, No. 8 (October 1986):26–29

Bullard, Robert D., and Wright, Beverly Hendrix

The Politics of Pollution: Implications for the Black Community. *Phylon* 47, No. 1 (March 1986):71–78

Bunk Johnson's Band (about)

Spicy Advice. Record review. Lewis Porter. *Black Perspective in Music* 14, No. 3 (Fall 1986):317–318

Burbridge, Lynn C.

Changes in Equal Employment Enforcement: What Enforcement Statistics Tell Us. *Review of Black Political Economy* 15, No. 1 (Summer 1986):71–80

Tax Reform: A Minimalist Approach for Assisting the Low-Income. *Urban League Review* 10, No. 2 (Winter 1986–87):101–112

Burg, B. R.

The Rhetoric of Miscegenation: Thomas Jefferson, Sally Hemings, and Their Historians. *Phylon* 47, No. 2 (June 1986):117–127

Burgess, Don

Uwa ndi Igbo: Journal of Igbo Life and Culture I. Book review. *Research in African Literatures* 17, No. 2 (Summer 1986): 288–291

Burnham, Linda

Black and Red—W. E. B. DuBois and the Afro-American Response to the Cold War—1944-1963. Book review. *Black Scholar* 17, No. 2 (March-April 1986):52–54

Burns, Khephra

Denzel. *Essence* 17, No. 7 (November 1986):54

Burrison, William

Another Look at *Lawd Today*: Richard Wright's Tricky Apprenticeship. Notes. *CLA Journal* 29, No. 4 (June 1986):424–441

Burroughs, Edgar Rice—Criticism and Interpretation

Lord Greystoke and the Darkest Africa: The Politics of the Tarzan Stories. John Newsinger. *Race and Class* 28, No. 2 (August 1986):59–71

Burrow, Rufus (Jr.)

Who Teaches Black Theology? Notes. *Journal of Religious Thought* 43, No. 2 (Fall-Winter 1986–87):7–18

Burwell, Bryan

With Style and Grace. *Black Enterprise* 16, No. 11 (June 1986):52

Bush, Olivia Ward (Banks)

Character Names in *Indian Trails* by Olivia Ward Bush (Banks): Clues to Afro Assimilation Into Long Island's Native Americans. Notes. Bernice F. Guillaume. *Afro-Americans* in *New York Life and History* 10, No. 2 (July 1986):45–53

Bush, Roland E.

Heroes are Grazing in My Garden. Book review. *Caribbean Review* 15, No. 1 (Winter 1986):41

Bushnell, Horace

Horace Bushnell: Sermons. Edited by Conrad Cherry. Reviewed by Kortright Davis. *Journal of Religious Thought* 43, No. 2 (Fall-Winter 1986–87):91–92

Business Consultants

Planning Designs for Success. Lloyd Gite. *Black Enterprise* 17, No. 5 (December 1986):37

Business—Directories

Opportunities for Success. Marsha Jones. *About Time* 14, No. 12 (December 1986):13–19

Business Education

Marketing Colleges. Ken Smikle. *Black Enterprise* 17, No. 4 (November 1986):24

This Dean Means Business: Marion Oliver Wants to Show Black Students the Advantages of Career in Business. Charles Whitaker. *Ebony* 41, No. 4 (February 1986):93

Business Enterprises

BE 100: The New Guys on the Block. Edmund Newton. *Black Enterprise* 16, No. 11 (June 1986):119

BE 100 Overview: A New Push for Profits. *Black Enterprise* 16, No. 11 (June 1986):91

Black Dollars: Taking Control. Jill Nelson. *Essence* 17, No. 5 (September 1986):65

The *Black Enterprise* List of Top 100 Black Businesses. *Black Enterprise* 16, No. 11 (June 1986):91

ColeJon's Hot Profits. Patricia A. Jones. *Black Enterprise* 16, No. 8 (March 1986):16

Market Structure and Minority Presence: Black-Owned Firms in Manufacturing. Arthur G. Woolf. *Review of Black Political Economy* 14, No. 4 (Spring 1986):79–89

Minority Firms: Growing in Value and Service. James M. Blount. *About Time* 14, No. 8 (August 1986):4

Providing a Healthier Workplace: Sheen and Shine, Inc. Marsha Jones. *About Time* 14, No. 8 (August 1986):28–29

Setting New Transportation Lanes: E. L. Lawson Trucking Company, Inc. Carolyne S. Blount. *About Time* 14, No. 8 (August 1986):30–31

A Sociological Analysis of Minority Business. Frank A. Fratoe. *Review of Black Political Economy* 15, No. 2 (Fall 1986):5–29

Trends and Prospects for Black Business. Andrew F. Brimmer. *Black Enterprise* 16, No. 12 (July 1986):29

Business Enterprises, International

Minority Business Development: An International Comparison. Gavin M. Chen. *Review of Black Political Economy* 15, No. 2 (Fall 1986):93–111

Business Enterprises—Conferences

Seeking a Big Agenda for Small Business. David C. Ruffin. *Black Enterprise* 17, No. 4 (November 1986):27

Business Enterprises—Finance

Government Agencies Working behind the Scenes. David C. Ruffin. *Black Enterprise* 16, No. 11 (June 1986):269–270

Linkages between Minority Business Characteristics and Minority Banks' Locations. John A. Cole and Lucy J. Reuben. *Review of Black Political Economy* 15, No. 2 (Fall 1986):73–92

Tapping the Money Pool. *Black Enterprise* 16, No. 11 (June 1986):232

Business Enterprises—Mortality

An Analysis of the Formation and Failure Rates of Minority-Owned Firms. Faith H. Ando. *Review of Black Political Economy* 15, No. 2 (Fall 1986):51–71

Business Enterprises—Set-Aside Programs

Fighting Fraud. Lynette Hazelton. *Black Enterprise* 17, No. 4 (November 1986):22

Businesses—Directories

Come, Grow with Us! Business and Service Directory. Marsha Jones. *About Time* 14, No. 8 (August 1986):15–22

Business Etiquette

Office Etiquette: The Right Response. Marianne Ilaw. *Black Enterprise* 16, No. 11 (June 1986):280

Business and Government

See Industry and State

Business—Interns

Internship Teaches Tangibles, Intangibles of Corporate Life. Shelia I. Payton. *Black Collegian* 16, No. 3 (January/February 1986):126–128

J. C. Penney's Leading Edge Internships. *Black Collegian* 16, No. 3 (January/February 1986):112–116

Business Leaders

Earl S. Washington: Rising in Defense. *Black Collegian* 16, No. 3 (January/February 1986):142

The Professional in Management: Cleve L. Killingsworth. Anita Johnson Sims. *About Time* 14, No. 12 (December 1986):11–12

Businessmen

A Day in the Life of a Franchise Owner. Marianne Ilaw. *Black Enterprise* 16, No. 7 (February 1986):128–132

Butler, Guy (editor)

The Re-interment on Buffelskop. Reviewed by Cherry Clayton. *Research in African Literatures* 17, No. 3 (Fall 1986): 404–406

Butler, Octavia

Black Women and the Science Fiction Genre. *Black Scholar* 17, No. 2 (March-April 1986):14–18

Butler, Robert James

The Function of Violence in Richard Wright's *Native Son*. *Black American Literature Forum* 20, Nos. 1–2 (Spring/Summer 1986):9–25

Buxton, Iowa—History

Exploring Buried Buxton: Archeology of an Abandoned Iowa Coal Mining Town with a Large Black Population. By David M. Gradwohl and Nancy M. Osborn. Reviewed by Maria Boynton. *Afro-Americans in New York Life and History* 10, No. 2 (July 1986): 65–68

Byrd, Manford (Jr.) (about)

Dr. Manford Byrd, Jr.: Cooling off the Hot Seat. Alex Poinsett. *Ebony* 41, No. 4 (February 1986):44

Byrd, Rudolph

The World of Richard Wright. Book review. *Callaloo* 9, No. 4 (Fall 1986):751–752

Caballero, Diana

Puerto Ricans and Bilingual Education. *Interracial Books for Children Bulletin* 17, Nos. 3–4 (1986):15–16

Cabezas, Omar

Fire from the Mountain: The Making of a Sandinista. Book review. David E. Lewis. *Black Scholar* 17, No. 1 (January-February 1986):49

Cabral, Amilcar (about)

On Revolutionary Nationalism: The Legacy of Cabral. Basil Davidson. *Race and Class* 27, No. 3 (Winter 1986):21–45

Cahill, Edward (joint author)

See Turner, William H.

Cailler, Bernadette

Assia Djebar: Romancière algérienne, cinéaste arabe. Book review. *Research in African Literatures* 17, No. 4 (Winter 1986): 579–581

Calabash Dance Theatre

The Calabash Dance Theatre. Illustrated. Abiodun McCray and Ayanna Fredricks. *Western Journal of Black Studies* 10, No. 1 (Spring 1986):17–18

Calderon, Ricardo Arias

Panama, Desastre...o Democracia. Reviewed by Neale Pearson. *Caribbean Review* 15, No. 1 (Winter 1986):26–27 +

Political Systems as Export Commodities: Democracy and the Role of the US in Central America. *Caribbean Review* 15, No. 1 (Winter 1986):21–23 +

Calendar, Egyptian

Africa's Contribution to World Civilization: The Exact Sciences. Notes. Bibliography. Cheikh Anta Diop. *Journal of African Civilizations* 8, No. 1 (June 1986):74–88

Call to Action

A Call to Action: Community Crusade for Learning. Joan Marie Allen. *About Time* 14, No. 11 (November 1986):22–24

Calomee, Gloria

Brazil and the Blacks of South America. *Crisis* 93, No. 6 (June/July 1986):37

Calypso Music

Street Life: Afro-American Culture in Urban Trinidad. By Michael Lieber. Reviewed by Keith Q. Warner. *CLA Journal* 29, No. 4 (June 1986):493–496

Valentino and Calypso. Norman Riley. *Crisis* 93, No. 2 (February 1986):14

Cameroon—Culture

Symbolic Structures: An Exploration of the Culture of the Dowayos. By Nigel Barley. Reviewed by Wyatt MacGaffey. *Research in African Literatures* 17, No. 2 (Summer 1986): 295-296

Cameroon—Folktales

Kamerunische Marchen: Text und Kontext in ethnosoziologischer und psychologischer Sicht. By Norbert Ndong. Reviewed by Tunde Okanlawon. *Research in African Literatures* 17, No. 2 (Summer 1986): 294

Cameroon—Literature—Bibliographies

A Bibliography of Cameroonian Literature. Bibliography. Notes. Richard Bjornson. *Research in African Literatures* 17, No. 1 (Spring 1986): 85-126

Cameroon—Literature—French Langauge

Dialectique de la ville de la campagne chez Gabrielle Roy et chez Mongo Beti. By Ekitike Behounde. Reviewed by Mildred Mortimer. *Research in African Literatures* 17, No. 4 (Winter 1986): 572-574

Cameroon—Women

The Changing Status of Women in Cameroon: An Overview. Mario Azevedo and Gwendolyn Spencer Prater. *Western Journal of Black Studies* 10, No. 4 (Winter 1986):195-204

Campaign Funds

Differences in Campaign Funds: A Racial Explanation. John Theilmann and Al Wilhite. *Review of Black Political Economy* 15, No. 1 (Summer 1986):45-58

Campbell, Bebe Moore

Computers and You: "How My Computer Has Put Punch in My Marriage!" *Essence* 17, No. 2 (July 1986):98

Games Lovers Play. *Essence* 17, No. 2 (July 1986):60

Where There's a Will...from Dropout to M. D. *Essence* 17, No. 6 (October 1986):79

Campbell, Patricia B.

Shadows on the Pond. Book review. *Interracial Books for Children Bulletin* 17, No. 2 (1986):19

What Works: Research about Teaching and Learning. Book review. *Interracial Books for Children Bulletin* 17, Nos. 3-4 (1986):37

Why Me? Book review. *Interracial Books for Children Bulletin* 17, No. 2 (1986):15

Campbell, Rita (about)

Catch a Rising Star: Savvy Rhode Island Talent Agent Polishes Up New Acts. Carol R. Scott. *Essence* 17, No. 2 (June 1986):18

Campbell, Thomas C., and Reierson, Gary B.

The Gift of Administration. Reviewed by James Hammond. *Journal of Religious Thought* 43, No. 1 (Spring-Summer 1986):128-129

Camper, Diane

Appointees May Tip Scales of Justice. *Black Enterprise* 17, No. 3 (October 1986):29-30

Canada—Race Relations

Canada. Herb Boyd. *Crisis* 93, No. 6 (June/July 1986):47-54

Canada—West Indians

Monarchial Liberty and Republican Slavery: West Indies Emancipation Celebrations in Upstate New York and Canada West. John R. McKivigan and Jason H. Silverman. *Afro-Americans in New York Life and History* 10, No.1 (January 1986):7-18

Cancer Prevention

The Anticancer Diet. Maudene Nelson. *Essence* 17, No. 2 (June 1986):66

Candler, Julie

Auto Accessories. *Black Enterprise* 17, No. 4 (November 1986):84

Utility Vehicles. *Black Enterprise* 17, No. 4 (November 1986):82

Cannon, Reuben (about)

Inside Hollywood. Ken Smikle. *Black Enterprise* 17, No. 5 (December 1986):48

Capital

Linkages between Minority Business Characteristics and Minority Banks' Locations. John A. Cole and Lucy J. Reuben. *Review of Black Political Economy* 15, No. 2 (Fall 1986):73-92

Capitalism

The Black Family and the Crisis of Capitalism. Angela Davis and Fania Davis. *Black Scholar* 17, No. 5 (September-October 1986):33-40

Estado empresario y luncha politica en Costa Rica. By Ana Sojo. Reviewed by Francisco A. Leguizamon. *Caribbean Review* 15, No. 2 (Spring 1986):45-46

Capitalism and Racism

Racial Prejudice in a Capitalist State: What Happened to the American Creed. Richard T. Schaefer. *Phylon* 47, No. 3 (September 1986):192-198

Career Changes

Longing for Longevity. Ken Smikle and Marianne Ilaw. *Black Enterprise* 17, No. 4 (November 1986):52

Career Education

A Learning Skills and Counseling Model for Developing Countries. Rudolph V. Green. *Journal of Negro Education* 55, No.2 (Spring 1986):214–221

Career Planning

See Vocational Guidance

Carew, Jan

Conversations with Diop and Tsegaye: The Nile Valley Revisited. Notes. *Journal of African Civilizations* 8, No. 1 (June 1986):19–27

Grenada: The Hour Will Strike Again. Book review. Cameron McCarthy. *Race and Class* 28, No. 2 (August 1986):89–91

Caribbean American Chamber of Commerce and Industry

Caribbean Commerce. Colin Channer. *Black Enterprise* 17, No. 3 (October 1986):22

Caricatures and Cartoons

Revolutionary Comics: Political Humor from Nicaragua. Roger Sanchez Flores. *Caribbean Review* 15, No. 1 (Winter 1986):16–17

Carkhum, Jacki

Educated People. Poem. *Essence* 17, No. 2 (June 1986):114

Carner, Gary

A Bibliography of Jazz and Blues Biographical Literature. *Black American Literature Forum* 20, Nos. 1–2 (Spring/Summer 1986):161–202

Carpenter, Delores Causion

The Professionalism of the Ministry of Women. Notes. *Journal of Religious Thought* 43, No. 1 (Spring-Summer 1986):59–75

Carpentier, Alejo (about)

Images et mythes d'Haiti. By Daniel-Henry Pageaux. Reviewed by Clarisse Zimra. *Research in African Literatures* 17, No. 4 (Winter 1986): 591–593

Carrick, Carol

Stay Away from Simon! Book review. Emily Strauss Watson. *Interracial Books for Children Bulletin* 17, No. 1 (1986):9

Carrington, Laura (about)

Meet Laura Carrington. *Black Collegian* 17, No. 1 (September/October 1986):40

Carroll, Diahann (about)

Diahann Carroll Tells All: Autobiography Details Stormy Nine-Year Love Affair with Sidney Poitier. *Ebony* 41, No. 8 (June 1986):126

Carson, Julia (about)

The Body Politic. Margo Walker. *Black Enterprise* 16, No. 11 (June 1986):50

Carter, John P.

A Pastoral Letter from John P. Carter. *Journal of Religious Thought* 43, No. 1 (Spring-Summer 1986):120–127

Carter, Kenneth (about)

The New Entrepreneur: Catering Magician. E. D. Smith. *Black Enterprise* 16, No. 11 (June 1986):301

Carter, Lawrence Edward, Sr.

Cheikh Anta Diop's First Visit to the United States. *Journal of African Civilizations* 8, No. 1 (June 1986):307–314

Carter, Robert (III) (about)

Management of Policy Benefits. Margo Walker. *Black Enterprise* 16, No. 11 (June 1986):65

Carter, Sharon

The Law...and Your Medical, Doctor and Hospital Rights. *About Time* 14, No. 4 (April 1986):22

Cartoons

See Caricatures and Cartoons

Caruthers, Candice

Money Merchants. *Black Enterprise* 17, No. 1 (August 1986):61–63

Psst! Have We Got a Deal for You! *Black Enterprise* 17, No. 4 (November 1986):86

Cassells, Cyrus

Sin. Book review. *Callaloo* 9, No. 1 (Winter 1986):243–247

These Are Not Brushstrokes. Poem. *Callaloo* 9, No. 1 (Winter 1986):18–23

To the Cypress Again and Again. Poem. *Callaloo* 9, No. 1 (Winter 1986):18–23

Cassese, Sid

Richard Pryor: No Laughing Matter. Interview. *Essence* 16, No. 11 (March 1986):78

Castles, Stephen

Ethnicity, Class and Gender in Australia. Book review. *Race and Class* 27, No. 4 (Spring 1986):94–96

Castration Complex in Literature

Castration Symbolism in Recent Black American Fiction. Notes. Richard K. Barksdale. *CLA Journal* 29, No. 4 (June 1986):400–413

Castro, Fidel—Interview

Fidel y la Religion: Conversaciones con Frei Betto. Interview. Reviewed by Paul E. Sigmund. *Caribbean Review* 15, No. 2 (Spring 1986):30–31

Caterers and Catering

The New Entrepreneur: Catering Magician. E. D. Smith. *Black Enterprise* 16, No. 11 (June 1986):301

Catholicism

Catholicism and Candomble: The Mystical Mix. Harriette Cole. *Essence* 16, No. 11 (March 1986):92

Catlett, Elizabeth (about)

Elizabeth Catlett. Illustrated. Mary Jane Hewitt. *International Review of African American Art* 7, No. 2 (1986):26–33

Cavanaugh, Ronald R. (joint author)

See Hall, T. William

Cayer, David A. (joint editor)

See Morgenstern, Dan

Cemeteries—New York (State)

A Beginning Investigation into the Afro-American Cemeteries of Ulster County, New York. Gail Schneider. *Afro-Americans in New York Life and History* 10, No.1 (January 1986):61–70

Censorship

A Guide to Political Censorship in South Africa. By Louise Silver. Reviewed by Neville Choonoo. *Research in African Literatures* 17, No. 3 (Fall 1986): 416–418

Center on Budget and Policy Priorities

Falling Behind: A Report on How Blacks Have Fared under Reagan. *Journal of Black Studies* 17, No. 2 (December 1986):148–171

Central America—History

Endless War: How We Got Involved in Central America—and What Can Be Done About It. By James Chace. Reviewed by Alexander H. McIntire, Jr. *Caribbean Review* 15, No. 1 (Winter 1986):44

Central American Defense Council

Nicaragua under Siege. Marlene Dixon and Susanne Jonas, editors. Reviewed by John A. Booth. *Caribbean Review* 15, No. 2 (Spring 1986):47

Central America—Politics and Government

Political Systems as Export Commodities: Democracy and the Role of the US in Central America. Ricardo Arias Calderon. *Caribbean Review* 15, No. 1 (Winter 1986):21–23+

Césaire, Aimé (about)

Aimé Césaire's Lesson about Decolonization in *La Tragédie de Roi Christophe*. Notes. Hunt Hawkins. *CLA Journal* 30, No. 2 (December 1986):144–153

Images et mythes d'Haiti. By Daniel-Henry Pageaux. Reviewed by Clarisse Zimra. *Research in African Literatures* 17, No. 4 (Winter 1986): 591–593

Modernism and Negritude: The Poetry and Poetics of Aimé Césaire. By James A. Arnold. Reviewed by Vera M. Kutzinski. *Callaloo* 9, No. 4 (Fall 1986):740–748

Soleil éclate. Jacqueline Leiner, editor. Reviewed by Bernard Aresu. *Research in African Literatures* 17, No. 4 (Winter 1986): 588–591

Chaane, Busi

Causes for Concern: British Criminal Justice on Trial? Book review. *Race and Class* 28, No. 1 (Summer 1986):103–107

Worlds Apart: Women under Immigration and Nationality Law. Book review. *Race and Class* 28, No. 1 (Summer 1986):103–107

Chace, James

Endless War: How We Got Involved in Central America—and What Can Be Done About It. Reviewed by Alexander H. McIntire, Jr. *Caribbean Review* 15, No. 1 (Winter 1986):44

Cham, Mbye B.

Senegalese Literature: A Critical History. Book review. *Research in African Literatures* 17, No. 4 (Winter 1986): 567–569

Chambers, Kimberly (joint author)

See Rowell, Charles H.

Champagne Productions Inc.

Automotive Luxury. Yvette Moore. *Black Enterprise* 17, No. 4 (November 1986):31

Chandler, Wayne B.

Trait-Influences in Meso-America: The African-Asian Connection. Notes. *Journal of African Civilizations* 8, No. 2 (December 1986):274–334

Channer, Colin

Caribbean Commerce. *Black Enterprise* 17, No. 3 (October 1986):22

Chapel Hill (N.C.)—History

Civil Rights Organization and the Indigenous Movement in Chapel Hill, N. C., 1960–1965. Marcellus Barksdale. *Phylon* 47, No. 1 (March 1986):29–42

Chapman, Audrey B.

Man Sharing: Dilemma or Choice. Book review. Henry Duvall. *About Time* 14, No. 12 (December 1986):29

Chapman, Michael

Douglas Blackburn. Book review. *Research in African Literatures* 17, No. 3 (Fall 1986): 406–408

Chapman, Sandra San Viki

Holding On. Poem. *Essence* 17, No. 4 (August 1986):148

Relationship. Poem. *Essence* 17, No. 7 (November 1986):132

Charleston, Lillian (joint author)

See Mannan, Golam

Charlotte, N.C.—Officials and Employees

Harvey Gantt: The First Black Mayor of Charlotte, N.C., Is Proving to Be the Most Popular Mayor as Well. Charles Whitaker. *Ebony* 41, No. 6 (April 1986):92

Cheatwood, Kiarri T.-H.

Elegies for Patrice. Book review. Gerald Barrax. *Callaloo* 9, No. 1 (Winter 1986):263–265

Checking Accounts

Handling a Lost Check. *Black Enterprise* 17, No. 1 (August 1986):22

Cheers, D. Michael

Jesse Jackson: Rebuilding Bridges to Africa. *Ebony* 42, No. 2 (December 1986):132

The Lady in Charge: Trudi Morrison Runs Day-to-Day Operations of U.S. Senate. *Ebony* 41, No. 12 (October 1986):117

Requiem for a Hero: "Touching the Face of God." *Ebony* 41, No. 7 (May 1986):82

Terence Todman: Top Diplomat Ambassador to Denmark. *Ebony* 41, No. 4 (February 1986):67

Chemain, Roger

La ville dans le roman africain. Reviewed by S. Ade Ojo. *Research in African Literatures* 17, No. 4 (Winter 1986): 574–576

Chen, Gavin M.

Minority Business Development: An International Comparison. *Review of Black Political Economy* 15, No. 2 (Fall 1986):93–111

Chenault, Julie

"What I Wanted to Be When I Grew Up." *Essence* 17, No. 1 (May 1986):80

Cherry, Connie

Salvador's Sumptuous Cuisine and Spirits. *Essence* 16, No. 11 (March 1986):88

Cherry, Conrad (editor)

Horace Bushnell: Sermons. Reviewed by Kortright Davis. *Journal of Religious Thought* 43, No. 2 (Fall-Winter 1986–87):91–92

Cherry, Dianne Lynne

News Coverage in Africa's Anglophone Press: Implications of Neocolonialism. *Western Journal of Black Studies* 10, No. 1 (Spring 1986):12–16

Chester, PA—Officials and Employees

Municipal Management. Kenneth Maurice Jones. *Black Enterprise* 16, No. 10 (May 1986):20

Chicago—Cook County Hospital

Cook County's Top Doctor: Dr. Agnes Lattimer Is the Only Black Woman to Head One of the Nation's Largest Hospitals. Charles Whitaker. *Ebony* 41, No. 11 (September 1986):44

Chicago—Politics

Harold Washington and the Politics of Race in Chicago. Manning Marable. *Black Scholar* 17, No. 6 (November-December 1986):14–23

Chicago—Public Schools

Dr. Manford Byrd, Jr.: Cooling off the Hot Seat. Alex Poinsett. *Ebony* 41, No. 4 (February 1986):44

Chicago—Writers

Richard Wright and the Chicago Renaissance. Robert Bone. *Callaloo* 9, No. 3 (Summer 1986):446–468

Childbirth

Black and White Children in America: Key Facts. Children's Defense Fund. Reviewed by Gayl Fowler. *Journal of Religious Thought* 43, No. 1 (Spring-Summer 1986):130

Childhood—Africa

Concepts of the Child in Some Nigerian Cultures. O. L. Okanlawon. *Journal of Black Psychology* 12, No. 2 (February 1986):61–70

Child Molesting

How to Protect Your Children from People They Trust. Marilyn Marshall. *Ebony* 42, No. 1 (November 1986):46

Child Rearing

Child Care by Cassette. Ken Smikle. *Black Enterprise* 16, No. 8 (March 1986):16

Children

Black and White Children in America: Key Facts. Children's Defense Fund. Reviewed by Gayl Fowler. *Journal of Religious Thought* 43, No. 1 (Spring-Summer 1986):130

Save the Children. Marian Wright Edelman. *Ebony* 41, No. 10 (August 1986):53

See also Missing Children

Children's Defense Fund

Black and White Children in America: Key Facts. Reviewed by Gayl Fowler. *Journal of Religious Thought* 43, No. 1 (Spring-Summer 1986):130

How to Shape Policy through Lobbying. David
C. Ruffin. *Black Enterprise* 17, No. 5 (December
1986):33

Children's Literature

African American Literature: A New Challenge.
Eloise Greenfield. *Interracial Books for Children
Bulletin* 17, No. 2 (1986):4–5

Interracial Books for Children—Bibliographies.
Interracial Books for Children Bulletin 17, No. 1
(1986):12–30

Children's Literature—Africa

Literature for Children and Young People in
Kenya. By Asenath Bole Odaga. Reviewed by
Nancy J. Schmidt. *Research in African Literatures*
17, No. 4 (Winter 1986): 609–610

Childress, Alice (about)

Images of Blacks in Plays by Black Women.
Elizabeth Brown-Guillory. *Phylon* 47, No. 3
(September 1986):230–237

Chinese Historical Society of Southern California

Linking Our Lives: Chinese American Women of
Los Angeles. Lillian Yeh. Book review. *Interracial
Books for Children Bulletin* 17, Nos. 3–4 (1986):34

Chinese—United States

Linking Our Lives: Chinese American Women of
Los Angeles. By the Chinese Historical Society of
Southern California. Reviewed by Lillian Yeh.
Interracial Books for Children Bulletin 17, Nos. 3–4
(1986):34

Chinweizu, and others

Gibb's Gibberish. *Research in African Literatures*
17, No. 1 (Spring 1986): 48–52

Chlamydia

Chlamydia: The "Silent Disease." Francesca
Simon. *Essence* 17, No. 1 (May 1986):28

Chomsky, Noam

Middle East Terrorism and the American
Ideological System. *Race and Class* 28, No. 1
(Summer 1986):1–28

Choonoo, Neville

A Guide to Political Censorship in South Africa.
Book review. *Research in African Literatures* 17,
No. 3 (Fall 1986): 416–418

Christian, Barbara T.

Coagulations: New and Selected Poems. Book
review. *Callaloo* 9, No. 1 (Winter 1986):235–239

Christian, Shirley

Nicaragua: Revolution in the Family. Book
review. Saul Landau. *Race and Class* 27, No. 3
(Winter 1986):95–99

Christianity—Philosophy

The Devil and Dr. Church: A Guide to Hell for
Atheists and True Believers. By F. Forrester
Church. Reviewed by Kortright Davis. *Journal of
Religious Thought* 43, No. 2 (Fall-Winter
1986–87):91

Christmann, Timothy J.

Navy: Unparalleled Opportunities. *Black Collegian*
16, No. 4 (March/April 1986):130–134

Christmas, Rachel J., and Salter, Dan Giles

Off the Beaten Path. *Essence* 16, No. 11 (March
1986):22

Chuck Davis Dance Company

Chuck Davis Dance Company. Kris DiLorenzo.
Crisis 93, No. 5 (May 1986):14–38

Church, F. Forrester

The Devil and Dr. Church: A Guide to Hell for
Atheists and True Believers. Reviewed by
Kortright Davis. *Journal of Religious Thought* 43,
No. 2 (Fall-Winter 1986–87):91

Church Founding

See Religion—Church Development

Church Management

The Gift of Administration. By Thomas C.
Campbell and Gary B. Reierson. Reviewed by
James Hammond. *Journal of Religious Thought* 43,
No. 1 (Spring-Summer 1986):128–129

Church and Social Problems

Return to the Spiritual Traditions of Black
Churches and Schools. *Ebony* 41, No. 10 (August
1986):160

Church and State

Do Vouchers Equal Choices for the Poor? David
C. Ruffin. *Black Enterprise* 17, No. 2 (September
1986):25

Fidel y la Religion: Conversaciones con Frei
Betto. Interview. Reviewed by Paul E. Sigmund.
Caribbean Review 15, No. 2 (Spring 1986):30–31

Nicaragua under Siege. Marlene Dixon and
Susanne Jonas, editors. Reviewed by John A.
Booth. *Caribbean Review* 15, No. 2 (Spring
1986):47

Religious Belief and Political Activism in Black
America: An Essay. Robert Michael Franklin.
Journal of Religious Thought 43, No. 2 (Fall-Winter
1986–87):63–72

Ritual, Paradox and Death in Managua:
Internacionalistas in Nicaragua. Alfred Padula.
Caribbean Review 15, No. 1 (Winter 1986):18–19

Cinema

See also Blacks in the Performing Arts

Cinema—Political Aspects

The Western Film Hollywood Myths and One Black Reality. Waliyy Gill. *Western Journal of Black Studies* 10, No. 1 (Spring 1986):1–5

Cityplace Development Corporation

How One Man Is Building the City of the Future. Lloyd Gite. *Black Enterprise* 17, No. 5 (December 1986):68

Civil Disturbances

A Social History of 20th Century Urban Riots. By James Upton. Reviewed by Earl Smith. *Phylon* 47, No. 1 (March 1986):101–103

Civilization, Ancient

The African Origin of Civilization: Myth or Reality. Notes. By Cheikh Anta Diop. Reviewed by A. J. Williams-Myers. *Journal of African Civilizations* 8, No. 1 (June 1986):118–126

The African Presence in Ancient America: Evidence from Physical Anthropology. Notes. Keith M. Jordon. *Journal of African Civilizations* 8, No. 2 (December 1986):136–151

Africa's Contribution to World Civilization: The Exact Sciences. Notes. Bibliography. Cheikh Anta Diop. *Journal of African Civilizations* 8, No. 1 (June 1986):74–88

The Beginnings of Man and Civilization. Cheikh Anta Diop. *Journal of African Civilizations* 8, No. 1 (June 1986):322–351

The Changing Perception of C. A. Diop and His Work: The Preeminence of a Scientific Spirit. Notes. James G. Spady. *Journal of African Civilizations* 8, No. 1 (June 1986):89–101

Cheikh Anta Diop and the New Concept of African History. Notes. John Henrik Clarke. *Journal of African Civilizations* 8, No. 1 (June 1986):110–117

Civilization or Barbarism: An Authentic Anthropology. Excerpt. Notes. Cheikh Anta Diop. *Journal of African Civilizations* 8, No. 1 (June 1986):161–225

Civilization or Barbarism: The Legacy of Cheikh Anta Diop. By Cheikh Anta Diop. Reviewed by Leonard Jeffries, Jr. *Journal of African Civilizations* 8, No. 1 (June 1986):146–160

The Cultural Unity of Black Africa: The Domains of Patriarchy and of Matriarchy in Classical Antiquity. Bibliography. By Cheikh Anta Diop. Reviewed by Asa G. Hilliard III. *Journal of African Civilizations* 8, No. 1 (June 1986):102–109

Death Shall Not Find Us Thinking That We Die. Notes. Ivan Van Sertima. *Journal of African Civilizations* 8, No. 1 (June 1986):7–16

Dr. Diop on Asia: Highlights and Insights. Notes. Runoko Rashidi. *Journal of African Civilizations* 8, No. 1 (June 1986):127–145

The Egyptian Presence in South America. Notes. R. A. Jairazbhoy. *Journal of African Civilizations* 8, No. 2 (December 1986):76–135

The First Americans. Notes. Legrand H. Clegg II. *Journal of African Civilizations* 8, No. 2 (December 1986):264–273

Further Conversations with the Pharaoh. Interview. Charles S. Finch. *Journal of African Civilizations* 8, No. 1 (June 1986):227–237

Interview with Cheikh Anta Diop. Interview. Notes. Bibliography. Shawna Moore. *Journal of African Civilizations* 8, No. 1 (June 1986):238–248

Iron in the Ancient Egyptian Empire. Notes. Bibliography. Cheikh Anta Diop. *Journal of African Civilizations* 8, No. 1 (June 1986):64–73

Men Out of Asia: A Review and Update of the Gladwin Thesis. Notes. By Harold Sterling Gladwin. Reviewed by Runoko Rashidi. *Journal of African Civilizations* 8, No. 2 (December 1986):248–263

Origin of the Ancient Egyptians. Notes. Cheikh Anta Diop. *Journal of African Civilizations* 8, No. 1 (June 1986):35–63

Pyramid—American and African: A Comparison. Notes. Beatrice Lumpkin. *Journal of African Civilizations* 8, No. 2 (December 1986):169–187

Trait-Influences in Meso-America: The African-Asian Connection. Notes. Wayne B. Chandler. *Journal of African Civilizations* 8, No. 2 (December 1986):274–334

Two Interviews with Cheikh Anta Diop. Interview. Listervelt Middleton and Nile Valley Executive Committee. *Journal of African Civilizations* 8, No. 1 (June 1986):284–302

Unexpected African Faces in Pre-Columbian America. Alexander Von Wuthenau. *Journal of African Civilizations* 8, No. 2 (December 1986):56–75

Civilization—Africa

Ten Years After: An Introduction and Overview. Ivan Van Sertima. *Journal of African Civilizations* 8, No. 2 (December 1986):5–27

Civil Rights

Affirmative Reaction. Errol T. Louis. *Black Enterprise* 17, No. 3 (October 1986):21

The Enforcement of Civil Rights Statutes: The Reagan Administration's Record. Barbara Wolvovitz and Jules Lobel. *Black Law Journal* 9, No. 3 (Winter 1986):252–262

The Erosion of Civil Rights Enforcement. Phyllis McClure. *Black Scholar* 17, No. 3 (May-June 1986):10–18

High Court Reviews Civil Rights. Frank Dexter Brown. *Black Enterprise* 16, No. 6 (January 1986):31

Civil Rights Activists

Civil Rights Lawyers Revisited. *Ebony* 42, No. 2 (December 1986):76

Dr. Mary Frances Berry: Educator-Activist Beats Drum for Civil Rights. Henry Duvall. *About Time* 14, No. 11 (November 1986):16–17

Earl B. Dickerson: An Appreciation. Walter W. Morrison. *Crisis* 93, No. 8 (October 1986):37

Eslanda Goode Robeson, Pan-Africanist. Barbara Ranby. *SAGE* 3, No. 2 (Fall 1986):22–26

Groundwork: Charles Hamilton Houston and the Struggle for Civil Rights. By Genna Rae McNeil. Reviewed by Marsha Jones. *About Time* 14, No. 2 (February 1986):18–20

Martin Luther King (Jr.) and the Paradox of Nonviolent Direct Action. James A. Colaiaco. *Phylon* 47, No. 1 (March 1986):16–28

Martin Luther King (Jr.) and the Quest for Nonviolent Social Change. Adam Fairclough. *Phylon* 47, No. 1 (March 1986):1–15

Modjeska A. Simkins: Profile of a Legend. Louis C. Bryan. *SAGE* 3, No. 1 (Spring 1986):56–57

The Struggle from Without: An Interview with South African Exile Tandi Gcabashe. *SAGE* 3, No. 2 (Fall 1986):48–51

Tribute to James Brown, Jr., Fighter for Justice. Jerry M. Guess. *Crisis* 93, No. 5 (May 1986):32–33

W. E. B. Du Bois: A Final Resting Place for an Afro-American Giant. Charles Whitaker. *Ebony* 42, No. 1 (November 1986):172

Civil Rights—History

The Black Middle Class in America. Thomas J. Durant (Jr.) and Joyce S. Louden. *Phylon* 47, No. 4 (December 1986):253–263

The Marxist Analyses of Manning Marable. Manning Marable. Reviewed by John Williams. *Phylon* 47, No. 3 (September 1986):248–250

The United States and South Africa: History, Civil Rights and the Legal and Cultural Vulnerability of Blacks. JoAnne Cornwell. *Phylon* 47, No. 4 (December 1986):285–293

Civil Rights Movement

At the River I Stand: Memphis, the 1968 Strike and Martin Luther King. By Joan Turner Beifuss. Reviewed by Cain H. Felder. *Journal of Religious Thought* 43, No. 2 (Fall-Winter 1986–87):93–94

Civil Rights Organization and the Indigenous Movement in Chapel Hill, N. C., 1960–1965. Marcellus Barksdale. *Phylon* 47, No. 1 (March 1986):29–42

Part of a Whole: The Independence of the Civil Rights Movement and Other Social Movements. Judith Rollins. *Phylon* 47, No. 1 (March 1986):61–70

Civil War, 1861–1865

See United States—Civil War, 1861–1865

Claiborne, Ron C.

Institutional Reform and the Enforcement of the Fair Housing Laws. *Black Scholar* 17, No. 3 (May-June 1986):42–48

Clark, J. P. (about)

J. P. Clark. By Robert M. Wren. Reviewed by Thomas R. Knipp. *Research in African Literatures* 17, No. 2 (Summer 1986): 278–281

Clark, Vernon L., and others

NCAA Rule 48: Racism or Reform? *Journal of Negro Education* 55, No.2 (Spring 1986):162–170

Clark, VeVe A. (joint author)

See Berrian, Brenda F.

Clarke, John Henrik

Cheikh Anta Diop and the New Concept of African History. Notes. *Journal of African Civilizations* 8, No. 1 (June 1986):110–117

Class Actions (Civil Procedure)

Remedies for Victim Group Isolation in the Work Place: Court Orders, Problem-Solving and Affirmative Action in the Post-*Stotts* Era. Paul J. Spiegelman. *Howard Law Journal* 29, No. 1 (1986):191–258

Class Consciousness

Buppies. Kenneth M. Jones. *Crisis* 93, No. 4 (April 1986):16–24

From Working Class to Middle Class: Ideology and Socialization. Luke Tripp. *Negro Educational Review* 37, Nos. 3–4 (July-October 1986):144–153

Claude, Judy

Poverty Patterns for Black Men and Women. *Black Scholar* 17, No. 5 (September-October 1986):20–23

Clay, William L.

Decimation of School Lunches. *About Time* 14, No. 5 (May 1986):9

Parental and Medical Leave. *About Time* 14, No. 4 (April 1986):19

Reagan Administration Tries to Hide Success of WIC Program. *About Time* 14, No. 3 (March 1986):19

South Africa: Challenge for Our Nation. *About Time* 14, No. 8 (August 1986):13

Tax Reform: Neither Fairness Nor Simplicity. *About Time* 14, No. 10 (October 1986):21

Claypool, Jane

Issues in American History: The Worker in America. Book review. Jan M. Goodman. *Interracial Books for Children Bulletin* 17, No. 2 (1986):13

Clayton, Cherry

The Re-interment on Buffelskop. Book review. *Research in African Literatures* 17, No. 3 (Fall 1986): 404–406

Clayton, Janet (joint author)

See Adams, Joyce Davis

Cleaning Services

Providing a Healthier Workplace: Sheen and Shine, Inc. Marsha Jones. *About Time* 14, No. 8 (August 1986):28–29

Clegg, Legrand H. (II)

The First Americans. Notes. *Journal of African Civilizations* 8, No. 2 (December 1986):264–273

Clements, Charles, M.D.

Witness to War: An American Doctor in El Salvador. Reviewed by Neale Pearson. *Caribbean Review* 15, No. 2 (Spring 1986):47–48

Cleveland, Lisa (joint author)

See Jordan, Jennifer

Cleveland, Odessa

Lifeless Heart. Poem. *Black American Literature Forum* 20, No. 3 (Fall 1986):314

Clothing Industry and Trade

The Body Politic. Margo Walker. *Black Enterprise* 16, No. 11 (June 1986):50

King-Size Entrepreneur Runs Queen-Size Dress Chain. *Ebony* 41, No. 8 (June 1986):53

Clothing in Literature

Clothes and Closure in Three Novels by Black Women. Mary Jane Lupton. *Black American Literature Forum* 20, No. 4 (Winter 1986):409–421

Coal Mining and Miners

Exploring Buried Buxton: Archeology of an Abandoned Iowa Coal Mining Town with a Large Black Population. By David M. Gradwohl and Nancy M. Osborn. Reviewed by Maria Boynton. *Afro-Americans in New York Life and History* 10, No. 2 (July 1986): 65–68

Coastal Environmental Control Inc.

Cleaning up in Waste Removal. Lloyd Gite. *Black Enterprise* 17, No. 3 (October 1986):33

Cobham-Sander, Rhonda

Class vs. Sex: The Problem of Values in the Modern Nigerian Novel. *Black Scholar* 17, No. 4 (July-August 1986):17–27

Coca-Cola Bottling Company

Bruce: The Boss. Ken Smikle. *Black Enterprise* 17, No. 2 (September 1986):36

Cashing in on Coke. Ken Smikle. *Black Enterprise* 16, No. 8 (March 1986):13

Cochran, Donnie (about)

The First Black Blue Angel: Lt. Cmdr. Donnie Cochran Makes Naval History as Member of Famed Precision Flying Team. Aldore Collier. *Ebony* 41, No. 8 (June 1986):27

Coetzee, J. M. (about)

Colonialism and the Novels of S. M. Coetzee. Notes. Stephen Watson. *Research in African Literatures* 17, No. 3 (Fall 1986): 370–392

Cognition

Is There an Afro-American Cognitive Style? Barbara J. Shade. *Journal of Black Psychology* 13, No. 1 (August 1986):13–16

Cohen, Carol Lee

Sally Ann Thunder Ann Whirlwind Crockett. Book review. Karen Mantlo. *Interracial Books for Children Bulletin* 17, No. 2 (1986):13

Coin Collecting

See Numismatics

Coins

Centennial Collectible. *Black Enterprise* 16, No. 11 (June 1986):52

Colaiaco, James A.

Martin Luther King (Jr.) and the Paradox of Nonviolent Direct Action. *Phylon* 47, No. 1 (March 1986):16–28

Colburn, Forrest D. (compiler)

First Impressions: Critics Look at the New Literature. *Caribbean Review* 15, No. 1 (Winter 1986):41–44

First Impressions: Critics Look at the New Literature. *Caribbean Review* 15, No. 2 (Spring 1986):45–48

Cold War

Black and Red—W. E. B. DuBois and the Afro-American Response to the Cold War—1944–1963. By Gerald Horne. Reviewed by Linda Burnham. *Black Scholar* 17, No. 2 (March-April 1986):52–54

Cole, Beverly P.

The Black Educator: An Endangered Species. *Journal of Negro Education* 55, No.3 (Summer 1986):326–334

Cole, Diane

Ten Time-Management Tips. *Essence* 17, No. 5 (September 1986):130

Cole, Harriette

Catholicism and Candomble: The Mystical Mix. *Essence* 16, No. 11 (March 1986):92

Creative Color in Interior Design. *Essence* 17, No. 2 (July 1986):100

Cole, John A., and Reuben, Lucy J.

Linkages between Minority Business Characteristics and Minority Banks' Locations. *Review of Black Political Economy* 15, No. 2 (Fall 1986):73–92

Cole, Mike

The Aboriginal Struggle: An Interview with Helen Boyle. *Race and Class* 27, No. 4 (Spring 1986):21–33

Cole, O. Jackson, and Washington, Valora

A Critical Analysis of the Assessment of the Effects of Head Start on Minority Children. *Journal of Negro Education* 55, No. 1 (Winter 1986):91–106

Cole, William S. (about)

Wind and Thunder. *Western Journal of Black Studies* 10, No. 4 (Winter 1986):193–194

ColeJon Mechanical Corporation

ColeJon's Hot Profits. Patricia A. Jones. *Black Enterprise* 16, No. 8 (March 1986):16

Coleman, James

The Quest for Wholeness in Toni Morrison's *Tar Baby. Black American Literature Forum* 20, Nos. 1–2 (Spring/Summer 1986):63–73

Coleman, Larry G.

See Gandy, Oscar H. (Jr.)

Coleman, Philip W.

The Effect of the Requirement of Expert Testimony on the Tenant's Ability to Prove Damages in a Breach of Warranty of Habitability Action. *Howard Law Journal* 29, No. 1 (1986):177–189

Coleman, Wanda

Emmett Till. Poem. *Callaloo* 9, No. 2 (Spring 1986):295–299

Coleman, Willette

WHMM-TV's Super Internship. *Black Collegian* 16, No. 3 (January/February 1986):118–124

Coleridge-Taylor, Samuel (about)

Samuel Coleridge-Taylor: A Postscript. Jeffrey Green and Paul McGilchrist. *Black Perspective in Music* 14, No. 3 (Fall 1986):259–266

Collective Bargaining

Justice and Dignity: Due Process Notions in the Administration of Collective Bargaining Agreement. Jeffrey D. Gilliam. *Black Law Journal* 9, No. 3 (Winter 1986):323–333

Collectors and Collecting

Investing by Collecting. Julianne Malveaux. *Essence* 17, No. 8 (December 1986):113

College Administrators

This Dean Means Business: Marion Oliver Wants to Show Black Students the Advantages of Career in Business. Charles Whitaker. *Ebony* 41, No. 4 (February 1986):93

College Language Association—Conference Reports

The College Language Association: Past, Present, Future Perfect. Ann Venture Young. *CLA Journal* 29, No. 4 (June 1986):391–399

In Memoriam: A Tribute to Professor Robert A. Smith. Ruthe T. Sheffey. *CLA Journal* 29, No. 4 (June 1986):483–485

College Language Association—Member Publications

Publications by CLA Members: 1985–86. Bibliography. Robert J. Hudson and Robert P. Smith (Jr.) *CLA Journal* 30, No. 2 (December 1986):241–251

College Presidents

Black Women College Presidents. *Ebony* 41, No. 4 (February 1986):108

Chief Academic Officers at Black Colleges and Universities: A Comparison by Gender. Lea E. Williams. *Journal of Negro Education* 55, No.4 (Fall 1986):443–452

College Sports

The Exploitation of the Black Athlete: Some Alternative Solutions. Editorial. Gary A. Sales *Journal of Negro Education* 55, No.4 (Fall 1986):439–442

NCAA Rule 48: Racism or Reform? Vernon L. Clark, Floyd Horton, and Robert L. Alford. *Journal of Negro Education* 55, No.2 (Spring 1986):162–170

College Students

Autonomy and Theoretical Orientation of Remedial and Non-Remedial College Students. James Koutrelakos. *Journal of Negro Education* 55, No. 1 (Winter 1986):29–37

Blacks in College. By J. Fleming. Reviewed by Herman Brown. *Journal of Negro Education* 55, No.2 (Spring 1986):237–239

Black Students in Higher Education. By C. Scully Stikes. Reviewed by Roberta N. Morse. *Journal of Negro Education* 55, No. 1 (Winter 1986):118–120

A Comparison of the Academic Performance of Black and White Freshman Students on an Urban Commuter Campus. Golam Mannan, Lillian Charleston, and Behrooz Saghafi. *Journal of Negro Education* 55, No.2 (Spring 1986):155–161

Enhancing Minority College Students' Performance on Educational Tests. Henry T. Frierson. *Journal of Negro Education* 55, No. 1 (Winter 1986):38–45

Entrepreneurs, Students of the 80's: Financing Their Educations and Making a Profit. William Ball. *Black Collegian* 17, No. 1 (September/October 1986):128–132

Role Model Advice to Students. Kuumba Kazi-Ferrouillet and Portia Ballard. *Black Collegian* 17, No. 1 (September/October 1986):115–120

See also Study, Method of

College Students—Attitudes

An Analysis of University of Ibadan Undergraduates' Attitudes toward Issues Incidental to the Yoruba Culture. Adedeji Awoniyi. *Negro Educational Review* 37, No. 2 (April 1986):62–70

Black and Blue on Campus. Errol T. Louis. *Essence* 17, No. 4 (August 1986):67

College Students—Employment

Evaluating Your Course Load. Jessica B. Harris. *Black Enterprise* 16, No. 7 (February 1986):103–104

College Students—Political Activity

Community Leadership and Black Former Activists of the 1960s. Luke Tripp. *Western Journal of Black Studies* 10, No. 2 (Summer 1986):86–89

From Working Class to Middle Class: Ideology and Socialization. Luke Tripp. *Negro Educational Review* 37, Nos. 3–4 (July-October 1986):144–153

Selected Correlates of Perceptions of Black Militancy. Richard D. Bucher. *Western Journal of Black Studies* 10, No. 2 (Summer 1986):79–85

Student Culture and Activism in Black South African Universities. M. O. Nkomo. Reviewed by Ernest F. Dube. *Journal of Negro Education* 55, No.2 (Spring 1986):240–244

Watch Jesse Run and Tell Me What You See: A First Look at Student Perceptions of the Jesse Jackson Presidential Candidacy. Oscar H. Gandy, Jr., and Larry G. Coleman. *Journal of Black Studies* 16, No. 3 (March 1986):293–306

College Students—Summer Jobs

Winter Hunt for a Summer Job. Sandra Schocket. *Black Collegian* 17, No. 2 (November/December 1986):67–71

College Students—Travel

Summer Abroad 1987: Test Your "Study Abroad" IQ. Shirley O. Henderson. *Black Collegian* 17, No. 2 (November/December 1986):59–62

Collier, Aldore

227—Marla's Masterpiece. *Ebony* 42, No. 2 (December 1986):92

Bonnie St. John: A Profile in Beauty, Brains, and Courage. *Ebony* 42, No. 1 (November 1986):134

Danny Glover: The Reluctant Movie Star. *Ebony* 41, No. 5 (March 1986):82

The First Black Blue Angel: Lt. Cmdr. Donnie Cochran Makes Naval History as Member of Famed Precision Flying Team. *Ebony* 41, No. 8 (June 1986):27

Janet: Hit Album Takes Another Jackson to the Top. *Ebony* 41, No. 11 (September 1986):29

New Edition: Teen Idols of the Music World Wow Fans with Soulful Young Sound and Fancy Steps. *Ebony* 41, No. 8 (June 1986):58

The Weaver Triplets: Following in the Footsteps of Big Brother Mike. *Ebony* 41, No. 9 (July 1986):48

The World's Greatest Woman Athlete: Jackie Joyner Shatters Heptathalon Record Twice in 26 Days. *Ebony* 41, No. 12 (October 1986):77

Collins, Carol C.

Black Progress: Reality or Illusion. Book review. Marianne Ilaw. *Black Enterprise* 16, No. 7 (February 1986):19–21

Collins, John

Musicmakers of West Africa. Book review. Jacqueline Cogdell DjeDje. *Black Perspective in Music* 14, No. 3 (Fall 1986):308–309

Collins, Joseph (joint author)

See Benjamin, Medea

Collins, June L.

Unnamed. Poem. *Essence* 17, No. 2 (July 1986):126

Collins, Patricia Hill

The Afro-American Work/Family Nexus: An Exploratory Analysis. *Western Journal of Black Studies* 10, No. 3 (Fall 1986):148–158

Colombia

Nature Strikes at Colombia. Bernard Diederich. *Caribbean Review* 15, No. 1 (Winter 1986):15

Colombia—Politics and Government

Betancur's Battles: The Man of Peace Takes Up the Sword. Bernard Diederich. *Caribbean Review* 15, No. 1 (Winter 1986):10–11+

Colombia in the Eighties: A Political Regime in Transition. Ricardo Santamaria Salamanca and Gabriel Silva Lujan. *Caribbean Review* 15, No. 1 (Winter 1986):12–14+

Colombia under Stress: A Presidency Lamed by Instability. Gary Hoskin. *Caribbean Review* 15, No. 1 (Winter 1986):7–9+

Colon, Linda (joint author)

See Froschl, Merle

Colonialism

Aimé Césaire's Lesson about Decolonization in *La Tragédie de Roi Christophe.* Notes. Hunt Hawkins. *CLA Journal* 30, No. 2 (December 1986):144–153

Colonialism and the Novels of S. M. Coetzee. Notes. Stephen Watson. *Research in African Literatures* 17, No. 3 (Fall 1986): 370–392

Expatriate Characters in the Early African Novel. L. Losambe. *Phylon* 47, No. 2 (June 1986):148–158

Spain and the Loss of America. By Timothy E. Anna. Reviewed by Joaquin Roy. *Caribbean Review* 15, No. 2 (Spring 1986):48

Colonization—Africa

Application of Memmi's Theory of the Colonizer and the Colonized to the Conflicts in Zimbabwe. Dickson A. Mungazi. *Journal of Negro Education* 55, No.4 (Fall 1986):518–534

Color in Interior Decoration

Creative Color in Interior Design. *Essence* 17, No. 2 (July 1986):100

Comedians

Richard Pryor Changes Direction. Charles Whitaker. *Ebony* 41, No. 9 (July 1986):132

Richard Pryor: No Laughing Matter. Interview. Sid Cassese. *Essence* 16, No. 11 (March 1986):78

Commerce

Trade and Growth: The First Annual W. Arthur Lewis Lecture. Lance Taylor. *Review of Black Political Economy* 14, No. 4 (Spring 1986):17–36

Commodity Exhanges

Finding Your Future in Commodities Trading. *Black Enterprise* 16, No. 12 (July 1986):24

Commonwealth Institute

Conference on the Acquisition and Bibliography of Commonwealth and Third World Literatures in English. Reviewed by Nancy J. Schmidt. *Research in African Literatures* 17, No. 3 (Fall 1986): 439–440

Commonwealth v. Richardson

Commonwealth v. Richardson: Voir Dire and the Consent Defense to an Interracial Rape in Pennsylvania—Finding Twelve Not-Too-Angry Men. James A. Buddie. *Black Law Journal* 9, No. 3 (Winter 1986):300–311

Communication

When Well-Tuned Professionals Talk—People Listen. Karen Brailsford. *Black Enterprise* 16, No. 11 (June 1986):282

Communism

See Marxism

Community Centers

See Social Settlements

Community Development

See Local Government

Community Life

The Black Universe in Contemporary Afro-American Fiction. Notes. Norman Harris. *CLA Journal* 30, No. 1 (September 1986):1–13

Community Organizations

Baden Street Settlement: Putting the Pieces Together. Marsha Jones. *About Time* 14, No. 9 (September 1986):14–17

Grassroots Development in Latin America and the Caribbean: Oral Histories of Social Change. By Robert Wasserstrom. Reviewed by Linda Miller. *Caribbean Review* 15, No. 1 (Winter 1986):41–42

The Professional Ideology and Grassroots Community Organizations: New York's South Bronx Community in Perspective. Notes. Charles Green. *Afro-Americans in New York Life and History* 10, No. 2 (July 1986): 29–44

Volunteerism Makes a Difference. Marsha Jones. *About Time* 14, No. 6 (June 1986):14–20

Community Organizers

Community Leadership and Black Former Activists of the 1960s. Luke Tripp. *Western Journal of Black Studies* 10, No. 2 (Summer 1986):86–89

Community and School

Black Students in Special Education: Issues and Implications for Community Involvement. Thomas Serwatka and others. *Negro Educational Review* 37, No. 1 (January 1986):17–26

Composers

The Black-American Composer and the Orchestra in the Twentieth Century. Olly Wilson. *Black Perspective in Music* 14, No. 1 (Winter 1986):26–34

Debussy and American Minstrelsy. Ann McKinley. *Black Perspective in Music* 14, No. 3 (Fall 1986):249–258

In Retrospect: Edmund Thornton Jenkins. Betty Hillmon. *Black Perspective in Music* 14, No. 2 (Spring 1986):143–180

Samuel Coleridge-Taylor: A Postscript. Jeffrey Green and Paul McGilchrist. *Black Perspective in Music* 14, No. 3 (Fall 1986):249–258

Computer-Assisted Instruction

The Match: Learning Styles of Black Children and Microcomputer Programming. Marjorie W. Lee. *Journal of Negro Education* 55, No. 1 (Winter 1986):78–90

Computer Education—Dissertations and Theses

Master's Theses in Progress in Selected Colleges and Universities. Mac A. Stewart. *Negro Educational Review* 37, Nos. 3–4 (July-October 1986):95–96, 107

Computer Industry

BE Company of the Year: Maxima. Errol Lewis. *Black Enterprise* 16, No. 11 (June 1986):130

Computers, Personal

Computers and You: "How My Computer Has Put Punch in My Marriage!" Bebe Moore Campbell. *Essence* 17, No. 2 (July 1986):98

Your PC—A Great Time-Saver. Sharon Y. Lopez. *Black Enterprise* 16, No. 11 (June 1986):278

Computer Software

Tracking Films by Computer. Elaine Wapples. *Black Enterprise* 17, No. 2 (September 1986):27

Computer Technology—Employment Opportunities

The Sure Things: Computer-Related Careers Programmed for Growth. Solomon J. Herbert. *Black Collegian* 17, No. 2 (November/December 1986):50–55

Conde, Marie

La parole des femmes: Essais sur des romancières des Antilles de langue française. Book review. John Williams. *Black Scholar* 17, No. 4 (July-August 1986):57

Conde, Maryse (about)

Return of a Native Daughter: An Interview with Paule Marshall and Maryse Conde. John Williams (translator). *SAGE* 3, No. 2 (Fall 1986):52–53

Conference on Empirical Research in Black Psychology

Proceedings of the Seventh Conference on Empirical Research in Black Psychology, November 12–15, 1982. Howard P. Ramseur. *SAGE* 3, No. 2 (Fall 1986):71

Conference Reports

Avery Research Center Sponsors First Major Conference. Myrtle G. Glascoe. *SAGE* 3, No. 1 (Spring 1986):67

The Black Woman Writer and the Diaspora, October 27–30, 1985. Linda Susan Beard. *SAGE* 3, No. 2 (Fall 1986):70–71

The Black Woman Writer and the Diaspora. Gloria T. Hull. *Black Scholar* 17, No. 2 (March-April 1986):2–4

The Commonwealth in Canada: Proceedings of the Second Triennial Conference of the Canadian Association for Commonwealth Literature and Language Studies. Ama Pararneswaran, editor. Reviewed by Alastair Niven. *Research in African Literatures* 17, No. 3 (Fall 1986): 435–439

Conference Keynote Address: Sisterhood and Survival. Audre Lorde. *Black Scholar* 17, No. 2 (March-April 1986):5–7

Conference on the Acquisition and Bibliography of Commonwealth and Third World Literatures in English. Commonwealth Institute. Reviewed by Nancy J. Schmidt. *Research in African Literatures* 17, No. 3 (Fall 1986): 439–440

Contemporary African Literature. Hal Wylie, Eileen Julien, and Russell J. Linnemann, editors. Reviewed by J. I. Okonkwo. *Research in African Literatures* 17, No. 3 (Fall 1986): 445–448

Interdisciplinary Dimensions of African Literature. Kofi Anyidoho, Abioseh M. Porter, Daniel Racine, and Janice Spleth, editors. Reviewed by C. L. Innes. *Research in African Literatures* 17, No. 3 (Fall 1986): 449–451

Mississippi's Native Son: An International Symposium on Richard Wright (1908–1960). Maryemma Graham. *SAGE* 3, No. 1 (Spring 1986):66

Proceedings of the Seventh Conference on Empirical Research in Black Psychology, November 12–15, 1982. Howard P. Ramseur. *SAGE* 3, No. 2 (Fall 1986):71

Tuskegee Airmen: A Continuing Legacy. Marsha Jones. *About Time* 14, No. 10 (October 1986):22

Conflict of Generations

Home Again. Renita Weems. *Essence* 17, No. 8 (December 1986):63

Where I'm Coming from. Jennifer Jordan and Lisa Cleveland. *Essence* 17, No. 1 (May 1986):86

Conford, Ellen

Why Me? Book review. Patricia B. Campbell. *Interracial Books for Children Bulletin* 17, No. 2 (1986):15

Congo—Poetry

La nouvelle génération de poètes congolais. By Leopold-Pindy Mamonsono. Reviewed by Daniel Whitman. *Research in African Literatures* 17, No. 4 (Winter 1986): 570–572

Congregationalist Church

Horace Bushnell: Sermons. Edited by Conrad Cherry. Reviewed by Kortright Davis. *Journal of Religious Thought* 43, No. 2 (Fall-Winter 1986–87):91–92

Congressional Black Caucus

Parren Mitchell: Interview. David Hatchett. *Crisis* 93, No. 2 (February 1986):34–40

Seeking Power beyond Their Numbers. David Hatchett. *Crisis* 93, No. 7 (August/September 1986):16

Conley, Larry

Facing the Challenge of Raising My Black Manchild. *Essence* 17, No. 7 (November 1986):116

Conrad, Joseph (about)

Conrad and Imperialism: Ideological Boundaries and Visionary Frontiers. By Benita Parry. Reviewed by Robert D. Hamner. *Research in African Literatures* 17, No. 1 (Spring 1986): 158–162

Joseph Conrad and Africa. By Henryk Zins. Reviewed by Martin Tucker. *Research in African Literatures* 17, No. 3 (Fall 1986): 440–442

Consent Decree

The Consent Degree as an Instrument for Desegregation in Higher Education. James J. Prestage and Jewel L. Prestage. *Urban League Review* 10, No. 2 (Winter 1986–87):113–130

Conservatism

The Ideology of the New Right. Edited Ruth Levitas. Reviewed by Paul Gordon. *Race and Class* 28, No. 1 (Summer 1986):95–97

Neo-Conservatives as Social Darwinists: Implications for Higher Education. Peter Sola, Joseph DeVitis, and John R. Danley. *Journal of Negro Education* 55, No. 1 (Winter 1986):3–20

Social Ethics and the Black Family. Maulana Karenga. *Black Scholar* 17, No. 5 (September-October 1986):41–54

Voting Rights, Government Responsibility, and Conservative Ideology. Alex Willingham. *Urban League Review* 10, No. 2 (Winter 1986–87):12–23

Voting Rights, Government Responsibility and Conservative Ideology. Alex Willingham. *Urban League Review* 10, No. 2 (Winter 1986–87):12–23

Consolidated Tenants League

The Consolidated Tenants League of Harlem: Black Self-Help vs. White, Liberal Intervention in Ghetto Housing, 1934–1944. Joel Schwartz. *Afro-Americans in New York Life and History* 10, No.1 (January 1986):31–51

Consortium for the Advancement of Private Higher Education

Marketing Colleges. Ken Smikle. *Black Enterprise* 17, No. 4 (November 1986):24

Construction Equipment

Moving Up with Heavy Equipment. Solomon Herbert. *Black Enterprise* 16, No. 10 (May 1986):29

Construction Workers

Black Hardhats and the Elite Craft Trade Unions. Michael Emerson Howard III. *Crisis* 93, No. 8 (October 1986):26–29

Convention Planning

Meeting Planners. Solomon J. Herbert. *Black Enterprise* 17, No. 1 (August 1986):14

Conwill, William L.

Training Parents in Child Behavior-Management Skills: A Group Approach. *Journal of Negro Education* 55, No. 1 (Winter 1986):67–77

Conyers, James E.

Black American Doctorates in Sociology: A Follow-up Study of their Social and Educational Origins. *Phylon* 47, No. 4 (December 1986):303–317

Cooke, Bobbette and George (about)

A Tale of Two Franchises. Joyce Davis Adams and Janet Clayton. *Black Enterprise* 16, No. 12 (July 1986):42–46

Cookery

The Traditional Family Dinner. Charlotte Lyons. *Ebony* 41, No. 10 (August 1986):108

Cookery, African

African Delights. Charlotte Lyons. *Ebony* 41, No. 3 (January 1986):110

Food: An African-Style Thanksgiving. *Essence* 17, No. 7 (November 1986):92

Cookery, Bahian

Salvador's Sumptuous Cuisine and Spirits. Connie Cherry. *Essence* 16, No. 11 (March 1986):88

Cookery, Cajun

Cajun Cuisine at Home. Charlotte Lyons. *Ebony* 41, No. 5 (March 1986):116

Cookery, East Indian

Food: Exotic East Indian and Thai Cookery. *Essence* 17, No. 2 (July 1986):85

Coolidge, David A. (Jr.)

Prophet Without Honor? The Reverend Jesse Jackson and the Palestinian Question. Notes. *Journal of Religious Thought* 43, No. 2 (Fall-Winter 1986–87):51–62

Cooper, Constance Carter

Strategies to Assure Certification and Retention of Black Teachers. *Journal of Negro Education* 55, No. 1 (Winter 1986):46–55

Cooper, James Fenimore—Criticism and Interpretation

Cooper's Leatherstocking: Romance and the Limits of Character. Notes. Bryant N. Wyatt. *CLA Journal* 29, No. 3 (March 1986):295–308

Ethnocentric Manifestations in Cooper's *Pioneers*, and *The Last of the Mohicans*. Chester H. Mills. *Journal of Black Studies* 16, No. 4 (June 1986):435–449

Copage, Eric

The Fat Boys Enjoy a Banquet of Rap and Roles. *Essence* 17, No. 2 (July 1986):34

Copyright

Protecting Your Ideas—and Your Money. Ernest E. Helms. *Black Enterprise* 17, No. 2 (September 1986):65

Cornwell, JoAnne

The United States and South Africa: History, Civil Rights and the Legal and Cultural Vulnerability of Blacks. *Phylon* 47, No. 4 (December 1986):285–293

Corporate Divestiture

Investing with a Conscience. Frank Dexter Brown. *Black Enterprise* 17, No. 3 (October 1986):91

Corporations

In Good Company: The 25 Best Places for Black to Work. *Black Enterprise* 16, No. 7 (February 1986):88–100

Corporations—Meetings

We've Got to Stop Meeting Like This. *Black Enterprise* 16, No. 9 (April 1986):63–66

Corporations—Profits

Employee Health Can Spell Profits for U.S. Corporations. Donna Horton. *About Time* 14, No. 8 (August 1986):14

Cortez, Jayne

Coagulations: New and Selected Poems. Book review. Barbara T. Christian. *Callaloo* 9, No. 1 (Winter 1986):235–239

When I Look at Wifredo Lam's Paintings. Poem. *Callaloo* 9, No. 1 (Winter 1986):26–27

Cosby, Bill (about)

TV's Top Mom and Dad: Bill Cosby, Phylicia Ayers-Allen Are Role Model Parents on Award-Winning Television Show. Robert E. Johnson. *Ebony* 41, No. 4 (February 1986):29

Cosmetics Industry

Millions in Makeup. Lloyd Gite. *Black Enterprise* 17, No. 5 (December 1986):28

M & M's New Markets. *Black Enterprise* 16, No. 6 (January 1986):26

Costa Rica—Economic History

What Price Equity? A Macroeconomic Evaluation of Government Policies in Costa Rica. By Fuat M. Andic. Reviewed by Irma T. De Alonso. *Caribbean Review* 15, No. 1 (Winter 1986):44

Costa Rica—Politics and Government

Estado empresario y lucha politica en Costa Rica. By Ana Sojo. Reviewed by Francisco A. Leguizamon. *Caribbean Review* 15, No. 2 (Spring 1986):45–46

Council for the Economic Development of Black Americans

The Price of Freedom. Kenneth Maurice Jones. *Black Enterprise* 16, No. 7 (February 1986):28

Council on Career Development for Minorities

Your Career Planning and Self-Development. *Black Collegian* 17, No. 1 (September/October 1986):102–107

Counseling

Enhancing One's Quality of Life. Marsha Jones. *About Time* 14, No. 4 (April 1986):16–18

Role Model Advice to Students. Kuumba Kazi-Ferrouillet and Portia Ballard. *Black Collegian* 17, No. 1 (September/October 1986):115–120

Counterclaims

See Set-Off and Counterclaim

Coupons (Retail Trade)

Cashing In on a Windfall of Coupons. *Ebony* 41, No. 11 (September 1986):72

Courlander, Harold

Kunta Kinte's Struggle to be African. *Phylon* 47, No. 4 (December 1986):294–302

Covey, Joan

African Sea Kings in America? Evidence from Early Maps. Bibliography. *Journal of African Civilizations* 8, No. 2 (December 1986):152–168

Cowhig, Ruth

Shakespeare in Sable: A History of Black Shakespearean Actors. Book review. *Research in African Literatures* 17, No. 2 (Summer 1986): 284–287

Cox, Edward L.

Free Coloreds in the Slave Societies of St. Kitts and Grenada, 1763–1833. Reviewed by Keith C. Simmonds. *Phylon* 47, No. 4 (December 1986):327–328

Cox, Ida (about)

Ida Cox. Wild Women Don't Have the Blues. Record review. Lewis Porter. *Black Perspective in Music* 14, No. 3 (Fall 1986):318–319

Crane, Hart—Criticism and Interpretation

Apo Koinou in Audre Lorde and the Moderns. Amitai F. Avi-ram. *Callaloo* 9, No. 1 (Winter 1986):192–208

Crapanzano, Vincent

Waiting: The Whites of South Africa. Reviewed by A. B. Assensoh. *Phylon* 47, No. 3 (September 1986):248

Credit

Financial Lessons for After School. Karen Brailsford. *Black Enterprise* 17, No. 3 (October 1986):57

Creoles

Bilingual Education and Creole Languages. Carole Berotte Joseph. *Interracial Books for Children Bulletin* 17, Nos. 3-4 (1986):13-14

Creque-Harris, Leah

Literature of the Diaspora by Women of Color. *SAGE* 3, No. 2 (Fall 1986):61-64

Crime and Criminals

Black Unemployment and Its Link to Crime. Samuel L. Myers, Jr. *Urban League Review* 10, No. 1 (Summer 1986):98-105

See also Murder

See also Rape

Criminal Behavior

Empirical Models of Criminal Behavior: How Significant a Factor Is Race? Kasabena Gyimah-Brempong. *Review of Black Political Economy* 15, No. 1 (Summer 1986):27-43

Criminology—Dissertations and Theses

Master's Theses in Progress in Selected Colleges and Universities. Mac A. Stewart. *Negro Educational Review* 37, Nos. 3-4 (July-October 1986):102, 113-114

Crisis Management

Managing through Tough Times. Sharon Y. Lopez. *Black Enterprise* 16, No. 6 (January 1986):57-58

Crockett-Smith, D. L.

Cowboy Diplomacy. Poem. *Black Scholar* 17, No. 1 (January-February 1986):12

Cowboy Eating His Children. Poem. *Black Scholar* 17, No. 1 (January-February 1986):13

Prometheus on de Range. Poem. *Black Scholar* 17, No. 1 (January-February 1986):12

Cross-Cultural Studies

The Dual Vision: Insights and Applications of Cross-Cultural Research. Bennetta Jules-Rosette. *Journal of Negro Education* 55, No. 2 (Spring 1986):125-141

Crosta, Suzanne

An Introduction to the French Caribbean Novel. Book review. *CLA Journal* 29, No. 4 (June 1986):497-500

Crowley, Daniel J.

Malagasy Tale Index. Book review. *Research in African Literatures* 17, No. 2 (Summer 1986): 308-309

Cuba—Art

The Mythical Landscapes of a Cuban Painter: Wilfredo Lam's *La Jungla*. Juan A. Martinez. *Caribbean Review* 15, No. 2 (Spring 1986):32-36

Cuba—Economic Development

Cuba as an Oil Trader: Petroleum Deals in a Falling Market. Jorge F. Perez-Lopez. *Caribbean Review* 15, No. 2 (Spring 1986):26-29+

Is the Cuban Economy Knowable? A National Accounting Parable. Jorge Salazar-Carrillo. *Caribbean Review* 15, No. 2 (Spring 1986):24-25

No Free Lunch: Food and Revolution in Cuba Today. By Medea Benjamin, Joseph Collins, and Michael Scott. Reviewed by James E. Austin. *Caribbean Review* 15, No. 2 (Spring 1986):45

Cuba—History

Slave Emancipation in Cuba. The Transition to Free Labor, 1866-1899. By Rebecca J. Scott. Reviewed by David Kyle. *Caribbean Review* 15, No. 2 (Spring 1986):47

Cuba—International Relations—Grenada

Grenadian Party Papers: Revealing an Imaginary Document. Short Story. Jorge I. Dominguez. *Caribbean Review* 15, No. 2 (Spring 1986):16-20

Report Redux: Thoughts on the Imaginary Document. Short Story. Nelson P. Valdes. *Caribbean Review* 15, No. 2 (Spring 1986):21-23

Cuba—Politics and Government

Crossing Swords: Rethinking Cuba. Barry B. Levine. *Caribbean Review* 15, No. 2 (Spring 1986):3

Did Fidel Fudge the Figures? Literacy and Health: The Cuban Model. Nicholas Eberstadt. *Caribbean Review* 15, No. 2 (Spring 1986):5-7+

Fidel y la Religion: Conversaciones con Frei Betto. Interview. Reviewed by Paul E. Sigmund. *Caribbean Review* 15, No. 2 (Spring 1986):30-31

Heroes are Grazing in My Garden. By Herbert Padilla. Reviewed by Roland E. Bush. *Caribbean Review* 15, No. 1 (Winter 1986):41

How to Figure Out Cuba: Development, Ideology and Mortality. Sergio Diaz-Briquets. *Caribbean Review* 15, No. 2 (Spring 1986):8-11+

Cuba—Race Relations

The Black Man in Cuban Society: From Colonial Times to the Revolution. Roberto Nodal. *Journal of Black Studies* 16, No. 3 (March 1986):251-267

Congo or Carabali? Race Relations in Socialist Cuba. Carlos Moore. *Caribbean Review* 15, No. 2 (Spring 1986):12-15+

Cullen, Countee (about)

Countee Cullen. By Alan R. Shucard. Reviewed by Jay R. Berry. *CLA Journal* 29, No. 3 (March 1986):372-377

Cults

A Sympathetic History of Jonestown: The Moore Family Involvement in Peoples Temple. By Rebecca Moore. Reviewed by Kortright Davis. *Journal of Religious Thought* 43, No. 2 (Fall-Winter 1986-87):92-93

Culture, Afro-American

Street Life: Afro-American Culture in Urban Trinidad. By Michael Lieber. Reviewed by Keith Q. Warner. *CLA Journal* 29, No. 4 (June 1986):493–496

Culture, Afro-Hispanic

The Human Legacy of Black Latin American Literature. Notes. Richard L. Jackson. *CLA Journal* 30, No. 2 (December 1986):154–170

Culture—Africa

The African Origin of Civilization: Myth or Reality. Notes. By Cheikh Anta Diop. Reviewed by A. J. Williams-Myers. *Journal of African Civilizations* 8, No. 1 (June 1986):118–126

Africa's Contribution to World Civilization: The Exact Sciences. Notes. Bibliography. Cheikh Anta Diop. *Journal of African Civilizations* 8, No. 1 (June 1986):74–88

Black-American Heritage? By David Tuesday Adamo. Reviewed by Emma S. Etuk. *Journal of Religious Thought* 43, No. 1 (Spring-Summer 1986):128

The Changing Perception of C. A. Diop and His Work: The Preeminence of a Scientific Spirit. Notes. James G. Spady. *Journal of African Civilizations* 8, No. 1 (June 1986):89–101

Civilization or Barbarism: An Authentic Anthropology. Excerpt. Notes. Cheikh Anta Diop. *Journal of African Civilizations* 8, No. 1 (June 1986):161–225

Civilization or Barbarism: The Legacy of Cheikh Anta Diop. By Cheikh Anta Diop. Reviewed by Leonard Jeffries, Jr. *Journal of African Civilizations* 8, No. 1 (June 1986):146–160

The Cultural Unity of Black Africa: The Domains of Patriarchy and of Matriarchy in Classical Antiquity. Bibliography. By Cheikh Anta Diop. Reviewed by Asa G. Hilliard III. *Journal of African Civilizations* 8, No. 1 (June 1986):102–109

Death Shall Not Find Us Thinking That We Die. Notes. Ivan Van Sertima. *Journal of African Civilizations* 8, No. 1 (June 1986):7–16

Further Conversations with the Pharaoh. Interview. Charles S. Finch. *Journal of African Civilizations* 8, No. 1 (June 1986):227–237

Interview with Cheikh Anta Diop. Interview. Notes. Bibliography. Shawna Moore. *Journal of African Civilizations* 8, No. 1 (June 1986):238–248

Interviews with Cheikh Anta Diop. Interview. Carlos Moore. *Journal of African Civilizations* 8, No. 1 (June 1986):249–283

Ten Years After: An Introduction and Overview. Ivan Van Sertima. *Journal of African Civilizations* 8, No. 2 (December 1986):5–27

Trait-Influences in Meso-America: The African-Asian Connection. Notes. Wayne B. Chandler. *Journal of African Civilizations* 8, No. 2 (December 1986):274–334

Culture—America

Unexpected African Faces in Pre-Columbian America. Alexander Von Wuthenau. *Journal of African Civilizations* 8, No. 2 (December 1986):56–75

Culverson, Donald

Standing Fast: The Autobiography of Roy Wilkins. Book review. *Western Journal of Black Studies* 10, No. 3 (Fall 1986):159–160

Cummings, Pat

Jimmy Lee Did It. Book review. Emily Leinster. *Interracial Books for Children Bulletin* 17, No. 1 (1986):8

Cummins, Jim

Bilingual Education and Anti-Racist Education. *Interracial Books for Children Bulletin* 17, Nos. 3–4 (1986):9–12

Cunningham, Calvin M.

A Career for the Future: Podiatric Medicine. *Black Collegian* 16, No. 4 (March/April 1986):102–107

Cybernetics—Social Aspects

The Impact of Cybernation Technology on Black Automotive Workers in the United States. By Samuel D. K. James. Reviewed by Julianne Malveaux. *Review of Black Political Economy* 15, No. 1 (Summer 1986):103–105

Dabydeen, David

Hogarth's Blacks: Images of Blacks in Eighteenth Century English Art. Book review. Roslyn Zalin. *Race and Class* 27, No. 4 (Spring 1986):99–100

Dadie, Bernard (about)

Images et mythes d'Haiti. By Daniel-Henry Pageaux. Reviewed by Clarisse Zimra. *Research in African Literatures* 17, No. 4 (Winter 1986): 591–593

Dailly, Christophe, and Kotchy, Barthelemy

Propos sur la littérature negro-africaine. Reviewed by Jonathan Ngate. *Research in African Literatures* 17, No. 4 (Winter 1986): 565–566

Dalton, Tracy

Heart Politics. Book review. *Interracial Books for Children Bulletin* 17, Nos. 3–4 (1986):38

Damali, Nia

Birth of a Poet. Poem. *Black American Literature Forum* 20, No. 3 (Fall 1986):303–305

Real Lovin. Poem. *Black American Literature Forum* 20, No. 3 (Fall 1986):305

Sassafras U.S.A. Poem. *Black American Literature Forum* 20, No. 3 (Fall 1986):305

Dance

African-American Soul Force: Dance, Music and Vera Mae Green. A. Lynn Bolles. *SAGE* 3, No. 2 (Fall 1986):32-34

Alvin Ailey American Dance Theatre. Kris DiLorenzo. *Crisis* 93, No. 2 (February 1986):16

The Calabash Dance Theatre. Illustrated. Abiodun McCray and Ayanna Fredricks. *Western Journal of Black Studies* 10, No. 1 (Spring 1986):17-18

Chuck Davis Dance Company. Kris DiLorenzo. *Crisis* 93, No. 5 (May 1986):14-38

A *Crisis* Report on Dance. Kris DiLorenzo. *Crisis* 93, No. 1 (January 1986):29

Joe Johnson and the Repertory Dance Theater of Los Angeles. L. Martina Young. *Crisis* 93, No. 6 (June/July 1986):2

Dance—Africa

An Example of Syncretic Drama from Malawi: Malipenga. Notes. Christopher F. Kamlongera. *Research in African Literatures* 17, No. 2 (Summer 1986): 197-210

Dance Reviews

Crossing the Lines. Choreographed by Lula Washington. Reviewed by Martha Young. *Crisis* 93, No. 7 (August/September 1986):14

Dancers

Gregory Hines: Dancer Wins Stardom as Chicago Vice Cop. *Ebony* 41, No. 12 (October 1986):100

Showstopper: Virginia Johnson, Long on Grace. Ruth Dolores Manuel. *Essence* 17, No. 2 (June 1986):31

Dandridge, Dorothy (about)

The Real-Life Tragedy of Dorothy Dandridge. Walter Leavy. *Ebony* 41, No. 11 (September 1986):136

Daniel, Joyce (about)

Interviews with Five Bajan Artists. Illustrated. *International Review of African American Art* 7, No. 1 (1986):45-55

Daniel, Walter C.

Black Journals of the United States. Book review. Karen Nadeski. *Western Journal of Black Studies* 10, No. 2 (Summer 1986):102

Danley, John R. (joint author)

See Sola, Peter Andre

Darby, Henry E., and Rowley, Margaret N.

King on Vietnam and Beyond. *Phylon* 47, No. 1 (March 1986):43-50

Darity, William (Jr.), and Myers, Samuel L. (Jr.)

Distress vs. Dependency: Changing Income Support Programs. *Urban League Review* 10, No. 2 (Winter 1986-87):24-33

Dating (Social Customs)

Games Lovers Play. Bebe Moore Campbell. *Essence* 17, No. 2 (July 1986):60

How Black Women Can Deal with the Black Male Shortage. *Ebony* 41, No. 7 (May 1986):29

Dauer, Alfons Michael

Tradition afrikanischer Blasorchester und Entstehung des Jazz (African Traditions of Wind Orchestras and the Origination of Jazz). Book review. Lewis Porter. *Black Perspective in Music* 14, No. 3 (Fall 1986):314-316

Daughters

See also Revolutionaries' Daughters

Davenport, Chester (about)

Savings and Loan of the Year: The Rebirth of Berkley Savings. Gordon Borell. *Black Enterprise* 16, No. 11 (June 1986):166

Davenport, Doris

Dessa Rose. Book review. *Black American Literature Forum* 20, No. 3 (Fall 1986):335-340

David, C. R.

Memory. Poem. *About Time* 14, No. 2 (February 1986):24

Talkin Bout Crossin Over. Poem. *About Time* 14, No. 2 (February 1986):24

Third World Plenty. Poem. *About Time* 14, No. 2 (February 1986):24

David, Mary T.

Drama of the Gods: A Study of Seven African Plays. Book review. *Research in African Literatures* 17, No. 2 (Summer 1986): 276-278

Davidson, Basil

On Revolutionary Nationalism: The Legacy of Cabral. *Race and Class* 27, No. 3 (Winter 1986):21-45

Davie, Frank (about)

Beauty Secret for Success. Solomon J. Herbert. *Black Enterprise* 16, No. 12 (July 1986):21

Davies, Carole Boyce, and Graves, Anne Adams (editors)

Ngambika: Studies of Women in African Literature. Book review. Iely Burkhead Mohamed. *SAGE* 3, No. 2 (Fall 1986):59-60

Davis, Angela (about)

Angela Davis: Talking Tough. Interview. Cheryll Y. Greene. *Essence* 17, No. 4 (August 1986):62

Davis, Angela and Davis, Fania

The Black Family and the Crisis of Capitalism. *Black Scholar* 17, No. 5 (September-October 1986):33-40

Davis, Carlton G., and others

Effects of Food Stamp Program Participation and Other Sociodemographic Characteristics on Food Expenditure Patterns of Elderly Minority Households. *Review of Black Political Economy* 15, No. 1 (Summer 1986):3–25

Davis, Charles T., and Gates, Henry Louis (Jr.) (editors)

The Slave's Narrative. Book review. William L. Andrews. *Black American Literature Forum* 20, Nos. 1–2 (Spring/Summer 1986):203–207

Davis, Fania (joint author)

See Davis, Angela

Davis, George (joint author)

See Nelson, Jill

Davis, Joyce M.

Dealing with Car Mechanics. *Essence* 17, No. 7 (November 1986):103

Davis, Kortright

The Devil and Dr. Church: A Guide to Hell for Atheists and True Believers. Book review. *Journal of Religious Thought* 43, No. 2 (Fall-Winter 1986–87):91

Horace Bushnell: Sermons. Book review. *Journal of Religious Thought* 43, No. 2 (Fall-Winter 1986–87):91–92

Religion: An Introduction. Book review. *Journal of Religious Thought* 43, No. 2 (Fall-Winter 1986–87):92

A Sympathetic History of Jonestown: The Moore Family Involvement in Peoples Temple. Book review. *Journal of Religious Thought* 43, No. 2 (Fall-Winter 1986–87):92–93

Davis, Thadious

For Alice Faye Jackson, from *The Vanishing Black Family in Memoriam* (January 1986). Poem. *Black American Literature Forum* 20, No. 3 (Fall 1986):301

For Flo Hyman, Captain of the Olympic Volleyball Team (1984). Poem. *Black American Literature Forum* 20, No. 3 (Fall 1986):299–300

Nomzamo. Poem. *Black American Literature Forum* 20, No. 3 (Fall 1986):302

Ramona Johnson Africa, MOVE Survivor. Poem. *Black American Literature Forum* 20, No. 3 (Fall 1986):300–301

Wright, Faulkner and the South: Reconstitution and Transfiguration. *Callaloo* 9, No. 3 (Summer 1986):469–478

Davis, Tonya Bolden

Black Books by Mail. *Black Enterprise* 17, No. 3 (October 1986):26

Collecting Black Art. *Black Enterprise* 17, No. 5 (December 1986):85

The Evidence of Things Not Seen. Book review. *Black Enterprise* 16, No. 11 (June 1986):38

Family and Nation. Book review. *Black Enterprise* 17, No. 3 (October 1986):17

The Hornes. Book review. *Black Enterprise* 17, No. 3 (October 1986):18

Kaffir Boy: The True Story of a Black Youth's Coming of Age in Apartheid South Africa. Book review. *Black Enterprise* 17, No. 5 (December 1986):20

Room and Board Meetings. *Black Enterprise* 16, No. 8 (March 1986):58

Where Did Our Love Go? The Rise and Fall of the Motown Sound. Book review. *Black Enterprise* 16, No. 11 (June 1986):35–37

Davis, Trudier

Black Women in the Fiction of James Baldwin. Book review. Ketu H. Katrak. *Black American Literature Forum* 20, No. 4 (Winter 1986):449–458

Davis, Winifred R.

The Civilian Navy: A Diversified Employer. *Black Collegian* 16, No. 3 (January/February 1986):144–150

Dawkins, Marvin P.

A Longitudinal Analysis of Variations in Mobility Goals across Race-Sex Groups. *Western Journal of Black Studies* 10, No. 1 (Spring 1986):34–43

Dawkins, Wayne

Suburban Housing. *Black Enterprise* 16, No. 8 (March 1986):14

Daynes, Byron W.

The Politics of Public Holidays: King's Day of Celebration. *Western Journal of Black Studies* 10, No. 2 (Summer 1986):90–101

De Alonso, Irma T.

What Price Equity? A Macroeconomic Evaluation of Government Policies in Costa Rica. Book review. *Caribbean Review* 15, No. 1 (Winter 1986):44

Dean, Jacquelyn M.

The Mythology of North America. Book review. *Interracial Books for Children Bulletin* 17, No. 1 (1986):9

Dearborn, MI—Race Relations

Dearborn Boycott. Margo Walker. *Black Enterprise* 17, No. 1 (August 1986):12

Debt

How to Get Out of Debt: Experts Offer Tips on Ways of Dealing with Your Financial Crisis. *Ebony* 41, No. 9 (July 1986):56

Debussy, Claude

Debussy and American Minstrelsy. Ann McKinley. *Black Perspective in Music* 14, No. 3 (Fall 1986):249–258

Decision-Making (Ethics)

Ethics, Education and Administrative Decisions: A Book of Readings. Edited by Peter Andre Sola. Reviewed by Joseph L. DeVitis. *Journal of Negro Education* 55, No.4 (Fall 1986):549–550

DeCosta-Willis, Miriam

Avenging Angels and Mute Mothers: Black Southern Women in Wright's Fictonal World. *Callaloo* 9, No. 3 (Summer 1986):540–549

Defense Industry—Employment Opportunities

Employment Opportunities in the Defense Industry: The Big Build-Up at the Cutting Edge. James Borders. *Black Collegian* 16, No. 3 (January/February 1986):140–141

Dejeux, Jean

Assia Djebar: Romancière algérienne, cinéaste arabe. Reviewed by Bernadette Cailler. *Research in African Literatures* 17, No. 4 (Winter 1986): 579–581

Bibliographie méthodique et critique de la littérature algérienne de langue française, 1945–1977. Reviewed by Eric Sellin. *Research in African Literatures* 17, No. 4 (Winter 1986): 581

de Lepervanche, Marie (joint editor)

See Bottomley, Gill

de Lerma, Dominique-René

Bibliography of Black Music. Volume 4: Theory, Education, and Related Studies. Book review. Doris E. McGinty. *Black Perspective in Music* 14, No. 2 (Spring 1986):186–187

The Life and Works of Nunes-Garcia. *Black Perspective in Music* 14, No. 2 (Spring 1986):93–102

Delivery of Goods

When It Has to Be There Now. *Black Enterprise* 16, No. 12 (July 1986):21

Dellums, Ronald V.

Welfare State vs. Warfare State: The Legislative Struggle for a Full-Employment Economy. *Black Scholar* 17, No. 6 (November-December 1986):38–51

Welfare State vs. Warfare State: The Legislative Struggle for Full Employment. *Urban League Review* 10, No. 1 (Summer 1986):49–60

Democracy—Central America

Political Systems as Export Commodities: Democracy and the Role of the US in Central America. Ricardo Arias Calderon. *Caribbean Review* 15, No. 1 (Winter 1986):21–23 +

Democracy—South America

Betancur's Battles: The Man of Peace Takes Up the Sword. Bernard Diederich. *Caribbean Review* 15, No. 1 (Winter 1986):10–11 +

Democratic Party

Blacks and the Democratic Party: The Dissolution of an Irreconcilable Marriage. Mfanya D. Tryman. *Black Scholar* 17, No. 6 (November-December 1986):28–32

Mayor Washington's Bid for Re-Election. Abdul Alkalimat. *Black Scholar* 17, No. 6 (November-December 1986):14–23

Protest and Politics: The Mississippi Freedom Democratic Party and the 1965 Congressional Challenge. Leslie Burl McLemore. *Negro Educational Review* 37, Nos. 3–4 (July-October 1986):130–143

Dennis, John (about)

John Dennis and the Religious Sublime. Notes. David M. Wheeler. *CLA Journal* 30, No. 2 (December 1986):210–218

Dent, David

Network for Newcomers. *Black Enterprise* 16, No. 9 (April 1986):20

New Ballot Battles. *Black Enterprise* 16, No. 7 (February 1986):28

Denyer, Tom

Obreros en la Corazon del Bruto. *Race and Class* 27, No. 4 (Spring 1986):53–68

dePass, Ty (joint author)

See Beal, Frances M.

Depression, Mental

Are You Blue? How to Beat Depression. Stephanie Renfrow Hamilton. *Essence* 17, No. 6 (October 1986):66

Depression—1929—Great Britain

The Worst of Times: An Oral History of the Great Depression in Britain. By Nigel Gray. Reviewed by Graham Murray. *Race and Class* 27, No. 4 (Spring 1986):103–104

D'Eramo, Francis J.

Parratt v. Taylor, and Liberty Interests under the Fourteenth Amendment. *Black Law Journal* 9, No. 3 (Winter 1986):312–322

Derricote, Toi

Fears of the Eighth Grade. Poem. *Callaloo* 9, No. 1 (Winter 1986):29

Hamtramck: The Polish Women. Poem. *Callaloo* 9, No. 1 (Winter 1986):30

Letter to Miss Glasser. Poem. *Callaloo* 9, No. 1 (Winter 1986):28

De Shields, Jimm, and Zaimaran, M.

The Third World Concept: Revisited. *Negro Educational Review* 37, No. 2 (April 1986):71–80

De Veaux, Alexis

DO-BE-DO-WOW! Jazz's Grand Divas. *Essence* 17, No. 6 (October 1986):54

Developers

Miracle on Clifton Street: Robert Vickers, Developer. Adolph Dupree. *About Time* 14, No. 8 (August 1986):8–12

Developing Countries

A Learning Skills and Counseling Model for Developing Countries. Rudolph V. Green. *Journal of Negro Education* 55, No.2 (Spring 1986):214–221

Developing Countries—Economic Conditions

The Third World Concept: Revisited. Jimm De Shields and M. Zaimaran. *Negro Educational Review* 37, No. 2 (April 1986):71–80

Developing Countries—Economic Policy

Grassroots Development in Latin America and the Caribbean: Oral Histories of Social Change. By Robert Wasserstrom. Reviewed by Linda Miller. *Caribbean Review* 15, No. 1 (Winter 1986):41–42

What Price Equity? A Macroeconomic Evaluation of Government Policies in Costa Rica. By Fuat M. Andic. Reviewed by Irma T. De Alonso. *Caribbean Review* 15, No. 1 (Winter 1986):44

Developing Countries—International Economic Relations

Crossing Swords: The Psychological Divide in the Caribbean Basin. Robert A. Pastor. *Caribbean Review* 15, No. 1 (Winter 1986):3

Developing Countries—Religion

Liberation Theology and Islamic Revivalism. Notes. Mohammad Yadegari. *Journal of Religious Thought* 43, No. 2 (Fall-Winter 1986–87):38–50

Devil

The Devil and Dr. Church: A Guide to Hell for Atheists and True Believers. By F. Forrester Church. Reviewed by Kortright Davis. *Journal of Religious Thought* 43, No. 2 (Fall-Winter 1986–87):91

DeVitis, Joseph L.

Ethics, Education and Administrative Decisions: A Book of Readings. Book review. *Journal of Negro Education* 55, No.4 (Fall 1986):549–550

DeVitis, Joseph L. (joint author)

See Sola, Peter Andre

De Young, Curtis Paul

History's Lesson. Poem. *Journal of Religious Thought* 43, No. 2 (Fall-Winter 1986–87):88–89

Diabetes

Diabetes: A Dread Disease You Might Have and Not Know It. Charles L. Sanders. *Ebony* 41, No. 12 (October 1986):53

Diagnostic Imaging

Flying High on Medical Tech. Marvin E. Perry. *Black Enterprise* 17, No. 1 (August 1986):19

Diagnostic Related Groups

Health Policy and the Black Aged. Wilbur H. Watson and others. *Urban League Review* 10, No. 2 (Winter 1986–87):63–71

Diallo, Djibril (about)

A Conversation with Djibril Diallo. Audrey Edwards. *Essence* 16, No. 11 (March 1986):40

Diaz-Briquets, Sergio

How to Figure Out Cuba: Development, Ideology and Mortality. *Caribbean Review* 15, No. 2 (Spring 1986):8–11 +

Dickerson, Earl B. (about)

Earl B. Dickerson: An Appreciation. Walter W. Morrison. *Crisis* 93, No. 8 (October 1986):37

Diederich, Bernard

Betancur's Battles: The Man of Peace Takes Up the Sword. *Caribbean Review* 15, No. 1 (Winter 1986):10–11 +

Nature Strikes at Colombia. *Caribbean Review* 15, No. 1 (Winter 1986):15

Diedrich, Maria

"My Love is Black as Yours is Fair":Premarital Love and Sexuality in the Antebellum Slave Narrative. *Phylon* 47, No. 3 (September 1986):238–247

Diet

Benefits of Water. Curtia James. *Essence* 17, No. 2 (July 1986):108

Diet Right! Bahamian Style. Janine C. McAdams. *Essence* 17, No. 4 (August 1986):124

How to Add Ten Years to Your Life. *Ebony* 41, No. 8 (June 1986):37

DiLorenzo, Kris

Alvin Ailey American Dance Theatre. *Crisis* 93, No. 2 (February 1986):16

The Blacks of Central America. *Crisis* 93, No. 6 (June/July 1986):29

Chuck Davis Dance Company. *Crisis* 93, No. 5 (May 1986):14–38

A *Crisis* Report on Dance. *Crisis* 93, No. 1 (January 1986):29

Rachel Lampert. *Crisis* 93, No. 3 (March 1986):12–48

Discrimination—The Arts

Racism in the Arts in Britain. *Race and Class* 28, No. 1 (Summer 1986):73–76

The Struggle for Black Arts in Britain. A. Sivanandan. *Race and Class* 28, No. 1 (Summer 1986):76–79

Discrimination—Education

Affirmative Action Defended: Exploding the Myths of a Slandered Policy. Carter A. Wilson. *Black Scholar* 17, No. 3 (May-June 1986):19–24

The Asian-American Success Myth. Deborah Wei. *Interracial Books for Children Bulletin* 17, Nos. 3–4 (1986):16–17

Bilingual Education and Anti-Racist Education. Jim Cummins. *Interracial Books for Children Bulletin* 17, Nos. 3–4 (1986):9–12

The Consent Decree as an Instrument for Desegregation in Higher Education. James J. Prestage and Jewel L. Prestage. *Urban League Review* 10, No. 2 (Winter 1986–87):113–130

Desegregation and Bilingual Education: Legal and Pedagogical Imperatives. Tony Baez. *Interracial Books for Children Bulletin* 17, Nos. 3–4 (1986):22–23

Education and the Separate But Equal Doctrine. John P. Muffler. *Black Scholar* 17, No. 3 (May-June 1986):35–41

The Five Most Important Problems Confronting Black Students Today. James H. Smith and others. *Negro Educational Review* 37, No. 2 (April 1986):52–61

Discrimination—Employment

Black Teachers' Salaries and the Federal Courts Before *Brown v. Board of Education*: One Beginning for Equity. Bruce Beezer. *Journal of Negro Education* 55, No.2 (Spring 1986):200–213

The Black Underclass: Theory and Reality. Creigs C. Beverly and Howard J. Stanback. *Black Scholar* 17, No. 5 (September-October 1986):24–32

Changes in Equal Employment Enforcement: What Enforcement Statistics Tell Us. Lynn C. Burbridge. *Review of Black Political Economy* 15, No. 1 (Summer 1986):71–80

Discrimination, Occupations and Income. Michael A. Lawrence and Jerry M. Guess. *Crisis* 93, No. 8 (October 1986):17

The Future of Affirmative Action in Higher Education. Richard P. Thornell. *Howard Law Journal* 29, No. 1 (1986):259–278

Guestworkers of the Sea: Racism in British Shipping. Paul Gordon and Danny Reilly. *Race and Class* 28, No. 2 (August 1986):73–82

Keeping Track: How Schools Structure Inequality. J. Oakes. Reviewed by Nancy L. Arnez. *Journal of Negro Education* 55, No.2 (Spring 1986):244–246

Long-Standing Problem of Poverty Must Be Solved. *Ebony* 41, No. 10 (August 1986):144

Notes on Implicit Contracts and the Racial Unemployment Differential. Vince Eagan. *Review of Black Political Economy* 15, No. 1 (Summer 1986):81–91

The *Pittsburgh Courier*, and Black Workers in 1942. Patrick S. Washburn. *Western Journal of Black Studies* 10, No. 3 (Fall 1986):109–118

Racial Employment and Earnings Differentials: The Impact of the Reagan Administration. Charles A. Register. *Review of Black Political Economy* 15, No. 1 (Summer 1986):59–69

Steel Suits Are Settled. Frederick H. Lowe. *Black Enterprise* 17, No. 4 (November 1986):22

    See also Employment—Reverse Discrimination

Discrimination—Employment—Laws and Legislation

Remedies for Victim Group Isolation in the Work Place: Court Orders, Problem-Solving and Affirmative Action in the Post-*Stotts* Era. Paul J. Spiegelman. *Howard Law Journal* 29, No. 1 (1986):191–258

Discrimination—Housing

Black-White Differences in Housing: An Analysis of Trend and Differentials, United States of America, 1960–1978. Ruhul Amin and A. G. Mariam. *Negro Educational Review* 37, No. 1 (January 1986):27–38

The Influence of Race on Rezoning Decisions: Equality of Treatment in Black and White Census Tracts, 1955–1980. Dudley S. Hinds and Nicholas Ordway. *Review of Black Political Economy* 14, No. 4 (Spring 1986):51–63

Institutional Reform and the Enforcement of the Fair Housing Laws. Ron C. Claiborne. *Black Scholar* 17, No. 3 (May-June 1986):42–48

Legal Comments: Discrimination in Housing. Grover G. Hankins. *Crisis* 93, No. 8 (October 1986):42–43

Discrimination—Laws and Legislation

Black America in the 1980s: Rhetoric vs. Reality. Alphine W. Jefferson. *Black Scholar* 17, No. 3 (May-June 1986):2–9

The Erosion of Civil Rights Enforcement. Phyllis McClure. *Black Scholar* 17, No. 3 (May-June 1986):10–18

Discrimination—Media and Communications

PUSH Eyes CBS Stations. Ken Smikle. *Black Enterprise* 16, No. 11 (June 1986):47

Disraeli, Benjamin—Criticism and Interpretation

Beyond "The Convent and the Cottage": A Reconsideration of Disraeli's *Sybil*. Notes. Michael McCully. *CLA Journal* 29, No. 3 (March 1986):318–335

Dissanayake, Wimal

Richard Wright: A View from the Third World. *Callaloo* 9, No. 3 (Summer 1986):481–489

Dissertations and Theses

Master's Theses in Progress in Selected Colleges and Universities. Mac A. Stewart. *Negro Educational Review* 37, Nos. 3–4 (July-October 1986):92–118

Distribution (Economic Theory)

Scheming for the Poor: The Politics of Redistribution in Latin America. By William Ascher. Reviewed by John Waterbury. *Caribbean Review* 15, No. 1 (Winter 1986):42–43

District of Columbia Court of Appeals—Decisions

Special Project on Landlord-Tenant Law in the District of Columbia Court of Appeals. *Howard Law Journal* 29, No. 1 (1986):1–189

Diversification in Industry

BE 100 Overview: A New Push for Profits. *Black Enterprise* 16, No. 11 (June 1986):91

Industry Overview: Magazine Monarchs. Ken Smikle. *Black Enterprise* 16, No. 11 (June 1986):212

Divi Hotels

The Divi Hotels: Hospitality with That Caribbean Touch. Kuumba Kazi-Ferrouillet. *Black Collegian* 17, No. 1 (September/October 1986):144–146

Divorce

Yours, Mine and Ours. Frances E. Ruffin. *Black Enterprise* 16, No. 8 (March 1986):34–36

Dixon, Harold E.

See Spaights, Ernest

Dixon, Marlene, and Jonas, Susanne (editors)

Nicaragua under Siege. Reviewed by John A. Booth. *Caribbean Review* 15, No. 2 (Spring 1986):47

Dixon, Melvin

The Alchemist's Dilemma. Poem. *Callaloo* 9, No. 1 (Winter 1986):31–33

Place, Places. Poem. *Callaloo* 9, No. 1 (Winter 1986):34

Djebar, Assia (about)

Assia Djebar: Romancière algérienne, cinéaste arabe. By Jean Dejeux. Reviewed by Bernadette Cailler. *Research in African Literatures* 17, No. 4 (Winter 1986): 579–581

DjéDjé, Jacqueline Cogdell

Kaiso! the Trinidad Calypso: A Study of the Calypso as Oral Literature. Book review. *Black Perspective in Music* 14, No. 3 (Fall 1986):309

The Mandinka Balafon: An Introduction with Notation for Teaching. Book review. *Black Perspective in Music* 14, No. 3 (Fall 1986):307–308

Musicmakers of West Africa. Book review. *Black Perspective in Music* 14, No. 3 (Fall 1986):308–309

Performance Practice: Ethnomusicological Perspective. Book review. *Black Perspective in Music* 14, No. 3 (Fall 1986):306–307

Dodson, Owen

Epitaph for a Negro Woman. Poem. *Essence* 17, No. 1 (May 1986):169

Doggett, Enid Ann

The Perils of Obsession. *Essence* 17, No. 2 (June 1986):80

Dole, Robert (about)

Senator Robert Dole: Interview. Paul Lindsey Johnson. *Crisis* 93, No. 7 (August/September 1986):30

Doll-Makers

Dealing in Dolls. Pamela Toussaint. *Essence* 17, No. 1 (May 1986):20

Dominguez, Jorge I.

Grenadian Party Papers: Revealing an Imaginary Document. Short Story. *Caribbean Review* 15, No. 2 (Spring 1986):16–20

Dorsey, David (joint compiler)

See Mayes, Janis A.

Dorsey, David. F. (Jr.)

Newspaper Columns by W. E. B. Du Bois. Book review. *CLA Journal* 30, No. 2 (December 1986):254–258

Douglas, Robert L. (Sr.)

Blacks and White T.V.: Afro-Americans in Television since 1948. Book review. *Western Journal of Black Studies* 10, No. 1 (Spring 1986):44–45

Dove, Rita

Anniversary. Poem. *Callaloo* 9, No. 1 (Winter 1986):46

Company. Poem. *Callaloo* 9, No. 1 (Winter 1986):50

The First Suite. *Black American Literature Forum* 20, No. 3 (Fall 1986):241–250

Headdress. Poem. *Callaloo* 9, No. 1 (Winter 1986):47

The House on Bishop Street. Poem. *Callaloo* 9, No. 1 (Winter 1986):45

Motherhood. Poem. *Callaloo* 9, No. 1 (Winter 1986):44

Nightmare. Poem. *Callaloo* 9, No. 1 (Winter 1986):49

One Volume Missing. Poem. *Callaloo* 9, No. 1 (Winter 1986):39

Promises. Poem. *Callaloo* 9, No. 1 (Winter 1986):43

Recovery. Poem. *Callaloo* 9, No. 1 (Winter 1986):48

Roast Possum. Poem. *Callaloo* 9, No. 1 (Winter 1986):41–42

Straw Hat. Poem. *Callaloo* 9, No. 1 (Winter 1986):37

Under the Viaduct, 1932. Poem. *Callaloo* 9, No. 1 (Winter 1986):38

Variation on Gaining a Son. Poem. *Callaloo* 9, No. 1 (Winter 1986):40

Dove, Rita (about)

A Conversation with Rita Dove. Stan Sanvel Rubin and Earl G. Ingersoll (editors). *Black American Literature Forum* 20, No. 3 (Fall 1986):227–240

Dove, Rita—Criticism and Interpretation

The Assembling Vision of Rita Dove. Robert McDowell. *Callaloo* 9, No. 1 (Winter 1986):61–70

The Poems of Rita Dove. Arnold Rampersad. *Callaloo* 9, No. 1 (Winter 1986):52–60

Dove, Theresa (joint author)

See Serwatka, Thomas

Dowayo—Ethnography

Symbolic Structures: An Exploration of the Culture of the Dowayos. By Nigel Barley. Reviewed by Wyatt MacGaffey. *Research in African Literatures* 17, No. 2 (Summer 1986): 295–296

Drama

Images of Blacks in Plays by Black Women. Elizabeth Brown-Guillory. *Phylon* 47, No. 3 (September 1986):230–237

Drama—Africa

Drama of the Gods: A Study of Seven African Plays. By Martin Owusu. Reviewed by Mary T. David. *Research in African Literatures* 17, No. 2 (Summer 1986): 276–278

Dramatists

Aimé Césaire's Lesson about Decolonization in *La Tragédie de Roi Christophe*. Notes. Hunt Hawkins. *CLA Journal* 30, No. 2 (December 1986):144–153

Athol Fugard. By Dennis Walder. Reviewed by Stephen Gray. *Research in African Literatures* 17, No. 2 (Summer 1986): 281–284

Melvin Van Peebles's Bold New Money Play. Interview. Knolly Moses. *Essence* 17, No. 2 (June 1986):12

Sweet Stock Picker: His Show Biz Success and Unorthodox Style Have Opened Up New Options for Melvin Van Peebles. Edmund Newton. *Black Enterprise* 17, No. 3 (October 1986):84

Drimmer, Frederick

The Elephant Man. Book review. Emily Strauss Watson. *Interracial Books for Children Bulletin* 17, Nos. 3–4 (1986):33

Drug Abuse

See Substance Abuse

Dual, J. Fred (Jr.) (about)

Innovative Dual Consulting. Lloyd Gite. *Black Enterprise* 17, No. 4 (November 1986):31

Dual and Associates

See Dual, J. Fred (Jr.)

Dube, Ernest F.

Student Culture and Activism in Black South African Universities. Book review. *Journal of Negro Education* 55, No.2 (Spring 1986):240–244

Dube, S. W. D. (editor)

Proceedings of the Symposium on Afro-American and African Poetry and the Teaching of Poetry in Schools. Reviewed by Ernest Mathabela. *Research in African Literatures* 17, No. 1 (Spring 1986): 133–137

Du Bois, W. E. B.

Newspaper Columns by W. E. B. Du Bois. Compiled and edited by Herbert Aptheker. Reviewed by David F. Dorsey (Jr.) *CLA Journal* 30, No. 2 (December 1986):254–258

Du Bois, W. E. B. (about)

Black and Red—W. E. B. DuBois and the Afro-American Response to the Cold War—1944–1963. By Gerald Horne. Reviewed by Linda Burnham. *Black Scholar* 17, No. 2 (March-April 1986):52–54

W. E. B. Du Bois: A Final Resting Place for an Afro-American Giant. Charles Whitaker. *Ebony* 42, No. 1 (November 1986):172

Duckett-Cain, Joy

Spotlight: Cool-Hand Mark. *Essence* 17, No. 2 (June 1986):76

Dumas, Léon-Gontran (about)

Léon-Gontran Dumas: L'homme et l'oeuvre. By Daniel Racine. Reviewed by Martin Steins. *Research in African Literatures* 17, No. 4 (Winter 1986): 587–588

Dunayevskaya, Raya

Women's Liberation and the Dialectics of Revolution: Reaching for the Future. Book review. Diane Lee. *SAGE* 3, No. 1 (Spring 1986):62–63

Duncan-Hall, Tricia

Debi Thomas—World Figure Skating Champion. *Black Collegian* 17, No. 1 (September/October 1986):49–52

Dunnaville, Norine (about)

Black Books by Mail. Tonya Bolden Davis. *Black Enterprise* 17, No. 3 (October 1986):26

Dupre, Beverly B.

Problems Regarding the Survival of Future Black Teachers in Education. *Journal of Negro Education* 55, No. 1 (Winter 1986):56-66

Dupree, Adolph

Behold a Leader: Jonathan David Farley. *About Time* 14, No. 12 (December 1986):8-9

Diagnosis of Art...Hidden Heritage: Afro-American Art, 1800–1950. Illustrated. *About Time* 14, No. 4 (April 1986):24-25

Dr. Dorothy Irene Height: Motivating the Strengths of Black Women. *About Time* 14, No. 6 (June 1986):8-23

Dust from the Ashes of Canaan: A Black Agenda Conference. *About Time* 14, No. 9 (September 1986):18-22

Eye of the Beholder: The Africans. *About Time* 14, No. 9 (September 1986):8-10

A Family Affair: Ben Richardson, Candidate for New York State Senate. *About Time* 14, No. 10 (October 1986):14-17

Film Festival: Reservations for 62,332. *About Time* 14, No. 1 (January 1986):16-17

As Gentle As the Wind: The Falcon Trap and Game Club. *About Time* 14, No. 12 (December 1986):20-24

Language of an Evening Star: Charlayne Hunter-Gault. *About Time* 14, No. 7 (July 1986):14-19

Miracle on Clifton Street: Robert Vickers, Developer. *About Time* 14, No. 8 (August 1986):8-12

A Number of Things. *About Time* 14, No. 3 (March 1986):8

Pursuit of Excellence: A Curriculum for Black Students to Select, Prepare for and Practice Careers. *About Time* 14, No. 11 (November 1986):I-XVI

Ronald Ervin McNair: First and One of a Kind. *About Time* 14, No. 6 (June 1986):12-13

Of Scholarship and Ice: Debi Thomas. *About Time* 14, No. 4 (April 1986):14

Some of Our Troops Are Missing: A Photo Essay on a South Africa Teach-In. *About Time* 14, No. 5 (May 1986):18-19

Durant, Thomas J. (Jr.), and Louden, Joyce S.

The Black Middle Class in America. *Phylon* 47, No. 4 (December 1986):253-263

Duvalier, Jean-Claude ("Baby Doc") (about)

No Dock for "Baby Doc." Kenneth Maurice Jones. *Black Enterprise* 16, No. 10 (May 1986):17

Duvall, Henry

AIDS...Fact or Fantasy? Impact on Black Children/Adults. *About Time* 14, No. 4 (April 1986):20-21

Daughter of Tutu Spreads Appeal to Dismantle Apartheid. *About Time* 14, No. 5 (May 1986):18-19

Dr. Mary Frances Berry: Educator-Activist Beats Drum for Civil Rights. *About Time* 14, No. 11 (November 1986):16-17

Howard University Jazz Ensemble. *About Time* 14, No. 12 (December 1986):27-28

Man Sharing: Dilemma or Choice. Book review. *About Time* 14, No. 12 (December 1986):29

Mixing Sports and School: Leo F. Miles. *About Time* 14, No. 5 (May 1986):23-24

Washington's Superstation: Howard University's WHUR-FM (96.3). *About Time* 14, No. 2 (February 1986):22-23

Dykes, J. Roger

Ritchie Herbert: Photography Major/Hockey Player. *About Time* 14, No. 5 (May 1986):24-25

Dyslexia

Dyslexia: Understanding Reading Problems. By John Savage. Reviewed by Emily Strauss Watson. *Interracial Books for Children Bulletin* 17, No. 2 (1986):15-16

Eady, Cornelius

Waffle House Girl. Poem. *Essence* 17, No. 1 (May 1986):93

Eagan, Vince

Notes on Implicit Contracts and the Racial Unemployment Differential. *Review of Black Political Economy* 15, No. 1 (Summer 1986):81-91

Early, Gerald

Working Girl Blues: Mothers, Daughters, and the Image of Billie Holiday in Kristin Hunter's *God Bless the Child. Black American Literature Forum* 20, No. 4 (Winter 1986):423-442

Eastman, Carol M.

Expressing a Swahili Sense of Humor: Siu Jokes. Notes. References. *Research in African Literatures* 17, No. 4 (Winter 1986): 474-495

Introduction: Swahili Verbal Arts. References. *Research in African Literatures* 17, No. 4 (Winter 1986): 459-463

Eaton and Associates

Out-of-Town Campaigns. *Black Enterprise* 16, No. 8 (March 1986):17

Eberstadt, Nicholas

Did Fidel Fudge the Figures? Literacy and Health: The Cuban Model. *Caribbean Review* 15, No. 2 (Spring 1986):5-7 +

Economic Community of West African States

Interviews with Cheikh Anta Diop. Interview. Carlos Moore. *Journal of African Civilizations* 8, No. 1 (June 1986):249–283

Economic Development

Blacks Make Moderate Gains in Employment. Andrew F. Brimmer. *Black Enterprise* 17, No. 4 (November 1986):36

The Economic State of Black America. Sidney M. Willhelm. *Journal of Black Studies* 17, No. 2 (December 1986):139–147

Inequality in Metropolitan Industrial Revenue Bond Programs. Gregory D. Squires. *Review of Black Political Economy* 14, No. 4 (Spring 1986):37–50

Nonprofits Going It Alone. Gwen McKinney. *Black Enterprise* 16, No. 11 (June 1986):272–274

The Push for Economic Development. David Hatchett. *Crisis* 93, No. 5 (May 1986):17–40

Trade and Growth: The First Annual W. Arthur Lewis Lecture. Lance Taylor. *Review of Black Political Economy* 14, No. 4 (Spring 1986):17–36

Washington: District of Commerce. Patricia A. Jones. *Black Enterprise* 16, No. 11 (June 1986):253

Economic Development—Africa

The Dilemma of the Contribution of African Women toward and the Benefits They Derive from Economic Development. Immaculate Mary Amuge. *Western Journal of Black Studies* 10, No. 4 (Winter 1986):205–210

Women and Development in Africa: A Bibliography. Barbara Kinley and Yolanda T. Moses. *SAGE* 3, No. 2 (Fall 1986):65–69

Economic Development—Economic Theory

Economic Structural Change: A Challenge for Full Employment. Bernard E. Anderson. *Urban League Review* 10, No. 1 (Summer 1986):41–48

Economic Forecasting

The *Black Enterprise* Annual Economic Outlook: Walking on an Economic Tightrope. *Black Enterprise* 16, No. 6 (January 1986):50–54

Seeking an Agenda for Economic Growth. Derek T. Dingle. *Black Enterprise* 16, No. 11 (June 1986):201

Trends, Prospects, and Strategies for Black Economic Progress. Andrew F. Brimmer. *Review of Black Political Economy* 14, No. 4 (Spring 1986):91–97

Trends and Prospects for Black Business. Andrew F. Brimmer. *Black Enterprise* 16, No. 12 (July 1986):29

Economic History

Welfare State vs. Warfare State: The Legislative Struggle for Full Employment. Ronald V. Dellums. *Urban League Review* 10, No. 1 (Summer 1986):49–60

Economic History—Central America

The Blacks of Central America. Kris DiLorenzo. *Crisis* 93, No. 6 (June/July 1986):29

Economic History—South America

Brazil and the Blacks of South America. Gloria Calomee. *Crisis* 93, No. 6 (June/July 1986):37

Economic Policy

A Brief Prescription for a Proactive Socioeconomic Agenda. Editorial. Douglas G. Glasgow. *Urban League Review* 10, No. 2 (Winter 1986–87):3–5

The Economic Demise of Blacks in America: A Prelude to Genocide? Sidney M. Willhelm. *Journal of Black Studies* 17, No. 2 (December 1986):201–254

Emerging Two-Tier Wage Systems: Employment Opportunity or Wage Attack? Julianne Malveaux. *Urban League Review* 10, No. 2 (Winter 1986–87):34–44

Falling Behind: A Report on How Blacks Have Fared under Reagan. Center on Budget and Policy Priorities. *Journal of Black Studies* 17, No. 2 (December 1986):148–171

Gramm-Rudman and the Politics of Deficit Reduction. Linda F. Williams. *Urban League Review* 10, No. 2 (Winter 1986–87):62–83

Regulatory Policy and Minority Concerns: The Impact of Changes in Telecommunications Policy. Georgia A. Persons. *Urban League Review* 10, No. 2 (Winter 1986–87):45–63

See also Social Policy

Economic Recovery and Tax Act of 1981

Tax Reform: A Minimalist Approach for Assisting the Low-Income. Lynn Burbridge. *Urban League Review* 10, No. 2 (Winter 1986–87):101–112

Economics—Economic Theory

The African-American Intellectual and the Struggle for Black Empowerment. Charles Green and Basil Wilson. *Western Journal of Black Studies* 10, No. 2 (Summer 1986):59–69

Economics—Study and Teaching

En defensa de Mexico: pensamiento economico politico. By Jesus Silva Herzog. Reviewed by Jorge Salazar-Carrillo. *Caribbean Review* 15, No. 2 (Spring 1986):46

Edelman, Marian Wright

Save the Children. *Ebony* 41. No. 10 (August 1986):53

Edelman, Marian Wright (about)

Civil Rights Lawyers Revisited. *Ebony* 42, No. 2 (December 1986):76

Education

A Black Elite. By Daniel C. Thompson. Reviewed by C. J. Wiltz. *Phylon* 47, No. 4 (December 1986):328–329

A Call to Action: Community Crusade for Learning. Joan Marie Allen. *About Time* 14, No. 11 (November 1986):22–24

Educational Specialists: Addressing a Child's Career Development. Marsha Jones. *About Time* 14, No. 11 (November 1986):18–21

The Education of Black Children and Youths: A Framework for Excellence. By Samuel L. Banks. Reviewed by Sandra Noel Smith. *Journal of Negro Education* 55, No.4 (Fall 1986):551–552

Education Is a Team Effort. James M. Blount. *About Time* 14, No. 11 (November 1986):4

Education on Trial: Strategies for the Future. Edited by William L. Johnston. Reviewed by Laurence R. Marcus. *Journal of Negro Education* 55, No.4 (Fall 1986):548–549

Ethics, Education and Administrative Decisions: A Book of Readings. Edited by Peter Andre Sola. Reviewed by Joseph L. DeVitis. *Journal of Negro Education* 55, No.4 (Fall 1986):549–550

How to Save Our High Schools. *Ebony* 41, No. 6 (April 1986):144

Is Failure Inevitable in Our Schools? Alexander R. Jones. *About Time* 14, No. 3 (March 1986):21

The Move to Educational Excellence Does Not Mean a Move to Educational Equality. John S. Swift, Jr. *Negro Educational Review* 37, Nos. 3–4 (July-October 1986):119–126

Neoliberalism and Black Education. John Martin Rich. *Journal of Negro Education* 55, No. 1 (Winter 1986):21–28

Share the Wealth: Who Will Teach the Black Children? E. Jeannie Barry. *Black Collegian* 16, No. 4 (March/April 1986):122

Sustaining Black Educational Progress: Challenges for the 1990s. Antoine M. Garibaldi. *Journal of Negro Education* 55, No.3 (Summer 1986):386–396

    See also Computer-Assisted Instruction

    See also Gifted Children—Education

    See also Special Education

Education, Bilingual

Bilingual Education and Anti-Racist Education. Jim Cummins. *Interracial Books for Children Bulletin* 17, Nos. 3–4 (1986):9–12

Bilingual Education and Creole Languages. Carole Berotte Joseph. *Interracial Books for Children Bulletin* 17, Nos. 3–4 (1986):13–14

Bilingual Education and the Law. Alan Jay Rom. *Interracial Books for Children Bulletin* 17, Nos. 3–4 (1986):24–25

Desegregation and Bilingual Education: Legal and Pedagogical Imperatives. Tony Baez. *Interracial Books for Children Bulletin* 17, Nos. 3–4 (1986):22–23

Equity in Education: The Case for Bilingual Education. Sonia Nieto. *Interracial Books for Children Bulletin* 17, Nos. 3–4 (1986):4–8

Guidelines for Evaluating Bilingual Classrooms. Sonia Nieto. *Interracial Books for Children Bulletin* 17, Nos. 3–4 (1986):26–28

The Parent-School Partnership and Bilingual Education. Luis Fuentes. *Interracial Books for Children Bulletin* 17, Nos. 3–4 (1986):20–21

Past Accomplishments, Current Needs: La Lucha Continúa. Sonia Nieto. *Interracial Books for Children Bulletin* 17, No. 2 (1986):6–8

Puerto Ricans and Bilingual Education. Diana Caballero. *Interracial Books for Children Bulletin* 17, Nos. 3–4 (1986):15–16

    See also English Language—Study and
    Teaching—Psychological Aspects.

Education, Bilingual—Bibliographies

Annotated Bibliography. Sonia Nieto. *Interracial Books for Children Bulletin* 17, Nos. 3–4 (1986):29–30

Education, Bilingual—Organizations

Organizational Resources. Sonia Nieto. *Interracial Books for Children Bulletin* 17, Nos. 3–4 (1986):31–32

Education, Compensatory

Educational Disadvantagement: Associated Factors, Current Interventions, and Implications. Donna M. Murphy. *Journal of Negro Education* 55, No.4 (Fall 1986):495–507

Education in the Post-Integration Era. Russell William Irvine. *Journal of Negro Education* 55, No.4 (Fall 1986):508–517

Education, Elementary

Sequence Memory and Organization in Recall of Black Third and Fifth Graders. Joan Gildemeister and Phillip Friedman. *Journal of Negro Education* 55, No.2 (Spring 1986):142–154

Education, Elementary—Dissertations and Theses

Master's Theses in Progress in Selected Colleges and Universities. Mac A. Stewart. *Negro Educational Review* 37, Nos. 3–4 (July-October 1986):100

Education, Higher

Autonomy and Theoretical Orientation of Remedial and Non-Remedial College Students. James Koutrelakos. *Journal of Negro Education* 55, No. 1 (Winter 1986):29–37

Black Students in Higher Education. By C. Scully Stikes. Reviewed by Roberta N. Morse. *Journal of Negro Education* 55, No. 1 (Winter 1986):118–120

A Comparison of the Academic Performance of Black and White Freshman Students on an Urban Commuter Campus. Golam Mannan, Lillian Charleston, and Behrooz Saghafi. *Journal of Negro Education* 55, No.2 (Spring 1986):155–161

Neo-Conservatives as Social Darwinists: Implications for Higher Education. Peter Sola, Joseph DeVitis, and John R. Danley. *Journal of Negro Education* 55, No. 1 (Winter 1986):3–20

Education, Preschool

Addressing Preschool Needs of Children. Marsha Jones. *About Time* 14, No. 5 (May 1986):10–13

A Critical Analysis of the Assessment of the Effects of Head Start on Minority Children. O. Jackson Cole. *Journal of Negro Education* 55, No. 1 (Winter 1986): 91–106

Education, Secondary—Dissertations and Theses

Master's Theses in Progress in Selected Colleges and Universities. Mac A. Stewart. *Negro Educational Review* 37, Nos. 3–4 (July-October 1986):108

Education—Africa

A Handbook for Teaching African Literature. By Elizabeth Gunner. Reviewed by Anne Walmsley. *Research in African Literatures* 17, No. 1 (Spring 1986): 149–153

Educational Exchanges

Cultural Awareness through Educational Exchange. Cheryl R. Gooch. *Black Collegian* 16, No. 3 (January/February 1986):104–106

Educational Fund Raising

Do Vouchers Equal Choices for the Poor? David C. Ruffin. *Black Enterprise* 17, No. 2 (September 1986):25

Educational Testing Services

The Black Educator: An Endangered Species. Beverly P. Cole. *Journal of Negro Education* 55, No.3 (Summer 1986):326–334

Educational Tests and Measurements

Assessment Strategies for Minority Groups. Sarla Sharma. *Journal of Black Studies* 17, No. 1 (September 1986):111–124

Enhancing Minority College Students' Performance on Educational Tests. Henry T. Frierson. *Journal of Negro Education* 55, No. 1 (Winter 1986):38–45

The Impact of National Testing on Ethnic Minorities: With Proposed Solutions. Peter A. Garcia. *Journal of Negro Education* 55, No.3 (Summer 1986):347–357

The Memorable Teacher: Implications for Teacher Selection. Sylvia T. Johnson and Sukai Prom-Jackson. *Journal of Negro Education* 55, No.3 (Summer 1986):272–283

Sequence Memory and Organization in Recall of Black Third and Fifth Graders. Joan Gildemeister and Phillip Friedman. *Journal of Negro Education* 55, No.2 (Spring 1986):142–154

Testing, Politics, and the Allocation of Opportunities. Bernard R. Gifford. *Journal of Negro Education* 55, No.3 (Summer 1986):422–432

See also Teacher Competency Testing

Educational Toys

Educational Toys for Kids. Peggy Ann Taylor. *Essence* 17, No. 7 (November 1986):106

What's New in Educational Toys? *Ebony* 42, No. 1 (November 1986):78

Education of Children

The Black Church as an Ally in the Education of Black Children. Notes. James D. Tyms. *Journal of Religious Thought* 43, No. 2 (Fall-Winter 1986–87):73–87

The Five Most Important Problems Confronting Black Students Today. James H. Smith and others. *Negro Educational Review* 37, No. 2 (April 1986):52–61

Education—Desegregation

The Consent Degree as an Instrument for Desegregation in Higher Education. James J. Prestage and Jewel L. Prestage. *Urban League Review* 10, No. 2 (Winter 1986–87):113–130

Education—Economic Aspects

Evaluating Your Course Load. Jessica B. Harris. *Black Enterprise* 16, No. 7 (February 1986):103–104

Education—Employment Opportunities

Educational Reform and Teacher Shortages: New Career Opportunities in Education. Walter M. Perkins. *Black Collegian* 16, No. 4 (March/April 1986):114–120

Education Equality Project

The Move to Educational Excellence Does Not Mean a Move to Educational Equality. John S. Swift, Jr. *Negro Educational Review* 37, Nos. 3–4 (July-October 1986):119–126

Education—Family Influences

The Parent-School Partnership and Bilingual Education. Luis Fuentes. *Interracial Books for Children Bulletin* 17, Nos. 3–4 (1986):20–21

The Relative Contribution of the Extended Family System to Schooling in Nigeria. E. E. Ezewu. *Journal of Negro Education* 55, No.2 (Spring 1986):222–228

Education—Laws and Legislation

The Consent Decree as an Instrument for Desegregation in Higher Education. James J. Prestage and Jewel L. Prestage. *Urban League Review* 10, No. 2 (Winter 1986–87):113–130

Desegregation and Bilingual Education: Legal and Pedagogical Imperatives. Tony Baez. *Interracial Books for Children Bulletin* 17, Nos. 3–4 (1986):22–23

Educational Disadvantagement: Associated Factors, Current Interventions, and Implications. Donna M. Murphy. *Journal of Negro Education* 55, No.4 (Fall 1986):495–507

English-Only Movement Fosters Divisiveness. Arnoldo Torres. *Interracial Books for Children Bulletin* 17, Nos. 3–4 (1986):18–19

Gramm-Rudman and Black Education. Gerald D. Jaynes. *Black Enterprise* 16, No. 10 (May 1986):39

More Busing Battles. Kenneth Maurice Jones. *Black Enterprise* 16, No. 10 (May 1986):18

Education and Politics

Black Public Policy. Nancy L. Arnez. *Journal of Black Studies* 16, No. 4 (June 1986):397–408

Education—Sociocultural Aspects

A Review of Urban Life in Kingston, Jamaica. By Diane J. Austin. Reviewed by Bernard D. Headley. *Caribbean Review* 15, No. 1 (Winter 1986):42

Education of Women

In the Company of Educated Women: A History of Women and Higher Education in America. By Barbara Miller Solomon. Reviewed by Patricia Bell-Scott. *Journal of Negro Education* 55, No. 1 (Winter 1986):116–117

The Professionalism of the Ministry of Women. Notes. Delores Causion Carpenter. *Journal of Religious Thought* 43, No. 1 (Spring-Summer 1986):59–75

Educators

Dr. Mary Frances Berry: Educator-Activist Beats Drum for Civil Rights. Henry Duvall. *About Time* 14, No. 11 (November 1986):16–17

Dr. Nathan Hare. Gregory Pete. *Crisis* 93, No. 3 (March 1986):30–46

J. Saunders Redding: Author, Scholar and Cultural Historian. Martin R. Stiles. *About Time* 14, No. 7 (July 1986):20–21

See also Public Schools—Principals

See also Public Schools—Superintendants

Edwards, Audrey

A Conversation with Djibril Diallo. *Essence* 16, No. 11 (March 1986):40

Oprah Winfrey: Stealing the Show. *Essence* 17, No. 6 (October 1986):50

Edwards, Mel (about)

Mel Edwards. Illustrated. Watson Hines. *International Review of African American Art* 7, No. 2 (1986):34–51

Edwards, Paul

Phillis Wheatley and Her Writings. Book review. *Research in African Literatures* 17, No. 1 (Spring 1986): 130–133

Effective Parenting Information for Children (EPIC)

Making Parenting a Priority. Anita Johnson Sims. *About Time* 14, No. 11 (November 1986):10–13

Egypt—History

Africa and the Discovery of America, Volume I. By Leo Wiener. Reviewed by Phillips Barry. *Journal of African Civilizations* 8, No. 2 (December 1986):197–201

The African Origin of Civilization: Myth or Reality. Notes. By Cheikh Anta Diop. Reviewed by A. J. Williams-Myers. *Journal of African Civilizations* 8, No. 1 (June 1986):118–126

The African Presence in Ancient America: Evidence from Physical Anthropology. Notes. Keith M. Jordon. *Journal of African Civilizations* 8, No. 2 (December 1986):136–151

Africa's Contribution to World Civilization: The Exact Sciences. Notes. Bibliography. Cheikh Anta Diop. *Journal of African Civilizations* 8, No. 1 (June 1986):74–88

The Beginnings of Man and Civilization. Cheikh Anta Diop. *Journal of African Civilizations* 8, No. 1 (June 1986):322–351

The Changing Perception of C. A. Diop and His Work: The Preeminence of a Scientific Spirit. Notes. James G. Spady. *Journal of African Civilizations* 8, No. 1 (June 1986):89–101

Cheikh Anta Diop and the New Concept of African History. Notes. John Henrik Clarke. *Journal of African Civilizations* 8, No. 1 (June 1986):110–117

Civilization or Barbarism: An Authentic Anthropology. Excerpt. Notes. Cheikh Anta Diop. *Journal of African Civilizations* 8, No. 1 (June 1986):161–225

Civilization or Barbarism: The Legacy of Cheikh Anta Diop. By Cheikh Anta Diop. Reviewed by Leonard Jeffries, Jr. *Journal of African Civilizations* 8, No. 1 (June 1986):146–160

The Cultural Unity of Black Africa: The Domains of Patriarchy and of Matriarchy in Classical Antiquity. Bibliography. By Cheikh Anta Diop. Reviewed by Asa G. Hilliard III. *Journal of African Civilizations* 8, No. 1 (June 1986):102–109

Dr. Diop on Asia: Highlights and Insights. Notes. Runoko Rashidi. *Journal of African Civilizations* 8, No. 1 (June 1986):127–145

The Egyptian Presence in South America. Notes. R. A. Jairazbhoy. *Journal of African Civilizations* 8, No. 2 (December 1986):76–135

Egypto-Nubian Presences in Ancient Mexico. Notes. Ivan Van Sertima. *Journal of African Civilizations* 8, No. 2 (December 1986):29–55

Further Conversations with the Pharaoh. Interview. Charles S. Finch. *Journal of African Civilizations* 8, No. 1 (June 1986):227–237

Interview with Cheikh Anta Diop. Interview. Notes. Bibliography. Shawna Moore. *Journal of African Civilizations* 8, No. 1 (June 1986):238–248

Interviews with Cheikh Anta Diop. Interview. Carlos Moore. *Journal of African Civilizations* 8, No. 1 (June 1986):249–283

Iron in the Ancient Egyptian Empire. Notes. Bibliography. Cheikh Anta Diop. *Journal of African Civilizations* 8, No. 1 (June 1986):64–73

Leo Wiener—A Plea for Re-Examination. Notes. David J. M. Muffett. *Journal of African Civilizations* 8, No. 2 (December 1986):188–196

Origin of the Ancient Egyptians. Notes. Cheikh Anta Diop. *Journal of African Civilizations* 8, No. 1 (June 1986):35–63

Pyramid—American and African: A Comparison. Notes. Beatrice Lumpkin. *Journal of African Civilizations* 8, No. 2 (December 1986):169–187

Two Interviews with Cheikh Anta Diop. Interview. Listervelt Middleton and Nile Valley Executive Committee. *Journal of African Civilizations* 8, No. 1 (June 1986):284–302

Egyptologists

The Changing Perception of C. A. Diop and His Work: The Preeminence of a Scientific Spirit. Notes. James G. Spady. *Journal of African Civilizations* 8, No. 1 (June 1986):89–101

Conversations with Diop and Tsegaye: The Nile Valley Revisited. Notes. Jan Carew. *Journal of African Civilizations* 8, No. 1 (June 1986):19–27

Death Shall Not Find Us Thinking That We Die. Notes. Ivan Van Sertima. *Journal of African Civilizations* 8, No. 1 (June 1986):7–16

Meeting the Pharoah: Conversations with Cheikh Anta Diop. Interview. Charles S. Finch. *Journal of African Civilizations* 8, No. 1 (June 1986):28–34

Egyptology

See Egyptologists

See Egypt—History

Ejizu, C.

African Religions in Western Conceptual Schemes: The Problem of Interpretation. Book review. *Journal of Religious Thought* 43, No. 2 (Fall-Winter 1986–87):90

Eko, Ebele

Beyond the Myth of Confrontation: A Comparative Study of African and African-American Female Protagonists. *Phylon* 47, No. 3 (September 1986):219–229

Changes in the Image of the African Woman: A Celebration. *Phylon* 47, No. 3 (September 1986):210–218

Oral Tradition: The Bridge to Africa in Paule Marshall's *Praisesong for the Widow*. *Western Journal of Black Studies* 10, No. 3 (Fall 1986):143–147

Election Districts

Effects of Multimember Districts on Black Representation in State Legislatures. Bernard Grofman and others. *Review of Black Political Economy* 14, No. 4 (Spring 1986):65–78

Election Law

Voting Rights, Government Responsibility and Conservative Ideology. Alex Willingham. *Urban League Review* 10, No. 2 (Winter 1986–87):12–23

Elections

Differences in Campaign Funds: A Racial Explanation. John Theilmann and Al Wilhite. *Review of Black Political Economy* 15, No. 1 (Summer 1986):45–58

A Family Affair: Ben Richardson, Candidate for New York State Senate. Adolph Dupree. *About Time* 14, No. 10 (October 1986):14–17

The Fight for the Fifth. Ann Kimbrough. *Black Enterprise* 17, No. 4 (November 1986):21

How to Get More Blacks into Congress: Enforcement of Voting Rights Act Regarded as the Most Important Step. Alex Poinsett. *Ebony* 41, No. 7 (May 1986):122

Mayor Washington's Bid for Re-Election. Abdul Alkalimat. *Black Scholar* 17, No. 6 (November-December 1986):2–13

The Political Stakes Are High. James M. Blount. *About Time* 14, No. 10 (October 1986):4

Political Update: An Analysis of Election '86. Carolyne S. Blount. *About Time* 14, No. 10 (October 1986):8–11

Protest and Politics: The Mississippi Freedom Democratic Party and the 1965 Congressional Challenge. Leslie Burl McLemore. *Negro Educational Review* 37, Nos. 3–4 (July-October 1986):130–143

Redefining Full Employment. Charles P. Henry and Bertram Gross. *Urban League Review* 10, No. 1 (Summer 1986):13–24

Solving the Unemployment Problem: A Case for Full Employment. Linda F. Williams. *Urban League Review* 10, No. 1 (Summer 1986):25–40

Employment Forecasting

Careers 1990: The Changing Workplace. Kuumba Kazi-Ferrouillet. *Black Collegian* 17, No. 1 (September/October 1986):81–87

Employment—Legislation

The Income and Jobs Action Bill: A Mandate for Full Employment. Charles A. Hayes. *Urban League Review* 10, No. 1 (Summer 1986):61–65

Welfare State vs. Warfare State: The Legislative Struggle for a Full-Employment Economy. Ronald V. Dellums. *Black Scholar* 17, No. 6 (November-December 1986):38–51

Welfare State vs. Warfare State: The Legislative Struggle for Full Employment. Ronald V. Dellums. *Urban League Review* 10, No. 1 (Summer 1986):49–60

Employment—Local Government

Jobs and the Quality of Life in Cities: Local Government's Role in Full Employment. Eugene "Gus" Newport. *Urban League Review* 10, No. 1 (Summer 1986):71–78

Employment Opportunities

The 25 Most Promising Careers for Blacks. Frank White III. *Ebony* 41, No. 12 (October 1986):67

Industry by Industry Assessment of the Job Outlook for the Class of 1986. *Black Collegian* 16, No. 4 (March/April 1986):72–128

The Top 100 Employers and the Majors in Demand, 1986–87. *Black Collegian* 17, No. 2 (November/December 1986):56–58

See also Defense Industry—Employment Opportunities

See also Engineering—Employment Opportunities

See also Space—Employment Opportunities

See also United States Air Force, Army, Coast Guard, Marines, Navy—Employment Opportunities

Employment—Reverse Discrimination

Reversing Affirmative Action: A Theoretical Construct. Mfanya Donald Tryman. *Journal of Negro Education* 55, No.2 (Spring 1986):185–199

Employment—State Government

Vision and Responsibility: The Role of States in Planning for Full Employment. Tom Bradley. *Urban League Review* 10, No. 1 (Summer 1986):66–70

Engineering Administration—Dissertations and Theses

Master's Theses in Progress in Selected Colleges and Universities. Mac A. Stewart. *Negro Educational Review* 37, Nos. 3–4 (July-October 1986):97–101, 108

Engineering—Employment Opportunities

1986 Comprehensive Employment Outlook for Engineering Students. Kuumba Kazi-Ferrouillet. *Black Collegian* 16, No. 3 (January/February 1986):162–163

The Black Collegian's Guide to Employers of Engineering and Technical Majors for 1986. *Black Collegian* 16, No. 3 (January/February 1986):164–178

Engineering Firms

Innovative Dual Consulting. Lloyd Gite. *Black Enterprise* 17, No. 4 (November 1986):31

The Real Road to Success. Lloyd Gite. *Black Enterprise* 16, No. 11 (June 1986):66

Engineering—Interns

Summer Engineering Opportunities. *Black Collegian* 16, No. 3 (January/February 1986):180–183

Engineering Schools

Black Engineering Schools: The Big Six. Frank White III. *Ebony* 41, No. 7 (May 1986):96

Engineering Students

The Minority Engineering Effort: A Spectrum of Organizations with One Unified Goal. Walter Perkins. *Black Collegian* 16, No. 3 (January/February 1986):152–161

Outstanding Student Engineers. *Black Collegian* 16, No. 3 (January/February 1986):184–190

Engineers

A Dream Fulfilled. Blair Walker. *Black Enterprise* 16, No. 9 (April 1986):25

Requiem for a Hero: "Touching the Face of God." D. Michael Cheers. *Ebony* 41, No. 7 (May 1986):82

Ronald Ervin McNair: First and One of a Kind. Adolph Dupree. *About Time* 14, No. 6 (June 1986):12–13

See also Electrical Engineers

Englander, Susan (joint author)

See Malveaux, Julianne

English—Dissertations and Theses

Master's Theses in Progress in Selected Colleges and Universities. Mac A. Stewart. *Negro Educational Review* 37, Nos. 3–4 (July-October 1986):100, 109

English Language—Grammar—Study and Teaching

The Transitive Vampire: A Handbook of Grammar for the Innocent, the Eager and the Damned. By Karen Elizabeth Gordon. Reviewed by Elizabeth J. Higgins. *CLA Journal* 30, No. 2 (December 1986):252–253

English Language—Study and Teaching—Psychological Aspects

English-Only Movement Fosters Divisiveness. Arnoldo Torres. *Interracial Books for Children Bulletin* 17, Nos. 3–4 (1986):18–19

Entertainers

An Evening with Bobby Short. Felicia Kessel. *Crisis* 93, No. 10 (December 1986):24–25

Josephine Baker: A Lifetime of Struggle and Romance. S. Brandi Barnes. *Black Collegian* 16, No. 3 (January/February 1986):98–102

Entrepreneurs

Act I: How to Write a Business Plan. Udayan Gupta. *Black Enterprise* 16, No. 7 (February 1986):135–138

Characteristics of Minorities Who Are Entering Self-Employment. Timothy Bates. *Review of Black Political Economy* 15, No. 2 (Fall 1986):31–49

Check It Out: Coat Checking and Matchmaking Pay Off. Janine C. McAdams. *Essence* 17, No. 6 (October 1986):109

Entrepreneurial Surgeon: Dr. Ernest Bates Nurses Ailing Firm to Fiscal Health. Mark McNamara. *Ebony* 41, No. 6 (April 1986):84

Entrepreneurs, Students of the 80's: Financing Their Educations and Making a Profit. William Ball. *Black Collegian* 17, No. 1 (September/October 1986):128–132

Moving Up with Heavy Equipment. Solomon Herbert. *Black Enterprise* 16, No. 10 (May 1986):29

The New Entrepreneur: Catering Magician. E. D. Smith. *Black Enterprise* 16, No. 11 (June 1986):301

Part-Time Payoff of Direct Sales. Elaine Gregg. *Black Enterprise* 16, No. 10 (May 1986):58

The Trumark of Excellence. Trudy Gallant. *Black Enterprise* 17, No. 1 (August 1986):39

Young, Black and in Business. Walter M. Perkins. *Black Collegian* 16, No. 4 (March/April 1986):51–62

The Young Tycoons. Lloyd Gite. *Black Enterprise* 16, No. 6 (January 1986):44–47

Environmental Policy

The Politics of Pollution: Implications for the Black Community. Robert D. Bullard and Beverly Hendrix Wright. *Phylon* 47, No. 1 (March 1986):71–78

EPIC

See Effective Parenting Information for Children

Epic Poetry

Heresy in Paradise and the Ghosts of Readers Past. Notes. Michael E. Bauman. *CLA Journal* 30, No. 1 (September 1986):59–68

The Identity of the Hero in the Liongo Epic. References. Joseph L. Mbele. *Research in African Literatures* 17, No. 4 (Winter 1986): 464–473

Kibabina's "Message About Zanzibar": The Art of Swahili Poetry. References. Appendix. Jan Feidel and Ibrahim Noor Shariff. *Research in African Literatures* 17, No. 4 (Winter 1986): 496–524

Equal Employment Opportunity Commission

Changes in Equal Employment Enforcement: What Enforcement Statistics Tell Us. Lynn C. Burbridge. *Review of Black Political Economy* 15, No. 1 (Summer 1986):71–80

Equipment Leasing

See Industrial Equipment Leases

Equity and Choice Act, The

Do Vouchers Equal Choices for the Poor? David C. Ruffin. *Black Enterprise* 17, No. 2 (September 1986):25

Erickson, Peter

The Love Poetry of June Jordan. *Callaloo* 9, No. 1 (Winter 1986):221–234

Errand Runners Inc.

When It Has to Be There Now. *Black Enterprise* 16, No. 12 (July 1986):21

Ervin, Janice (about)

Turning Fun into Fortune. *Black Enterprise* 16, No. 7 (February 1986):79–87

Ethics

The Devil and Dr. Church: A Guide to Hell for Atheists and True Believers. By F. Forrester Church. Reviewed by Kortright Davis. *Journal of Religious Thought* 43, No. 2 (Fall-Winter 1986–87):91

Ethiopia—British Influences

Shakespeare in Ethiopia. Notes. Richard Pankhurst. *Research in African Literatures* 17, No. 2 (Summer 1986): 169–196

Ethnic Groups

The Impact of National Testing on Ethnic Minorities: With Proposed Solutions. Peter A. Garcia. *Journal of Negro Education* 55, No. 3 (Summer 1986):347–357

Ethnology

The Dual Vision: Insights and Applications of Cross-Cultural Research. Bennetta Jules-Rosette. *Journal of Negro Education* 55, No. 2 (Spring 1986):125–141

Ethridge, J. E., Construction Inc.

BE 100: The New Guys on the Block. Edmund Newton. *Black Enterprise* 16, No. 11 (June 1986):119

Etuk, Emma S.

Black-American Heritage? Book review. *Journal of Religious Thought* 43, No. 1 (Spring-Summer 1986):128

Europe, Eastern

Black Journalists Visit Eastern Europe. Terry E. Johnson. *Black Scholar* 17, No. 1 (January-February 1986):35–37

Evans, Arthur S. (Jr.), and Giles, Michael W.

Effects of Percent Black on Blacks' Perceptions of Relative Power and Social Distance. *Journal of Black Studies* 17, No. 1 (September 1986):3–14

Everett, Joyce E.

Between Women: Domestics and Their Employers. Book review. *SAGE* 3, No. 1 (Spring 1986):61

Everett, Percival

The Bear as Symbol. *Callaloo* 9, No. 2 (Spring 1986):349–353

Eviction

Constructive Eviction—An Illusive Tenant Remedy? Sydney M. Knight. *Howard Law Journal* 29, No. 1 (1986):13–26

Evidence, Expert

The Effect of the Requirement of Expert Testimony on the Tenant's Ability to Prove Damages in a Breach of Warranty of Habitability Action. Philip W. Coleman. *Howard Law Journal* 29, No. 1 (1986):177–189

Evil

See Good and Evil

Ewing, Patrick (about)

Patrick Ewing: Can This Man Save the Knicks? Walter Leavy. *Ebony* 41, No. 4 (February 1986):59

Executives

Bruce: The Boss. Ken Smikle. *Black Enterprise* 17, No. 2 (September 1986):36

The Corporate Pioneers. Paul Lindsay Johnson. *Crisis* 93, No. 4 (April 1986):26–30

Corporate Profile: Success among the Suds. Joyce Davis Adams. *Black Enterprise* 16, No. 11 (June 1986):242

How to Make It in the White Corporate World. Charles Whitaker. *Ebony* 41, No. 5 (March 1986):102

A Perennial Favorite. Robert A. Monroe. *Crisis* 93, No. 4 (April 1986):38

Expatriation

Doris Lessing. By Lorna Sage. Reviewed by Roberta Rubenstein. *Research in African Literatures* 17, No. 3 (Fall 1986): 411–413

Expatriate Characters in the Early African Novel. L. Losambe. *Phylon* 47, No. 2 (June 1986):148–158

Home and Exile and Other Selections. Reviewed by James Booth. *Research in African Literatures* 17, No. 3 (Fall 1986): 398–401

Rereading *Banjo*: Claude McKay and the French Connection. Notes. Robert P. Smith (Jr.) *CLA Journal* 30, No. 1 (September 1986):46–58

Tessere per un mosaico africano. By Itala Vivan. Reviewed by Jane Wilkinson. *Research in African Literatures* 17, No. 3 (Fall 1986): 425–426

Export Contrcls

Cuba as an Oil Trader: Petroleum Deals in a Falling Market. Jorge F. Perez-Lopez. *Caribbean Review* 15, No. 2 (Spring 1986):26–29+

Ezewu, E. E.

The Relative Contribution of the Extended Family System to Schooling in Nigeria. *Journal of Negro Education* 55, No.2 (Spring 1986):222–228

Faber, Doris

Margaret Thatcher: Britain's "Iron Lady." Book review. Carole M. Martin. *Interracial Books for Children Bulletin* 17, No. 2 (1986):15

Fabre, Genevieve

Drumbeats, Masks, and Metaphor: Contemporary Afro-American Theatre. Book review. Errol Hill. *Black American Literature Forum* 20, No. 4 (Winter 1986):459–462

Fabre, Michel

La rive noire: De Harlem à la Seine. Reviewed by Clarisse Zimra. *Research in African Literatures* 17, No. 4 (Winter 1986): 601–603

The World of Richard Wright. Book review. Rudolph Byrd. *Callaloo* 9, No. 4 (Fall 1986):751–752

Factories

Obreros en la Corazon del Bruto. Tom Denyer. *Race and Class* 27, No. 4 (Spring 1986):53–68

Fagan, Helen Alexander (about)

Alabama Super Mom Rears Officers, Gentlemen and Scholars. *Ebony* 41, No. 6 (April 1986):101

Fairchild, Halford H., and others

Impact of *Roots*: Evidence from the National Survey of Black Americans. *Journal of Black Studies* 16, No. 3 (March 1986):307–318

Fairclough, Adam

Martin Luther King (Jr.) and the Quest for Nonviolent Social Change. *Phylon* 47, No. 1 (March 1986):1–15

Fair Housing Act

Institutional Reform and the Enforcement of the Fair Housing Laws. Ron C. Claiborne. *Black Scholar* 17, No. 3 (May-June 1986):42–48

Faith

Coming to Faith: My Testimony. Loretta A. Kelly. *Essence* 16, No. 11 (March 1986):56

Falcon Trap and Game Club

As Gentle As the Wind: The Falcon Trap and Game Club. Adolph Dupree. *About Time* 14, No. 12 (December 1986):20–24

Family

Black Love and the Extended Family Concept Should Be Priorities. *Ebony* 41, No. 10 (August 1986):158

The Crisis of the Black Family. *Ebony* 41, No. 10 (August 1986):30

The Enduring Family: Long-Term Marriages, Happy Households and Successful Children Are Not Unusual. Marilyn Marshall. *Ebony* 41, No. 10 (August 1986):78

It's In Our Hands! Maxine Childress Brown. *About Time* 14, No. 7 (July 1986):9

Social Ethics and the Black Family. Maulana Karenga. *Black Scholar* 17, No. 5 (September-October 1986):41–54

The Ten Biggest Myths about the Black Family. Lerone Bennett (Jr.) *Ebony* 41, No. 10 (August 1986):134

See also Parenting

Family Farms

Four Brothers: Farming Is Their Business. *Ebony* 41, No. 8 (June 1986):46

Family Finance

See Home Economics

Family Law

Parental and Medical Leave. William L. Clay. *About Time* 14, No. 4 (April 1986):19

Family Life Education

The Future of the Black Community: Human Capital, Family Aspirations, and Individual Motivation. Clifton R. Wharton, Jr. *Review of Black Political Economy* 14, No. 4 (Spring 1986):9–16

Family in Literature

Pieces of Days. Wilhelmina R. Wynn. *Callaloo* 9, No. 2 (Spring 1986):391–403

Family Policy

Family and Nation. By Daniel Patrick Moynihan. Reviewed by Tonya Bolden Davis. *Black Enterprise* 17, No. 3 (October 1986):17

Family Relationships

Loving a Troubled Man. Janice C. Simpson. *Essence* 17, No. 6 (October 1986):75

Family—Religious Life

Return to the Spiritual Traditions of Black Churches and Schools. *Ebony* 41, No. 10 (August 1986):160

Family Reunions

National Black Family Celebration. Marsha Jones. *About Time* 14, No. 10 (October 1986):23

Family Structure

Africanity and the Black Family: The Development of a Theoretical Model. By Wade W. Nobles. Reviewed by S. M. Khatib. *Journal of Black Psychology* 13, No. 1 (August 1986):24–26

The Afro-American Work/Family Nexus: An Exploratory Analysis. Patricia Hill Collins. *Western Journal of Black Studies* 10, No. 3 (Fall 1986):148–158

The Black Family and the Crisis of Capitalism. Angela Davis and Fania Davis. *Black Scholar* 17, No. 5 (September-October 1986):33–40

Characteristics of the Black Family. Carolyne S. Blount. *About Time* 14, No. 3 (March 1986):4

The Cultural Unity of Black Africa: The Domains of Patriarchy and of Matriarchy in Classical Antiquity. Bibliography. By Cheikh Anta Diop. Reviewed by Asa G. Hilliard III. *Journal of African Civilizations* 8, No. 1 (June 1986):102–109

Dr. Ann Creighton Zollar: Assessing the Urban Black Family Experience. Carolyne S. Blount. *About Time* 14, No. 3 (March 1986):10–13

From Teenage Parenthood to Polygamy: Case Studies in Black Polygamous Family Formation. Joseph W. Scott. *Western Journal of Black Studies* 10, No. 4 (Winter 1986):172–179

The Impact of Unemployment on the Social Well-Being of the Black Family. Essie Tramel Seck. *Urban League Review* 10, No. 1 (Summer 1986):87–97

Labor of Love, Labor of Sorrow: Black Women, Work, and the Family from Slavery to the Present. Book review. *Race and Class* 28, No. 2 (August 1986):96–97

The Political Economy of Black Family Life. Robert Staples. *Black Scholar* 17, No. 5 (September-October 1986):2–11

Understanding the Black Family: A Guide for Scholarship and Research. By Wade W. Nobles and Lawford Goddard. *Journal of Black Psychology* 13, No. 1 (August 1986):20–23

See also Parenting

See also Single-Parent Families

Famines—Africa

A Conversation with Djibril Diallo. Audrey Edwards. *Essence* 16, No. 11 (March 1986):40

The Politics of Neglect: The U.S. Response to Africa's Famine. Cherri D. Waters. *Urban League Review* 10, No. 2 (Winter 1986–87):131–148

Fanon, Frantz (about)

Black Soul, White Artifact: Fanon's Clinical Psychology and Social Theory. By Jack McCulloch. Reviewed by Hal Wylie. *Research in African Literatures* 17, No. 4 (Winter 1986): 599–601

Frantz Fanon and Black Consciousness in Azania (South Africa). Thomas K. Ranuga. *Phylon* 47, No. 3 (September 1986):182–191

Holy Violence: The Revolutionary Thought of Frantz Fanon. By Marie Perinbam. Reviewed by Hal Wylie. *Research in African Literatures* 17, No. 4 (Winter 1986): 597–599

Farley, Jonathan David (about)

Behold a Leader: Jonathan David Farley. Adolph Dupree. *About Time* 14, No. 12 (December 1986):8–9

Farley, Reynolds

Blacks and Whites: Narrowing the Gap? Book review. Louis Kushnick. *Race and Class* 27, No. 3 (Winter 1986):106–108

Farmers

Four Brothers: Farming Is Their Business. *Ebony* 41, No. 8 (June 1986):46

Rice, Rice and More Rice: Ephron Lewis' Arkansas Farm Yields the Long, Medium and Short of It. *Ebony* 42, No. 2 (December 1986):100

Farnsworth, Robert M.

Melvin B. Tolson 1898–1966: Plain Talk and Poetic Prophecy. Book review. Raymond Nelson. *Callaloo* 9, No. 1 (Winter 1986):270–272

Farrakhan, Louis (about)

Religious Belief and Political Activism in Black America: An Essay. Robert Michael Franklin. *Journal of Religious Thought* 43, No. 2 (Fall-Winter 1986–87):63–72

Farris, Christine King

The Young Martin: From Childhood through College. *Ebony* 41, No. 3 (January 1986):56

Fascism

The Anti-Fascist Movement: Lessons We Must Learn. Lis Fekete. *Race and Class* 28, No. 1 (Summer 1986):79–85

Fat Boys

The Fat Boys Enjoy a Banquet of Rap and Roles. Eric Copage. *Essence* 17, No. 2 (July 1986):34

Fathers

Facing the Challenge of Raising My Black Manchild. Larry Conley. *Essence* 17, No. 7 (November 1986):116

Fathers Who Walk Away. Walter Leavy. *Ebony* 41, No. 10 (August 1986):53

Save the Fathers: Black Fathers of Today Must Fight to Regain Traditional Strengths of the Past. Alvin F. Poussaint. *Ebony* 41, No. 10 (August 1986):43

Faulkner, William

Vision in Spring. Reviewed by Elizabeth J. Higgins. *CLA Journal* 29, No. 4 (June 1986):490–492

Faulkner, William—Criticism and Interpretation

In Defense of Reverend Hightower: It is Never Too Late. Notes. Robert L. Feldman. *CLA Journal* 29, No. 3 (March 1986):352–367

The Origin of Faulkner's Art. By Judith L. Sensibar. Reviewed by Elizabeth J. Higgins. *CLA Journal* 29, No. 4 (June 1986):490–492

Wright, Faulkner and the South: Reconstitution and Transfiguration. Thadious M. Davis. *Callaloo* 9, No. 3 (Summer 1986):469–478

Fauset, Jessie Redmon

Plum Bun: A Novel without a Moral. Book review. Beth Brown. *Black Scholar* 17, No. 4 (July-August 1986):58–59

Fauset, Jessie Redmon—Criticism and Interpretation

Clothes and Closure in Three Novels by Black Women. Mary Jane Lupton. *Black American Literature Forum* 20, No. 4 (Winter 1986):409–421

Fax, Elton C.

It's Been a Beautiful But Rugged Journey. *Black American Literature Forum* 20, No. 3 (Fall 1986):273–288

Feagin, Joe

Slavery Unwilling to Die: The Background of Black Oppression in the 1980s. *Journal of Black Studies* 17, No. 2 (December 1986):173–200

Feasts and Rituals

The Feast of Good Death: An Afro-Catholic Emancipation Celebration in Brazil. Sheila S. Walker. *SAGE* 3, No. 2 (Fall 1986):27–31

Federal Budget

Gramm-Rudman and the Politics of Deficit Reduction. Linda F. Williams. *Urban League Review* 10, No. 2 (Winter 1986–87):72–83

Federal Communications Commission

In Support of Black Media. Ken Smikle. *Black Enterprise* 17, No. 5 (December 1986):25

Federal Communications Commission—Regulatory Policy

Regulatory Policy and Minority Concerns: The Impact of Changes in Telecommunications Policy. Georgia A. Persons. *Urban League Review* 10, No. 2 (Winter 1986–87):45–62

Feidel, Jan, and Shariff, Ibrahim Noor

Kibabina's "Message About Zanzibar": The Art of Swahili Poetry. References. Appendix. *Research in African Literatures* 17, No. 4 (Winter 1986): 496–524

Fekete, Liz

The Anti Fascist Movement: Lessons We Must Learn. *Race and Class* 28, No. 1 (Summer 1986):79–85

Beating Time: Riot 'n' Race 'n' Rock 'n' Roll. Book review. *Race and Class* 28, No. 2 (August 1986):91–93

Singin' and Swingin' and Gettin' Merry Like Christmas. Book review. *Race and Class* 27, No. 4 (Spring 1986):106–107

Felder, Cain H.

At the River I Stand: Memphis, the 1968 Strike and Martin Luther King. Book review. *Journal of Religious Thought* 43, No. 2 (Fall-Winter 1986–87):93–94

Feldman, Robert L.

In Defense of Reverend Hightower: It is Never Too Late. Notes. *CLA Journal* 29, No. 3 (March 1986):352–367

Feminism—Religious Aspects

The Color of Feminism: Or Speaking the Black Woman's Tongue. Notes. Delores S. Williams. *Journal of Religious Thought* 43, No. 1 (Spring-Summer 1986):42–58

The Professionalism of the Ministry of Women. Notes. Delores Causion Carpenter. *Journal of Religious Thought* 43, No. 1 (Spring-Summer 1986):59–75

Ferebee, Gideon (Jr.)

Refugee. Poem. *Black American Literature Forum* 20, No. 3 (Fall 1986):311

Feuser, Willfried F.

Commonwealth Literatur. Book review. *Research in African Literatures* 17, No. 3 (Fall 1986): 430–433

Fiction

The Bridge. Maya Angelou. *Essence* 16, No. 11 (March 1986):66

Fido, Elaine Savory

The Truthful Lie: Essays in a Sociology of African Drama. Book review. *Research in African Literatures* 17, No. 2 (Summer 1986): 273–275

Fields, Kim (about)

Fields in Bloom. Nikki Grimes. *Essence* 17, No. 4 (August 1986):84

Film Festivals

Film Festival: Reservations for 62,332. Adolph Dupree. *About Time* 14, No. 1 (January 1986):16–17

Film and Filmmakers

African Literature on Film: A Preliminary Bibliography/Filmography. Notes. Nancy J. Schmidt. Notes. *Research in African Literatures* 17, No. 2 (Summer 1986): 261–266

Film Industry

A *Crisis* Report on Film. Paul Lindsay Johnson. *Crisis* 93, No. 1 (January 1986):21–24

Film Producers and Directors

Black Directors. *Ebony* 42, No. 2 (December 1986):43

Coast to Coast Salute to Black Filmmakers: New York Gala Kicks off the Nationwide Drive for Home for This Film Group. *Ebony* 41, No. 12 (October 1986):91

Inside Hollywood. Ken Smikle. *Black Enterprise* 17, No. 5 (December 1986):48

Spike Lee's Declaration of Independence. David Frechette. *Black Enterprise* 17, No. 5 (December 1986):56

Film Reviews

The Color Purple. Directed by Steven Spielberg. *Interracial Books for Children Bulletin* 17, No. 2 (1986):20–21

The Color Purple. Directed by Steven Spielberg. Reviewed by JoNina M. Abron. *Black Scholar* 17, No. 2 (March-April 1986):54

The Color Purple. Directed by Steven Spielberg. Reviewed by Marsha Jones. *About Time* 14, No. 1 (January 1986):18–19

The Color Purple. Produced and directed by Steven Spielberg. Reviewed by Lynn Norment. *Ebony* 41, No. 4 (February 1986):146

The Color Purple. Reviewed by Herb Boyd. *Crisis* 93, No. 2 (February 1986):10

Crossroads. *About Time* 14, No. 3 (March 1986):22–23

Eyes on the Prize: America's Civil Rights Years, 1954–1965. Produced by Blackside, Inc. Reviewed by Shelley Moore. *Crisis* 93, No. 10 (December 1986):12–13

Namibia: Africa's Last Colony. Reviewed by Roland S. Jefferson. *Black Scholar* 17, No. 1 (January-February 1986):46–47

Native Son. Reviewed by Christopher Vaughn. *Essence* 17, No. 8 (December 1986):30

Nicaragua. Directed by Marc Karlin. Reviewed by John Bevan. *Race and Class* 27, No. 3 (Winter 1986):99–102

Rocky IV—Mindless Jingoism. Reviewed by Albert V. Schwartz. *Interracial Books for Children Bulletin* 17, No. 1 (1986):11

Round Midnight. By Bertrand Tavernier. Reviewed by Nelson George. *Essence* 17, No. 7 (November 1986):36

She's Gotta Have It. By Spike Lee. Reviewed by Marsha Jones. *About Time* 14, No. 10 (October 1986):24–25

Spike Lee's "She's Gotta Have It." Reviewed by Paul Linsey Johnson. *Crisis* 93, No. 8 (October 1986):11–12

Under the Cherry Moon. Reviewed by Herb Boyd. *Crisis* 93, No. 7 (August/September 1986):11

Finance, Personal

Cashing In on a Windfall of Coupons. *Ebony* 41, No. 11 (September 1986):72

Financial Lessons for After School. Karen Brailsford. *Black Enterprise* 17, No. 3 (October 1986):57

Fired! Creating a Financial Safety Net Now Can Prevent Serious Injuries if You're Handed the Pink Slip. Denise Lamaute. *Black Enterprise* 17, No. 3 (October 1986):111

How to Get Out of Debt: Experts Offer Tips on Ways of Dealing with Your Financial Crisis. *Ebony* 41, No. 9 (July 1986):56

Living Well on... Lloyd Gite. *Black Enterprise* 16, No. 10 (May 1986):44

Testing Your Financial I. Q. Sheryl Hilliard. *Black Enterprise* 17, No. 3 (October 1986):105

Yours, Mine and Ours. Frances E. Ruffin. *Black Enterprise* 16, No. 8 (March 1986):34–36

Financial Advisers

Melvin Van Peebles's Bold New Money Play. Interview. Knolly Moses. *Essence* 17, No. 2 (June 1986):12

Sweet Stock Picker: His Show Biz Success and Unorthodox Style Have Opened Up New Options for Melvin Van Peebles. Edmund Newton. *Black Enterprise* 17, No. 3 (October 1986):84

Financial Services

Brokers Go for Growth. Ken Smikle. *Black Enterprise* 16, No. 10 (May 1986):18

Finch, Charles S.

Further Conversations with the Pharaoh. Interview. *Journal of African Civilizations* 8, No. 1 (June 1986):227–237

Meeting the Pharoah: Conversations with Cheikh Anta Diop. Interview. *Journal of African Civilizations* 8, No. 1 (June 1986):28–34

Finkelman, Paul

Slavery in the Courtroom: An Annotated Bibliography of American Cases. Reviewed by Mary Frances Berry. *Afro-Americans in New York Life and History* 10, No. 2 (July 1986):65

Finney, Nikky

Chariots. Poem. *Essence* 17, No. 4 (August 1986):144

Firearms—Laws and Regulations

Controlling and Regulating Handguns—A Way to Save Black Lives. Robert Berkley Harper. *Black Law Journal* 9, No. 3 (Winter 1986):229–251

First California Funding

Mortgage Money for Minorities. Solomon J. Herbert. *Black Enterprise* 17, No. 1 (August 1986):19

Fisher, Hilary

Passbook Number F.47927: Women and Mau Mau in Kenya. Book review. *Race and Class* 27, No. 4 (Spring 1986):96–97

Fleissner, Robert F.

...And Ladies of the Club. Book review. *CLA Journal* 29, No. 4 (June 1986):486–489

Fleming, J.

Blacks in College. Reviewed by Herman Brown. *Journal of Negro Education* 55, No.2 (Spring 1986):237–239

Flores, Roger Sanchez

Revolutionary Comics: Political Humor from Nicaragua. *Caribbean Review* 15, No. 1 (Winter 1986):16–17

Florida—History

The First New African States in North America. Imari A. Obadele. *Black Collegian* 16, No. 3 (January/February 1986):86–97

Flowers, Arthur

Which Way Black America? *Essence* 17, No. 8 (December 1986):54

Flowers, Harold (about)

Civil Rights Lawyers Revisited. *Ebony* 42, No. 2 (December 1986):76

Floyd, Samuel A. (Jr.)

Books on Black Music by Black Authors: A Bibliography. *Black Perspective in Music* 14, No. 3 (Fall 1986):215–232

Foley, John Miles

Oral-Formulaic Theory and Research: An Introduction and Annotated Bibliography. Reviewed by Dan Ben-Amos. *Research in African Literatures* 17, No. 2 (Summer 1986): 309–310

Folk-Dance—Barbados

1627 and All That Sort of Thing. Illustrated. *International Review of African American Art* 7, No. 1 (1986):29–31

Folk Literature

The Bantu-Speaking Heritage of the United States. By Winifred Kellersberger. Reviewed by Joseph E. Holloway. *Phylon* 47, No. 2 (June 1986):167–168

Folklore—Africa

Oral-Formulaic Theory and Research: An Introduction and Annotated Bibliography. By John Miles Foley. Reviewed by Dan Ben-Amos. *Research in African Literatures* 17, No. 2 (Summer 1986): 309–310

Food Industry and Trade

Cashing in on Chips. Lloyd Gite. *Black Enterprise* 16, No. 12 (July 1986):14

Food—Prices

Effects of Food Stamp Program Participation and Other Sociodemographic Characteristics on Food Expenditure Patterns of Elderly Minority Households. Carlton G. Davis and others. *Review of Black Political Economy* 15, No. 1 (Summer 1986):3–25

Food Stamp Program

Effects of Food Stamp Program Participation and Other Sociodemographic Characteristics on Food Expenditure Patterns of Elderly Minority Households. Carlton G. Davis and others. *Review of Black Political Economy* 15, No. 1 (Summer 1986):3–25

Food Supply

No Free Lunch: Food and Revolution in Cuba Today. By Medea Benjamin, Joseph Collins, and Michael Scott. Reviewed by James E. Austin. *Caribbean Review* 15, No. 2 (Spring 1986):45

Football

Mixing Sports and School: Leo F. Miles. Henry Duvall. *About Time* 14, No. 5 (May 1986):23–24

The Top 15—An Overview of Black College Football. Donald F. Staffo. *Black Collegian* 17, No. 2 (November/December 1986):29–35

Football Players

Ebony Visits Payton's Place. Illustrated. *Ebony* 41, No. 11 (September 1986):92

Herschel Walker: Pro Football's New Million-Dollar Man. Walter Leavy. *Ebony* 42, No. 1 (November 1986):156

William A. Perry: The Man behind the "Fridge." Walter Leavy. *Ebony* 41, No. 12 (October 1986):29

Ford Motor Company

A First for Ford. Jay Koblenz. *Black Enterprise* 16, No. 12 (July 1986):16

Foreclosures

Rights of a Tenant When the Landlord Defaults on the Mortgage. Anna E. Blackburne. *Howard Law Journal* 29, No. 1 (1986):27–39

Foreign Policy

See International Relations

Foreign Service

See Diplomatic and Consular Service

Foreign Service Officers

Black Americans as Participants in the Foreign Service. Daniel Brantley. *Crisis* 93, No. 9 (November 1986):31–33

Forster, Imogen

To Bury Our Fathers: A Novel of Nicaragua. Book review. *Race and Class* 27, No. 4 (Spring 1986):92–93

Fosse, Bob

Big Deal. Theater review. Charles E. Rogers. *Essence* 17, No. 1 (May 1986):44

Sweet Charity. Theater review. *Crisis* 93, No. 7 (August/September 1986):10

Fowler, Gayl

Black and White Children in America: Key Facts. Book review. *Journal of Religious Thought* 43, No. 1 (Spring-Summer 1986):130

10 Super Sunday Schools in the Black Community. Book review. *Journal of Religious Thought* 43, No. 2 (Fall-Winter 1986–87):93

Those Preachin' Women: Sermons by Black Women Preachers. Book review. *Journal of Religious Thought* 43, No. 1 (Spring-Summer 1986):129–130

Fox, Robert E.

Derek Walcott: History as Dis-ease. *Callaloo* 9, No. 2 (Spring 1986):331–340

France—Colonies

Ideologies of Race and Sex in Literature: Racism and Antiracism in the African Francophone Novel. Notes. E. P. Abanime. *CLA Journal* 30, No. 2 (December 1986):125–143

Franchises (Retail Trade)

Doing Chicken Right. Sam Fulwood. *Black Enterprise* 17, No. 4 (November 1986):60

Of Financing and Franchising. Kenneth Maurice Jones. *Black Enterprise* 16, No. 9 (April 1986):52–56

Harvey Buys Pepsi Plant. Gordon Borrell. *Black Enterprise* 16, No. 11 (June 1986):48

A Tale of Two Franchises. Joyce Davis Adams and Janet Clayton. *Black Enterprise* 16, No. 12 (July 1986):42–46

Francis, Reynold S.

Don't Leave Me. Poem. *Essence* 17, No. 4 (August 1986):138

Franklin, Aretha

Aretha. Record review. Norman Riley. *Crisis* 93, No. 10 (December 1986):8–9

Franklin, Clyde W. (II)

Conceptual and Logical Issues in Theory and Research Related to Black Masculinity. *Western Journal of Black Studies* 10, No. 4 (Winter 1986):161–166

Franklin, R. Edward

Love's Own Answer. Poem. *Essence* 17, No. 2 (June 1986):121

Franklin, Robert M. (Jr.)

An Ethic of Hope: The Moral Thought of Martin Luther King, Jr. *About Time* 14, No. 1 (January 1986):10–26

Franklin, Robert Michael

Religious Belief and Political Activism in Black America: An Essay. *Journal of Religious Thought* 43, No. 2 (Fall-Winter 1986–87):63–72

Franklin, V. P.

Black Marxism: The Making of the Black Radical Tradition. Book review. *Phylon* 47, No. 3 (September 1986):250–251

Fratoe, Frank A.

A Sociological Analysis of Minority Business. *Review of Black Political Economy* 15, No. 2 (Fall 1986):5–29

Fraud

Fighting Fraud. Lynette Hazelton. *Black Enterprise* 17, No. 4 (November 1986):22

Frazier, E. Franklin (about)

The Sociological Tradition of E. Franklin Frazier: Implications for Black Studies. Clovis E. Semmes. *Journal of Negro Education* 55, No.4 (Fall 1986):484–494

Frechette, David

Spike Lee's Declaration of Independence. *Black Enterprise* 17, No. 5 (December 1986):56

Fredricks, Ayanna (joint author)

See McCray, Abiodun

Freedmen's Bureau

Gideonites and Freedmen: Adult Literacy Education at Port Royal, 1862–1865. John R. Rachal. *Journal of Negro Education* 55, No.4 (Fall 1986):453–469

Freeman, Donald J. (joint author)

See Porter, Andrew C.

Fresh, Doug E. (about)

Doug E. Fresh: "The Show" Must Go On. Charles E. Rogers. *Black Collegian* 16, No. 4 (March/April 1986):42–46

Fridkin, Sid

Bajan Places and Faces. Illustrated. *International Review of African American Art* 7, No. 1 (1986):65–71

Fried, Eunice

Island Liqueurs. *Black Enterprise* 16, No. 10 (May 1986):88

Friedman, Carol

A Moment's Notice: Portraits of American Jazz Musicians. Book review. George L. Starks, Jr. *Black Perspective in Music* 14, No. 3 (Fall 1986):312–313

Friedman, Phillip (joint author)

See Gildemeister, Joan

Frierson, Henry T.

Enhancing Minority College Students' Performance on Educational Tests. *Journal of Negro Education* 55, No. 1 (Winter 1986):38–45

Froschl, Merle, and others

Including All of Us: An Early Childhood Curriculum about Disability. Book review. Emily Strauss Watson. *Interracial Books for Children Bulletin* 17, Nos. 3–4 (1986):37–38

Fuentes, Luis

The Parent-School Partnership and Bilingual Education. *Interracial Books for Children Bulletin* 17, Nos. 3–4 (1986):20–21

Winter Green. Poem. *Black American Literature Forum* 20, No. 3 (Fall 1986):306–307

Garrison, Zina (about)

Zina Garrison: Aiming for the Top in Tennis. Marilyn Marshall. *Ebony* 41, No. 8 (June 1986):79

Garvey, Julius

Remembering...Marcus Garvey. *Essence* 17, No. 7 (November 1986):63

Garvey, Marcus (about)

Marcus Garvey and the Harlem Renaissance. Notes. John Runcie. *Afro-Americans in New York Life and History* 10, No. 2 (July 1986): 7–28

The Poetical Works of Marcus Garvey. By Tony Martin. Reviewed by Joanne Veal Gabbin. *Afro-Americans in New York Life and History* 10, No.1 (January 1986):72–74

Remembering...Marcus Garvey. Julius Garvey. *Essence* 17, No. 7 (November 1986):63

Gary, Lawrence E.

Drinking, Homicide, and the Black Male. *Journal of Black Studies* 17, No. 1 (September 1986):15–31

Gaston, John C.

The Destruction of the Young Black Male: The Impact of Popular Culture and Organized Sports. *Journal of Black Studies* 16, No. 4 (June 1986):369–384

Gates, Henry Louis (editor)

Our Nig; Or, Sketches from the Life of a Free Black. Reviewed by Beth Brown. *CLA Journal* 29, No. 3 (March 1986):383–386

Gates, Henry Louis (Jr.) (joint editor)

See Davis, Charles T.

Gayle, Misani

Aruba: Taking It "Poko Poko." *Black Enterprise* 16, No. 10 (May 1986):72

Tobago: A Veritable Enchanted Isle. *Black Enterprise* 16, No. 10 (May 1986):82

Gcabashe, Tandi (about)

The Struggle from Without: An Interview with South African Exile Tandi Gcabashe. *SAGE* 3, No. 2 (Fall 1986):48–51

G & C Equipment Corporation

Moving Up with Heavy Equipment. Solomon Herbert. *Black Enterprise* 16, No. 10 (May 1986):29

Generals

See United States Army, etc.

Generation Gap

See Conflict of Generations

Genet, Jean (about)

Jean Genet and the Black Panther Party. Robert Sandarg. *Journal of Black Studies* 16, No. 3 (March 1986):269–282

Geneva—International Summit

Jesse Jackson Takes His Peace Program to Geneva. Don Rojas. *Black Scholar* 17, No. 1 (January-February 1986):31–34

Reflections on the Geneva Summit: The Perspective of a Journalist from the Developing World. Don Rojas. *Black Scholar* 17, No. 1 (January-February 1986):26–30

Geography, Ancient—Maps

African Sea Kings in America? Evidence from Early Maps. Bibliography. Joan Covey. *Journal of African Civilizations* 8, No. 2 (December 1986):152–168

George, Nelson

A Conversation with Ishmael Reed. Interview. *Essence* 17, No. 2 (July 1986):38

Round Midnight. Film review. *Essence* 17, No. 7 (November 1986):36

Where Did Our Love Go? The Rise and Fall of the Motown Sound. Book review. Tonya Bolden Davis. *Black Enterprise* 16, No. 11 (June 1986):35–37

Gerard, Albert

Essais d'histoire littéraire africaine. Reviewed by Mohamadou Kane. *Research in African Literatures* 17, No. 4 (Winter 1986): 563–565

Ghana—Theater

Come to Laugh: A Study of African Traditional Theatre in Ghana. By Kwabena N. Bame. Reviewed by Alain Ricard. *Research in African Literatures* 17, No. 2 (Summer 1986): 287

Gibbs, James

"Larsony" With a Difference: An Examination of a Paragraph from *Toward the Decolonization of African Literature*. Notes. *Research in African Literatures* 17, No. 1 (Spring 1986): 39–47

Wole Soyinka's *The Road*. Book review. *Research in African Literatures* 17, No. 4 (Winter 1986): 617–620

Gibbs, James (about)

Gibb's Gibberish. Chinweizu, Onwuchekwa Jemie, and Ihechukwu Madubuike. *Research in African Literatures* 17, No. 1 (Spring 1986):48–52

Gibbs, Marla (about)

227—Marla's Masterpiece. Aldore Collier. *Ebony* 42, No. 2 (December 1986):92

Gibson, Ashton, and Barrow, Jocelyn

The Unequal Struggle. Book review. Paul Okojie. *Race and Class* 28, No. 2 (August 1986):93–95

Gibson, Donald B.

Richard Wright's Black Boy and the Trauma of Autobiographical Rebirth. *Callaloo* 9, No. 3 (Summer 1986):492–498

Gibson, G. Robert (about)

Tracking Films by Computer. Elaine Wapples. *Black Enterprise* 17, No. 2 (September 1986):27

Giddings, Ann L.

Abandonment. *Howard Law Journal* 29, No. 1 (1986):117–125

Giddings, Paula

The Struggle from Without: An Interview with South African Exile Tandi Gcabashe. *SAGE* 3, No. 2 (Fall 1986):48–51

When and Where I Enter: The Impact of Black Women on Race and Sex in America. Book review. Eleanor Smith. *Western Journal of Black Studies* 10, No. 1 (Spring 1986):45–46

Giddins, Gary

A Moment's Notice: Portraits of American Jazz Musicians. Book review. George L. Starks, Jr. *Black Perspective in Music* 14, No. 3 (Fall 1986):312–313

Rhythm-A-Ning: Jazz Tradition and Innovation in the 80's. Book review. George L. Starks, Jr. *Black Perspective in Music* 14, No. 2 (Spring 1986):187

Gifford, Bernard R.

Excellence and Equity in Teacher Competency Testing: A Policy Perspective. *Journal of Negro Education* 55, No.3 (Summer 1986):251–271

Testing, Politics, and the Allocation of Opportunities. *Journal of Negro Education* 55, No.3 (Summer 1986):422–432

Gifted Children—Education

Enhancing the Intellectual Potential of the Minority Gifted: A Shared Responsibility. Cecilia Steppe-Jones and others. *Negro Educational Review* 37, Nos. 3–4 (July-October 1986):127–129

Gikandi, Simon

Kikuyu People: A Brief Outline of their Customs and Traditions. Book review. *Research in African Literatures* 17, No. 2 (Summer 1986): 299–301

Wole Soyinka's *The Road*. Reviewed by James Gibbs. *Research in African Literatures* 17, No. 4 (Winter 1986): 617–620

Gildemeister, Joan, and Friedman, Phillip

Sequence Memory and Organization in Recall of Black Third and Fifth Graders. *Journal of Negro Education* 55, No.2 (Spring 1986):142–154

Giles, Michael W. (joint author)

See Evans, Arthur S.

Gilkes, Cheryl Townsend

The Role of Women in the Sanctified Church. Notes. *Journal of Religious Thought* 43, No. 1 (Spring-Summer 1986):24–41

Gill, Waliyy

The Western Film Hollywood Myths and One Black Reality. *Western Journal of Black Studies* 10, No. 1 (Spring 1986):1–5

Gillespie, Dizzie (about)

Dizzy Gillespie: He Just Keeps Bopping Along. Marilyn Marshall. *Ebony* 41, No. 11 (September 1986):50

Gillespie, Fern

Black Theater. *Crisis* 93, No. 1 (January 1986):35–46

Gilliam, Jeffrey D.

Justice and Dignity: Due Process Notions in the Administration of Collective Bargaining Agreement. *Black Law Journal* 9, No. 3 (Winter 1986):323–333

Gillis-Olion, Marion, and others

Strategies for Interacting with Black Parents of Handicapped Children. *Negro Educational Review* 37, No. 1 (January 1986):8–16

Gite, Lloyd

The Benefits of Leasing. *Black Enterprise* 17, No. 2 (September 1986):27

Black Men and Suicide. *Essence* 17, No. 7 (November 1986):64

Cashing in on Chips. *Black Enterprise* 16, No. 12 (July 1986):14

Cleaning up in Waste Removal. *Black Enterprise* 17, No. 3 (October 1986):33

Fairy Tales Come True. *Black Enterprise* 17, No. 3 (October 1986):24

Historian with a Mission. *Black Enterprise* 17, No. 1 (August 1986):57

Homes on the Range. *Black Enterprise* 16, No. 9 (April 1986):22

How One Man Is Building the City of the Future. *Black Enterprise* 17, No. 5 (December 1986):68

Innovative Dual Consulting. *Black Enterprise* 17, No. 4 (November 1986):31

Living Well on... *Black Enterprise* 16, No. 10 (May 1986):44

Millions in Makeup. *Black Enterprise* 17, No. 5 (December 1986):28

Planning Designs for Success. *Black Enterprise* 17, No. 5 (December 1986):37

The Power of the Press. *Black Enterprise* 17, No. 3 (October 1986):33

The Real Road to Success. *Black Enterprise* 16, No. 11 (June 1986):66

A Window of Opportunity. *Black Enterprise* 16, No. 10 (May 1986):29

The Young Tycoons. *Black Enterprise* 16, No. 6 (January 1986):44–47

Gladwin, Harold Sterling (about)

Men Out of Asia: A Review and Update of the Gladwin Thesis. Notes. Reviewed by Runoko Rashidi. *Journal of African Civilizations* 8, No. 2 (December 1986):248–263

Glascoe, Myrtle G.

Avery Research Center Sponsors First Major Conference. *SAGE* 3, No. 1 (Spring 1986):67

Glasgow, Douglas G.

A Brief Prescription for a Proactive Socioeconomic Agenda. Editorial. *Urban League Review* 10, No. 2 (Winter 1986–87):3–5

A Brief Prescription for a Proactive Socioeconomic Agenda. *Urban League Review* 10, No. 2 (Winter 1986–87):3–5

Glover, Danny (about)

Danny Glover: The Reluctant Movie Star. Aldore Collier. *Ebony* 41, No. 5 (March 1986):82

Goddard, Angela

Turning Fun into Fortune. *Black Enterprise* 16, No. 7 (February 1986):72–76

Goddard, Lawford (joint author)

See Nobles, Wade W.

Goertz, Margaret E. (joint author)

See Anrig, Gregory R.

Golden, Marita

A Woman's Place. *Essence* 17, No. 4 (August 1986):88

Goldfarb, Russell M.

Rosamond Vincy of *Middlemarch*. Notes. *CLA Journal* 30, No. 1 (September 1986):83–99

Goldstein, Erwin (joint author)

See Smith, James H.

Gomez, Jewelle

Black Women Heroes: Here's Reality, Where's the Fiction? *Black Scholar* 17, No. 2 (March-April 1986):8–13

Gooch, Cheryl R.

Cultural Awareness through Educational Exchange. *Black Collegian* 16, No. 3 (January/February 1986):104–106

Good and Evil

The Devil and Dr. Church: A Guide to Hell for Atheists and True Believers. By F. Forrester Church. Reviewed by Kortright Davis. *Journal of Religious Thought* 43, No. 2 (Fall-Winter 1986–87):91

Goodman, Jan M.

Issues in American History: The Worker in America. Book review. *Interracial Books for Children Bulletin* 17, No. 2 (1986):13

Gordimer, Nadine (about)

Nadine Gordimer: Politics and the Order of Art. Reviewed by Sheila Roberts. *Research in African Literatures* 17, No. 3 (Fall 1986): 408–411

Gordimer, Nadine—Criticism and Interpretation

Nadine Gordimer's "A Chip of Glass Ruby": A Commentary on Apartheid Society. Evelyn Schroth. *Journal of Black Studies* 17, No. 1 (September 1986):85–90

The Short Fiction of Nadine Gordimer. Notes. Martin Trump. *Research in African Literatures* 17, No. 3 (Fall 1986): 341–369

Gordon, Karen Elizabeth

The Transitive Vampire: A Handbook of Grammar for the Innocent, the Eager and the Damned. Reviewed by Elizabeth J. Higgins. *CLA Journal* 30, No. 2 (December 1986):252–253

Gordon, Paul

The Ideology of the New Right. Book review. *Race and Class* 28, No. 1 (Summer 1986):95–97

Race and Labour in Twentieth Century Britain. Book review. *Race and Class* 28, No. 2 (August 1986):102–103

Gordon, Paul, and Reilly, Danny

Guestworkers of the Sea: Racism in British Shipping. *Race and Class* 28, No. 2 (August 1986):73–82

Gordon, Paul (joint editor)

See Scraton, Phil

Goree

Goree. Shelley Moore. *Crisis* 93, No. 6 (June/July 1986):18

Gorman, G. E.

A Bibliography of Criticism of Southern African Literature in English. Book review. *Research in African Literatures* 17, No. 3 (Fall 1986): 419–421

Goslinga, Marian (compiler)

Recent Books on the Region and its Peoples. Bibliography. *Caribbean Review* 15, No. 1 (Winter 1986):45–48

Recent Books on the Region and its Peoples.
Bibliography. *Caribbean Review* 15, No. 2 (Spring
1986):49–52

Gotech Inc.

The Real Road to Success. Lloyd Gite. *Black
Enterprise* 16, No. 11 (June 1986):66

Government and Politics—Africa

A Comparative Study of Zambia and
Mozambique: Africanization, Professionalization,
and Bureaucracy in the African Postcolonial State.
Mokubung O. Nkomo. *Journal of Black Studies* 16,
No. 3 (March 1986):319–342

Government Regulation of Commerce

Regulatory Policy and Minority Concerns: The
Impact of Changes in Telecommunications Policy.
Georgia A. Persons. *Urban League Review* 10, No.
2 (Winter 1986–87):45–62

Governors

Great Moments in Black History: The First Black
Governor. Lerone Bennett, Jr. *Ebony* 42, No. 1
(November 1986):116

Gradwohl, David M., and Osborn, Nancy M.

Exploring Buried Buxton: Archeology of an
Abandoned Iowa Coal Mining Town with a Large
Black Population. Book review. *Afro-Americans in
New York Life and History* 10, No. 2 (July 1986):
65–68

Grafton, Michael E.

Are You Still My Mother? Book review.
Interracial Books for Children Bulletin 17, Nos. 3–4
(1986):38

What If They Saw Me Now? Book review.
Interracial Books for Children Bulletin 17, No. 2
(1986):17

Graham, Maryemma

Mississippi's Native Son: An International
Symposium on Richard Wright (1908–1960).
SAGE 3, No. 1 (Spring 1986):66

**Grambling State University
(Louisiana)—Curricula**

Teacher Education at Grambling State University:
A Move Toward Excellence. Thelma L. Spencer.
Journal of Negro Education 55, No.3 (Summer
1986):293–303

Gramm-Rudman-Hollings Act

Gramm-Rudman and Black Education. Gerald D.
Jaynes. *Black Enterprise* 16, No. 10 (May 1986):39

Gramm-Rudman and the Politics of Deficit
Reduction. Linda F. Williams. *Urban League
Review* 10, No. 2 (Winter 1986–87):72–83

Grandsaigne, J. de (editor)

African Short Stories in English: An Anthology.
Reviewed by Adewale Maja-Pearce. *Research in
African Literatures* 17, No. 4 (Winter 1986):
620–622

Grant, Carl A., and Grant, Gloria W.

Increasing the Educational Opportunities of Black
Students by Training Teachers in Multicultural
Curriculum Development. *Western Journal of
Black Studies* 10, No. 1 (Spring 1986):29–33

Grant, Gloria W. (joint author)

See Grant, Carl A.

Grant, Paul

Faith in the City: A Call for Action by Church
and Nation. Book review. *Race and Class* 27, No.
4 (Spring 1986):97–98

Grant, Winifred (about)

Moving Forward in Stationery. Margo Walker.
Black Enterprise 16, No. 11 (June 1986):66

Grant's Office Supplies Inc.

See Grant, Winifred

Graves, Anne Adams (joint editor)

See Davies, Carole Boyce

Gray, Fred D. (Jr.)

Jurisdiction of the Landlord and Tenant Branch of
the Superior Court of the District of Columbia.
Howard Law Journal 29, No. 1 (1986):137–147

Gray, Fred D. (Jr.) (about)

Civil Rights Lawyers Revisited. *Ebony* 42, No. 2
(December 1986):76

Gray, Lorene E.

Life after Rape. *Essence* 17, No. 5 (September
1986):68

Gray, Nigel

The Worst of Times: An Oral History of the
Great Depression in Britain. Book review.
Graham Murray. *Race and Class* 27, No. 4 (Spring
1986):103–104

Gray, Stephen

Athol Fugard. Book review. *Research in African
Literatures* 17, No. 2 (Summer 1986): 281–284

Douglas Blackburn. Reviewed by Michael
Chapman. *Research in African Literatures* 17, No.
3 (Fall 1986): 406–408

An Interview with Doris Lessing. *Research in
African Literatures* 17, No. 3 (Fall 1986): 329–340

Gray, William H. (about)

Gray Tours South Africa. Dewayne Wickham.
Black Enterprise 16, No. 9 (April 1986):20

Shades of Gray. David C. Ruffin. *Black Enterprise* 16, No. 8 (March 1986):28–33

Great Britain—Colonies

Application of Memmi's Theory of the Colonizer and the Colonized to the Conflicts in Zimbabwe. Dickson A. Mungazi. *Journal of Negro Education* 55, No.4 (Fall 1986):518–534

Slave Populations of the British Caribbean 1807–1834. By B. W. Higman. Reviewed by Bonham C. Richardson. *Caribbean Review* 15, No. 2 (Spring 1986):46

Great Britain—History

The Black Abolitionists Papers. Volume I: The British Isles, 1830–1865. C. Peter Ripley, editor. Reviewed by Alexa Benson Henderson. *Phylon* 47, No. 2 (June 1986):168–169

Literature and Imperialism. Bart Moore-Gilbert, editor. Reviewed by Robert D. Hamner. *Research in African Literatures* 17, No. 1 (Spring 1986): 162–165

On Living in an Old Country: The National Past in Contemporary Britain. By Patrick Wright. Reviewed by Nancy Murray. *Race and Class* 28, No. 1 (Summer 1986):93–95

Great Britain—Indians

Ayahs, Lascars and Princes: Indians in Britain 1700–1947. By Rozina Visram. Reviewed by Angela Sherlock. *Race and Class* 28, No. 2 (August 1986):106–107

Great Britain—Legal System

Causes for Concern: British Criminal Justice on Trial? Edited by Phil Scraton and Paul Gordon. Reviewed by Busi Chaane. *Race and Class* 28, No. 1 (Summer 1986):103–107

Great Britain—Race Relations

Anti-Racists and Other Demons: The Press and Ideology in Thatcher's Britain. Nancy Murray. *Race and Class* 27, No. 3 (Winter 1986):1–19

Beyond Accountability: Labour and Policing after the 1985 Rebellions. Lee Bridges. *Race and Class* 27, No. 4 (Spring 1986):78–85

Black Politics and Urban Crisis in Britain. By Brian D. Jacobs. Reviewed by Lee Bridges. *Race and Class* 28, No. 2 (August 1986):99–102

Britain's Gulags. A. Sivanandan. *Race and Class* 27, No. 3 (Winter 1986):81–85

"Diverse Reports" and the Meaning of "Racism." Kenneth Leech. *Race and Class* 28, No. 2 (August 1986):82–88

Guestworkers of the Sea: Racism in British Shipping. Paul Gordon and Danny Reilly. *Race and Class* 28, No. 2 (August 1986):73–82

The Local Politics of Race. By Gideon Ben-Tovim and others. Reviewed by Lee Bridges. *Race and Class* 28, No. 2 (August 1986):99–102

Race and Labour in Twentieth Century Britain. Edited by Kenneth Lunn. Reviewed by Paul Gordon. *Race and Class* 28, No. 2 (August 1986):102–103

Racism in the Arts in Britain. *Race and Class* 28, No. 1 (Summer 1986):73–76

Reporting the "riots." Nancy Murray. *Race and Class* 27, No. 3 (Winter 1986):86–90

The Struggle for Black Arts in Britain. A. Sivanandan. *Race and Class* 28, No. 1 (Summer 1986):76–79

Greek Letter Societies

The Power Concept of Alpha Kappa Alpha Sorority. Carolyne S. Blount. *About Time* 14, No. 6 (June 1986):18–19

Green, Charles

The Professional Ideology and Grassroots Community Organizations: New York's South Bronx Community in Perspective. Notes. *Afro-Americans in New York Life and History* 10, No. 2 (July 1986): 29–44

Green, Charles, and Wilson, Basil

The African-American Intellectual and the Struggle for Black Empowerment. *Western Journal of Black Studies* 10, No. 2 (Summer 1986):59–69

Green, Constance M.

Great Expectations: How to Read Your Boss' Mind and Become a Star Performer. *Black Enterprise* 16, No. 8 (March 1986):41–42

Landing That Job. *Black Enterprise* 16, No. 7 (February 1986):121–126

Steel Artistry in Trinidad. *Black Enterprise* 17, No. 3 (October 1986):119

Vieques: Puerto Rico's Hideaway. *Black Enterprise* 16, No. 10 (May 1986):78

Working Smart! *Black Enterprise* 16, No. 11 (June 1986):277

Green, Geraldine Clark

God Bless the Children. Poem. *About Time* 14, No. 11 (November 1986):15

Heaven. Poem. *About Time* 14, No. 11 (November 1986):15

I Am the King of This Castle. Poem. *About Time* 14, No. 11 (November 1986):15

Were Only Men Created after God's Image. *About Time* 14, No. 11 (November 1986):15

Green, Jeffrey, and McGilchrist, Paul

Samuel Coleridge-Taylor: A Postscript. *Black Perspective in Music* 14, No. 3 (Fall 1986):259–266

Green, Kerry

Career Stop-Outs: A Leave of Absence Can Be a Smart Move If You Plan Carefully. *Essence* 17, No. 7 (November 1986):123

Green, Leonard

Sterling A. Brown: Building the Black Aesthetic Tradition. Book review. *Black American Literature Forum* 20, No. 3 (Fall 1986):327–334

Green, Lil (about)

Chicago 1940–1947. Record review. Lewis Porter. *Black Perspective in Music* 14, No. 3 (Fall 1986):318–319

Green, Rudolph V.

A Learning Skills and Counseling Model for Developing Countries. *Journal of Negro Education* 55, No.2 (Spring 1986):214–221

Green, Vera Mae (about)

African-American Soul Force: Dance, Music and Vera Mae Green. A. Lynn Bolles. *SAGE* 3, No. 2 (Fall 1986):32–34

Greene, Cheryll Y.

Angela Davis: Talking Tough. Interview. *Essence* 17, No. 4 (August 1986):62

Greene, Graham

Getting to Know the General, The Story of an Involvement. Reviewed by Neale Pearson. *Caribbean Review* 15, No. 1 (Winter 1986):26–27 +

Greene, Jimmy James (about)

Jimmy James Greene. Illustrated. *Black Collegian* 17, No. 2 (November/December 1986):72–73

Greenfield, Eloise

African American Literature: A New Challenge. *Interracial Books for Children Bulletin* 17, No. 2 (1986):4–5

Greenwood, Monique

Status Symbols. *Black Enterprise* 16, No. 10 (May 1986):63

Gregg, Elaine

Martin Luther King, Jr.: To the Mountaintop. Book review. *Black Enterprise* 16, No. 6 (January 1986):18

Part-Time Payoff of Direct Sales. *Black Enterprise* 16, No. 10 (May 1986):58

Grenada

Grenada: The Hour Will Strike Again. By Jan Carew. Reviewed by Cameron McCarthy. *Race and Class* 28, No. 2 (August 1986):89–91

Grenada—American Invasion, 1983—Fiction

Grenadian Party Papers: Revealing an Imaginary Document. Short Story. Jorge I. Dominguez. *Caribbean Review* 15, No. 2 (Spring 1986):16–20

Report Redux: Thoughts on the Imaginary Document. Short Story. Nelson P. Valdes. *Caribbean Review* 15, No. 2 (Spring 1986):21–23

Grenada—History

Free Colored in the Slave Societies of St. Kitts and Grenada, 1763–1833. By Edward L. Cox. Reviewed by Keith C. Simmonds. *Phylon* 47, No. 4 (December 1986):327–328

Grensing, Lin

Tips for Effective Delegation. *About Time* 14, No. 8 (August 1986):32–33

Gridley, Mark C.

Jazz Styles: History and Analysis. Book review. George L. Starks, Jr. *Black Perspective in Music* 14, No. 2 (Spring 1986):188–189

Griffith, Ivelaw L.

Law and the Political Environment in Guyana. Book review. *Black Scholar* 17, No. 3 (May-June 1986):58

Griffiths, Gareth

The History and Historiography of Commonwealth Literature. Book review. *Research in African Literatures* 17, No. 3 (Fall 1986): 433–435

Griggs, Sutton E. (about)

Saving the Day: The Recordings of Reverend Sutton E. Griggs. Steven C. Tracy. *Phylon* 47, No. 2 (June 1986):159–166

Grigsby, Brandford and Company, Inc.

See Grigsby, Calvin

Grigsby, Calvin (about)

Money Merchants. Candice Caruthers. *Black Enterprise* 17, No. 1 (August 1986):61–63

Grimes, Nikki

Fields in Bloom. *Essence* 17, No. 4 (August 1986):84

Grofman, Bernard, and others

Effects of Multimember Districts on Black Representation in State Legislatures. *Review of Black Political Economy* 14, No. 4 (Spring 1986):65–78

Grooming

See Personal Appearance

Gross, Bertram

See Henry, Charles P.

Grossman, Zoltan

Inside the Philippine Resistance. *Race and Class* 28, No. 2 (August 1986):1–29

Group Insurance Administration

Management of Policy Benefits. Margo Walker. *Black Enterprise* 16, No. 11 (June 1986):65

Grubb, Henry J.

The Black Prole and Whitespeak: Black English from an Orwellian Perspective. *Race and Class* 27, No. 3 (Winter 1986):67–80

Gudmundson, Lowell

Mexico: A History. Book review. *Caribbean Review* 15, No. 1 (Winter 1986):43

Guernsey, JoAnn Bren

Journey to Almost There. Book review. Betty Bacon. *Interracial Books for Children Bulletin* 17, No. 2 (1986):18

Guerrilla Warfare

Inside the Philippine Resistance. Zoltan Grossman. *Race and Class* 28, No. 2 (August 1986):1–29

Witness to War: An American Doctor in El Salvador. By Charles Clements, M.D. Reviewed by Neale Pearson. *Caribbean Review* 15, No. 2 (Spring 1986):47–48

See also Revolutionaries

Guess, Jerry M.

Tribute to James Brown, Jr., Fighter for Justice. *Crisis* 93, No. 5 (May 1986):32–33

Guess, Jerry M. (joint author)

See Lawrence, Michael A.

Guidance and Counseling—Dissertations and Theses

Master's Theses in Progress in Selected Colleges and Universities. Mac A. Stewart. *Negro Educational Review* 37, Nos. 3–4 (July-October 1986):100

Guillaume, Bernice F.

Character Names in *Indian Trails* by Olivia Ward Bush (Banks): Clues to Afro Assimilation Into Long Island's Native Americans. Notes. *Afro-Americans in New York Life and History* 10, No. 2 (July 1986): 45–53

Guillaume, Rhaoul (about)

The Real Road to Success. Lloyd Gite. *Black Enterprise* 16, No. 11 (June 1986):66

Gunner, Elizabeth

A Handbook for Teaching African Literature. Reviewed by Anne Walmsley. *Research in African Literatures* 17, No. 1 (Spring 1986): 149–153

Gupta, Udayan

Act I: How to Write a Business Plan. *Black Enterprise* 16, No. 7 (February 1986):135–138

Gurnah, Ahmed

Race, Power and Resistance. Book review. *Race and Class* 28, No. 1 (Summer 1986):99–103

Guthrie, Carlton and Michael (about)

The Trumark of Excellence. Trudy Gallant. *Black Enterprise* 17, No. 1 (August 1986):39

Guyana—Law and Politics

Law and the Political Environment in Guyana. By Randolph W. James and Harold A. Lutchman. Reviewed by Ivelaw L. Griffith. *Black Scholar* 17, No. 3 (May-June 1986):58

Guyana Massacre

See Jonestown (Guyana) Massacre, 1978

Guyonneau, Christine H.

Francophone Women Writers from Sub-Saharan Africa, Bibliography. *Callaloo* 9, No. 2 (Spring 1986):404–431

Francophone Women Writers from Sub-Saharan Africa and Its Diaspora. *Callaloo* 9, No. 4 (Fall 1986):694–736

Guyonneau, Christine H. (joint compiler)

See Mayes, Janis A.

Gwartney-Gibbs, Patricia A., and Taylor, Patricia A.

Black Women Workers' Earnings Progress in Three Industrial Sectors, 1970–1980. *SAGE* 3, No. 1 (Spring 1986):20–25

Gyimah-Brempong, Kasabena

Empirical Models of Criminal Behavior: How Significant a Factor Is Race? *Review of Black Political Economy* 15, No. 1 (Summer 1986):27–43

Habit

How to Kick Your Bad Habits. Frank White III. *Ebony* 41, No. 11 (September 1986):86

Hair Care Industry

Beauty Secret for Success. Solomon J. Herbert. *Black Enterprise* 16, No. 12 (July 1986):21

Hairston, Deborah W.

There's No Place Like Home. *Black Enterprise* 17, No. 3 (October 1986):99

Haiti—History—American Occupation, 1915-1934

The NAACP and the American Occupation of Haiti. Leon D. Pamphile. *Phylon* 47, No. 1 (March 1986):91–100

Haiti—Literature

Essays on Haitian Literature. By Leon-Francois Hoffmann. Reviewed by Maurice A. Lubin. *Research in African Literatures* 17, No. 4 (Winter 1986): 593–595

Images et mythes d'Haiti. By Daniel-Henry Pageaux. Reviewed by Clarisse Zimra. *Research in African Literatures* 17, No. 4 (Winter 1986): 591–593

So Spoke the Uncle. By Jean Price-Mars. Reviewed by Michel-Rolph Trouillot. *Research in African Literatures* 17, No. 4 (Winter 1986): 596–597

Haiti—Politics and Government

No Dock for "Baby Doc." Kenneth Maurice Jones. *Black Enterprise* 16, No. 10 (May 1986):17

Hakutani, Yoshinobu, and Kiuchi, Toru

The Critical Reception of Richard Wright in Japan: An Annotated Bibliography. *Black American Literature Forum* 20, Nos. 1–2 (Spring/Summer 1986):27–61

Hale, Clara (Mother) (about)

Clara (Mother) Hale: Healing Baby "Junkies" with Love. Herschel Johnson. *Ebony* 41, No. 7 (May 1986):58

Hale, Gene (about)

Moving Up with Heavy Equipment. Solomon Herbert. *Black Enterprise* 16, No. 10 (May 1986):29

Hale, Percy (about)

Cashing in on Chips. Lloyd Gite. *Black Enterprise* 16, No. 12 (July 1986):14

Hale House

See Hale, Clara (Mother)

Haley, Alex

We Must Honor Our Ancestors. *Ebony* 41, No. 10 (August 1986):134

Hall, Barbara

Blacks in America: A Photographic Record. Illustrated. *About Time* 14, No. 1 (January 1986):14–15

Hall, Edmond (about)

Edmond Hall. Rompin' in '44. Record review. Lewis Porter. *Black Perspective in Music* 14, No. 3 (Fall 1986):317–318

Hall, Ronald E.

Myth of the Black Male Shortage. *Black Collegian* 17, No. 2 (November/December 1986):16–18

Hall, Samuel M.

The Placement Office Can Help You Launch Your Career. *Black Collegian* 17, No. 1 (September/October 1986):108–112

Hall, Shelly L.

When Earth Comes to Water. Poem. *Callaloo* 9, No. 1 (Winter 1986):71

Hall, T. William, and others

Religion: An Introduction. Reviewed by Kortright Davis. *Journal of Religious Thought* 43, No. 2 (Fall-Winter 1986–87):92

Halperin, John

The Life of Jane Austen. Reviewed by Louis D. Mitchell. *CLA Journal* 30, No. 1 (September 1986):104–106

Hamer, Alice (about)

Historian with a Mission. Lloyd Gite. *Black Enterprise* 17, No. 1 (August 1986):57

Hamilton, Edwin

Can the School System Produce Its Own Leaders? *Negro Educational Review* 37, No. 2 (April 1986):81–87

Illiterate America. Book review. *Journal of Negro Education* 55, No. 1 (Winter 1986):117–118

Hamilton, Russell G.

Literature Africana Literature Necessaria, II—Moçambique, Cabo Verde, Guiné-Bissau, Sao Tomé e Principe. Reviewed by Gerald Moser. *Research in African Literatures* 17, No. 3 (Fall 1986):422–425

Sobre Literatura Moçambicana. Book review. *Research in African Literatures* 17, No. 3 (Fall 1986): 422–425

Hamilton, Stephanie Renfrow

Are You Blue? How to Beat Depression. *Essence* 17, No. 6 (October 1986):66

Hamilton, Virginia

Junius Over Far. Book review. Daphne Muse. *Interracial Books for Children Bulletin* 17, Nos. 3–4 (1986):34

Hammond, James

The Gift of Administration. Book review. *Journal of Religious Thought* 43, No. 1 (Spring-Summer 1986):128–129

Hamner, Robert D.

Conrad and Imperialism: Ideological Boundaries and Visionary Frontiers. Book review. *Research in African Literatures* 17, No. 1 (Spring 1986): 158–162

Literature and Imperialism. Book review. *Research in African Literatures* 17, No. 1 (Spring 1986): 162–165

Handcraft

Partners in Craft. Dan Giles Salter. *Essence* 16, No. 11 (March 1986):16

Handicapped

Bonnie St. John: A Profile in Beauty, Brains, and Courage. Aldore Collier. *Ebony* 42, No. 1 (November 1986):134

Including All of Us: An Early Childhood Curriculum about Disability. By Merle Froschl and others. Reviewed by Emily Strauss Watson. *Interracial Books for Children Bulletin* 17, Nos. 3–4 (1986):37–38

Where There's a Will: Bonnie's Story. Bill Rhoden. *Essence* 17, No. 1 (May 1986):82

Handicapped—Home Care

Strategies for Interacting with Black Parents of Handicapped Children. Marion Gillis-Olion and others. *Negro Educational Review* 37, No. 1 (January 1986):8–16

Hankins, Grover G.

Legal Comments. *Crisis* 93, No. 5 (May 1986):34–35

Legal Comments: Discrimination in Housing. *Crisis* 93, No. 8 (October 1986):42–43

Legal Comments: Peremptory Challenge. *Crisis* 93, No. 7 (August/September 1986):44–45

Legal Comments: South African Economic Conditions. *Crisis* 93, No. 9 (November 1986):46–48

Legal Comments: United States Supreme Court. *Crisis* 93, No. 10 (December 1986):30

Hanson, Ken (about)

Turning Fun into Fortune. *Black Enterprise* 16, No. 7 (February 1986):79–87

Hanson, Marjorie

Gleanings from the Desegregation Research. Essay Review. *Journal of Negro Education* 55, No. 1 (Winter 1986):107–115

Hardee, John

See Quebec, Ike

Hare, Nathan (about)

Dr. Nathan Hare. Gregory Pete. *Crisis* 93, No. 3 (March 1986):30–46

Haring, Lee

Malagasy Tale Index. Reviewed by Daniel J. Crowley. *Research in African Literatures* 17, No. 2 (Summer 1986): 308–309

Harlem—History

The Consolidated Tenants League of Harlem: Black Self-Help vs. White, Liberal Intervention in Ghetto Housing, 1934–1944. Joel Schwartz. *Afro-Americans in New York Life and History* 10, No.1 (January 1986):31–51

Harlem—Renaissance

Countee Cullen. By Alan R. Shucard. Reviewed by Jay R. Berry. *CLA Journal* 29, No. 3 (March 1986):372–377

Marcus Garvey and the Harlem Renaissance. Notes. John Runcie. *Afro-Americans in New York Life and History* 10, No. 2 (July 1986): 7–28

Rereading *Banjo*: Claude McKay and the French Connection. Notes. Robert P. Smith (Jr.) *CLA Journal* 30, No. 1 (September 1986):46–58

The Sage in Harlem: H. L. Mencken and the Black Writers of the 1920s. By Charles Scruggs. Reviewed by John Edgar Tidwell. *Black American Literature Forum* 20, No. 3 (Fall 1986):341–344

Harlow, Barbara

Nostalgia for the Present: An Anthology of Writings. Book review. *Black American Literature Forum* 20, No. 3 (Fall 1986):317–326

Palestine and Modern Arab Poetry. Book review. *Race and Class* 27, No. 3 (Winter 1986):102–103

Harper, Janice A. (joint author)

See Steppe-Jones, Cecilia

Harper, Michael S.

Arthritis Dance. Poem. *Callaloo* 9, No. 1 (Winter 1986):75

Fanny's Kitchen. Poem. *Callaloo* 9, No. 2 (Spring 1986):324–325

A Father's Song. Poem. *Callaloo* 9, No. 1 (Winter 1986):72

Free Association: Some Practical Symbols. Poem. *Callaloo* 9, No. 2 (Spring 1986):328–330

Hinton's Silkscreens. Poem. *Callaloo* 9, No. 2 (Spring 1986):326–327

Loyalty. Poem. *Callaloo* 9, No. 1 (Winter 1986):73–74

Harper, Michael S.—Criticism and Interpretation

Their Long Scars Touch Ours. Joseph A. Brown. *Callaloo* 9, No. 1 (Winter 1986):209–220

Harper, Robert Berkley

Controlling and Regulating Handguns—A Way to Save Black Lives. *Black Law Journal* 9, No. 3 (Winter 1986):229–251

Harrell, Jules P. (joint author)

See Singleton, Edward G.

Harris, Christy E.

The Duty of a Modern Landlord and Tenant to Protect His Tenants from Crime. *Howard Law Journal* 29, No. 1 (1986):149–163

Harris, Elizabeth (about)

Queen of Arts. Fatima Shaik. *Essence* 17, No. 2 (July 1986):15

Harris, Jessica B.

Evaluating Your Course Load. *Black Enterprise* 16, No. 7 (February 1986):103–104

India's Jewels: Delhi City and the State of Rajasthan. *Black Enterprise* 17, No. 1 (August 1986):65

Wild, Wet and Wonderful. *Black Enterprise* 16, No. 10 (May 1986):86

Harris, Jessica B. (about)

Turning Fun into Fortune. *Black Enterprise* 16, No. 7 (February 1986):79–87

Harris, Norman

Blacks in Vietnam: A Holistic Perspective through Fiction and Journalism. *Western Journal of Black Studies* 10, No. 3 (Fall 1986):121–131

The Black Universe in Contemporary Afro-American Fiction. Notes. *CLA Journal* 30, No. 1 (September 1986):1–13

Harris, Ron

What Do Men Want in Bed? *Essence* 17, No. 7 (November 1986):59

Harris, Virgil L. (about)

Insurance Company of the Year: Premium Profits. Nathan McCall. *Black Enterprise* 16, No. 11 (June 1986):182

Harris Brown Gallery

Queen of Arts. Fatima Shaik. *Essence* 17, No. 2 (July 1986):15

Harrison, Donald, and Blanchard, Terence

Nascence. Record review. Norman Riley. *Crisis* 93, No. 9 (November 1986):9

Harvey, Louis-Charles

Black Gospel Music and Black Theology. Notes. *Journal of Religious Thought* 43, No. 2 (Fall-Winter 1986-87):19–37

Harvey, William R. (about)

Harvey Buys Pepsi Plant. Gordon Borrell. *Black Enterprise* 16, No. 11 (June 1986):48

Hass, John Edward (editor)

Ragtime: Its History, Composers, and Music. Book review. George L. Starks, Jr. *Black Perspective in Music* 14, No. 3 (Fall 1986):313–314

Hassinger, Maren (about)

Maren Hassinger. Illustrated. Watson Hines. *International Review of African American Art* 7, No. 2 (1986):60–63

Hatchett, David

A Conflict of Reasons and Remedies. *Crisis* 93, No. 3 (March 1986):36–47

Is There a Black Foreign Policy? *Crisis* 93, No. 9 (November 1986):14–19

Parren Mitchell: Interview. *Crisis* 93, No. 2 (February 1986):34

The Push for Economic Development. *Crisis* 93, No. 5 (May 1986):17–40

Seeking Power beyond Their Numbers. *Crisis* 93, No. 7 (August/September 1986):16

Havill, Juanita

Jamaica's Find. Book review. Judy Rogers. *Interracial Books for Children Bulletin* 17, Nos. 3–4 (1986):35

Hawkins, Augustus F.

Whatever Happened to Full Employment? *Urban League Review* 10, No. 1 (Summer 1986):9–12

Hawkins, Hunt

Aimé Césaire's Lesson about Decolonization in *La Tragédie de Roi Christophe*. Notes. *CLA Journal* 30, No. 2 (December 1986):144–153

Hawthorne, Nathaniel—Criticism and Interpretation

Hawthorne's Beatrice Rappaccini: Unlocking her Paradoxical Nature with a Shelleyean Key. Notes. Martin F. Kearney. *CLA Journal* 29, No. 3 (March 1986):309–317

Hayden, Robert—Criticism and Interpretation

Changing Permanences. Vera M. Kutzinski. *Callaloo* 9, No. 1 (Winter 1986):171–183

Hayes, Charles A.

The Income and Jobs Action Bill: A Mandate for Full Employment. *Urban League Review* 10, No. 1 (Summer 1986):61–65

Hayes, Dianne

The MBA is Still a Hot Item. *Black Collegian* 17, No. 2 (November/December 1986):81–85

Hayes, Janice

School Discipline and Your Child. *Essence* 17, No. 6 (October 1986):104

Haynes, John

Okigbo's Technique in "Distances I." Notes. Bibliography. *Research in African Literatures* 17, No. 1 (Spring 1986): 73–84

Hazardous Wastes

See Pollution

Hazelton, Lynette

Fighting Fraud. *Black Enterprise* 17, No. 4 (November 1986):22

Money Saved Is Money Earned. *Black Enterprise* 16, No. 8 (March 1986):56

Head, Bessie (about)

Bessie Head in Gaborone, Botswana: An Interview. Linda Susan Beard. *SAGE* 3, No. 2 (Fall 1986):44–47

Feminist Perspectives in African Fiction: Bessie Head and Buchi Emecheta. Nancy Topping Bazin. *Black Scholar* 17, No. 2 (March-April 1986):34–40

Headley, Bernard D.

A Review of Urban Life in Kingston, Jamaica. Book review. *Caribbean Review* 15, No. 1 (Winter 1986):42

Health

The Politics of Pollution: Implications for the Black Community. Robert D. Bullard and Beverly Hendrix Wright. *Phylon* 47, No. 1 (March 1986):71–78

Health Care

Did Fidel Fudge the Figures? Literacy and Health: The Cuban Model. Nicholas Eberstadt. *Caribbean Review* 15, No. 2 (Spring 1986):5–7 +

Health Policy and the Black Aged. Nelson McGhee, Jr., and others. *Urban League Review* 10, No. 2 (Winter 1986–87):63–71

How to Deal with Ten Serious Health Problems. Alex Poinsett. *Ebony* 41, No. 5 (March 1986):144

How to Figure Out Cuba: Development, Ideology and Mortality. Sergio Diaz-Briquets. *Caribbean Review* 15, No. 2 (Spring 1986):8–11 +

Taking Responsibility for Our Health Care. Editorial. Carolyne S. Blount. *About Time* 14, No. 4 (April 1986):4

Witness to War: An American Doctor in El Salvador. By Charles Clements, M.D. Reviewed by Neale Pearson. *Caribbean Review* 15, No. 2 (Spring 1986):47–48

See also Preventive Medicine

Health Care, Preventive

Hypertension: Shriners Join Fight against the "Silent Killer." *Ebony* 42, No. 1 (November 1986):128

Health Care—Corporations

Employee Health Can Spell Profits for U.S. Corporations. Donna Horton. *About Time* 14, No. 8 (August 1986):14

Health Care—Costs

Reducing Costs with Health Care. Marsha Jones. *About Time* 14, No. 4 (April 1986):12–13

Health Care—Education

Saving Lives through Public Education. Kelly Papa. *About Time* 14, No. 6 (June 1986):21

Health Care Facilities

Cook County's Top Doctor: Dr. Agnes Lattimer Is the Only Black Woman to Head One of the Nation's Largest Hospitals. Charles Whitaker. *Ebony* 41, No. 11 (September 1986):44

Health Care Professionals

Historian with a Mission. Lloyd Gite. *Black Enterprise* 17, No. 1 (August 1986):57

Health Maintenance Organizations

More Health and Wealth. Joyce Davis Adams. *Black Enterprise* 16, No. 10 (May 1986):20

Health Policy

Dumping Health Care for Poor Americans. David C. Ruffin. *Black Enterprise* 16, No. 9 (April 1986):29

Health Policy and the Black Aged. Wilbur H. Watson and others. *Urban League Review* 10, No. 2 (Winter 1986–87):63–71

Health-Reach

More Health and Wealth. Joyce Davis Adams. *Black Enterprise* 16, No. 10 (May 1986):20

Health Services Industry

Entrepreneurial Surgeon: Dr. Ernest Bates Nurses Ailing Firm to Fiscal Health. Mark McNamara. *Ebony* 41, No. 6 (April 1986):84

Hearn, Oscar (Jr.) (about)

Florida Man Sheds 197 Pounds to Become Body-Building Champ. *Ebony* 42, No. 2 (December 1986):86

Hedgley, David R. (Jr.) (about)

NASA Computer Whiz: Doing It His Way, Maverick Mathematician David R. Hedgley (Jr.), Comes Up with the Right Answers. *Ebony* 41, No. 5 (March 1986):62

Heggoy, Alf Andrew (editor)

Through Foreign Eyes: Western Attitudes toward North Africa. Reviewed by Aouicha E. Hilliard. *Research in African Literatures* 17, No. 4 (Winter 1986): 584–587

Height, Dorothy Irene (about)

Dr. Dorothy Irene Height: Motivating the Strengths of Black Women. Adolph Dupree. *About Time* 14, No. 6 (June 1986):8–23

Heilbut, Anthony

The Gospel Sound. Good News and Bad Times. Book review. André Prévos. *Black Perspective in Music* 14, No. 2 (Spring 1986):191

Heintze, M. R.

Private Black Colleges in Texas: 1865–1954. Reviewed by Antoine M. Garibaldi. *Journal of Negro Education* 55, No.2 (Spring 1986):239–240

Hell

The Devil and Dr. Church: A Guide to Hell for Atheists and True Believers. By F. Forrester Church. Reviewed by Kortright Davis. *Journal of Religious Thought* 43, No. 2 (Fall-Winter 1986–87):91

Hellenbrand, Harold

Speech, after Silence: Alice Walker's *The Third Life of Grange Copeland*. *Black American Literature Forum* 20, Nos. 1–2 (Spring/Summer 1986):113–128

Helms, Ernest E.

Protecting Your Ideas—and Your Money. *Black Enterprise* 17, No. 2 (September 1986):65

Hemodynamics Inc.

Flying High on Medical Tech. Marvin E. Perry. *Black Enterprise* 17, No. 1 (August 1986):19

Hemphill, Essex

The Edge. Poem. *Callaloo* 9, No. 1 (Winter 1986):76–78

The Note. Poem. *Callaloo* 9, No. 2 (Spring 1986):302

Henderson, Alexa Benson

The Black Abolitionists Papers. Volume I: The British Isles, 1830–1865. Book review. *Phylon* 47, No. 2 (June 1986):168–169

Henderson, Shirley O.

Summer Abroad 1987: Test Your "Study Abroad" IQ. *Black Collegian* 17, No. 2 (November/December 1986):59–62

Summer Study in the Caribbean. *Black Collegian* 16, No. 3 (January/February 1986):108–110

Hendriksen, Aage

De uboendige: Om Ibsen—Blixen—hverdagens virkelighed—det ubevidste. Reviewed by Casey Bjerregaard Black. *Research in African Literatures* 17, No. 1 (Spring 1986): 155–158

Hendrix, Wanzo F., and Nelson, William J.

Recruitment: A Significant and Overlooked Component of Black College Survival. *Western Journal of Black Studies* 10, No. 2 (Summer 1986):55–58

Hendryx, Nona (about)

Nona Hendryx Turns on "the Heat." Charles E. Rogers. *Black Collegian* 16, No. 3 (January/February 1986):59–62

Henry, Charles P.

The Menu. Editorial. *Urban League Review* 10, No. 1 (Summer 1986):5–7

A Piece of the Pie. *Crisis* 93, No. 5 (May 1986):20–41

Henry, Charles P., and Gross, Bertram

Redefining Full Employment. *Urban League Review* 10, No. 1 (Summer 1986):13–24

Hen's Teeth Square

Center of Attraction. Donna Mugen. *Black Enterprise* 16, No. 8 (March 1986):17

Herbert, Ritchie (about)

Ritchie Herbert: Photography Major/Hockey Player. J. Roger Dykes. *About Time* 14, No. 5 (May 1986):24–25

Herbert, Solomon J.

Beauty Secret for Success. *Black Enterprise* 16, No. 12 (July 1986):21

Blacks in Energy Meet. *Black Enterprise* 16, No. 11 (June 1986):48

Careers in Orthotics and Prosthetics. *Black Collegian* 16, No. 4 (March/April 1986):94–99

A Meeting of Marketers. *Black Enterprise* 17, No. 2 (September 1986):18

Meeting Planners. *Black Enterprise* 17, No. 1 (August 1986):14

Mortgage Money for Minorities. *Black Enterprise* 17, No. 1 (August 1986):19

Moving Up with Heavy Equipment. *Black Enterprise* 16, No. 10 (May 1986):29

Quality Control over Metal. *Black Enterprise* 17, No. 5 (December 1986):37

The Sure Things: Computer-Related Careers Programmed for Growth. *Black Collegian* 17, No. 2 (November/December 1986):50–55

Heresies, Christian

Heresy in Paradise and the Ghosts of Readers Past. Notes. Michael E. Bauman. *CLA Journal* 30, No. 1 (September 1986):59–68

Heroines in Literature

Rosamond Vincy of *Middlemarch*. Notes. Russell M. Goldfarb. *CLA Journal* 30, No. 1 (September 1986):83–99

Herson, Maurice

African Refugees: Reflections on the African Refugee Problem. Book review. *Race and Class* 27, No. 4 (Spring 1986):104–105

Herzig, Alison Cragin

Shadows on the Pond. Book review. Patricia B. Campbell. *Interracial Books for Children Bulletin* 17, No. 2 (1986):19

Herzog, Jesus Silva

En defensa de Mexico: pensamiento economico politico. Reviewed by Jorge Salazar-Carrillo. *Caribbean Review* 15, No. 2 (Spring 1986):46

Hesse-Biber, Sharlene

The Black Woman Worker: A Minority Group Perspective on Women at Work. *SAGE* 3, No. 1 (Spring 1986):26–34

Hewitt, Mary Jane

Elizabeth Catlett. Illustrated. *International Review of African American Art* 7, No. 2 (1986):26–33

H. H. Roberts Mortuary, Inc.

Legacy of Success: A Young Mortician Inherits Her Father's Dream. Janine C. McAdams. *Essence* 17, No. 4 (August 1986):16

Hickey, Bernard

A Sense of Place: Essays in Post-Colonial Literature. Book review. *Research in African Literatures* 17, No. 3 (Fall 1986): 426–430

Higgins, Elizabeth J.

Charlotte Bronte: The Self Conceived. Book review. *CLA Journal* 29, No. 3 (March 1986):368–371

The Origin of Faulkner's Art. Book review. *CLA Journal* 29, No. 4 (June 1986):490–492

The Transitive Vampire: A Handbook of Grammar for the Innocent, the Eager and the Damned. Book review. *CLA Journal* 30, No. 2 (December 1986):252–253

Vision in Spring. Book review. *CLA Journal* 29, No. 4 (June 1986):490–492

Higginsen, Vy

Mama I Want to Sing. Theater review. Cecilia Loving-Sloane. *Crisis* 93, No. 8 (October 1986):12–13

Highwater, Jamake

The Ceremony of Innocence. Book review. Doris Seale. *Interracial Books for Children Bulletin* 17, No. 1 (1986):6

Higman, B. W.

Slave Populations of the British Caribbean 1807–1834. Reviewed by Bonham C. Richardson. *Caribbean Review* 15, No. 2 (Spring 1986):46

Hill, Donna

First Your Penny. Book review. Emily Strauss Watson. *Interracial Books for Children Bulletin* 17, No. 2 (1986):17–18

Hill, Errol

Drumbeats, Masks, and Metaphor: Contemporary Afro-American Theatre. Book review. *Black American Literature Forum* 20, No. 4 (Winter 1986):459–462

Shakespeare in Sable: A History of Black Shakespearean Actors. Reviewed by Ruth Cowhig. *Research in African Literatures* 17, No. 2 (Summer 1986): 284–287

Hill, Robert B.

Youth Employment and Training Programs: The YEDPA Years. Book review. *Review of Black Political Economy* 15, No. 1 (Summer 1986):107–112

Hill, Tanya Adrienne

Ambiguity in Leases. *Howard Law Journal* 29, No. 1 (1986):63–75

Hilliard, Aouicha E.

Through Foreign Eyes: Western Attitudes toward North Africa. Book review. *Research in African Literatures* 17, No. 4 (Winter 1986): 584–587

Hilliard, Asa G. (III)

The Cultural Unity of Black Africa: The Domains of Patriarchy and of Matriarchy in Classical Antiquity. Bibliography. Book review. *Journal of African Civilizations* 8, No. 1 (June 1986):102–109

From Hurdles to Standards of Quality in Teacher Testing. *Journal of Negro Education* 55, No.3 (Summer 1986):304–315

Hilliard, Sheryl Lee

Black Enterprise Professional Exchange. *Black Enterprise* 17, No. 4 (November 1986):69

Testing Your Financial I. Q. *Black Enterprise* 17, No. 3 (October 1986):105

Hillmon, Betty

In Retrospect: Edmund Thornton Jenkins. *Black Perspective in Music* 14, No. 2 (Spring 1986):143–180

Hinds, Dudley S., and Ordway, Nicholas

The Influence of Race on Rezoning Decisions: Equality of Treatment in Black and White Census Tracts, 1955–1980. *Review of Black Political Economy* 14, No. 4 (Spring 1986):51–63

Hines, Gregory (about)

Gregory Hines: Dancer Wins Stardom as Chicago Vice Cop. *Ebony* 41, No. 12 (October 1986):100

Hines, Watson

Maren Hassinger. Illustrated. *International Review of African American Art* 7, No. 2 (1986):60–63

Mel Edwards. Illustrated. *International Review of African American Art* 7, No. 2 (1986):34–51

Historians

The Changing Perception of C. A. Diop and His Work: The Preeminence of a Scientific Spirit. Notes. James G. Spady. *Journal of African Civilizations* 8, No. 1 (June 1986):89–101

Cheikh Anta Diop and the New Concept of African History. Notes. John Henrik Clarke. *Journal of African Civilizations* 8, No. 1 (June 1986):110–117

Conversations with Diop and Tsegaye: The Nile Valley Revisited. Notes. Jan Carew. *Journal of African Civilizations* 8, No. 1 (June 1986):19–27

Death Shall Not Find Us Thinking That We Die. Notes. Ivan Van Sertima. *Journal of African Civilizations* 8, No. 1 (June 1986):7–16

Further Conversations with the Pharaoh. Interview. Charles S. Finch. *Journal of African Civilizations* 8, No. 1 (June 1986):227–237

Historian with a Mission. Lloyd Gite. *Black Enterprise* 17, No. 1 (August 1986):57

Interview with Cheikh Anta Diop. Interview. Notes. Bibliography. Shawna Moore. *Journal of African Civilizations* 8, No. 1 (June 1986):238–248

Meeting the Pharoah: Conversations with Cheikh Anta Diop. Interview. Charles S. Finch. *Journal of African Civilizations* 8, No. 1 (June 1986):28–34

Men Out of Asia: A Review and Update of the Gladwin Thesis. Notes. By Harold Sterling Gladwin. Reviewed by Runoko Rashidi. *Journal of African Civilizations* 8, No. 2 (December 1986):248–263

The Rhetoric of Miscegenation: Thomas Jefferson, Sally Hemings, and Their Historians. B. R. Burg. *Phylon* 47, No. 2 (June 1986):117–127

History, Afro-American

Roots...Still Working. Sydney H. Gallwey. *About Time* 14, No. 2 (February 1986):14–17

History—Asia

Dr. Diop on Asia: Highlights and Insights. Notes. Runoko Rashidi. *Journal of African Civilizations* 8, No. 1 (June 1986):127–145

History—Oral Tradition

Grassroots Development in Latin America and the Caribbean: Oral Histories of Social Change. By Robert Wasserstrom. Reviewed by Linda Miller. *Caribbean Review* 15, No. 1 (Winter 1986):41–42

Oral-Formulaic Theory and Research: An Introduction and Annotated Bibliography. By John Miles Foley. Reviewed by Dan Ben-Amos. *Research in African Literatures* 17, No. 2 (Summer 1986): 309–310

History—Study and Teaching

Mexico: A History. By Robert Ryal Miller. Reviewed by Lowell Gudmundson. *Caribbean Review* 15, No. 1 (Winter 1986):43

Hockey

Ritchie Herbert: Photography Major/Hockey Player. J. Roger Dykes. *About Time* 14, No. 5 (May 1986):24–25

Hodge, Warren (joint author)

See Serwatka, Thomas

Hoffmann, Léon-François

Essays on Haitian Literature. Reviewed by Maurice A. Lubin. *Research in African Literatures* 17, No. 4 (Winter 1986): 593–595

Hogan, Lawrence D.

A Tradition of Black Journalism. *About Time* 14, No. 2 (February 1986):11–13

Holcomb, Betty

The Healing Connection: A Look at Holistic Ways to Treat and Cure Illness. *Essence* 17, No. 6 (October 1986):14

Holidays

Celebrating Kwanzaa Now! *Essence* 17, No. 8 (December 1986):99

Holidays—United States

See Martin Luther King (Jr.) Holiday

Holistic Medicine

The Healing Connection: A Look at Holistic Ways to Treat and Cure Illness. Betty Holcomb. *Essence* 17, No. 6 (October 1986):14

Hollister, Robinson G. (Jr.) (joint editor)

See Betsey, Charles L.

Holloway, Joseph E.

The Bantu-Speaking Heritage of the United States. Book review. *Phylon* 47, No. 2 (June 1986):167–168

Holman, M. Carl (about)

Government Agencies Working behind the Scenes. David C. Ruffin. *Black Enterprise* 16, No. 11 (June 1986):269–270

Holmes, Barbara J.

Do Not Buy the Conventional Wisdom: Minority Teachers Can Pass the Tests. *Journal of Negro Education* 55, No.3 (Summer 1986):335–346

Holmes, Roosevelt L. (joint author)

See Gillis-Olion, Marion

Home Economics

Blue Collar/White Collar Success: Husband and Wife Pool Resources for the Good Life. *Ebony* 41, No. 10 (August 1986):96

Living Well on... Lloyd Gite. *Black Enterprise* 16, No. 10 (May 1986):44

Homeless

The Homeless. Joan Marie Allen. *About Time* 14, No. 10 (October 1986):18–20

Homer, Ronald (about)

Bank of the Year: Banking on Boston. Gregg Patterson. *Black Enterprise* 16, No. 11 (June 1986):150

Homicide

See Murder

Honduras—History

Witness to War: An American Doctor in El Salvador. By Charles Clements, M.D. Reviewed by Neale Pearson. *Caribbean Review* 15, No. 2 (Spring 1986):47–48

Hope, Akua Lezli

Leaving Is a Little Death. Poem. *Black American Literature Forum* 20, No. 3 (Fall 1986):262–263

Hord, Fred L.

Belly Dancer. Poem. *Black American Literature Forum* 20, No. 3 (Fall 1986):270

The Black Axe: Cleaving for Song. Poem. *Black American Literature Forum* 20, No. 3 (Fall 1986):268–269

How Could I Not Love You? Poem. *Black American Literature Forum* 20, No. 3 (Fall 1986):267–268

Nuptials. Poem. *Black American Literature Forum* 20, No. 3 (Fall 1986):267

Horn, Andrew

South African Theater: Ideology and Rebellion. Notes. *Research in African Literatures* 17, No. 2 (Summer 1986): 211–233

Horne, Gerald

Black and Red—W. E. B. DuBois and the Afro-American Response to the Cold War—1944–1963. Book review. Linda Burnham. *Black Scholar* 17, No. 2 (March-April 1986):52–54

Horne Family

The Hornes. By Gail Lumet Buckley. Reviewed by Tonya Bolden Davis. *Black Enterprise* 17, No. 3 (October 1986):18

Horoscopes

How Much Can Your Horoscope Really Tell You? *Ebony* 41, No. 6 (April 1986):74

Horta, José Ramos

The Struggle in East Timor: An Interview with José Ramos Horta. *Race and Class* 28, No. 1 (Summer 1986):86–90

Horton, Donna

Employee Health Can Spell Profits for U.S. Corporations. *About Time* 14, No. 8 (August 1986):14

Horton, Floyd (joint author)

See Clark, Vernon L.

Hoskin, Gary

Colombia under Stress: A Presidency Lamed by Instability. *Caribbean Review* 15, No. 1 (Winter 1986):7–9+

Hospitality Industry

The Hospitality Industry: Still Growing Strong. Thonnia Lee. *Black Collegian* 17, No. 1 (September/October 1986):137–147

House, Amelia Blossom

Fall. Poem. *Essence* 17, No. 1 (May 1986):164

Firecircle. Poem. *Essence* 17, No. 8 (December 1986):124

For South Africa. Poem. *Essence* 17, No. 7 (November 1986):158

House Buying

Real Estate: Home, Sweet Home. Constance Mitchell. *Black Enterprise* 16, No. 11 (June 1986):290

There's No Place Like Home. Deborah W. Hairston. *Black Enterprise* 17, No. 3 (October 1986):99

House Remodeling

Renovating Your Home the Smart Way. Denise Lamaute. *Black Enterprise* 16, No. 8 (March 1986):21–22

Housing

See also Landlord and Tenant

Housing, Cooperative

The Co-Op King. Derek T. Dingle and Dewayne Wickham. *Black Enterprise* 16, No. 9 (April 1986):45–50

There's No Place Like Home. Deborah W. Hairston. *Black Enterprise* 17, No. 3 (October 1986):99

Housing—Abandonment

Abandonment. Ann L. Giddings. *Howard Law Journal* 29, No. 1 (1986):117–125

Housing—Finance

Mortgage Money for Minorities. Solomon J. Herbert. *Black Enterprise* 17, No. 1 (August 1986):19

Housing—Harlem

The Consolidated Tenants League of Harlem: Black Self-Help vs. White, Liberal Intervention in Ghetto Housing, 1934–1944. Joel Schwartz. *Afro-Americans in New York Life and History* 10, No.1 (January 1986):31–51

Housing Policy

Suburban Housing. Wayne Dawkins. *Black Enterprise* 16, No. 8 (March 1986):14

Housing—Research

Black-White Differences in Housing: An Analysis of Trend and Differentials, United States of America, 1960–1978. Ruhul Amin and A. G. Mariam. *Negro Educational Review* 37, No. 1 (January 1986):27–38

Houston, Whitney (about)

Whitney Houston: The Joys and Dangers of Sudden Success. Lynn Norment. *Ebony* 41, No. 9 (July 1986):126

Howard, Michael Emerson (III)

Black Hardhats and the Elite Craft Trade Unions. *Crisis* 93, No. 8 (October 1986):26–29

Howard University—Jazz Ensemble

Howard University Jazz Ensemble. Henry Duvall. *About Time* 14, No. 12 (December 1986):27–28

Howard University—Radio Station

Washington's Superstation: Howard University's WHUR-FM (96.3). Henry Duvall. *About Time* 14, No. 2 (February 1986):22–23

Howard University—Television Station

WHMM-TV's Super Internship. Willette Coleman. *Black Collegian* 16, No. 3 (January/February 1986):118–124

Howe, Florence

Myths of Coeducation. Book review. *Interracial Books for Children Bulletin* 17, No. 1 (1986):10

Howell, Diane C.

Exculpatory Clauses in Leases. *Howard Law Journal* 29, No. 1 (1986):95–102

Howland, Jacob

Black Boy: A Story of Soul-Making and a Quest for the Real. *Phylon* 47, No. 2 (June 1986):117–127

Hoytt, Eleanor Hinton

International Council of Women of the Darker Races: Historical Notes from Margaret Murray Washington. *SAGE* 3, No. 2 (Fall 1986):54–55

Hudson, Robert J., and Smith, Robert P. (Jr.)

Publications by CLA Members: 1985–86. Bibliography. *CLA Journal* 30, No. 2 (December 1986):241–251

Hudson-Withers, Clenora

Toni Morrison's World of Topsy-Turvydom: A Methodological Explication of New Black Literary Criticism. *Western Journal of Black Studies* 10, No. 3 (Fall 1986):132–136

Huggins, Nathan

Report to the Ford Foundation on Afro-American Studies. Book review. Molefi K. Asante. *Journal of Black Studies* 17, No. 2 (December 1986):255–262

Hughes, C. Alvin

Let Us Do Our Part: The New York City Based Negro Labor Victory Committee, 1941–1945. *Afro-Americans in New York Life and History* 10, No.1 (January 1986):19–29

Hughes, Langston

Aunt Sue's Stories. Poem. *Essence* 16, No. 11 (March 1986):122

Hughes, Langston—Criticism and Interpretation

Langston Hughes's *Fine Clothes to the Jew*. Arnold Rampersad. *Callaloo* 9, No. 1 (Winter 1986):144–158

Hull, Gloria T.

The Black Woman Writer and the Diaspora. *Black Scholar* 17, No. 2 (March-April 1986):2–4

Hull, Gloria T. (editor)

Give Us Each Day: The Diary of Alice Dunbar-Nelson. Book review. Elizabeth Brown-Guillory. *SAGE* 3, No. 2 (Fall 1986):57–59

Human Capital

The Future of the Black Community: Human Capital, Family Aspirations, and Individual Motivation. Clifton R. Wharton, Jr. *Review of Black Political Economy* 14, No. 4 (Spring 1986):9–16

Humanism in Literature

The Human Legacy of Black Latin American Literature. Notes. Richard L. Jackson. *CLA Journal* 30, No. 2 (December 1986):154–170

Humanities

See also Liberal Arts

Humor in Education

The Transitive Vampire: A Handbook of Grammar for the Innocent, the Eager and the Damned. By Karen Elizabeth Gordon. Reviewed by Elizabeth J. Higgins. *CLA Journal* 30, No. 2 (December 1986):252–253

Humorists, Nicaraguan

Revolutionary Comics: Political Humor from Nicaragua. Roger Sanchez Flores. *Caribbean Review* 15, No. 1 (Winter 1986):16–17

Hunger

No Free Lunch: Food and Revolution in Cuba Today. By Medea Benjamin, Joseph Collins, and Michael Scott. Reviewed by James E. Austin. *Caribbean Review* 15, No. 2 (Spring 1986):45

Hunt, Richard (about)

Richard Hunt. Illustrated. Samella Lewis. *International Review of African American Art* 7, No. 2 (1986):16–21

Hunter, Kristin—Criticism and Interpretation

Working Girl Blues: Mothers, Daughters, and the Image of Billie Holiday in Kristin Hunter's *God Bless the Child*. Gerald Early. *Black American Literature Forum* 20, No. 4 (Winter 1986):423–442

Hunter-Gault, Charlayne (about)

Language of an Evening Star: Charlayne Hunter-Gault. Adolph Dupree. *About Time* 14, No. 7 (July 1986):14–19

Hussain, Sinjari

Notes on the Kurdish Struggle. *Race and Class* 27, No. 3 (Winter 1986):92–94

Hyclak, Thomas J. (joint author)

See Stewart, James B.

Hypertension

Hypertension: Shriners Join Fight against the "Silent Killer." *Ebony* 42, No. 1 (November 1986):128

Ice Cream Industry

Cream of Vegetables. Vernon Smith. *Black Enterprise* 17, No. 2 (September 1986):18

A Tale of Two Franchises. Joyce Davis Adams and Janet Clayton. *Black Enterprise* 16, No. 12 (July 1986):42–46

Ice Skating

Debi Thomas—World Figure Skating Champion. Tricia Duncan-Hall. *Black Collegian* 17, No. 1 (September/October 1986):49–52

Of Scholarship and Ice: Debi Thomas. Adolph Dupree. *About Time* 14, No. 4 (April 1986):14

With Style and Grace. Bryan Burwell. *Black Enterprise* 16, No. 11 (June 1986):52

Ideology, Political

Voting Rights, Government Responsibility and Conservative Ideology. Alex Willingham. *Urban League Review* 10, No. 2 (Winter 1986–87):12–23

Ifemesia, Chieka (editor)

Uwa ndi Igbo: Journal of Igbo Life and Culture I. Reviewed by Don Burgess. *Research in African Literatures* 17, No. 2 (Summer 1986): 288–291

Igbalajobi, Muyiwa

The Effect of Ridicule on the Academic Performance of Secondary School Students. *Negro Educational Review* 37, No. 1 (January 1986):39–45

Igbo—Language and Culture

Igbo Language and Culture II. F. C. Ogbalu and E. N. Emenanjo, editors. Reviewed by Kalu Ogbaa. *Research in African Literatures* 17, No. 2 (Summer 1986): 291–293

Uwa ndi Igbo: Journal of Igbo Life and Culture I. Chieka Ifemesia, editor. Reviewed by Don Burgess. *Research in African Literatures* 17, No. 2 (Summer 1986): 288–291

Igbo—Music

Conversation with Israel Anyahuru. Joshua Uzoigwe. *Black Perspective in Music* 14, No. 2 (Spring 1986):126–142

Igbo—Religion

African Religions in Western Conceptual Schemes: The Problem of Interpretation. Reviewed by C. Ejizu. *Journal of Religious Thought* 43, No. 2 (Fall-Winter 1986–87):90

Ikeler, A. Abbott

That Peculiar Book: Critics, Common Readers and *The Way We Live Now*. Notes. *CLA Journal* 30, No. 2 (December 1986):219–240

Ikonne, Chidi

René Maran, the Black Frenchman: A Bio-Critical Study. Book review. *Research in African Literatures* 17, No. 4 (Winter 1986): 603–605

Ilaw, Marianne

Black Progress: Reality or Illusion. Book review. *Black Enterprise* 16, No. 7 (February 1986):19–21

A Busy Night with a Big-City Doctor. *Black Enterprise* 16, No. 9 (April 1986):58–60

A Day in the Life of a Franchise Owner. *Black Enterprise* 16, No. 7 (February 1986):128–132

Memory Games. *Black Enterprise* 16, No. 11 (June 1986):280

The Myth of Black Progress. Book review. *Black Enterprise* 16, No. 7 (February 1986):19–21

Office Etiquette: The Right Response. *Black Enterprise* 16, No. 11 (June 1986):280

On Their Own: Women Traveling Solo. *Black Enterprise* 16, No. 8 (March 1986):68

When It's More than Just a Job. *Black Enterprise* 16, No. 10 (May 1986):54

Ilaw, Marianne (joint author)

See Smikle, Ken

Illiteracy

See Literacy

Iman

Iman in Africa: Supermodel Rediscovers Her Roots. *Ebony* 42, No. 1 (November 1986):62

Immigration—Economic Aspects

The Effects of Immigrants, Women, and Teenagers on the Relative Earnings of Black Males. James B. Stewart and Thomas J. Hyclak. *Review of Black Political Economy* 15, No. 1 (Summer 1986):93–101

Minority Business Development: An International Comparison. Gavin M. Chen. *Review of Black Political Economy* 15, No. 2 (Fall 1986):93–111

Immigration—Latin America

Adventurers and Proletarians: The Story of Migrants in Latin America. By Magnus Mörner. Reviewed by Frances Webber. *Race and Class* 28, No. 2 (August 1986):103–105

Immigration—Women

Strangers and Sisters: Women, Race and Immigration. Edited by Selma James. Reviewed by Jenny Bourne. *Race and Class* 27, No. 4 (Spring 1986):100–103

Worlds Apart: Women under Immigration and Nationality Law. By Women, Immigration and Nationality Group. Reviewed by Busi Chaane. *Race and Class* 28, No. 1 (Summer 1986):103–107

Imperialism

Conrad and Imperialism: Ideological Boundaries and Visionary Frontiers. By Benita Parry. Reviewed by Robert D. Hamner. *Research in African Literatures* 17, No. 1 (Spring 1986): 158–162

Literature and Imperialism. Bart Moore-Gilbert, editor. Reviewed by Robert D. Hamner. *Research in African Literatures* 17, No. 1 (Spring 1986): 162–165

See also Colonization—Africa

Imperialism—Africa

On Revolutionary Nationalism: The Legacy of Cabral. Basil Davidson. *Race and Class* 27, No. 3 (Winter 1986):21–45

Income

Black Visibility, Early Political Victories, and Income Inequality. Pamela Irving Jackson and Gail E. Marhewka. *Journal of Black Studies* 17, No. 1 (September 1986):33–48

See also Wages

Income Distribution

Black Income Mirrors Status in Economy. Andrew F. Brimmer. *Black Enterprise* 17, No. 2 (September 1986):33

The Effects of Immigrants, Women, and Teenagers on the Relative Earnings of Black Males. James B. Stewart and Thomas J. Hyclak. *Review of Black Political Economy* 15, No. 1 (Summer 1986):93–101

Racial Employment and Earnings Differentials: The Impact of the Reagan Administration. Charles A. Register. *Review of Black Political Economy* 15, No. 1 (Summer 1986):59–69

Scheming for the Poor: The Politics of Redistribution in Latin America. By William Ascher. Reviewed by John Waterbury. *Caribbean Review* 15, No. 1 (Winter 1986):42–43

Tax Reform: A Minimalist Approach for Assisting the Low-Income. Lynn Burbridge. *Urban League Review* 10, No. 2 (Winter 1986–87):101–112

Trends, Prospects, and Strategies for Black Economic Progress. Andrew F. Brimmer. *Review of Black Political Economy* 14, No. 4 (Spring 1986):91–97

Income and Jobs Action Bill

The Income and Jobs Action Bill: A Mandate for Full Employment. Charles A. Hayes. *Urban League Review* 10, No. 1 (Summer 1986):61–65

Income Maintenance Programs

Distress vs. Dependency: Changing Income Support Programs. William Darity, Jr., and Samuel Myers, Jr. *Urban League Review* 10, No. 2 (Winter 1986–87):24–33

Income Tax Preparation

Taking the Sting Out of Filing Taxes. Denise Lamaute. *Black Enterprise* 16, No. 9 (April 1986):33–34

Tax Tips for the Entrepreneur. Wanda Whitmore. *Black Enterprise* 16, No. 8 (March 1986):63

Incorporation

Finance You, Inc. Denise Lamaute. *Black Enterprise* 16, No. 11 (June 1986):265–266

India—Description and Travel

India's Jewels: Delhi City and the State of Rajasthan. Jessica B. Harris. *Black Enterprise* 17, No. 1 (August 1986):65

Indianola, MS—Public Schools

The Power of Protesting. Dan Berube. *Black Enterprise* 17, No. 3 (October 1986):22

Indians—Afro-Indian Communities

Social-Scientific Perspectives on the Afro-American Arts. Rhett S. Jones. *Black American Literature Forum* 20, No. 4 (Winter 1986):443–447

Indians of Central America—Art

Pyramid—American and African: A Comparison. Notes. Beatrice Lumpkin. *Journal of African Civilizations* 8, No. 2 (December 1986):169–187

Indians of Central America—Languages

Africa and the Discovery of America, Volume I. By Leo Wiener. Reviewed by Phillips Barry. *Journal of African Civilizations* 8, No. 2 (December 1986):197–201

Mandinga Voyages across the Atlantic. Notes. Harold G. Lawrence. *Journal of African Civilizations* 8, No. 2 (December 1986):202–247

Trait-Influences in Meso-America: The African-Asian Connection. Notes. Wayne B. Chandler. *Journal of African Civilizations* 8, No. 2 (December 1986):274–334

Indians of Mexico

Egypto-Nubian Presences in Ancient Mexico. Notes. Ivan Van Sertima. *Journal of African Civilizations* 8, No. 2 (December 1986):29–55

Ten Years After: An Introduction and Overview. Ivan Van Sertima. *Journal of African Civilizations* 8, No. 2 (December 1986):5–27

Indians of Mexico—Art

Unexpected African Faces in Pre-Columbian America. Alexander Von Wuthenau. *Journal of African Civilizations* 8, No. 2 (December 1986):56–75

Indians of North America—Afro-Indian Communities

Character Names in *Indian Trails* by Olivia Ward Bush (Banks): Clues to Afro Assimilation Into Long Island's Native Americans. Notes. Bernice F. Guillaume. *Afro-Americans in New York Life and History* 10, No. 2 (July 1986):45–53

Indians of North America—History

Amerindian Resistance: The Gathering of the Fires. Jan Nederveen Pieterse. *Race and Class* 27, No. 4 (Spring 1986):35–51

Indians of South America—Folktales

Leo Wiener—A Plea for Re-Examination. Notes. David J. M. Muffett. *Journal of African Civilizations* 8, No. 2 (December 1986):188–196

Indians of South America—Religion and Mythology

The Egyptian Presence in South America. Notes. R. A. Jairazbhoy. *Journal of African Civilizations* 8, No. 2 (December 1986):76–135

Indonesia—Resistance Movements

The Struggle in East Timor: An Interview with José Ramos Horta. *Race and Class* 28, No. 1 (Summer 1986):86–90

Industrial Equipment Leases

The Benefits of Leasing. Lloyd Gite. *Black Enterprise* 17, No. 2 (September 1986):27

Industrial Hygiene

Employee Health Can Spell Profits for U.S. Corporations. Donna Horton. *About Time* 14, No. 8 (August 1986):14

Industrial Revenue Bonds

Inequality in Metropolitan Industrial Revenue Bond Programs. Gregory D. Squires. *Review of Black Political Economy* 14, No. 4 (Spring 1986):37–50

Industry

See also Diversification in Industry

Industry—Social Aspects

The Corporate Pioneers. Paul Lindsay Johnson. *Crisis* 93, No. 4 (April 1986):26–30

Industry and State

When Private Companies Do Public Work. Britt Robson. *Black Enterprise* 16, No. 7 (February 1986):140–144

Infants—Mortality

Did Fidel Fudge the Figures? Literacy and Health: The Cuban Model. Nicholas Eberstadt. *Caribbean Review* 15, No. 2 (Spring 1986):5–7 +

How to Figure Out Cuba: Development, Ideology and Mortality. Sergio Diaz-Briquets. *Caribbean Review* 15, No. 2 (Spring 1986):8–11 +

Ingersoll, Earl G. (joint editor)

See Rubin, Stan Sanvel

Innes, C. L.

Interdisciplinary Dimensions of African Literature. Book review. *Research in African Literatures* 17, No. 3 (Fall 1986): 449–451

Innovative Technical Systems, Inc.

The Young Tycoons. Lloyd Gite. *Black Enterprise* 16, No. 6 (January 1986):44–47

Insurance, Disability

Insuring Your Income against Disability. Denise Lamaute. *Black Enterprise* 17, No. 4 (November 1986):39–40

Insurance Agents

The Maestro of Marketing. Jacqueline Moore. *Black Enterprise* 16, No. 12 (July 1986):32

Insurance Companies

The *Black Enterprise* List of Black Insurance Companies. *Black Enterprise* 16, No. 11 (June 1986):178

Insurance Company of the Year: Premium Profits. Nathan McCall. *Black Enterprise* 16, No. 11 (June 1986):182

Insurance Overview: A Change of Policy. Shawn Kennedy. *Black Enterprise* 16, No. 11 (June 1986):175

Management of Policy Benefits. Margo Walker. *Black Enterprise* 16, No. 11 (June 1986):65

Inter-American Foundation

Grassroots Development in Latin America and the Caribbean: Oral Histories of Social Change. By Robert Wasserstrom. Reviewed by Linda Miller. *Caribbean Review* 15, No. 1 (Winter 1986):41–42

Interior Decoration

See Color in Interior Decoration

Interior Design—Offices

Designing the Office of the 80s. *Black Enterprise* 16, No. 6 (January 1986):61

International Council of Women of the Darker Races

International Council of Women of the Darker Races: Historical Notes from Margaret Murray Washington. Eleanor Hinton Hoytt. *SAGE* 3, No. 2 (Fall 1986):54–55

International Relations—Cultural Exchanges

Black Journalists Visit Eastern Europe. Terry E. Johnson. *Black Scholar* 17, No. 1 (January-February 1986):35–37

International Relief

Deadline: Foreign Aid to the Third World. David C. Ruffin. *Black Enterprise* 16, No. 12 (July 1986):19

International Trade

See Commerce

Interstate Landscaping Company

BE 100: The New Guys on the Block. Edmund Newton. *Black Enterprise* 16, No. 11 (June 1986):119

Investment Bankers

Money Merchants. Candice Caruthers. *Black Enterprise* 17, No. 1 (August 1986):61–63

Investment Clubs

For Members Only: There's Strength in Numbers for Those Who Pool Their Resources through Investment Clubs. *Black Enterprise* 17, No. 3 (October 1986):75

Investments

Black Dollars: Taking Control. Jill Nelson. *Essence* 17, No. 5 (September 1986):65

Bold Money. By Melvin Van Peebles. Reviewed by Denise Lamaute. *Black Enterprise* 17, No. 3 (October 1986):88

Investing by Collecting. Julianne Malveaux. *Essence* 17, No. 8 (December 1986):113

Investing in Commercial Real Estate. Denise Lamaute. *Black Enterprise* 16, No. 11 (June 1986):71–72

Investing with a Conscience. Frank Dexter Brown. *Black Enterprise* 17, No. 3 (October 1986):91

Make Your Money Grow with Investments. Brenda D. Neal. *Black Enterprise* 16, No. 7 (February 1986):43

Status Symbols. Monique Greenwood. *Black Enterprise* 16, No. 10 (May 1986):63

Take Stock? Anyone Can Invest in the Stock Market. *Essence* 17, No. 6 (October 1986):116

Trading Places. Derek T. Dingle. *Black Enterprise* 17, No. 3 (October 1986):51

Investment Trusts

Tapping the Magic of Mutual Funds. Denise Lamaute. *Black Enterprise* 17, No. 2 (September 1986):29–30

Iowa—Coal Mining

Exploring Buried Buxton: Archeology of an Abandoned Iowa Coal Mining Town with a Large Black Population. By David M. Gradwohl and Nancy M. Osborn. Reviewed by Maria Boynton. *Afro-Americans in New York Life and History* 10, No. 2 (July 1986): 65–68

Irby, Edith (about)

Breakthroughs Are Her Business: Edith Irby. Charles Whitaker. *Ebony* 41, No. 8 (June 1986):90

Iron—Metallurgy

Iron in the Ancient Egyptian Empire. Notes. Bibliography. Cheikh Anta Diop. *Journal of African Civilizations* 8, No. 1 (June 1986):64–73

Irons, Edward D., and Moore, Gilbert W.

Black Managers: The Case of the Banking Industry. Book review. Willene A. Johnson. *Review of Black Political Economy* 14, No. 4 (Spring 1986):103–108

Irvine, Russell William

Education in the Post-Integration Era. *Journal of Negro Education* 55, No.4 (Fall 1986):508–517

Islam

Liberation Theology and Islamic Revivalism. Notes. Mohammad Yadegari. *Journal of Religious Thought* 43, No. 2 (Fall-Winter 1986–87):38–50

Israel-Arab War, 1967-

Middle East Terrorism and the American Ideological System. Noam Chomsky. *Race and Class* 28, No. 1 (Summer 1986):1–28

Israel—Black American Attitudes

Prophet Without Honor? The Reverend Jesse Jackson and the Palestinian Question. Notes. David A. Coolidge, Jr. *Journal of Religious Thought* 43, No. 2 (Fall-Winter 1986–87):51–62

Iteso—Oral Literature

Iteso Thought Patterns in Tales. By Grace Akello. Reviewed by John Lamphear. *Research in African Literatures* 17, No. 2 (Summer 1986): 298–299

Iverem, Esther

Some Places in America Scare You More. Poem. *Black American Literature Forum* 20, No. 3 (Fall 1986):256

The Time. Poem. *Black American Literature Forum* 20, No. 3 (Fall 1986):254–255

Tsunami. Poem. *Black American Literature Forum* 20, No. 3 (Fall 1986):254–256

Ivory, Steven

Where the Money Goes. *Crisis* 93, No. 5 (May 1986):28–33

Ivory Coast—Description and Travel

Abidjan, Côte d'Ivoire: Tradition and Modernity at the Crossroads of West Africa. Patricia A. Jones. *Black Enterprise* 17, No. 3 (October 1986):117–118

Jackson, Gale

My Mother Usta Sing Love Songs. Poem. *Essence* 17, No. 1 (May 1986):93

Needles, Threads. *Callaloo* 9, No. 2 (Spring 1986):314–323

Jackson, Janet (about)

Janet: Hit Album Takes Another Jackson to the Top. Aldore Collier. *Ebony* 41, No. 11 (September 1986):29

Jackson, Jesse L. (about)

The Jesse Jackson Phenomenon: The Crisis of Purpose in Afro-American Politics. By Adolph Reed. Reviewed by Shirley Washington. *Black Scholar* 17, No. 6 (November-December 1986):52–53

Jesse Jackson: Rebuilding Bridges to Africa. D. Michael Cheers. *Ebony* 42, No. 2 (December 1986):132

Jesse Jackson Takes His Peace Program to Geneva. Don Rojas. *Black Scholar* 17, No. 1 (January-February 1986):31–34

Jesse Jackson and Television: Black Image Presentation and Affect in the 1984 Democratic Campaign Debates. Bishetta D. Merritt. *Journal of Black Studies* 16, No. 4 (June 1986):347–367

Prophet Without Honor? The Reverend Jesse Jackson and the Palestinian Question. Notes. David A. Coolidge (Jr.) *Journal of Religious Thought* 43, No. 2 (Fall-Winter 1986–87):51–62

Religious Belief and Political Activism in Black America: An Essay. Robert Michael Franklin. *Journal of Religious Thought* 43, No. 2 (Fall-Winter 1986–87):63–72

Watch Jesse Run and Tell Me What You See: A First Look at Student Perceptions of the Jesse Jackson Presidential Candidacy. Oscar H. Gandy, Jr., and Larry G. Coleman. *Journal of Black Studies* 16, No. 3 (March 1986):293–306

Jackson, Kirk

UNB Merger Announced. *Black Enterprise* 17, No. 5 (December 1986):26

Jackson, Pamela Irving, and Marhewka, Gail E.

Black Visibility, Early Political Victories, and Income Inequality. *Journal of Black Studies* 17, No. 1 (September 1986):33–48

Jackson, Reggie (about)

Reggie Jackson: More than Just a Baseball Superstar. Walter Leavy. *Ebony* 41, No. 9 (July 1986):104

Jackson, Reuben M.

The Murder City Blues. Poem. *Black American Literature Forum* 20, No. 3 (Fall 1986):308

Jackson, Richard (joint author)

See Berrian, Brenda F.

Jackson, Richard L.

The Human Legacy of Black Latin American Literature. Notes. *CLA Journal* 30, No. 2 (December 1986):154–170

Jacobs, Brian D.

Black Politics and Urban Crisis in Britain. Book review. Lee Bridges. *Race and Class* 28, No. 2 (August 1986):99–102

Jacobs, Sylvia M.

"Say Africa When You Pray": The Activities of Early Black Baptist Women Missionaries among Liberian Women and Children. *SAGE* 3, No. 2 (Fall 1986):16–21

Jain, Jasbir

The Unfolding of a Text: Soyinka's *Death and the King's Horseman*. Notes. *Research in African Literatures* 17, No. 2 (Summer 1986): 252–260

Jairazbhoy, R. A.

The Egyptian Presence in South America. Notes. *Journal of African Civilizations* 8, No. 2 (December 1986):76–135

Jamaica—Business Enterprises

Partners in Craft. Dan Giles Salter. *Essence* 16, No. 11 (March 1986):16

Jamaica—Culture and Society

A Review of Urban Life in Kingston, Jamaica. By Diane J. Austin. Reviewed by Bernard D. Headley. *Caribbean Review* 15, No. 1 (Winter 1986):42

Jamaica—Description and Travel

Jamaica: Homespun Charm, Quiet Elegance and Joyful Sounds. E. D. SMith. *Black Enterprise* 16, No. 10 (May 1986):76

James, Curtia

Art and Culture: The Bahian Way of Living. *Essence* 16, No. 11 (March 1986):90

Benefits of Water. *Essence* 17, No. 2 (July 1986):108

Sample the Spice of Salvador. *Essence* 16, No. 11 (March 1986):86

James, Luther

Theatre funding. *Crisis* 93, No. 2 (February 1986):13

James, Randolph W. and Lutchman, Harold A.

Law and the Political Environment in Guyana. Book review. Ivelaw L. Griffith. *Black Scholar* 17, No. 3 (May-June 1986):58

James, Samuel D. K.

The Impact of Cybernation Technology on Black Automotive Workers in the United States. Book review. Julianne Malveaux. *Review of Black Political Economy* 15, No. 1 (Summer 1986):103–105

James, Selma

Strangers and Sisters: Women, Race and Immigration. Book review. Jenny Bourne. *Race and Class* 27, No. 4 (Spring 1986):100–103

James, Sharpe (about)

A Sharpe Change. Errol T. Louis. *Black Enterprise* 17, No. 1 (August 1986):11

A "Sharpe" Change in Newark. Alex Poinsett. *Ebony* 41, No. 11 (September 1986):128

Janitorial Services

See Cleaning Services

Jarvis, Yvonne (about)

Life after Rape. Lorene E. Gray. *Essence* 17, No. 5 (September 1986):68

Jaynes, Gerald D.

Gramm-Rudman and Black Education. *Black Enterprise* 16, No. 10 (May 1986):39

Jefferson, Alphine W.

Black America in the 1980s: Rhetoric vs. Reality. *Black Scholar* 17, No. 3 (May-June 1986):2–9

Jefferson, Roland S.

Namibia: Africa's Last Colony. Film review. *Black Scholar* 17, No. 1 (January-February 1986):46–47

Jefferson, Thomas (about)

The Rhetoric of Miscegenation: Thomas Jefferson, Sally Hemings, and Their Historians. B. R. Burg. *Phylon* 47, No. 2 (June 1986):117–127

Jeffries, Leonard, Jr.

Civilization or Barbarism: The Legacy of Cheikh Anta Diop. Book review. *Journal of African Civilizations* 8, No. 1 (June 1986):146–160

Jemie, Onwuchekwa

See Chinweizu, and others

Jenkins, Christine

Gleanings. Book review. *Interracial Books for Children Bulletin* 17, No. 1 (1986):8

Julie's Daughter. Book review. *Interracial Books for Children Bulletin* 17, No. 1 (1986):7–8

Jenkins, Edmund Thornton (about)

In Retrospect: Edmund Thornton Jenkins. Betty Hillmon. *Black Perspective in Music* 14, No. 2 (Spring 1986):143–180

Jennings, Kenneth

The Teacher Rebellion. Book review. *Negro Educational Review* 37, Nos. 3–4 (July-October 1986):154–155

Jessup, Lynne

The Mandinka Balafon: An Introduction with Notation for Teaching. Book review. Jacqueline Cogdell DjeDje. *Black Perspective in Music* 14, No. 3 (Fall 1986):307–308

Jewell, Terri L.

Covenant. Poem. *Black American Literature Forum* 20, No. 3 (Fall 1986):259–260

Gasoline on the Roof. Poem. *Black American Literature Forum* 20, No. 3 (Fall 1986):257–259

Jewelry as an Investment

Getting Your Money's Worth in Fine Jewelry. Denise Lamaute. *Black Enterprise* 16, No. 10 (May 1986):33–34

Jewish-Arab Relations

Prophet Without Honor? The Reverend Jesse Jackson and the Palestinian Question. Notes. David A. Coolidge (Jr.) *Journal of Religious Thought* 43, No. 2 (Fall-Winter 1986–87):51–62

Jewish-Black Relations

The Post-Civil Rights Transformation of the Relationship between Blacks and Jews in the United States. Huey L. Perry and Ruth B. White. *Phylon* 47, No. 1 (March 1986):51–60

Jewish Poetry

Spanning Two Languages: The Legacy of Isaac and Joseph. Chris Searle. *Race and Class* 28, No. 1 (Summer 1986):29–42

Jews—Great Britain

Spanning Two Languages: The Legacy of Isaac and Joseph. Chris Searle. *Race and Class* 28, No. 1 (Summer 1986):29–42

Jeyifo, Biodun

The Truthful Lie: Essays in a Sociology of African Drama. Reviewed by Elaine Savory Fido. *Research in African Literatures* 17, No. 2 (Summer 1986): 273–275

Job Interviews

"A" to "Z" of Job Search. Toya L. Robinson. *Black Collegian* 16, No. 4 (March/April 1986):82–83

How to Begin the Job-Search Process in Your Chosen Field. Dale Moran. *Black Collegian* 17, No. 2 (November/December 1986):39–43

Job Satisfaction

Longing for Longevity. Ken Smikle and Marianne Ilaw. *Black Enterprise* 17, No. 4 (November 1986):52

Job Termination

See Employees, Dismissal of

Job Training

See Occupational Training

Job Training Partnership Act

Seeking Realistic Solutions to Welfare. Margaret Simms. *Black Enterprise* 17, No. 1 (August 1986):25

Job Vacancies

The Effects of Immigrants, Women, and Teenagers on the Relative Earnings of Black Males. James B. Stewart and Thomas J. Hyclak. *Review of Black Political Economy* 15, No. 1 (Summer 1986):93–101

Jochannon, Yosef ben (about)

Dr. Yosef ben Jochannon: Interview. Paul Lindsey Johnson. *Crisis* 93, No. 6 (June/July 1986):42–45

Johnson, Adrienne M.

The Political Legacy of Dr. King. *Crisis* 93, No. 2 (February 1986):26

Johnson, Bob (about)

The Best "Deal" in Town: Bob Johnson Chevrolet. Anita Johnson Sims. *About Time* 14, No. 8 (August 1986):24–26

Johnson, Charles

Sorcerer's Apprentice. Book review. Joe Johnson. *Crisis* 93, No. 5 (May 1986):12–38

Johnson, Donna

Riding Mass Transit. *Black Enterprise* 16, No. 7 (February 1986):26

Johnson, Gil (about)

Mortgage Money for Minorities. Solomon J. Herbert. *Black Enterprise* 17, No. 1 (August 1986):19

Johnson, Herschel

Clara (Mother) Hale: Healing Baby "Junkies" with Love. *Ebony* 41, No. 7 (May 1986):58

Johnson, Joe

Brothers and Keepers. Book review. *Crisis* 93, No. 3 (March 1986):14–48

A *Crisis* Report on Literature. *Crisis* 93, No. 1 (January 1986):11

The Evidence of Things Not Seen. Book review. *Crisis* 93, No. 3 (March 1986):14–48

Going to the Territory. Book review. *Crisis* 93, No. 10 (December 1986):10

History of the Negro Race in America from 1619 to 1880: Negroes as Slaves, as Soldiers, as Citizens. Book review. *Crisis* 93, No. 4 (April 1986):12–14

The Hornes: An American Family. Book review. *Crisis* 93, No. 8 (October 1986):14–16

The Life of Langston Hughes: Volume I: 1902–41. Book review. *Crisis* 93, No. 9 (November 1986):12–13

The Price of a Ticket. Book review. *Crisis* 93, No. 2 (February 1986):12

In Pursuit of Power: Southern Blacks and Electoral Politics, 1965–1982. Book review. *Crisis* 93, No. 7 (August/September 1986):12–13

Race, Class and Power in Brazil. Book review. *Crisis* 93, No. 6 (June/July 1986):16

Sorcerer's Apprentice. Book review. *Crisis* 93, No. 5 (May 1986):12–38

Johnson, Joe (about)

Joe Johnson and the Repertory Dance Theater of Los Angeles. L. Martina Young. *Crisis* 93, No. 6 (June/July 1986):2

Johnson, Lemuel A.

African Literature Today No. 14: Insiders and Outsiders. Book review. *Research in African Literatures* 17, No. 3 (Fall 1986): 442–444

Strong Breeds: Wole Soyinka and the Head of the Head of State in *A Play of Giants*. *Callaloo* 9, No. 2 (Spring 1986):354–370

Johnson, Martin

Up Swings Jazz. *Essence* 17, No. 6 (October 1986):36

Johnson, Paul Lindsay

The Corporate Pioneers. *Crisis* 93, No. 4 (April 1986):26–30

A *Crisis* Report on Film. *Crisis* 93, No. 1 (January 1986):21–24

Dr. Yosef ben Jochannon: Interview. Paul Lindsay Johnson. *Crisis* 93, No. 6 (June/July 1986):42–45

Senator Robert Dole: Interview. *Crisis* 93, No. 7 (August/September 1986):30

Spike Lee's "She's Gotta Have It." Film review. *Crisis* 93, No. 8 (October 1986):11–12

Johnson, Robert E.

TV's Top Mom and Dad: Bill Cosby, Phylicia Ayers-Allen Are Role Model Parents on Award-Winning Television Show. *Ebony* 41, No. 4 (February 1986):29

Johnson, Rosalind J.

Grooming for Success. *Black Collegian* 17, No. 1 (September/October 1986):55–56

Johnson, Rose Marie (about)

Crisis Interview: Rose Marie Johnson. *Crisis* 93, No. 4 (April 1986):34–37

Johnson, Sylvia T.

Teacher Testing and Assessment. Editorial. *Journal of Negro Education* 55, No.3 (Summer 1986):247–250

Changes in Family Structures. *About Time* 14, No. 3 (March 1986):14–18

The Color Purple. Film review. *About Time* 14, No. 1 (January 1986):18–19

Come, Grow with Us! Business and Service Directory. *About Time* 14, No. 8 (August 1986):15–22

Educational Specialists: Addressing a Child's Career Development. *About Time* 14, No. 11 (November 1986):18–21

Enhancing One's Quality of Life. *About Time* 14, No. 4 (April 1986):16–18

Groundwork: Charles Hamilton Houston and the Struggle for Civil Rights. Book review. *About Time* 14, No. 2 (February 1986):18–20

Is Black Bad? Poem. *About Time* 14, No. 1 (January 1986):21

Martin Luther King, Jr. Poem. *About Time* 14, No. 1 (January 1986):21

Moneta Sleet, Jr.: Pulitzer Prize Photojournalist. *About Time* 14, No. 10 (October 1986):12–13

National Black Family Celebration. *About Time* 14, No. 10 (October 1986):23

Opportunities for Success. *About Time* 14, No. 12 (December 1986):13–19

Our Time Has Come. Poem. *About Time* 14, No. 1 (January 1986):21

Providing a Healthier Workplace: Sheen and Shine, Inc. *About Time* 14, No. 8 (August 1986):28–29

Reducing Costs with Health Care. *About Time* 14, No. 4 (April 1986):12–13

She's Gotta Have It. Film review. *About Time* 14, No. 10 (October 1986):24–25

Tuskegee Airmen: A Continuing Legacy. *About Time* 14, No. 10 (October 1986):22

Volunteerism Makes a Difference. *About Time* 14, No. 6 (June 1986):14–20

Jones, Patricia A.

Abidjan, Côte d'Ivoire: Tradition and Modernity at the Crossroads of West Africa. *Black Enterprise* 17, No. 3 (October 1986):117–118

Career Counseling. *Crisis* 93, No. 8 (October 1986):19

ColeJon's Hot Profits. *Black Enterprise* 16, No. 8 (March 1986):16

Washington: District of Commerce. *Black Enterprise* 16, No. 11 (June 1986):253

Jones, Rhett S.

Social-Scientific Perspectives on the Afro-American Arts. *Black American Literature Forum* 20, No. 4 (Winter 1986):443–447

Jonestown (Guyana) Massacre, 1978

A Sympathetic History of Jonestown: The Moore Family Involvement in Peoples Temple. By Rebecca Moore. Reviewed by Kortright Davis. *Journal of Religious Thought* 43, No. 2 (Fall-Winter 1986–87):92–93

Jones-Wilson, Faustine

Implications from the 1985 Thompson Lecture. Editorial. *Journal of Negro Education* 55, No. 2 55, No. 2 (Spring 1986):123–124

Jordaan, Ken

Slavery in Dutch South Africa. Book review. *Race and Class* 27, No. 3 (Winter 1986):104–105

Jordan, Cassandra L.

The Sickle Cell Disease Crisis. *About Time* 14, No. 7 (July 1986):22–23

Jordan, Jennifer, and Cleveland, Lisa

Where I'm Coming from. *Essence* 17, No. 1 (May 1986):86

Jordan, June

An Always Lei of Ginger Blossoms for the First Lady of Hawai'i: Queen Lili'uokalani. Poem. *Callaloo* 9, No. 1 (Winter 1986):79–80

Living Room. Book review. Joanne V. Gabbin. *Callaloo* 9, No. 1 (Winter 1986):240–242

Poem for Buddy. Poem. *Callaloo* 9, No. 2 (Spring 1986):341–344

Relativity. Poem. *Essence* 17, No. 1 (May 1986):169

Jordan, June (about)

The Love Poetry of June Jordan. Peter Erickson. *Callaloo* 9, No. 1 (Winter 1986):221–234

Jordan, Sandra Dickerson

Focus on the 1984 Bail Reform Act: Pretrial Detention Permitted. *Black Law Journal* 9, No. 3 (Winter 1986):280–295

Jorden, William J.

Panama Odyssey. Reviewed by Ambler H. Moss, Jr. *Caribbean Review* 15, No. 1 (Winter 1986):43–44

Panama Odyssey. Reviewed by Neale Pearson. *Caribbean Review* 15, No. 1 (Winter 1986):26–27+

Jordon, Keith M.

The African Presence in Ancient America: Evidence from Physical Anthropology. Notes. *Journal of African Civilizations* 8, No. 2 (December 1986):136–151

Joseph, Carole Berotte

Bilingual Education and Creole Languages. *Interracial Books for Children Bulletin* 17, Nos. 3–4 (1986):13–14

Kavanagh, Robert Mshengu

Theater and Cultural Struggle in South Africa. Reviewed by Ian Steadman. *Research in African Literatures* 17, No. 2 (Summer 1986): 267–271

Kazi-Ferrouillet, Kuumba

1986 Comprehensive Employment Outlook for Engineering Students. *Black Collegian* 16, No. 3 (January/February 1986):162–163

Careers 1990: The Changing Workplace. *Black Collegian* 17, No. 1 (September/October 1986):81–87

The Divi Hotels: Hospitality with That Caribbean Touch. *Black Collegian* 17, No. 1 (September/October 1986):144–146

Kazi-Ferrouillet, Kuumba, and Ballard, Portia

Role Model Advice to Students. *Black Collegian* 17, No. 1 (September/October 1986):115–120

Kearney, Martin F.

Hawthorne's Beatrice Rappaccini: Unlocking her Paradoxical Nature with a Shelleyean Key. Notes. *CLA Journal* 29, No. 3 (March 1986):309–317

Kein, Sybil

Bessie Smith. Poem. *Essence* 17, No. 2 (July 1986):121

Kellersberger, Winifred

The Bantu-Speaking Heritage of the United States. Reviewed by Joseph E. Holloway. *Phylon* 47, No. 2 (June 1986):167–168

Kellico Checkers

Check It Out: Coat Checking and Matchmaking Pay Off. Janine C. McAdams. *Essence* 17, No. 6 (October 1986):109

Kellner, Bruce (editor)

The Harlem Renaissance: A Historical Dictionary for the Era. Book review. Arnold Rampersad. *Callaloo* 9, No. 4 (Fall 1986):749–750

Kelly, Lily M. (joint author)

See Singleton, Edward G.

Kelly, Loretta A.

Coming to Faith: My Testimony. *Essence* 16, No. 11 (March 1986):56

Kendrick, Dolores

Now Is the Thing to Praise. Book review. Gerald Barrax. *Callaloo* 9, No. 1 (Winter 1986):248–254

Kendrick, Gerald D.

Fools and Other Stories. Book review. *Black Scholar* 17, No. 4 (July-August 1986):57–58

Kennedy, Adrienne

Funny House of the Negro. Theater review. Cecilia Loving-Sloane. *Crisis* 93, No. 8 (October 1986):14

Kennedy, C. L. (about)

Cream of Vegetables. Vernon Smith. *Black Enterprise* 17, No. 2 (September 1986):18

Kennedy, C. L., All-Premium Ice Cream

See Kennedy, C. L.

Kennedy, James H.

Political Liberalization, Black Consciousness, and Recent Afro-Brazilian Literary Production. *Phylon* 47, No. 3 (September 1986):199–209

Kennedy, Jayne (about)

The New Jayne Kennedy: Wife, Mother, Woman. Laura B. Randolph. *Ebony* 41, No. 5 (March 1986):132

Kennedy, Shawn

Insurance Overview: A Change of Policy. *Black Enterprise* 16, No. 11 (June 1986):175

Kenney, William Howland (III)

The Influence of Black Vaudeville on Early Jazz. *Black Perspective in Music* 14, No. 3 (Fall 1986):233–248

Kentucky Fried Chicken Corporation

Doing Chicken Right. Sam Fulwood. *Black Enterprise* 17, No. 4 (November 1986):60

Kenya—History

Introduction: Swahili Verbal Arts. References. Carol M. Eastman. *Research in African Literatures* 17, No. 4 (Winter 1986): 459–463

Kenya—Language and Culture

Kikuyu People: A Brief Outline of their Customs and Traditions. By E. N. Mugo. Reviewed by Simon Gikandi. *Research in African Literatures* 17, No. 2 (Summer 1986): 299–301

Kenya—Literature

Literature for Children and Young People in Kenya. By Asenath Bole Odaga. Reviewed by Nancy J. Schmidt. *Research in African Literatures* 17, No. 4 (Winter 1986): 609–610

Un anglo d'Africa: Il Kenya visto dai suoi scrittori. Silvana Bottignole, translator. Reviewed by Jane Wilkinson. *Research in African Literatures* 17, No. 1 (Spring 1986): 142–144

The Writer in a Neocolonial State. Ngugi wa Thiong'o. *Black Scholar* 17, No. 4 (July-August 1986):2–10

Kenya—Mau Mau

Passbook Number F.47927: Women and Mau Mau in Kenya. By Muthoni Likimani. Reviewed by Hilary Fisher. *Race and Class* 27, No. 4 (Spring 1986):96–97

Kenya—Swahili Languages

Expressing a Swahili Sense of Humor: Siu Jokes. Notes. References. Carol M. Eastman. *Research in African Literatures* 17, No. 4 (Winter 1986): 474–495

Kessel, Felicia

An Evening with Bobby Short. *Crisis* 93, No. 10 (December 1986):24–25

Who Can Speak for South Africa? *Crisis* 93, No. 9 (November 1986):28

Kgositsile, Keorapetse

Culture and Resistance in South Africa. *Black Scholar* 17, No. 4 (July-August 1986):28–31

Khatib, S. M.

Africanity and the Black Family: The Development of a Theoretical Model. Book review. *Journal of Black Psychology* 13, No. 1 (August 1986):24–26

African Psychology: Towards Its Reclamation, Reascension and Revitalization. Book review. *Journal of Black Psychology* 13, No. 1 (August 1986):17–19

Understanding the Black Family: A Guide for Scholarship and Research. Book review. *Journal of Black Psychology* 13, No. 1 (August 1986):20–23

Kibreab, Gaim

African Refugees: Reflections on the African Refugee Problem. Book review. Maurice Herson. *Race and Class* 27, No. 4 (Spring 1986):104–105

Kikuyu—Oral Literature

Kikuyu People: A Brief Outline of their Customs and Traditions. By E. N. Mugo. Reviewed by Simon Gikandi. *Research in African Literatures* 17, No. 2 (Summer 1986): 299–301

Killam, G. D.

A Guide to Twentieth Century Literature in English. Book review. *Research in African Literatures* 17, No. 3 (Fall 1986): 430

Killam, G. D. (editor)

Critical Perspectives on Ngugi wa Thiong'o. Reviewed by D. A. Maughan Brown. *Research in African Literatures* 17, No. 4 (Winter 1986): 614–617

Killingsworth, Cleve L. (about)

The Professional in Management: Cleve L. Killingsworth. Anita Johnson Sims. *About Time* 14, No. 12 (December 1986):11–12

Kimbrough, Ann

Deals on Wheels. *Black Enterprise* 16, No. 9 (April 1986):25

The Fight for the Fifth. *Black Enterprise* 17, No. 4 (November 1986):21

Savings and Loan Overview: Staying Nifty, Thrifty—and Wise. *Black Enterprise* 16, No. 11 (June 1986):159

King, B. B. (about)

On the Road with B. B. King: After 38 Years, the Legendary Monarch of the Blues Is Still a Roadrunning Troubadour. Walter Leavy. *Ebony* 41, No. 8 (June 1986):141

King, Coretta Scott

Martin's Legacy. *Ebony* 41, No. 3 (January 1986):105

King, Martin Luther (Jr.)

"I Have a Dream." *Ebony* 41, No. 3 (January 1986):40–42

The Living King: Selected Quotes from His Speeches and Books. *Ebony* 41, No. 3 (January 1986):64

Statement at Hunter College. *Black Collegian* 16, No. 3 (January/February 1986):36–38

See also Martin Luther King (Jr.) Holiday

King, Martin Luther (Jr.) (about)

At the River I Stand: Memphis, the 1968 Strike and Martin Luther King. By Joan Turner Beifuss. Reviewed by Cain H. Felder. *Journal of Religious Thought* 43, No. 2 (Fall-Winter 1986–87):93–94

An Ethic of Hope: The Moral Thought of Martin Luther King, Jr. Robert M. Franklin, Jr. *About Time* 14, No. 1 (January 1986):10–26

Important Dates in the Life of Martin Luther King (Jr.) *Ebony* 41, No. 3 (January 1986):44

King on Vietnam and Beyond. Henry E. Darby and Margaret N. Rowley. *Phylon* 47, No. 1 (March 1986):43–50

Martin Luther King, Jr.: The Making of a Martyr. William R. Witherspoon. *Black Collegian* 16, No. 3 (January/February 1986):64–78

Martin Luther King (Jr.) and the Paradox of Nonviolent Direct Action. James A. Colaiaco. *Phylon* 47, No. 1 (March 1986):16–28

Martin Luther King (Jr.) and the Quest for Nonviolent Social Change. Adam Fairclough. *Phylon* 47, No. 1 (March 1986):1–15

Martin's Legacy. Coretta Scott King. *Ebony* 41, No. 3 (January 1986):105

The Political Legacy of Dr. King. Adrienne M. Johnson. *Crisis* 93, No. 2 (February 1986):26

What Martin Luther King Means to Me. *Ebony* 41, No. 3 (January 1986):74

The Young Martin: From Childhood through College. Christine King Farris. *Ebony* 41, No. 3 (January 1986):56

King, Martin Luther (Jr.)—Commemorative Stamps

The World Honors Martin Luther King (Jr.) through Commemorative Stamps. *Ebony* 41, No. 3 (January 1986):82

King, Martin Luther (Jr.)—Criticism and Interpretation

Martin Luther King, Jr.'s "Beloved Community" Ideal and the Apartheid System in South Africa. Lewis V. Baldwin. *Western Journal of Black Studies* 10, No. 4 (Winter 1986):211–222

King, Martin Luther (Jr.)—Photographs

Memorable Photos of Martin Luther King (Jr.) *Ebony* 41, No. 3 (January 1986):86

King, Martin Luther (Jr.)—Statues and Monuments

In Memory of Martin Luther King (Jr.) *Ebony* 41, No. 3 (January 1986):64

Kingston, New York—History

A Beginning Investigation into the Afro-American Cemeteries of Ulster County, New York. Gail Schneider. *Afro-Americans in New York Life and History* 10, No.1 (January 1986):61–70

Kinley, Barbara, and Moses, Yolanda T.

Women and Development in Africa: A Bibliography. *SAGE* 3, No. 2 (Fall 1986):65–69

Kinte, Kunta (about)

Kunta Kinte's Struggle to be African. Harold Courlander.*Phylon* 47, No. 4 (December 1986):294–302

Kipury, Naomi

Oral Literature of the Maasai. Reviewed by Clement Abiaziem Okafor. *Research in African Literatures* 17, No. 2 (Summer 1986): 301–304

Kishwar, Madhu

Gandhi on Women. *Race and Class* 28, No. 1 (Summer 1986):43–61

Kiuchi, Toru (joint author)

See Hakutani, Yoshinobu

Knapp, Herbert, and Knapp, Mary

Red, White and Blue Paradise, The American Canal Zone in Panama. Reviewed by Neale Pearson. *Caribbean Review* 15, No. 1 (Winter 1986):26–27 +

Knapp, Mary (joint author)

See Knapp, Herbert

Knight, Octavia B. (joint author)

See Steppe-Jones, Cecilia

Knight, Sydney M.

Constructive Eviction—An Illusive Tenant Remedy? *Howard Law Journal* 29, No. 1 (1986):13–26

Knipp, Thomas R.

J. P. Clark. Book review. *Research in African Literatures* 17, No. 2 (Summer 1986): 278–281

Koblenz, Jay

Auto Overview: The Autocrats. *Black Enterprise* 16, No. 11 (June 1986):191

Exotic Roadsters. *Black Enterprise* 17, No. 4 (November 1986):78

A First for Ford. *Black Enterprise* 16, No. 12 (July 1986):16

Kolko, Gabriel

Anatomy of a War: Vietnam, the United States and the Modern Historical Experience. Book review. Saul Landau. *Race and Class* 28, No. 1 (Summer 1986):91–93

Komunyakaa, Yusef

Boy Wearing a Dead Man's Clothes. Poem. *Callaloo* 9, No. 1 (Winter 1986):81–82

Communique. Poem. *Callaloo* 9, No. 1 (Winter 1986):83–84

From Crescent City Blues. Poem. *Callaloo* 9, No. 2 (Spring 1986):301

Lightshow. Poem. *Callaloo* 9, No. 1 (Winter 1986):86

Nothing Big. Poem. *Callaloo* 9, No. 1 (Winter 1986):85

Two Cranial Murals. Poem. *Callaloo* 9, No. 2 (Spring 1986):300

Kone, A., et al.

Littérature et méthodologie. Reviewed by Mineke Schipper. *Research in African Literatures* 17, No. 4 (Winter 1986): 566–567

Kool and the Gang

Kool and the Gang: Hottest Group of the '80s. Lynn Norment. *Ebony* 42, No. 1 (November 1986):70

Kotchy, Barthelemy (joint author)

See Dailly, Christophe

Kotin, Leslie

Preventing PMS. *Essence* 17, No. 8 (December 1986):14

Kotze, Sandra (joint compiler)

See Richter, Barbara

Koutrelakos, James

Autonomy and Theoretical Orientation of Remedial and Non-Remedial College Students. *Journal of Negro Education* 55, No. 1 (Winter 1986):29–37

Kozol, Jonathan

Illiterate America. Book review. *Journal of Negro Education* 55, No. 1 (Winter 1986):117–118

Illiterate America. Book review. Sharon Shervington. *Black Enterprise* 17, No. 2 (September 1986):15

Kpelle—Language and Culture

The Language of Secrecy. By Beryl Bellman. Reviewed by William P. Murphy. *Research in African Literatures* 17, No. 2 (Summer 1986): 296–298

Kroger, Terry (compiler)

New Books on Music. *Black Perspective in Music* 14, No. 2 (Spring 1986):181–184

New Books on Music. *Black Perspective in Music* 14, No. 3 (Fall 1986):303–305

Ku Klux Klan

The Ku Klux Klan: Reasons for Support or Opposition among White Respondents. Rick Seltzer and Grace M. Lopes. *Journal of Black Studies* 17, No. 1 (September 1986):91–109

Kurds

Notes on the Kurdish Struggle. Sinjari Hussain. *Race and Class* 27, No. 3 (Winter 1986):92–94

Kushnick, Louis

Blacks and Whites: Narrowing the Gap? Book review. *Race and Class* 27, No. 3 (Winter 1986):106–108

The Myth of Black Progress. Book review. *Race and Class* 27, No. 3 (Winter 1986):106–108

Kutzinski, Vera M.

Changing Permanences. *Callaloo* 9, No. 1 (Winter 1986):171–183

Modernism and Negritude: The Poetry and Poetics of Aime Cesaire. Book reviw. *Callaloo* 9, No. 4 (Fall 1986):740–748

Kuumba

Black Theater Stages a Comeback. *Ebony* 42, No. 1 (November 1986):54

Kuzwayo, Ellen

Call Me Woman. Book review. Angus Richmond. *Race and Class* 27, No. 4 (Spring 1986):90–92

Kwanzaa

Celebrating Kwanzaa Now! *Essence* 17, No. 8 (December 1986):99

Kyle, David

Slave Emancipation in Cuba. The Transition to Free Labor, 1866–1899. Book review. *Caribbean Review* 15, No. 2 (Spring 1986):47

Labelle, Patti (about)

The Other Patti LaBelle: Wife, Mother and World Class Cook. Laura B. Randolph. *Ebony* 41, No. 6 (April 1986):31

Labor and Laboring Classes

Issues in American History: The Worker in America. By Jane Claypool. Reviewed by Jan M. Goodman. *Interracial Books for Children Bulletin* 17, No. 2 (1986):13

Race and Labour in Twentieth Century Britain. Edited by Kenneth Lunn. Reviewed by Paul Gordon. *Race and Class* 28, No. 2 (August 1986):102–103

Labor Unions

The Art of Diplomacy: Bob Brown and Local 435. Joan Marie Allen. *About Time* 14, No. 12 (December 1986):9–10

Dorothy Bolden, Organizer of Domestic Workers: She Was Born Poor but She Would Not Bow Down. Imani-Shelia Newsome. *SAGE* 3, No. 1 (Spring 1986):53–55

Latino Caucuses in U.S. Labour Unions. Hector Ramos. *Race and Class* 27, No. 4 (Spring 1986):69–78

Let Us Do Our Part: The New York City Based Negro Labor Victory Committee, 1941–1945. C. Alvin Hughes. *Afro-Americans in New York Life and History* 10, No.1 (January 1986):19–29

See also American Federation of State, County and Municipal Employees

See also Building Trades

See also Collective Bargaining

Labor Unions—Employment Policies

Labor's Role in Support of Full Employment. William Lucy. *Urban League Review* 10, No. 1 (Summer 1986):79–86

Labor Unions—Officials and Employees

At the Bargaining Table. Joyce Davis Adams. *Black Enterprise* 17, No. 1 (August 1986):52–54

Ladner, Joyce A.

Black Women Face the 21st Century: Major Issues and Problems. *Black Scholar* 17, No. 5 (September-October 1986):12–19

LaDuke, Betty

June Beer: Nicaraguan Artist. *SAGE* 3, No. 2 (Fall 1986):35–39

La Guma, Alex (about)

Alex La Guma Revolutionary Intellectual. Daniel Garcia Santos. *Black Scholar* 17, No. 4 (July-August 1986):55–56

Lam, Wilfredo (about)

The Mythical Landscapes of a Cuban Painter: Wilfredo Lam's *La Jungla*. Juan A. Martinez. *Caribbean Review* 15, No. 2 (Spring 1986):32–36

Lamaute, Denise

Bold Money. Book review. *Black Enterprise* 17, No. 3 (October 1986):88

Finance You, Inc. *Black Enterprise* 16, No. 11 (June 1986):265–266

Finding the Best Bets in Bonds. *Black Enterprise* 17, No. 5 (December 1986):39–40

Fired! Creating a Financial Safety Net Now Can Prevent Serious Injuries if You're Handed the Pink Slip. *Black Enterprise* 17, No. 3 (October 1986):111

Getting Your Money's Worth in Fine Jewelry. *Black Enterprise* 16, No. 10 (May 1986):33–34

How to Minimize Relocation Costs. *Black Enterprise* 17, No. 1 (August 1986):21–22

The Ins and Outs of Buying a Foreign Car. *Black Enterprise* 17, No. 4 (November 1986):80

Insuring Your Income against Disability. *Black Enterprise* 17, No. 4 (November 1986):39–40

Investing in Commercial Real Estate. *Black Enterprise* 16, No. 11 (June 1986):71–72

Renovating Your Home the Smart Way. *Black Enterprise* 16, No. 8 (March 1986):21–22

Taking the Sting Out of Filing Taxes. *Black Enterprise* 16, No. 9 (April 1986):33–34

Tapping the Magic of Mutual Funds. *Black Enterprise* 17, No. 2 (September 1986):29–30

Winning at the Stock Options Game. *Black Enterprise* 16, No. 12 (July 1986):23–24

Winning the Tax Revolution. *Black Enterprise* 17, No. 5 (December 1986):62

Lampert, Rachel (about)

Rachel Lampert. Kris DiLorenzo. *Crisis* 93, No. 3 (March 1986):12–48

Lamphear, John

Iteso Thought Patterns in Tales. Book review. *Research in African Literatures* 17, No. 2 (Summer 1986): 298–299

Landau, Saul

Anatomy of a War: Vietnam, the United States and the Modern Historical Experience. Book review. *Race and Class* 28, No. 1 (Summer 1986):91–93

Nicaragua: Revolution in the Family. Book review. *Race and Class* 27, No. 3 (Winter 1986):95–99

Land Developers

How One Man Is Building the City of the Future. Lloyd Gite. *Black Enterprise* 17, No. 5 (December 1986):68

Landlord and Tenant

The Duty of a Modern Landlord and Tenant to Protect His Tenants from Crime. Christy E. Harris. *Howard Law Journal* 29, No. 1 (1986):149–163

The Effect of the Requirement of Expert Testimony on the Tenant's Ability to Prove Damages in a Breach of Warranty of Habitability Action. Philip W. Coleman. *Howard Law Journal* 29, No. 1 (1986):177–189

Jurisdiction of the Landlord and Tenant Branch of the Superior Court of the District of Columbia. Fred D. Gray, Jr. *Howard Law Journal* 29, No. 1 (1986):137–147

Notice to Quit. Alonzo L. Llorens. *Howard Law Journal* 29, No. 1 (1986):1–11

Protective Orders. Sharon Y. Vaughn. *Howard Law Journal* 29, No. 1 (1986):127–135

Rights of a Tenant When the Landlord Defaults on the Mortgage. Anna E. Blackburne. *Howard Law Journal* 29, No. 1 (1986):27–39

Special Project on Landlord-Tenant Law in the District of Columbia Court of Appeals. *Howard Law Journal* 29, No. 1 (1986):1–189

A Tenant's Right to Counterclaim for a Period Predating Landlord's Claim. Angela J. Moffitt. *Howard Law Journal* 29, No. 1 (1986):41–61

Lane, J. Eric

Legends and History of the Luba. Book review. *Research in African Literatures* 17, No. 2 (Summer 1986): 306–308

Lane, Pinkie Gordon

I Never Scream: New and Selected Poems. Book review. Lillian D. Roland. *Black American Literature Forum* 20, No. 3 (Fall 1986):294–298

Poems to My Father. *Black American Literature Forum* 20, No. 3 (Fall 1986):289–293

Lang, Marvel

Black Student Retention at Black Colleges and Universities: Problems, Issues, and Alternatives. *Western Journal of Black Studies* 10, No. 2 (Summer 1986):48–54

Language

The Black Prole and Whitespeak: Black English from an Orwellian Perspective. Henry J. Grubb. *Race and Class* 27, No. 3 (Winter 1986):67–80

Language—Bibliographies

Publications by CLA Members: 1985–86. Bibliography. Robert J. Hudson and Robert P. Smith (Jr.) *CLA Journal* 30, No. 2 (December 1986):241–251

Language and Culture

The Dual Vision: Insights and Applications of Cross-Cultural Research. Bennetta Jules-Rosette. *Journal of Negro Education* 55, No. 2 (Spring 1986):125–141

Origin of the Ancient Egyptians. Notes. Cheikh Anta Diop. *Journal of African Civilizations* 8, No. 1 (June 1986):35–63

The Third World Concept: Revisited. Jimm De Shields and M. Zaimaran. *Negro Educational Review* 37, No. 2 (April 1986):71–80

Language—Dissertations and Theses

Master's Theses in Progress in Selected Colleges and Universities. Mac A. Stewart. *Negro Educational Review* 37, Nos. 3–4 (July-October 1986):101

Language—Etymology

Africa and the Discovery of America, Volume I. By Leo Wiener. Reviewed by Phillips Barry. *Journal of African Civilizations* 8, No. 2 (December 1986):197–201

Mandinga Voyages across the Atlantic. Notes. Harold G. Lawrence. *Journal of African Civilizations* 8, No. 2 (December 1986):202–247

Language—Grammar

Linguistic Description and Literary Interpretation. Notes. Rei R. Noguchi. *CLA Journal* 30, No. 2 (December 1986):171–183

The Transitive Vampire: A Handbook of Grammar for the Innocent, the Eager and the Damned. By Karen Elizabeth Gordon. Reviewed by Elizabeth J. Higgins. *CLA Journal* 30, No. 2 (December 1986):252–253

Language and Literature

The Bantu-Speaking Heritage of the United States. By Winifred Kellersberger. Reviewed by Joseph E. Holloway. *Phylon* 47, No. 2 (June 1986):167–168

Ideology or Pedagogy: The Linguistic Indigenisation of African Literature. Al-Amin M. Mazrui. *Race and Class* 28, No. 1 (Summer 1986):63–72

Interdisciplinary Dimensions of African Literature. Kofi Anyidoho, Abioseh M. Porter, Daniel Racine, and Janice Spleth, editors. Reviewed by C. L. Innes. *Research in African Literatures* 17, No. 3 (Fall 1986): 449–451

John Dennis and the Religious Sublime. Notes. David M. Wheeler. *CLA Journal* 30, No. 2 (December 1986):210–218

"To Hear New Utterance Flow": Language Before the Fall in *Paradise Lost*. Notes. Leonard Mustazzi. *CLA Journal* 30, No. 2 (December 1986):184–209

Language and Logic

Linguistic Description and Literary Interpretation. Notes. Rei R. Noguchi. *CLA Journal* 30, No. 2 (December 1986):171–183

Language—Teaching

Tapping Potential: English and Language Arts for the Black Learner. Edited by Charlotte K. Brooks. Reviewed by Hawthorne Faison. *Black Scholar* 17, No. 3 (May-June 1986):60

Lankford, Richard (about)

Georgia's Reverend Sheriff: Richard Lankford Finds Joy in Preaching the Gospel and Keeping the Peace. Marilyn Marshall. *Ebony* 41, No. 5 (March 1986):92

Lannoy, Violet Dias

The Bewitched. *Callaloo* 9, No. 2 (Spring 1986):279–294

Larger Sizes, Inc.

King-Size Entrepreneur Runs Queen-Size Dress Chain. *Ebony* 41, No. 8 (June 1986):53

Larsen, Nella—Criticism and Interpretation

Nella Larsen's Use of the Near-White Female in *Quicksand*, and *Passing*. Vashti Crutcher Lewis. *Western Journal of Black Studies* 10, No. 3 (Fall 1986):137–142

Passing for What? Aspects of Identity in Nella Larsen's Novels. Cheryl Wall. *Black American Literature Forum* 20, Nos. 1–2 (Spring/Summer 1986):97–111

Larsson, Cloyte Murdock

Land of the Till Murder Revisited: Former *Ebony* Staffer Returns after 30 Years to Report on "The New Mississippi." *Ebony* 41, No. 5 (March 1986):53

Lasky, Kathryn

Night Journey. Book review. Suzi Wizowaty. *Interracial Books for Children Bulletin* 17, Nos. 3–4 (1986):35–36

Latin America—Bibliographies

Recent Books on the Region and its Peoples. Bibliography. Compiled by Marian Goslinga. *Caribbean Review* 15, No. 1 (Winter 1986):45–48

Recent Books on the Region and its Peoples. Bibliography. Compiled by Marian Goslinga. *Caribbean Review* 15, No. 2 (Spring 1986):49–52

Latin America—Black Literature

The Human Legacy of Black Latin American Literature. Notes. Richard L. Jackson. *CLA Journal* 30, No. 2 (December 1986):154–170

Herschel Walker: Pro Football's New Million-Dollar Man. *Ebony* 42, No. 1 (November 1986):156

Michael Spinks: The New King of the Ring. *Ebony* 41, No. 5 (March 1986):35

On the Road with B. B. King: After 38 Years, the Legendary Monarch of the Blues Is Still a Roadrunning Troubadour. *Ebony* 41, No. 8 (June 1986):141

Patrick Ewing: Can This Man Save the Knicks? *Ebony* 41, No. 4 (February 1986):59

The Real-Life Tragedy of Dorothy Dandridge. *Ebony* 41, No. 11 (September 1986):136

Reggie Jackson: More than Just a Baseball Superstar. *Ebony* 41, No. 9 (July 1986):104

Sade: The Story behind the Exotic Singing Sensation. *Ebony* 41, No. 7 (May 1986):155

William A. Perry: The Man behind the "Fridge." *Ebony* 41, No. 12 (October 1986):29

Lee, Diane

Women's Liberation and the Dialectics of Revolution: Reaching for the Future. Book review. *SAGE* 3, No. 1 (Spring 1986):62–63

Lee, Jeanne M.

Toad Is the Uncle of Heaven. Book review. Valerie Ooka Pang. *Interracial Books for Children Bulletin* 17, No. 1 (1986):9

Lee, John D.

The Easy Love of Friends. Poem. *Essence* 17, No. 2 (July 1986):114

Lee, Marjorie W.

The Match: Learning Styles of Black Children and Microcomputer Programming. *Journal of Negro Education* 55, No. 1 (Winter 1986):78–90

Lee, Spike

She's Gotta Have It. Film review. Marsha Jones. *About Time* 14, No. 10 (October 1986):24–25

Spike Lee's "She's Gotta Have It." Film review. Paul Lindsey Johnson. *Crisis* 93, No. 8 (October 1986):11–12

Lee, Spike (about)

Spike Lee's Declaration of Independence. David Frechette. *Black Enterprise* 17, No. 5 (December 1986):56

Lee, Thonnia

The Hospitality Industry: Still Growing Strong. *Black Collegian* 17, No. 1 (September/October 1986):137–147

Leech, Kenneth

Black Religion and Black Radicalism: An Interpretation of the Religious History of Afro-American People. Book review. *Race and Class* 28, No. 2 (August 1986):97–99

"Diverse Reports" and the Meaning of "Racism." *Race and Class* 28, No. 2 (August 1986):82–88

Leftwich, Joseph (about)

Spanning Two Languages: The Legacy of Isaac and Joseph. Chris Searle. *Race and Class* 28, No. 1 (Summer 1986):29–42

Legislators

Defending Voting Rights in the Alabama Black Belt. Frances M. Beal. *Black Scholar* 17, No. 3 (May-June 1986):34

New Forms of Leadership. Carolyne S. Blount. *About Time* 14, No. 2 (February 1986):8–26

     See also United States Congress

Legislators—State

The Body Politic. Margo Walker. *Black Enterprise* 16, No. 11 (June 1986):50

Legislators—United States

Parren Mitchell: Interview. David Hatchett. *Crisis* 93, No. 2 (February 1986):34–40

Parren Mitchell's Sixteen Years: A Legislative Legacy. David C. Ruffin. *Black Enterprise* 16, No. 11 (June 1986):59–60

Senator Robert Dole: Interview. Paul Lindsey Johnson. *Crisis* 93, No. 7 (August/September 1986):30

Shades of Gray. David C. Ruffin. *Black Enterprise* 16, No. 8 (March 1986):28–33

Whole Wheat. David C. Ruffin. *Black Enterprise* 17, No. 1 (August 1986):48

Leguizamon, Francisco A.

Estado empresario y lucha politica en Costa Rica. Book review. *Caribbean Review* 15, No. 2 (Spring 1986):45–46

Leiner, Jacqueline (editor)

Soleil éclate. Reviewed by Bernard Aresu. *Research in African Literatures* 17, No. 4 (Winter 1986): 588–591

Leinster, Emily

Don't Be My Valentine. Book review. *Interracial Books for Children Bulletin* 17, No. 1 (1986):6

Home in the Sky. Book review. *Interracial Books for Children Bulletin* 17, No. 1 (1986):8–9

Jimmy Lee Did It. Book review. *Interracial Books for Children Bulletin* 17, No. 1 (1986):8

Vol. 1: The Black Achievers Coloring Book; Vol. 2: The Black Achievers Activity Book. Book review. *Interracial Books for Children Bulletin* 17, No. 2 (1986):17

Leinster, Emily, and Leinster Sasha

Living in Two Worlds. Book review. *Interracial Books for Children Bulletin* 17, Nos. 3–4 (1986):33–34

Leinster, Sasha (joint author)

See Leinster, Emily

Lemelle, Anthony J.

Beyond Black Power: The Contradiction between Capital and Liberty. *Western Journal of Black Studies* 10, No. 2 (Summer 1986):70–76

Leonard, Neil

The Jazzman's Verbal Usage. *Black American Literature Forum* 20, Nos. 1–2 (Spring/Summer 1986):151–160

LeSeur, Geta

One Mother, Two Daughters: The Afro-American and the Afro-Caribbean Female *Bildungsroman*. *Black Scholar* 17, No. 2 (March-April 1986):26–33

Lessing, Doris (about)

Doris Lessing. By Lorna Sage. Reviewed by Roberta Rubenstein. *Research in African Literatures* 17, No. 3 (Fall 1986): 411–413

An Interview with Doris Lessing. Stephen Gray. *Research in African Literatures* 17, No. 3 (Fall 1986): 329–340

Levine, Barry B.

Crossing Swords: Rethinking Cuba. *Caribbean Review* 15, No. 2 (Spring 1986):3

Levitas, Ruth

The Ideology of the New Right. Book review. Paul Gordon. *Race and Class* 28, No. 1 (Summer 1986):95–97

Lewis, Carol Anita

Ask Winnie Mandela. Poem. *Essence* 17, No. 7 (November 1986):151

Lula's Chil Grown. Poem. *Essence* 17, No. 7 (November 1986):151

Lewis, David E.

Fire from the Mountain: The Making of a Sandinista. Book review. *Black Scholar* 17, No. 1 (January-February 1986):49

Lewis, Ephron (about)

Rice, Rice and More Rice: Ephron Lewis' Arkansas Farm Yields the Long, Medium and Short of It. *Ebony* 42, No. 2 (December 1986):100

Lewis, Errol

BE Company of the Year: Maxima. *Black Enterprise* 16, No. 11 (June 1986):130

Lewis, John (about)

The Fight for the Fifth. Ann Kimbrough. *Black Enterprise* 17, No. 4 (November 1986):21

Lewis, Samella

George Smith. Illustrated. *International Review of African American Art* 7, No. 2 (1986):6–15

Richard Hunt. Illustrated. *International Review of African American Art* 7, No. 2 (1986):16–21

Lewis, Tracey Pamela (about)

Tracey at the Bat. Timothy W. Smith. *Black Enterprise* 17, No. 2 (September 1986):52

Lewis, Vashti Crutcher

Nella Larsen's Use of the Near-White Female in *Quicksand*, and *Passing*. *Western Journal of Black Studies* 10, No. 3 (Fall 1986):137–142

Lexau, Joan M.

Don't Be My Valentine. Book review. Emily Leinster. *Interracial Books for Children Bulletin* 17, No. 1 (1986):6

Leyden, William

Strength for the Fight: A History of Blacks in the Military. Book review. *Negro Educational Review* 37, Nos. 3–4 (July-October 1986):155–156

Liberal Arts Careers

The Liberal Arts Make a Comeback. Lauran M. Nohe. *Black Collegian* 17, No. 1 (September/October 1986):124–126

Liberalism

Neoliberalism and Black Education. John Martin Rich. *Journal of Negro Education* 55, No. 1 (Winter 1986):21–28

Liberation Theology

Fidel y la Religion: Conversaciones con Frei Betto. Interview. Reviewed by Paul E. Sigmund. *Caribbean Review* 15, No. 2 (Spring 1986):30–31

Liberation Theology and Islamic Revivalism. Notes. Mohammad Yadegari. *Journal of Religious Thought* 43, No. 2 (Fall-Winter 1986–87):38–50

Ritual, Paradox and Death in Managua: Internacionalistas in Nicaragua. Alfred Padula. *Caribbean Review* 15, No. 1 (Winter 1986):18–19

Who Teaches Black Theology? Notes. Rufus Burrow (Jr.) *Journal of Religious Thought* 43, No. 2 (Fall-Winter 1986–87):7–18

Liberia—Culture

The Language of Secrecy. By Beryl Bellman. Reviewed by William P. Murphy. *Research in African Literatures* 17, No. 2 (Summer 1986): 296–298

Liberia—Missionaries

"Say Africa When You Pray": The Activities of Early Black Baptist Women Missionaries among Liberian Women and Children. Sylvia M. Jacobs. *SAGE* 3, No. 2 (Fall 1986):16–21

Lieber, Michael

Street Life: Afro-American Culture in Urban Trinidad. Reviewed by Keith Q. Warner. *CLA Journal* 29, No. 4 (June 1986):493–496

Lieutenant-Governors

L. Douglas Wilder: Virginia's Lieutenant Governor. Lynn Norment. *Ebony* 41, No. 6 (April 1986):67

Life Expectancy

Black and White Children in America: Key Facts. Children's Defense Fund. Reviewed by Gayl Fowler. *Journal of Religious Thought* 43, No. 1 (Spring-Summer 1986):130

How to Figure Out Cuba: Development, Ideology and Mortality. Sergio Diaz-Briquets. *Caribbean Review* 15, No. 2 (Spring 1986):8–11+

Likimani, Muthoni

Passbook Number F.47927: Women and Mau Mau in Kenya. Book review. Hilary Fisher. *Race and Class* 27, No. 4 (Spring 1986):96–97

Linguistics

The African Origin of Civilization: Myth or Reality. Notes. By Cheikh Anta Diop. Reviewed by A. J. Williams-Myers. *Journal of African Civilizations* 8, No. 1 (June 1986):118–126

Further Conversations with the Pharaoh. Interview. Charles S. Finch. *Journal of African Civilizations* 8, No. 1 (June 1986):227–237

Ideology or Pedagogy: The Linguistic Indigenisation of African Literature. Al-Amin M. Mazrui. *Race and Class* 28, No. 1 (Summer 1986):63–72

Interview with Cheikh Anta Diop. Interview. Notes. Bibliography. Shawna Moore. *Journal of African Civilizations* 8, No. 1 (June 1986):238–248

The Language of Secrecy. By Beryl Bellman. Reviewed by William P. Murphy. *Research in African Literatures* 17, No. 2 (Summer 1986): 296–298

Linguistic Description and Literary Interpretation. Notes. Rei R. Noguchi. *CLA Journal* 30, No. 2 (December 1986):171–183

Origin of the Ancient Egyptians. Notes. Cheikh Anta Diop. *Journal of African Civilizations* 8, No. 1 (June 1986):35–63

Linnemann, Russell J. (joint editor)

See Wylie, Hal

Lipsitz, George

Grass Roots Activists and Social Change: The Story of Ivory Perry. *CAAS Newsletter* 9, No. 2 (1986):1

Lipski, John M.

The Negros Congos of Panama: Afro-Hispanic Creole Language and Culture. *Journal of Black Studies* 16, No. 4 (June 1986):409–428

Liqueurs

Island Liqueurs. Eunice Fried. *Black Enterprise* 16, No. 10 (May 1986):88

Literacy

Did Fidel Fudge the Figures? Literacy and Health: The Cuban Model. Nicholas Eberstadt. *Caribbean Review* 15, No. 2 (Spring 1986):5–7+

Gideonites and Freedmen: Adult Literacy Education at Port Royal, 1862–1865. John R. Rachal. *Journal of Negro Education* 55, No.4 (Fall 1986):453–469

How to Figure Out Cuba: Development, Ideology and Mortality. Sergio Diaz-Briquets. *Caribbean Review* 15, No. 2 (Spring 1986):8–11+

Illiterate America. By Jonathan Kozol. Reviewed by Edwin Hamilton. *Journal of Negro Education* 55, No. 1 (Winter 1986):117–118

Illiterate America. By Jonathan Kozol. Reviewed by Sharon Shervington. *Black Enterprise* 17, No. 2 (September 1986):15

A Look at Tomorrow's Issues Today. David C. Ruffin. *Black Enterprise* 16, No. 7 (February 1986):35

Literary Criticism

Gibb's Gibberish. Chinweizu, Onwuchekwa Jemie, and Ihechukwu Madubuike. *Research in African Literatures* 17, No. 1 (Spring 1986):48–52

Linguistic Description and Literary Interpretation. Notes. Rei R. Noguchi. *CLA Journal* 30, No. 2 (December 1986):171–183

Soyinka as a Literary Critic. Notes. Obiajuru Maduakor. *Research in African Literatures* 17, No. 1 (Spring 1986): 1–38

Toni Morrison's World of Topsy-Turvydom: A Methodological Explication of New Black Literary Criticism. Clenora Hudson-Withers. *Western Journal of Black Studies* 10, No. 3 (Fall 1986):132–136

Literary Criticism—Feminist Perspectives

Rousseau's Julie; Or, the Maternal Odyssey. Notes. Ruth Ohayon. *CLA Journal* 30, No. 1 (September 1986):69–82

Some Implications of Womanist Theory. Sherley A. Williams. *Callaloo* 9, No. 2 (Spring 1986):303–308

Literature, Afro-American

African American Literature: A New Challenge. Eloise Greenfield. *Interracial Books for Children Bulletin* 17, No. 2 (1986):4–5

Beyond the Myth of Confrontation: A Comparative Study of African and African-American Female Protagonists. Ebele Eko. *Phylon* 47, No. 3 (September 1986):219–229

The Black Universe in Contemporary Afro-American Fiction. Notes. Norman Harris. *CLA Journal* 30, No. 1 (September 1986):1–13

Castration Symbolism in Recent Black American Fiction. Notes. Richard K. Barksdale. *CLA Journal* 29, No. 4 (June 1986):400–413

A *Crisis* Report on Literature. Joe Johnson. *Crisis* 93, No. 1 (January 1986):11

Images of Blacks in Plays by Black Women. Elizabeth Brown-Guillory. *Phylon* 47, No. 3 (September 1986):230–237

La rive noire: De Harlem à la Seine. By Michel Fabre. Reviewed by Clarisse Zimra. *Research in African Literatures* 17, No. 4 (Winter 1986): 601–603

"My Love is Black as Yours is Fair":Premarital Love and Sexuality in the Antebellum Slave Narrative. *Phylon* 47, No. 3 (September 1986):238–247

Race and Poetry: Two Anthologies of the Twenties. Notes. Vilma R. Potter. *CLA Journal* 29, No. 3 (March 1986):276–287

Literature, Afro-American—Bibliographies

Publishers Listing of Black Interest Books. *Black Scholar* 17, No. 4 (July-August 1986):33–49

Studies in Afro-American Literature: An Annual Annotated Bibliography, 1985. Charles H. Rowell and Kimberly Chambers. *Callaloo* 9, No. 4 (Fall 1986):583–622

Literature—Addresses, Essays, Lectures

The Black Woman Writer and the Diaspora. Gloria T. Hull. *Black Scholar* 17, No. 2 (March-April 1986):2–4

The College Language Association: Past, Present, Future Perfect. Ann Venture Young. *CLA Journal* 29, No. 4 (June 1986):391–399

Conference Keynote Address: Sisterhood and Survival. Audre Lorde. *Black Scholar* 17, No. 2 (March-April 1986):5–7

Literature and Imperialism. Bart Moore-Gilbert, editor. Reviewed by Robert D. Hamner. *Research in African Literatures* 17, No. 1 (Spring 1986): 162–165

Olive Schreiner and After: Essays on Southern African Literature in Honor of Guy Butler. Malvern van Wyk Smith and Don Maclennan, editors. Reviewed by Dennis Walder. *Research in African Literatures* 17, No. 3 (Fall 1986): 401–404

The Truthful Lie: Essays in a Sociology of African Drama. By Biodun Jeyifo. Reviewed by Elaine Savory Fido. *Research in African Literatures* 17, No. 2 (Summer 1986): 273–275

Literature—Africa

Beyond the Myth of Confrontation: A Comparative Study of African and African-American Female Protagonists. Ebele Eko. *Phylon* 47, No. 3 (September 1986):219–229

Ideology or Pedagogy: The Linguistic Indigenisation of African Literature. Al-Amin M. Mazrui. *Race and Class* 28, No. 1 (Summer 1986):63–72

Ngambika: Studies of Women in African Literature. Edited by Carole Boyce Davies and Anne Adams Graves. Reviewed by Iely Burkhead Mohamed. *SAGE* 3, No. 2 (Fall 1986):59–60

The Writer in a Neocolonial State. Ngugi wa Thiong'o. *Black Scholar* 17, No. 4 (July-August 1986):2–10

Literature—Africa—Anthologies

Un anglo d'Africa: Il Kenya visto dai suoi scrittori. Silvana Bottignole, translator. Reviewed by Jane Wilkinson. *Research in African Literatures* 17, No. 1 (Spring 1986): 142–144

Literature—Africa—Bibliographies

African Literature on Film: A Preliminary Bibliography/Filmography. Notes. Nancy J. Schmidt. Notes. *Research in African Literatures* 17, No. 2 (Summer 1986): 261–266

An Annotated Bibliography of Swahili Fiction and Drama Published between 1975 and 1984. Notes. References. Elena Zubkova Bertoncini. *Research in African Literatures* 17, No. 4 (Winter 1986): 525–562

Bibliographies for African Studies, 1980–1983. Yvette Scheven, compiler. Reviewed by Nancy J. Schmidt. *Research in African Literatures* 17, No. 1 (Spring 1986): 145–146

Francophone Women Writers from Sub-Saharan Africa, Bibliography. Christine H. Guyonneau. *Callaloo* 9, No. 2 (Spring 1986):404–431

Francophone Women Writers from Sub-Saharan Africa and Its Diaspora. Christine H. Guyonneau. *Callaloo* 9, No. 4 (Fall 1986):694–736

Literature for Children and Young People in Kenya. By Asenath Bole Odaga. Reviewed by Nancy J. Schmidt. *Research in African Literatures* 17, No. 4 (Winter 1986): 609–610

Literature of the Diaspora by Women of Color. Leah Creque-Harris. *SAGE* 3, No. 2 (Fall 1986):61–64

Littératures africaines à la Bibliotèque Nationale, 1973–1983. Paulette Lordereau, compiler. Reviewed by Hans E. Panofsky. *Research in African Literatures* 17, No. 4 (Winter 1986): 605–606

Studies in African Literatures and Oratures: An Annual Annotated Bibliography, 1985. Janice A. Mayes and other. *Callaloo* 9, No. 4 (Fall 1986):673–693

Literature—Africa—English Language

African Short Stories in English: An Anthology. J. de Grandsaigne, editor. Reviewed by Adewale Maja-Pearce. *Research in African Literatures* 17, No. 4 (Winter 1986): 620–622

A Bibliography of Criticism of Southern African Literature in English. Barbara Richter and Sandra Kotze, compilers. Reviewed by G. E. Gorman. *Research in African Literatures* 17, No. 3 (Fall 1986): 419–421

Literature—Africa—French Language

Bibliographie méthodique et critique de la littérature algérienne de langue française, 1945-1977. By Jean Dejeux. Reviewed by Eric Sellin. *Research in African Literatures* 17, No. 4 (Winter 1986): 581

Essais d'histoire littéraire africaine. By Albert Gerard. Reviewed by Mohamadou Kane. *Research in African Literatures* 17, No. 4 (Winter 1986): 563-565

Ideologies of Race and Sex in Literature: Racism and Antiracism in the African Francophone Novel. Notes. E. P. Abanime. *CLA Journal* 30, No. 2 (December 1986):125-143

La nouvelle génération de poètes congolais. By Leopold-Pindy Mamonsono. Reviewed by Daniel Whitman. *Research in African Literatures* 17, No. 4 (Winter 1986): 570-572

Propos sur la littérature negro-africaine. By Christophe Dailly and Barthelemy Kotchy. Reviewed by Jonathan Ngate. *Research in African Literatures* 17, No. 4 (Winter 1986): 565-566

Senegalese Literature: A Critical History. By Dorothy Blair. Reviewed by Mbye B. Cham. *Research in African Literatures* 17, No. 4 (Winter 1986): 567-569

Through Foreign Eyes: Western Attitudes toward North Africa. Alf Andrew Heggoy, editor. Reviewed by Aouicha E. Hilliard. *Research in African Literatures* 17, No. 4 (Winter 1986): 584-587

Literature—Africa—History and Criticism

African Literature Today No. 14: Insiders and Outsiders. Eldred Durosimi Jones, editor. Reviewed by Lemuel A. Johnson. *Research in African Literatures* 17, No. 3 (Fall 1986): 442-444

Contemporary African Literature. Hal Wylie, Eileen Julien, and Russell J. Linnemann, editors. Reviewed by J. I. Okonkwo. *Research in African Literatures* 17, No. 3 (Fall 1986): 445-448

A Handbook for Teaching African Literature. By Elizabeth Gunner. Reviewed by Anne Walmsley. *Research in African Literatures* 17, No. 1 (Spring 1986): 149-153

Interdisciplinary Dimensions of African Literature. Kofi Anyidoho, Abioseh M. Porter, Daniel Racine, and Janice Spleth, editors. Reviewed by C. L. Innes. *Research in African Literatures* 17, No. 3 (Fall 1986): 449-451

Olive Schreiner and After: Essays on Southern African Literature in Honor of Guy Butler. Malvern van Wyk Smith and Don Maclennan, editors. Reviewed by Dennis Walder. *Research in African Literatures* 17, No. 3 (Fall 1986): 401-404

Propos sur la littérature negro-africaine. By Christophe Dailly and Barthelemy Kotchy. Reviewed by Jonathan Ngate. *Research in African Literatures* 17, No. 4 (Winter 1986): 565-566

Senegalese Literature: A Critical History. By Dorothy Blair. Reviewed by Mbye B. Cham. *Research in African Literatures* 17, No. 4 (Winter 1986): 567-569

A Sense of Place: Essays in Post-Colonial Literature. Britta Olinder, editor. Reviewed by Bernard Hickey. *Research in African Literatures* 17, No. 3 (Fall 1986): 426-430

Soyinka as a Literary Critic. Notes. Obiajuru Maduakor. *Research in African Literatures* 17, No. 1 (Spring 1986): 1-38

Tessere per un mosaico africano. By Itala Vivan. Reviewed by Jane Wilkinson. *Research in African Literatures* 17, No. 3 (Fall 1986): 425-426

Literature—Africa—Portuguese Language

Literature Africana Literature Necessaria, II—Moçambique, Cabo Verde, Guiné-Bissau, Sao Tomé e Principe. Reviewed by Gerald Moser. *Research in African Literatures* 17, No. 3 (Fall 1986):422-425

Sobre Literatura Moçambicana. By Orlando Mendes. Reviewed by Russell G. Hamilton. *Research in African Literatures* 17, No. 3 (Fall 1986): 422-425

Literature—Africa—Study and Teaching

A Teacher's Guide to African Literature. By H. L. B. Moody. Reviewed by Carl Wood. *Research in African Literatures* 17, No. 4 (Winter 1986): 606-609

Teaching Literature in Africa: Principles and Techniques. By Emmanuel Ngara. Reviewed by Florence Stratton. *Research in African Literatures* 17, No. 3 (Fall 1986): 451-453

Literature—Africa—Theses and Dissertations

A List of B.A. Degree Projects in African Literature Completed in the English Department, University of Jos, Nigeria (1979-1984). J. O. J. Nwachukwu-Agbada. *Research in African Literatures* 17, No. 1 (Spring 1986): 127-129

Literature—Commonwealth

The Commonwealth in Canada: Proceedings of the Second Triennial Conference of the Canadian Association for Commonwealth Literature and Language Studies. Ama Parameswaran, editor. Reviewed by Alastair Niven. *Research in African Literatures* 17, No. 3 (Fall 1986): 435-439

Commonwealth Literatur. Jurgen Schafer, editor. Reviewed by Willfried F. Feuser. *Research in African Literatures* 17, No. 3 (Fall 1986): 430-433

Conference on the Acquisition and Bibliography of Commonwealth and Third World Literatures in English. Commonwealth Institute. Reviewed by Nancy J. Schmidt. *Research in African Literatures* 17, No. 3 (Fall 1986): 439-440

The History and Historiography of Commonwealth Literature. Dieter Riemenschneider, editor. Reviewed by Gareth Griffiths. Book review. *Research in African Literatures* 17, No. 3 (Fall 1986): 433-435

La rive noire: De Harlem à la Seine. By Michel
Fabre. Reviewed by Clarisse Zimra. *Research in
African Literatures* 17, No. 4 (Winter 1986):
601–603

Literature—East Africa

East African Literature: An Anthology. Arne
Zettersten, editor. Reviewed by Peter Nazareth.
Research in African Literatures 17, No. 1 (Spring
1986): 140–142

Literature—English Language

A Guide to Twentieth Century Literature in
English. Harry Blamires, editor. Reviewed by G.
D. Killam. *Research in African Literatures* 17, No.
3 (Fall 1986): 430

Literature—French Language

La rive noire: De Harlem à la Seine. By Michel
Fabre. Reviewed by Clarisse Zimra. *Research in
African Literatures* 17, No. 4 (Winter 1986):
601–603

Literature—North Africa—French Language

Le personnage féminin dans le roman maghrébin
de langue française des indépendances à 1980:
Representations et fonctions. By Anne-Marie
Nisbet. Reviewed by Charlotte H. Bruner.
Research in African Literatures 17, No. 4 (Winter
1986):576–579

Literature—South America—Bibliographies

Studies in Caribbean and South American
Literature: An Annual Annotated Bibliography,
1985. Brenda F. Berrian and others. *Callaloo* 9,
No. 4 (Fall 1986):623–672

Literature—Study and Teaching

Littérature et méthodologie. By A. Kone, et al.
Reviewed by Mineke Schipper. *Research in African
Literatures* 17, No. 4 (Winter 1986): 566–567

Propos sur la littérature negro-africaine. By
Christophe Dailly and Barthelemy Kotchy.
Reviewed by Jonathan Ngate. *Research in African
Literatures* 17, No. 4 (Winter 1986): 565–566

Llewellyn, J. Bruce (about)

Bruce: The Boss. Ken Smikle. *Black Enterprise* 17,
No. 2 (September 1986):36

Llorens, Alonzo L.

Notice to Quit. *Howard Law Journal* 29, No. 1
(1986):1–11

Lloyd, Hortense D.

Martin Luther King, Jr.: To the Mountaintop.
Book review. *Negro Educational Review* 37, No. 1
(January 1986):46–47

Lloyd, R. Grann

Defining the Situation: The Obligation of Schools
to Motivate Students. *Negro Educational Review*
37, Nos. 3–4 (July-October 1986):90–91

Living the Dream: Martin Luther King, Jr., Day
or Hypocrite Day? *Negro Educational Review* 37,
No. 1 (January 1986):2–7

Lobbying

How to Shape Policy through Lobbying. David
C. Ruffin. *Black Enterprise* 17, No. 5 (December
1986):33

Lobbyists

Randall Robinson: Interview. Frank McCoy.
Crisis 93, No. 9 (November 1986):20

Lobel, Jules (joint author)

See Wolvovitz, Barbara

Local Government

Jobs and the Quality of Life in Cities: Local
Government's Role in Full Employment. Eugene
"Gus" Newport. *Urban League Review* 10, No. 1
(Summer 1986):71–78

Locke, Alain (about)

The Race Consciousness of Alain Locke. Yvonne
Ochillo. *Phylon* 47, No. 3 (September
1986):173–181

Lockhart, Keith (about)

Golden Nuggets. Ken Smikle. *Black Enterprise* 17,
No. 3 (October 1986):26

Lockhart and Pettus Inc.

See Lockhart, Keith

Long Island (New York)—History

Character Names in *Indian Trails* by Olivia Ward
Bush (Banks): Clues to Afro Assimilation Into
Long Island's Native Americans. Notes. Bernice F.
Guillaume. *Afro-Americans in New York Life and
History* 10, No. 2 (July 1986):45–53

Longmyer, Kenneth (about)

When It's More than Just a Job. Marianne Ilaw.
Black Enterprise 16, No. 10 (May 1986):54

Lopes, Grace M. (joint author)

See Seltzer, Rick

Lopez, Sharon Y.

Managing the Cuckoo's Nest. *Black Enterprise* 17,
No. 2 (September 1986):45

Managing through Tough Times. *Black Enterprise*
16, No. 6 (January 1986):57–58

St. Lucia: Communing with Nature. *Black
Enterprise* 16, No. 10 (May 1986):70

We've Got to Stop Meeting Like This. *Black
Enterprise* 16, No. 9 (April 1986):63–66

Your PC—A Great Time-Saver. *Black Enterprise*
16, No. 11 (June 1986):278

Lorde, Audre

Berlin Is Hard on Colored Girls. Poem. *Callaloo* 9, No. 1 (Winter 1986):89

Conference Keynote Address: Sisterhood and Survival. *Black Scholar* 17, No. 2 (March-April 1986):5-7

Our Dead Behind Us. Book review. Joseph A. Brown. *Callaloo* 9, No. 4 (Fall 1986):737-739

Sisters in Arms. Poem. *Callaloo* 9, No. 1 (Winter 1986):87-88

Lorde, Audre (joint author)

See Joseph, Gloria I.

Lorde, Audre—Criticism and Interpretation

Apo Koinou in Audre Lorde and the Moderns. Amitai F. Avi-ram. *Callaloo* 9, No. 1 (Winter 1986):192-208

Lordereau, Paulette (compiler)

Littératures africaines à la Bibliotèque Nationale, 1973-1983. Reviewed by Hans E. Panofsky. *Research in African Literatures* 17, No. 4 (Winter 1986): 605-606

Losambe, L.

Expatriate Characters in the Early African Novel. *Phylon* 47, No. 2 (June 1986):148-158

Lotz, Rainer E.

In Retrospect: Will Garland and the Negro Operetta Company. *Black Perspective in Music* 14, No. 3 (Fall 1986):290-303

Louden, Joyce S. (joint author)

See Durant, Thomas J. (Jr.)

Louis, Errol T.

An Accountant and His Finances. *Black Enterprise* 17, No. 3 (October 1986):42

Affirmative Reaction. *Black Enterprise* 17, No. 3 (October 1986):21

Black and Blue on Campus. *Essence* 17, No. 4 (August 1986):67

The Price Is Right in Sales. *Black Enterprise* 16, No. 7 (February 1986):67-70

A Sharpe Change. *Black Enterprise* 17, No. 1 (August 1986):11

Louisiana Consent Decree

The Consent Decree as an Instrument for Desegregation in Higher Education. James J. Prestage and Jewel L. Prestage. *Urban League Review* 10, No. 2 (Winter 1986-87):113-130

Louisiana—Political History

Great Moments in Black History: The First Black Governor. Lerone Bennett, Jr. *Ebony* 42, No. 1 (November 1986):116

Louisiana State University System—Race Discrimination

The Consent Decree as an Instrument for Desegregation in Higher Education. James J. Prestage and Jewel L. Prestage. *Urban League Review* 10, No. 2 (Winter 1986-87):113-130

Love—Social History

An Historical Look at Male-Female Relationships in the Black Community. Shelley Moore. *Crisis* 93, No. 10 (December 1986):20

"My Love is Black as Yours is Fair":Premarital Love and Sexuality in the Antebellum Slave Narrative. *Phylon* 47, No. 3 (September 1986):238-247

Lovett-Scott, Margie

AIDS...Fact or Fantasy? A Devastating Disease. *About Time* 14, No. 4 (April 1986):20

Loving-Sloane, Cecilia

Blood Knot. Theater review. *Crisis* 93, No. 3 (March 1986):10

Blues for a Gospel Queen. Theater review. *Crisis* 93, No. 10 (December 1986):9-10

Boys of Winter. Theater review. *Crisis* 93, No. 3 (March 1986):10

Funny House of the Negro. Theater review. *Crisis* 93, No. 8 (October 1986):14

Jonah and the Wonderdog. Theater review. *Crisis* 93, No. 6 (June/July 1986):10-11

Jonin'. Theater review. *Crisis* 93, No. 3 (March 1986):11-48

Lady Day at Emerson's Bar and Grill. Theater review. *Crisis* 93, No. 10 (December 1986):9-10

The Life and Times of Malcolm X. Theater review. *Crisis* 93, No. 9 (November 1986):11

Mama I Want to Sing. Theater review. *Crisis* 93, No. 8 (October 1986):12-13

Mumbo Jumbo Theater Company. *Crisis* 93, No. 8 (October 1986):13-14

Sweet Charity. Theater review. *Crisis* 93, No. 7 (August/September 1986):10

Theatre. *Crisis* 93, No. 4 (April 1986):10-12

Lowe, Frederick H.

Proper Pay for Parents. *Black Enterprise* 16, No. 12 (July 1986):14

Radio Buys Settle Suits. *Black Enterprise* 16, No. 8 (March 1986):14

Steel Suits Are Settled. *Black Enterprise* 17, No. 4 (November 1986):22

Luba—Language and Culture

Legends and History of the Luba. By Harold Womersley. Reviewed by J. Eric Lane. *Research in African Literatures* 17, No. 2 (Summer 1986): 306-308

Lubin, Maurice A.

Essays on Haitian Literature. Book review. *Research in African Literatures* 17, No. 4 (Winter 1986): 593–595

Lucy, William

Labor's Role in Support of Full Employment. *Urban League Review* 10, No. 1 (Summer 1986):79–86

Lujan, Gabriel Silva (joint author)

See Salamanca, Ricardo Santamaria

Luke

At the Edge. Poem. *Callaloo* 9, No. 1 (Winter 1986):93

Stories about Chrone. Poem. *Callaloo* 9, No. 1 (Winter 1986):90–92

Lukens Inc.—Discriminatory Policies

Steel Suits Are Settled. Frederick H. Lowe. *Black Enterprise* 17, No. 4 (November 1986):22

Lumpkin, Beatrice

Pyramid—American and African: A Comparison. Notes. *Journal of African Civilizations* 8, No. 2 (December 1986):169–187

Lunn, Kenneth

Race and Labour in Twentieth Century Britain. Book review. Paul Gordon. *Race and Class* 28, No. 2 (August 1986):102–103

Lupton, Mary Jane

Clothes and Closure in Three Novels by Black Women. *Black American Literature Forum* 20, No. 4 (Winter 1986):409–421

Lutchman, Harold A. (joint author)

See James, Randolph W.

Lyons, Charlotte

African Delights. *Ebony* 41, No. 3 (January 1986):110

Cajun Cuisine at Home. *Ebony* 41, No. 5 (March 1986):116

The Traditional Family Dinner. *Ebony* 41, No. 10 (August 1986):108

Lyons, Peggy

Urban-Suburban Interdistrict Transfer Program. *About Time* 14, No. 5 (May 1986):30–31

Maasai—Oral Literature

Oral Literature of the Maasai. By Naomi Kipury. Reviewed by Clement Abiaziem Okafor. *Research in African Literatures* 17, No. 2 (Summer 1986): 301–304

MacCann, Donnerae

An Interview with Haki Madhubuti. *Interracial Books for Children Bulletin* 17, No. 2 (1986):9–11

MacClintock, Dorcas

African Images: A Look at Animals in Africa. Book review. Geraldine L. Wilson. *Interracial Books for Children Bulletin* 17, No. 2 (1986):13–14

Maceba Affairs

Black Theater Stages a Comeback. *Ebony* 42, No. 1 (November 1986):54

MacGaffey, Wyatt

Le Roi Nyamwezi, la Droite et la Gauche: Révision Comparative des Classifications Dualistes. Book review. *Research in African Literatures* 17, No. 2 (Summer 1986): 304–306

Symbolic Structures: An Exploration of the Culture of the Dowayos. Book review. *Research in African Literatures* 17, No. 2 (Summer 1986): 295–296

Machlin, Paul S.

Stride: The Music of Fats Waller. Book review. Eileen Southern. *Black Perspective in Music* 14, No. 2 (Spring 1986):194

Mackey, Nathaniel

Dogon Eclipse. Poem. *Callaloo* 9, No. 1 (Winter 1986):96–97

The Sleeping Rocks. Poem. *Callaloo* 9, No. 1 (Winter 1986):94–95

Solomon's Outer Wall. Poem. *Callaloo* 9, No. 1 (Winter 1986):98–99

Maclennan, Don (joint editor)

See Smith, Malvern van Wyk

Madagascar—Folklore

Malagasy Tale Index. By Lee Haring. Reviewed by Daniel J. Crowley. *Research in African Literatures* 17, No. 2 (Summer 1986): 308–309

Madhubuti, Haki (about)

An Interview with Haki Madhubuti. Donnerae MacCann. *Interracial Books for Children Bulletin* 17, No. 2 (1986):9–11

Maduakor, Obiajuru

Soyinka as a Literary Critic. Notes. *Research in African Literatures* 17, No. 1 (Spring 1986): 1–38

Madubuike, Ihechukwu

See Chinweizu, and others

Maja-Pearce, Adewale

African Short Stories in English: An Anthology. Book review. *Research in African Literatures* 17, No. 4 (Winter 1986): 620–622

Major, Reggie

A Question of Sedition: The Federal Government's Investigation of the Black Press during World War II. Book review. *Black Scholar* 17, No. 5 (September-October 1986):58–59

Malagasy—Language and Culture

Malagasy Tale Index. By Lee Haring. Reviewed by Daniel J. Crowley. *Research in African Literatures* 17, No. 2 (Summer 1986): 308–309

Malawi—Dance-Drama

An Example of Syncretic Drama from Malawi: Malipenga. Notes. Christopher F. Kamlongera. *Research in African Literatures* 17, No. 2 (Summer 1986): 197–210

Malcolm X (about)

From Sinners to Saints: The Confessions of Saint Augustine and Malcolm X. Notes. Winston A. Van Horne. *Journal of Religious Thought* 43, No. 1 (Spring-Summer 1986):76–101

Male-Female Relationships

Black Singles Face to Face. Diane Weathers. *Essence* 17, No. 8 (December 1986):58

Come out with Your Hands Up: How Black Men and Women Really Feel about Each Other. Jill Nelson and George Davis. *Essence* 17, No. 2 (July 1986):54

The Perils of Obsession. Enid Ann Doggett. *Essence* 17, No. 2 (June 1986):80

Tensions between Black Men and Women. Lynn Norment. *Ebony* 41, No. 10 (August 1986):153

What Do Men Want in Bed? Ron Harris. *Essence* 17, No. 7 (November 1986):59

Malekebu, Flora Zeto (about)

Black Women Missionaries: A Letter from Flora Zeto Malekebu to Lucy Hale Tapley. Jacqueline Jones Royster. *SAGE* 3, No. 1 (Spring 1986):58–60

Mallarmé, Stéphane—Criticism and Interpretation

Apo Koinou in Audre Lorde and the Moderns. Amitai F. Avi-ram. *Callaloo* 9, No. 1 (Winter 1986):192–208

Malveaux, Julianne

Emerging Two-Tier Wage Systems: Employment Opportunity or Wage Attack? *Urban League Review* 10, No. 2 (Winter 1986–87):34–44

The Impact of Cybernation Technology on Black Automotive Workers in the United States. Book review. *Review of Black Political Economy* 15, No. 1 (Summer 1986):103–105

Investing by Collecting. *Essence* 17, No. 8 (December 1986):113

Labor of Love, Labor of Sorrow. Book review. *Black Scholar* 17, No. 2 (March-April 1986):51–52

Malveaux, Julianne, and Englander, Susan

Race and Class in Nursing Occupations. *SAGE* 3, No. 1 (Spring 1986):41–45

Malveaux, Julianne M. (joint editor)

See Simms, Margaret C.

Mamonsono, Leopold-Pindy

La nouvelle génération de poètes congolais. Reviewed by Daniel Whitman. *Research in African Literatures* 17, No. 4 (Winter 1986): 570–572

Management—Delegation

Tips for Effective Delegation. Lin Grensing. *About Time* 14, No. 8 (August 1986):32–33

Mandela, Nelson

Nelson Mandela: The Struggle Is My Life. Book review. Genevieve H. Wilson. *About Time* 14, No. 9 (September 1986):23–25

Mandela, Nelson (about)

The Mandelas: First Family of South Africa's Freedom Fight. Illustrated. *Ebony* 41, No. 11 (September 1986):66

Winnie Mandela: Part of My Soul Went with Him. Edited by Anne Benjamin. Reviewed by Jeanne M. Woods. *Black Enterprise* 17, No. 5 (December 1986):19

Mandela, Winnie (about)

See Mandela, Nelson

Mandinga

See Mandingo (African People)

Mandingo (African People)

Mandinga Voyages across the Atlantic. Notes. Harold G. Lawrence. *Journal of African Civilizations* 8, No. 2 (December 1986):202–247

Mandinka—Music

The Mandinka Balafon: An Introduction with Notation for Teaching. By Lynne Jessup. Reviewed by Jacqueline Cogdell DjeDje. *Black Perspective in Music* 14, No. 3 (Fall 1986):307–308

Manganyi, N. Chabani

Sol Plaatje: South African Nationalist, 1876–1932. Book review. *Research in African Literatures* 17, No. 3 (Fall 1986): 393–395

Manganyi, N. Chabani (editor)

Bury Me at the Marketplace: Selected Letters of Es'kia Mphahlele, 1943–1980. Reviewed by Brian Worsfold. *Research in African Literatures* 17, No. 3 (Fall 1986): 395–398

Mannan, Golam, and others

A Comparison of the Academic Performance of Black and White Freshman Students on an Urban Commuter Campus. *Journal of Negro Education* 55, No.2 (Spring 1986):155–161

Man—Origin

The African Origin of Civilization: Myth or Reality. Notes. By Cheikh Anta Diop. Reviewed by A. J. Williams-Myers. *Journal of African Civilizations* 8, No. 1 (June 1986):118–126

The Beginnings of Man and Civilization. Cheikh Anta Diop. *Journal of African Civilizations* 8, No. 1 (June 1986):322–351

Civilization or Barbarism: An Authentic Anthropology. Excerpt. Notes. Cheikh Anta Diop. *Journal of African Civilizations* 8, No. 1 (June 1986):161–225

Civilization or Barbarism: The Legacy of Cheikh Anta Diop. By Cheikh Anta Diop. Reviewed by Leonard Jeffries, Jr. *Journal of African Civilizations* 8, No. 1 (June 1986):146–160

Conversations with Diop and Tsegaye: The Nile Valley Revisited. Notes. Jan Carew. *Journal of African Civilizations* 8, No. 1 (June 1986):19–27

Death Shall Not Find Us Thinking That We Die. Notes. Ivan Van Sertima. *Journal of African Civilizations* 8, No. 1 (June 1986):7–16

Dr. Diop on Asia: Highlights and Insights. Notes. Runoko Rashidi. *Journal of African Civilizations* 8, No. 1 (June 1986):127–145

Further Conversations with the Pharaoh. Interview. Charles S. Finch. *Journal of African Civilizations* 8, No. 1 (June 1986):227–237

Interview with Cheikh Anta Diop. Interview. Notes. Bibliography. Shawna Moore. *Journal of African Civilizations* 8, No. 1 (June 1986):238–248

Meeting the Pharoah: Conversations with Cheikh Anta Diop. Interview. Charles S. Finch. *Journal of African Civilizations* 8, No. 1 (June 1986):28–34

Origin of the Ancient Egyptians. Notes. Cheikh Anta Diop. *Journal of African Civilizations* 8, No. 1 (June 1986):35–63

Two Interviews with Cheikh Anta Diop. Interview. Listervelt Middleton and Nile Valley Executive Committee. *Journal of African Civilizations* 8, No. 1 (June 1986):284–302

Mantlo, Karen

Sally Ann Thunder Ann Whirlwind Crockett. Book review. *Interracial Books for Children Bulletin* 17, No. 2 (1986):13

Manuel, Ruth Dolores

Showstopper: Virginia Johnson, Long on Grace. *Essence* 17, No. 2 (June 1986):31

Manuel, V. Phillip

The National Technical Association: Sixty Years Young. *Black Collegian* 17, No. 2 (November/December 1986):38

Manufacturing

Market Structure and Minority Presence: Black-Owned Firms in Manufacturing. Arthur G. Woolf. *Review of Black Political Economy* 14, No. 4 (Spring 1986):79–89

Mapanje, Jack, and White, Landeg, editors

Oral Poetry from Africa. Reviewed by Oyekan Owomoyela. *Research in African Literatures* 17, No. 1 (Spring 1986): 137–140

Maps, Early

African Sea Kings in America? Evidence from Early Maps. Bibliography. Joan Covey. *Journal of African Civilizations* 8, No. 2 (December 1986):152–168

Marable, Manning

Black American Politics: From the Washington Marches to Jesse Jackson, vol. 1. Book review. Sanford A. Wright. *Black Scholar* 17, No. 1 (January-February 1986):45–46

Harold Washington and the Politics of Race in Chicago. *Black Scholar* 17, No. 6 (November-December 1986):14–23

The Marxist Analyses of Manning Marable. Reviewed by John Williams. *Phylon* 47, No. 3 (September 1986):248–250

Race, Reform and Rebellion: The Second Reconstruction in Black America. Reviewed by Earl Smith. *Phylon* 47, No. 1 (March 1986):101–103

Maran, René (about)

René Maran, the Black Frenchman: A Bio-Critical Study. By Femi Ojo-Ade. Reviewed by Chidi Ikonne. *Research in African Literatures* 17, No. 4 (Winter 1986): 603–605

Marcus, Laurence R.

Education on Trial: Strategies for the Future. Book review. *Journal of Negro Education* 55, No.4 (Fall 1986):548–549

Mardis, John W. (about)

Insurance Company of the Year: Premium Profits. Nathan McCall. *Black Enterprise* 16, No. 11 (June 1986):182

Marhewka, Gail E. (joint author)

See Jackson, Pamela Irving

Mariam, A. G. (joint author)

See Amin, Ruhul

Marketing

Positioning Yourself for Marketing. Lucius Millander. *Black Enterprise* 16, No. 7 (February 1986):56–62

The Price Is Right in Sales. Errol T. Louis. *Black Enterprise* 16, No. 7 (February 1986):67–70

Marketing of Insurance

The Maestro of Marketing. Jacqueline Moore. *Black Enterprise* 16, No. 12 (July 1986):32

Marketing—Professional Associations

A Meeting of Marketers. Solomon J. Herbert. *Black Enterprise* 17, No. 2 (September 1986):18

Marriage

A Creative Marriage: Artists Michael and Michelle Nero Singletary Share a Passion for Each Other and Painting. *Ebony* 41, No. 9 (July 1986):96

Love Can Be Lasting. Trudy S. Moore. *Ebony* 42, No. 2 (December 1986):123

    See also Sex Roles in Marriage

    See also Weddings

Marriage, Interracial

Ideologies of Race and Sex in Literature: Racism and Antiracism in the African Francophone Novel. Notes. E. P. Abanime. *CLA Journal* 30, No. 2 (December 1986):125–143

Marriage—Economic Aspects

Blue Collar/White Collar Success: Husband and Wife Pool Resources for the Good Life. *Ebony* 41, No. 10 (August 1986):96

Long Distance Love: Thousands of Married Couples in the U.S. Live Happily Apart. *Ebony* 41, No. 5 (March 1986):156

Marsalis, Branford (about)

Royal Garden Blues. Record review. Norman Riley. *Crisis* 93, No. 9 (November 1986):9

The Young Lions. Norman Riley. *Crisis* 93, No. 9 (November 1986):8–9

Marsalis, Wynton

Why We Must Preserve Our Jazz Heritage. *Ebony* 41, No. 4 (February 1986):131

Marsalis, Wynton (about)

J Mood. Record review. Norman Riley. *Crisis* 93, No. 9 (November 1986):9

The Young Lions. Norman Riley. *Crisis* 93, No. 9 (November 1986):8–9

Marsh, Clifton E.

From Black Muslims to Muslims. Reviewed by Sulayman S. Nyang. *Phylon* 47, No. 2 (June 1986):169–170

Marshall, Marilyn

Bowling for Fame and Fortune. *Ebony* 41, No. 4 (February 1986):157

Dizzy Gillespie: He Just Keeps Bopping Along. *Ebony* 41, No. 11 (September 1986):50

The Enduring Family: Long-Term Marriages, Happy Households and Successful Children Are Not Unusual. *Ebony* 41, No. 10 (August 1986):78

Georgia's Reverend Sheriff: Richard Lankford Finds Joy in Preaching the Gospel and Keeping the Peace. *Ebony* 41, No. 5 (March 1986):92

How to Protect Your Children from People They Trust. *Ebony* 42, No. 1 (November 1986):46

Keshia Knight Pulliam: Coping with Success at Seven. *Ebony* 42, No. 2 (December 1986):27

Zina Garrison: Aiming for the Top in Tennis. *Ebony* 41, No. 8 (June 1986):79

Marshall, Paule (about)

Return of a Native Daughter: An Interview with Paule Marshall and Maryse Conde. John Williams (translator). *SAGE* 3, No. 2 (Fall 1986):52–53

Marshall, Paule—Criticism and Interpretation

Oral Tradition: The Bridge to Africa in Paule Marshall's *Praisesong for the Widow*. Ebele O. Eko. *Western Journal of Black Studies* 10, No. 3 (Fall 1986):143–147

Paule Marshall's *Praisesong for the Widow*: The Reluctant Heiress, or Whose Life Is It Anyway? *Black American Literature Forum* 20, No. 4 (Winter 1986):371–392

Marshall, Trevor

The Growth of an Artistic Tradition in Barbados. Illustrated. *International Review of African American Art* 7, No. 1 (1986):4–25

Marshment, Margaret

Unheard Words: Women and Literature in Africa, the Arab World, Asia, the Caribbean and Latin America. *Race and Class* 28, No. 1 (Summer 1986):97–99

Martin, Carole M.

Betty Friedan: A Voice for Women's Rights. Book review. *Interracial Books for Children Bulletin* 17, No. 2 (1986):19

Margaret Thatcher: Britain's "Iron Lady." Book review. *Interracial Books for Children Bulletin* 17, No. 2 (1986):15

The Oval Amulet. Book review. *Interracial Books for Children Bulletin* 17, No. 2 (1986):16

Martin, Joel (about)

A Meeting of Marketers. Solomon J. Herbert. *Black Enterprise* 17, No. 2 (September 1986):18

Martin, Sallie (about)

Sallie Martin: At 90, the "Mother of Gospel" Is Being Hailed from Coast to Coast. *Ebony* 41, No. 5 (March 1986):76

Martin, Sandy D.

Black Baptist Women and African Mission Work, 1870–1925. *SAGE* 3, No. 1 (Spring 1986):16–19

Martin, Sharon S.

Healing through Acupuncture. *Black Collegian* 16, No. 4 (March/April 1986):90–93

Martin, Thad

The Black Vietnam Vet: Still Looking for Respect. *Ebony* 41, No. 6 (April 1986):122

Turnaround at Meharry Medical College Has Managed to Overcome Serious Problems with a New Mood on the Campus. *Ebony* 41, No. 5 (March 1986):42

Who's Stealing Our Children. *Ebony* 41, No. 4 (February 1986):139

Martin, Tony

The Poetical Works of Marcus Garvey. Reviewed by Joanne Veal Gabbin. *Afro-Americans in New York Life and History* 10, No.1 (January 1986):72–74

Martinez, Juan A.

The Mythical Landscapes of a Cuban Painter: Wilfredo Lam's *La Jungla*. *Caribbean Review* 15, No. 2 (Spring 1986):32–36

Martin Luther King Jr. Holiday

The Crusade for a King Holiday. *Ebony* 41, No. 3 (January 1986):36–38

The Politics of Public Holidays: King's Day of Celebration. Byron W. Daynes. *Western Journal of Black Studies* 10, No. 2 (Summer 1986):90–101

The Real Meaning of the King Holiday. *Ebony* 41, No. 3 (January 1986):31

Martin Luther King Jr. Holiday—Political Aspects

Living the Dream: Martin Luther King, Jr., Day or Hypocrite Day? R. Grann Lloyd. *Negro Educational Review* 37, No. 1 (January 1986):2–7

Marxism

Black Marxism: The Making of the Black Radical Tradition. By Cedric J. Robinson. Reviewed by V. P. Franklin. *Phylon* 47, No. 3 (September 1986):250–251

The Marxist Analyses of Manning Marable. Manning Marable. Reviewed by John Williams. *Phylon* 47, No. 3 (September 1986):248–250

Maryland—Officials and Employees

Parren Mitchell's Sixteen Years: A Legislative Legacy. David C. Ruffin. *Black Enterprise* 16, No. 11 (June 1986):59–60

Mason, Nia

The Visual Arts. *Crisis* 93, No. 2 (February 1986):50–53

Mass Transit

Riding Mass Transit. Donna Johnson. *Black Enterprise* 16, No. 7 (February 1986):26

Maternity Leave

See Parental Leave

Mathabane, Mark

Kaffir Boy: The True Story of a Black Youth's Coming of Age in Apartheid South Africa. Book review. Tonya Bolden Davis. *Black Enterprise* 17, No. 5 (December 1986):20

Mathabela, Ernest

Proceedings of the Symposium on Afro-American and African Poetry and the Teaching of Poetry in Schools. Book review. *Research in African Literatures* 17, No. 1 (Spring 1986): 133–137

Mathematicians

NASA Computer Whiz: Doing It His Way, Maverick Mathematician David R. Hedgley (Jr.), Comes Up with the Right Answers. *Ebony* 41, No. 5 (March 1986):62

Mathematics—Dissertations and Theses

Master's Theses in Progress in Selected Colleges and Universities. Mac A. Stewart. *Negro Educational Review* 37, Nos. 3–4 (July-October 1986):103–106, 115–117

Mathematics—History

Africa's Contribution to World Civilization: The Exact Sciences. Notes. Bibliography. Cheikh Anta Diop. *Journal of African Civilizations* 8, No. 1 (June 1986):74–88

Mathews, Tom (joint author)

See Wilkins, Roy

Matsikidze, Isabella P.

Prayersong for the Waiting. Poem. *Black Scholar* 17, No. 4 (July-August 1986):50

Who Do You Say I Am? Poem. *Black Scholar* 17, No. 4 (July-August 1986):50

Maturation (Psychology)

Where I'm Coming from. Jennifer Jordan and Lisa Cleveland. *Essence* 17, No. 1 (May 1986):86

Maxima Corporation

BE Company of the Year: Maxima. Errol Lewis. *Black Enterprise* 16, No. 11 (June 1986):130

Mayes, Janis A. (compiler) and others

Studies in African Literatures and Oratures: An Annual Annotated Bibliography, 1985. *Callaloo* 9, No. 4 (Fall 1986):673–693

Mayfield, Janice and Dana (about)

A Window of Opportunity. Lloyd Gite. *Black Enterprise* 16, No. 10 (May 1986):29

Mayors

Black Gains Tied Directly to Pursuit of Peace. Frances M. Beal. *Black Scholar* 17, No. 1 (January-February 1986):8–11

Former Mayors: Is There Life after City Hall? *Ebony* 42, No. 2 (December 1986):36

Harold Washington and the Politics of Race in Chicago. Manning Marable. *Black Scholar* 17, No. 6 (November-December 1986):14–23

Harvey Gantt: The First Black Mayor of Charlotte, N.C., Is Proving to Be the Most Popular Mayor as Well. Charles Whitaker. *Ebony* 41, No. 6 (April 1986):92

Mayor Sidney Barthelemy: New Orleans' Gentle Giant. *Ebony* 41, No. 9 (July 1986):120

Mayor Washington's Bid for Re-Election. Abdul Alkalimat. *Black Scholar* 17, No. 6 (November-December 1986):2–13

A Piece of the Pie. Charles P. Henry. *Crisis* 93, No. 5 (May 1986):20–41

A Sharpe Change. Errol T. Louis. *Black Enterprise* 17, No. 1 (August 1986):11

A "Sharpe" Change in Newark. Alex Poinsett. *Ebony* 41, No. 11 (September 1986):128

Washington: District of Commerce. Patricia A. Jones. *Black Enterprise* 16, No. 11 (June 1986):253

Mazrui, Al-Amin M.

Ideology or Pedagogy: The Linguistic Indigenisation of African Literature. *Race and Class* 28, No. 1 (Summer 1986):63–72

Mbele, Joseph L.

The Identity of the Hero in the Liongo Epic. References. *Research in African Literatures* 17, No. 4 (Winter 1986): 464–473

McAdams, Janine C.

After-School Specialist: Former Teacher Knows Her ABCs. *Essence* 17, No. 7 (November 1986):119

Check It Out: Coat Checking and Matchmaking Pay Off. *Essence* 17, No. 6 (October 1986):109

Diet Right! Bahamian Style. *Essence* 17, No. 4 (August 1986):124

Legacy of Success: A Young Mortician Inherits Her Father's Dream. *Essence* 17, No. 4 (August 1986):16

Personal Best: Her PR Agency Put Their Best Foot Forward. *Essence* 17, No. 8 (December 1986):109

McAdams, Janine C. (joint author)

See Williams, Monte

McAdams, Janine C., and Ray, Elaine C.

Making the Grade: The *Essence* Guide to College Survival. *Essence* 17, No. 4 (August 1986):67

McCall, Nathan

Insurance Company of the Year: Premium Profits. *Black Enterprise* 16, No. 11 (June 1986):182

Revving Up for Sales. *Black Enterprise* 17, No. 4 (November 1986):44

McCarthy, Cameron

Grenada: The Hour Will Strike Again. Book review. 89–91

McClean, Cynthia

The Bahamas: Eleuthera and Abaco. *Black Enterprise* 16, No. 10 (May 1986):80

McClure, Phyllis

The Erosion of Civil Rights Enforcement. *Black Scholar* 17, No. 3 (May-June 1986):10–18

McCoy, Frank

Randall Robinson: Interview. *Crisis* 93, No. 9 (November 1986):20

McCray, Abiodun, and Fredricks, Ayanna

The Calabash Dance Theatre. Illustrated. *Western Journal of Black Studies* 10, No. 1 (Spring 1986):17–18

McCulloch, Jack

Black Soul, White Artifact: Fanon's Clinical Psychology and Social Theory. Reviewed by Hal Wylie. *Research in African Literatures* 17, No. 4 (Winter 1986): 599–601

McCully, Michael

Beyond "The Convent and the Cottage": A Reconsideration of Disraeli's *Sybil*. Notes. *CLA Journal* 29, No. 3 (March 1986):318–335

McDade, Dianna (about)

A Tale of Two Franchises. Joyce Davis Adams and Janet Clayton. *Black Enterprise* 16, No. 12 (July 1986):42–46

McDonald, J. Fred

Blacks and White T.V.: Afro-Americans in Television since 1948. Book review. Robert L. Douglas, Sr. *Western Journal of Black Studies* 10, No. 1 (Spring 1986):44–45

McDowell, Robert

The Assembling Vision of Rita Dove. *Callaloo* 9, No. 1 (Winter 1986):61–70

McElroy, Colleen J.

With Bill Pickett at the 101 Ranch. Poem. *Callaloo* 9, No. 1 (Winter 1986):100

McGhee, Nelson (Jr.) (joint author)

See Watson, Wilbur H.

McGilchrist, Paul (joint author)

See Green, Jeffrey

McGinty, Doris E.

Bibliography of Black Music. Volume 4: Theory, Education, and Related Studies. Book review. *Black Perspective in Music* 14, No. 2 (Spring 1986):186–187

The Motown Story. Book review. *Black Perspective in Music* 14, No. 3 (Fall 1986):310–311

The Music of Black Americans: A History. Book review. *Black Perspective in Music* 14, No. 2 (Spring 1986):185–186

Popular Music, 1920–1979; A Revised Cumulation. Book review. *Black Perspective in Music* 14, No. 3 (Fall 1986):311–312

McGuire, Phillip

Black Music Critics and the Classic Blues Singers. *Black Perspective in Music* 14, No. 2 (Spring 1986):103–125

McIntire, Alexander H., Jr.

Endless War: How We Got Involved in Central America—and What Can Be Done About It. Book review. *Caribbean Review* 15, No. 1 (Winter 1986):44

McIntosh, Emily and Maurice (about)

Love Can Be Lasting. Trudy S. Moore. *Ebony* 42, No. 2 (December 1986):123

McKay, Claude

Banana Bottom. Book review. Hazel Waters. *Race and Class* 28, No. 2 (August 1986):106–107

McKay, Claude (about)

Rereading *Banjo*: Claude McKay and the French Connection. Notes. Robert P. Smith (Jr.) *CLA Journal* 30, No. 1 (September 1986):46–58

McKeever, Herman

WORK—Night Comes. Poem. *Black American Literature Forum* 20, No. 3 (Fall 1986):310

McKinley, Ann

Debussy and American Minstrelsy. *Black Perspective in Music* 14, No. 3 (Fall 1986):249–258

McKinney, Gwen

Nonprofits Going It Alone. *Black Enterprise* 16, No. 11 (June 1986):272–274

Post under Protest. *Black Enterprise* 17, No. 5 (December 1986):26

The Price of History. *Black Enterprise* 16, No. 11 (June 1986):48

The Rainbow Convention. *Black Enterprise* 17, No. 1 (August 1986):12

Reaching beyond the Outer Limits. *Black Enterprise* 17, No. 1 (August 1986):44–46

The State of Statehood. *Black Enterprise* 16, No. 6 (January 1986):21

Talks Held with Japan. *Black Enterprise* 17, No. 5 (December 1986):30

McKivigan, John R., and Silverman, Jason H.

Monarchial Liberty and Republican Slavery: West Indies Emancipation Celebrations in Upstate New York and Canada West. *Afro-Americans in New York Life and History* 10, No.1 (January 1986): 7–18

McLemore, Andrew (about)

The Benefits of Leasing. Lloyd Gite. *Black Enterprise* 17, No. 2 (September 1986):27

McLemore, Leslie Burl

Protest and Politics: The Mississippi Freedom Democratic Party and the 1965 Congressional Challenge. *Negro Educational Review* 37, Nos. 3–4 (July-October 1986):130–143

McMorris, Frances A.

Ensuring Our Health. *Essence* 17, No. 5 (September 1986):13

McNair, Ronald E. (about)

A Dream Fulfilled. Blair Walker. *Black Enterprise* 16, No. 9 (April 1986):25

Requiem for a Hero: "Touching the Face of God." D. Michael Cheers. *Ebony* 41, No. 7 (May 1986):82

Ronald Ervin McNair: First and One of a Kind. Adolph Dupree. *About Time* 14, No. 6 (June 1986):12–13

McNamara, Mark

Entrepreneurial Surgeon: Dr. Ernest Bates Nurses Ailing Firm to Fiscal Health. *Ebony* 41, No. 6 (April 1986):84

McNeely, Kenneth P.

Rent Control. *Howard Law Journal* 29, No. 1 (1986):165–175

McNeil, Genna Rae

Groundwork: Charles Hamilton Houston and the Struggle for Civil Rights. Book review. Marsha Jones. *About Time* 14, No. 2 (February 1986):18–20

McNeil, Regina Clark (joint author)

See Anrig, Gregory R.

McPherson, James Alan—Criticism and Interpretation

I Yam What You Is and You Is What I Yam. Herman Beavers. *Callaloo* 9, No. 4 (Fall 1986):565–577

McWalters, Peter (about)

Peter McWalters: Acting Superintendent of Rochester Schools. James M. Blount. *About Time* 14, No. 5 (May 1986):14–21

McWorter, Gerald A.

On Ranking Professional Achievement in Black Studies: A Reply to Carlos Brossard. *Journal of Negro Education* 55, No.2 (Spring 1986):229–235

Mechanics—History

Africa's Contribution to World Civilization: The Exact Sciences. Notes. Bibliography. Cheikh Anta Diop. *Journal of African Civilizations* 8, No. 1 (June 1986):74–88

Media and Communications

The Use of Communications Media in Four Novels by Richard Wright. John A. Williams. *Callaloo* 9, No. 3 (Summer 1986):529–539

See also Radio Broadcasting

See also Television

Media and Communications—Africa—English Language

News Coverage in Africa's Anglophone Press: Implications of Neocolonialism. Dianne Lynne Cherry. *Western Journal of Black Studies* 10, No. 1 (Spring 1986):12–16

Media and Communications—Interns

WHMM-TV's Super Internship. Willette Coleman. *Black Collegian* 16, No. 3 (January/February 1986):118–124

Media and Communications—Political Aspects

The American Press and the Repairing of the Philippines. Cedric J. Robinson. *Race and Class* 28, No. 2 (August 1986):31–44

Anti-Racists and Other Demons: The Press and Ideology in Thatcher's Britain. Nancy Murray. *Race and Class* 27, No. 3 (Winter 1986):1–19

The Black Press and Political Alliances: The Turning Point, 1928. J. William Snorgrass. *Western Journal of Black Studies* 10, No. 3 (Fall 1986):103–108

Media and Communications—Race Relations

The *Pittsburgh Courier*, and Black Workers in 1942. Patrick S. Washburn. *Western Journal of Black Studies* 10, No. 3 (Fall 1986):109–118

Post under Protest. Gwen McKinney. *Black Enterprise* 17, No. 5 (December 1986):26

See also Blacks in the Performing Arts

Medical Research

See also Syphilis—Research

Medical Research—Africa

Historian with a Mission. Lloyd Gite. *Black Enterprise* 17, No. 1 (August 1986):57

Medical Schools

Preparing for Medical School One Step at a Time. Jack Tinker. *Black Collegian* 16, No. 4 (March/April 1986):108–112

Turnaround at Meharry Medical College Has Managed to Overcome Serious Problems with a New Mood on the Campus. Thad Martin. *Ebony* 41, No. 5 (March 1986):42

Medical Service Industry

Flying High on Medical Tech. Marvin E. Perry. *Black Enterprise* 17, No. 1 (August 1986):19

Medicine—History

Africa's Contribution to World Civilization: The Exact Sciences. Notes. Bibliography. Cheikh Anta Diop. *Journal of African Civilizations* 8, No. 1 (June 1986):74–88

Medicine—Laws and Legislation

The Law...and Your Medical, Doctor and Hospital Rights. Sharon Carter. *About Time* 14, No. 4 (April 1986):22

Medicine as a Profession

A Career for the Future: Podiatric Medicine. Calvin M. Cunningham. *Black Collegian* 16, No. 4 (March/April 1986):102–107

Careers in Orthotics and Prosthetics. Solomon J. Herbert. *Black Collegian* 16, No. 4 (March/April 1986):94–99

Meharry Medical College

Turnaround at Meharry Medical College Has Managed to Overcome Serious Problems with a New Mood on the Campus. Thad Martin. *Ebony* 41, No. 5 (March 1986):42

Meltzer, Milton

Betty Friedan: A Voice for Women's Rights. Book review. Carole M. Martin. *Interracial Books for Children Bulletin* 17, No. 2 (1986):19

Memmi, Albert (about)

Application of Memmi's Theory of the Colonizer and the Colonized to the Conflicts in Zimbabwe. Dickson A. Mungazi. *Journal of Negro Education* 55, No.4 (Fall 1986):518–534

Memorandums

Memos That Do the Job. Sharon Shervington. *Black Enterprise* 16, No. 11 (June 1986):278

Memory

Memory Games. Marianne Ilaw. *Black Enterprise* 16, No. 11 (June 1986):280

Memphis (Tennessee)—History

At the River I Stand: Memphis, the 1968 Strike and Martin Luther King. By Joan Turner Beifuss. Reviewed by Cain H. Felder. *Journal of Religious Thought* 43, No. 2 (Fall-Winter 1986–87):93–94

Memphis (Tennessee)—Public Schools

A Bittersweet Victory: Public School Desegregation in Memphis. Roger Biles. *Journal of Negro Education* 55, No.4 (Fall 1986):470–483

Mendes, Orlando

Sobre Literatura Moçambicana. Reviewed by Russell G. Hamilton. *Research in African Literatures* 17, No. 3 (Fall 1986): 422–425

Men—Diseases

Your Man's Sexual Health. Reginald D. Ware. *Essence* 17, No. 7 (November 1986):16

Men—Mental Health

Black Men and Suicide. Lloyd Gite. *Essence* 17, No. 7 (November 1986):64

Men—Psychology

Conceptual and Logical Issues in Theory and Research Related to Black Masculinity. Clyde W. Franklin II. *Western Journal of Black Studies* 10, No. 4 (Winter 1986):161–166

The Destruction of the Young Black Male: The Impact of Popular Culture and Organized Sports. John C. Gaston. *Journal of Black Studies* 16, No. 4 (June 1986):369–384

Mental Health

See Depression

Mergers and Acquisitions

Cashing in on Coke. Ken Smikle. *Black Enterprise* 16, No. 8 (March 1986):13

Deals on Wheels. Ann Kimbrough. *Black Enterprise* 16, No. 9 (April 1986):25

Deals of the Year. Derek T. Dingle. *Black Enterprise* 17, No. 5 (December 1986):77

Insurance Overview: A Change of Policy. Shawn Kennedy. *Black Enterprise* 16, No. 11 (June 1986):175

Merritt, Bishetta D.

Jesse Jackson and Television: Black Image Presentation and Affect in the 1984 Democratic Campaign Debates. *Journal of Black Studies* 16, No. 4 (June 1986):347–367

Merritt, Robert (about)

The Power of Protesting. Dan Berube. *Black Enterprise* 17, No. 3 (October 1986):22

Metal-Stamping

The Trumark of Excellence. Trudy Gallant. *Black Enterprise* 17, No. 1 (August 1986):39

Metal-Work

Quality Control over Metal. Solomon J. Herbert. *Black Enterprise* 17, No. 5 (December 1986):37

Methodist Church—Clergy

A Pastoral Letter from John P. Carter. John P. Carter. *Journal of Religious Thought* 43, No. 1 (Spring-Summer 1986):120–127

Metuh, Ikenga E.

African Religions in Western Conceptual Schemes: The Problem of Interpretation. Reviewed by C. Ejizu. *Journal of Religious Thought* 43, No. 2 (Fall-Winter 1986–87):90

Mexican Americans

Time and Assimilation Clock. Irene I. Blea. *About Time* 14, No. 1 (January 1986):22

Mexican Americans—Employment

Latino Caucuses in U.S. Labour Unions. Hector Ramos. *Race and Class* 27, No. 4 (Spring 1986):69–78

Obreros en la Corazon del Bruto. Tom Denyer. *Race and Class* 27, No. 4 (Spring 1986):53–68

Mexico—Civilization—African Influences

Egypto-Nubian Presences in Ancient Mexico. Notes. Ivan Van Sertima. *Journal of African Civilizations* 8, No. 2 (December 1986):29–55

Mexico—Economic History

En defensa de Mexico: pensamiento economico politico. By Jesus Silva Herzog. Reviewed by Jorge Salazar-Carrillo. *Caribbean Review* 15, No. 2 (Spring 1986):46

Mexico—History

Mexico: A History. By Robert Ryal Miller. Reviewed by Lowell Gudmundson. *Caribbean Review* 15, No. 1 (Winter 1986):43

Meyer, Howard N.

American Reformers. Book review. *Interracial Books for Children Bulletin* 17, No. 1 (1986):10

Mickens, Marsha (about)

At the Bargaining Table. Joyce Davis Adams. *Black Enterprise* 17, No. 1 (August 1986):52–54

Microelectronics—Research

Reaching beyond the Outer Limits. Gwen McKinney. *Black Enterprise* 17, No. 1 (August 1986):44–46

Middle Classes

Attitudes of the New Black Middle-Class. Norman Riley. *Crisis* 93, No. 10 (December 1986):14

Middle East

See Arab Countries

Middleton, Listervelt, and Nile Valley Executive Committee

Two Interviews with Cheikh Anta Diop. Interview. *Journal of African Civilizations* 8, No. 1 (June 1986):284–302

Migalski, Michael (joint author)

See Grofman, Bernard

Migrations, Ancient

Africa and the Discovery of America, Volume I. By Leo Wiener. Reviewed by Phillips Barry. *Journal of African Civilizations* 8, No. 2 (December 1986):197–201

The African Presence in Ancient America: Evidence from Physical Anthropology. Notes. Keith M. Jordon. *Journal of African Civilizations* 8, No. 2 (December 1986):136–151

African Sea Kings in America? Evidence from Early Maps. Bibliography. Joan Covey. *Journal of African Civilizations* 8, No. 2 (December 1986):152–168

The Egyptian Presence in South America. Notes. R. A. Jairazbhoy. *Journal of African Civilizations* 8, No. 2 (December 1986):76–135

Egypto-Nubian Presences in Ancient Mexico. Notes. Ivan Van Sertima. *Journal of African Civilizations* 8, No. 2 (December 1986):29–55

The First Americans. Notes. Legrand H. Clegg II. *Journal of African Civilizations* 8, No. 2 (December 1986):264–273

Leo Wiener—A Plea for Re-Examination. Notes. David J. M. Muffett. *Journal of African Civilizations* 8, No. 2 (December 1986):188–196

Mandinga Voyages across the Atlantic. Notes. Harold G. Lawrence. *Journal of African Civilizations* 8, No. 2 (December 1986):202–247

Men Out of Asia: A Review and Update of the Gladwin Thesis. Notes. By Harold Sterling Gladwin. Reviewed by Runoko Rashidi. *Journal of African Civilizations* 8, No. 2 (December 1986):248–263

Pyramid—American and African: A Comparison. Notes. Beatrice Lumpkin. *Journal of African Civilizations* 8, No. 2 (December 1986):169–187

Ten Years After: An Introduction and Overview. Ivan Van Sertima. *Journal of African Civilizations* 8, No. 2 (December 1986):5–27

Trait-Influences in Meso-America: The African-Asian Connection. Notes. Wayne B. Chandler. *Journal of African Civilizations* 8, No. 2 (December 1986):274–334

Unexpected African Faces in Pre-Columbian America. Alexander Von Wuthenau. *Journal of African Civilizations* 8, No. 2 (December 1986):56–75

Miklowitz, Gloria D.

The War between the Classes. Book review. Valerie Ooka Pang. *Interracial Books for Children Bulletin* 17, Nos. 3–4 (1986):33

Miles, Leo F. (about)

Mixing Sports and School: Leo F. Miles. Henry Duvall. *About Time* 14, No. 5 (May 1986):23–24

Miles, Patrice

Conversations with Black Youths: A Round Table. *Essence* 17, No. 1 (May 1986):72

Phylicia and Ahmad: Off-Camera and Personal. *Essence* 17, No. 2 (July 1986):85

Military History

Strength for the Fight: A History of Blacks in the Military. By Bernard C. Nalty. Reviewed by William Leyden. *Negro Educational Review* 37, Nos. 3–4 (July-October 1986):155

Military Policy

  See War, Limited

Millander, Lucius

Positioning Yourself for Marketing. *Black Enterprise* 16, No. 7 (February 1986):56–62

Riding the Ratings. *Black Enterprise* 16, No. 6 (January 1986):26

Miller, E. Ethelbert

From the Mines of South Africa. Poem. *Western Journal of Black Studies* 10, No. 3 (Fall 1986):120

Tomorrow. Poem. *Western Journal of Black Studies* 10, No. 3 (Fall 1986):120

The Weather. Poem. *Western Journal of Black Studies* 10, No. 3 (Fall 1986):119

Miller, Howard J.

Miller Curriculum Development Process Model: A Systematic Approach to Curriculum Development in Black Studies. *Western Journal of Black Studies* 10, No. 1 (Spring 1986):19–28

Miller, James A.

Amiri Baraka in the 1980's. *Callaloo* 9, No. 1 (Winter 1986):184–192

Bigger Thomas's Quest for Voice and Audience in Richard Wright's *Native Son*. *Callaloo* 9, No. 3 (Summer 1986):501–506

The House of Si Abd Allah: The Oral History of a Moroccan Family. Book review. *Research in African Literatures* 17, No. 4 (Winter 1986): 582–584

Miller, Linda

Grassroots Development in Latin America and the Caribbean: Oral Histories of Social Change. Book review. *Caribbean Review* 15, No. 1 (Winter 1986):41–42

Miller, Robert Ryal

Mexico: A History. Reviewed by Lowell Gudmundson. *Caribbean Review* 15, No. 1 (Winter 1986):43

Miller Curriculum Development

Miller Curriculum Development Process Model: A Systematic Approach to Curriculum Development in Black Studies. Howard J. Miller. *Western Journal of Black Studies* 10, No. 1 (Spring 1986):19–28

Mills, Chester H.

Ethnocentric Manifestations in Cooper's *Pioneers*, and *The Last of the Mohicans. Journal of Black Studies* 16, No. 4 (June 1986):435–449

Milton, John (about)

Heresy in Paradise and the Ghosts of Readers Past. Notes. Michael E. Bauman. *CLA Journal* 30, No. 1 (September 1986):59–68

"To Hear New Utterance Flow": Language Before the Fall in *Paradise Lost*. Notes. Leonard Mustazzi. *CLA Journal* 30, No. 2 (December 1986):184–209

Mingus, Charles (about)

The Complete Candid Charles Mingus. Record review. Lewis Porter. *Black Perspective in Music* 14, No. 3 (Fall 1986):319–321

Minneapolis—History

Phyllis Wheatley House: A History of the Minneapolis Black Settlement House, 1924 to 1940. Howard Jacob Karger. *Phylon* 47, No. 1 (March 1986):79–90

Minorities in the Motion Picture Industry

Coast to Coast Salute to Black Filmmakers: New York Gala Kicks off the Nationwide Drive for Home for This Film Group. *Ebony* 41, No. 12 (October 1986):91

Minority Business Development Agency

Government Agencies Working behind the Scenes. David C. Ruffin. *Black Enterprise* 16, No. 11 (June 1986):269–270

Minority Business Legal Defense and Education Fund

Parren Mitchell's Sixteen Years: A Legislative Legacy. David C. Ruffin. *Black Enterprise* 16, No. 11 (June 1986):59–60

Minstrels

Debussy and American Minstrelsy. Ann McKinley. *Black Perspective in Music* 14, No. 3 (Fall 1986):249–258

Miscegenation

The Rhetoric of Miscegenation: Thomas Jefferson, Sally Hemings, and Their Historians. B. R. Burg. *Phylon* 47, No. 2 (June 1986):117–127

Missing Children

Who's Stealing Our Children. Thad Martin. *Ebony* 41, No. 4 (February 1986):139

Missionaries—Africa

Black Baptist Women and African Mission Work, 1870–1925. Sandy D. Martin. *SAGE* 3, No. 1 (Spring 1986):16–19

Black Women Missionaries: A Letter from Flora Zeto Malekebu to Lucy Hale Tapley. Jacqueline Jones Royster. *SAGE* 3, No. 1 (Spring 1986):58–60

"Say Africa When You Pray": The Activities of Early Black Baptist Women Missionaries among Liberian Women and Children. Sylvia M. Jacobs. *SAGE* 3, No. 2 (Fall 1986):16–21

Mississippi Freedom Democratic Party

Protest and Politics: The Mississippi Freedom Democratic Party and the 1965 Congressional Challenge. Leslie Burl McLemore. *Negro Educational Review* 37, Nos. 3–4 (July-October 1986):130–143

MississippiState Supreme Court

A Mississippi First: Black Judge Serves on State Supreme Court. *Ebony* 41, No. 4 (February 1986):37

Mitchell, Bert (about)

An Accountant and His Finances. Errol T. Louis. *Black Enterprise* 17, No. 3 (October 1986):42

Mitchell, Constance

Real Estate: Home, Sweet Home. *Black Enterprise* 16, No. 11 (June 1986):290

Mitchell, Ella Pearson (editor)

Those Preachin' Women: Sermons by Black Women Preachers. Book review. Renita J. Weems. *SAGE* 3, No. 2 (Fall 1986):56–57

Those Preachin' Women: Sermons by Black Women Preachers. Reviewed by Gayl Fowler. *Journal of Religious Thought* 43, No. 1 (Spring-Summer 1986):129–130

Mitchell, Louis D.

Letters to Alice: On First Reading Jane Austen. Book review. *CLA Journal* 30, No. 1 (September 1986):104–106

The Life of Jane Austen. Book review. *CLA Journal* 30, No. 1 (September 1986):104–106

Mitchell, Parren (about)

Parren Mitchell: Interview. David Hatchett. *Crisis* 93, No. 2 (February 1986):34–40

Parren Mitchell's Sixteen Years: A Legislative Legacy. David C. Ruffin. *Black Enterprise* 16, No. 11 (June 1986):59–60

Mitchell-Kernan, Claudia

Race, Class and Power in Brazil. Book review. Joe Johnson. *Crisis* 93, No. 6 (June/July 1986):16

Mitchell/Titus and Company

See Mitchell, Bert

M& M Products

M & M's New Markets. *Black Enterprise* 16, No. 6 (January 1986):26

Mobil Corporation

Making It Happen in Corporate America: Mobil and the Council on Career Development for Minorities, Inc. Work Together. J. D. Shattuck. *Black Collegian* 16, No. 4 (March/April 1986):86–87

Modeling as a Profession

So You Want to Be a Fashion Model. Hilton Als. *Essence* 17, No. 1 (May 1986):25

Models, Fashion

Iman in Africa: Supermodel Rediscovers Her Roots. *Ebony* 42, No. 1 (November 1986):62

Sade: The Story behind the Exotic Singing Sensation. Walter Leavy. *Ebony* 41, No. 7 (May 1986):155

Moeti, Moitsadi

The Origins of Forced Labor in the Witwatersrand. *Phylon* 47, No. 4 (December 1986):276–284

Moffett, George D. (III)

The Limits of Victory, The Ratification of the Panama Canal Treaties. Reviewed by Neale Pearson. *Caribbean Review* 15, No. 1 (Winter 1986):26–27 +

Moffitt, Angela J.

A Tenant's Right to Counterclaim for a Period Predating Landlord's Claim. *Howard Law Journal* 29, No. 1 (1986):41–61

Moglen, Helen

Charlotte Bronte: The Self Conceived. Reviewed by Elizabeth J. Higgins. *CLA Journal* 29, No. 3 (March 1986):368–371

Mohamed, Iely Burkhead

Ngambika: Studies of Women in African Literature. Book review. *SAGE* 3, No. 2 (Fall 1986):59–60

Monk, Thelonious (about)

The Complete Thelonious Monk. Record review. Lewis Porter. *Black Perspective in Music* 14, No. 3 (Fall 1986):319–321

Monroe, Robert A.

A Perennial Favorite. *Crisis* 93, No. 4 (April 1986):38

Same Questions, Different Answers. *Black Collegian* 17, No. 1 (September/October 1986):66–71

Moody, H. L. B.

A Teacher's Guide to African Literature. Reviewed by Carl Wood. *Research in African Literatures* 17, No. 4 (Winter 1986): 606–609

Moore, Carlos

Congo or Carabali? Race Relations in Socialist Cuba. *Caribbean Review* 15, No. 2 (Spring 1986):12–15 +

Interviews with Cheikh Anta Diop. Interview. *Journal of African Civilizations* 8, No. 1 (June 1986):249–283

Moore, Gilbert W. (joint author)

See Irons, Edward D.

Moore, Jacqueline

The Maestro of Marketing. *Black Enterprise* 16, No. 12 (July 1986):32

NFBPA Holds Conference. *Black Enterprise* 16, No. 12 (July 1986):16

Moore, Lenard D.

Dinin' Out at the Midway Cafe, 1975. Poem. *Black American Literature Forum* 20, No. 3 (Fall 1986):266

The Way I Think It Should Be. Poem. *Black American Literature Forum* 20, No. 3 (Fall 1986):266

Moore, Melba (about)

Melba Moore. Charles E. Rogers. *Black Collegian* 17, No. 2 (November/December 1986):45–47

Moore, Rebecca

A Sympathetic History of Jonestown: The Moore Family Involvement in Peoples Temple. Reviewed by Kortright Davis. *Journal of Religious Thought* 43, No. 2 (Fall-Winter 1986–87):92–93

Moore, Shawna

Interview with Cheikh Anta Diop. Interview. Notes. Bibliography. *Journal of African Civilizations* 8, No. 1 (June 1986):238–248

Moore, Shelley

Dakar, Senegal: A City of Many Moods—from Blue to Indigo. *Black Enterprise* 16, No. 9 (April 1986):67–68

Eyes on the Prize: America's Civil Rights Years, 1954–1965. Film review. *Crisis* 93, No. 10 (December 1986):12–13

Goree. *Crisis* 93, No. 6 (June/July 1986):18

An Historical Look at Male-Female Relationships in the Black Community. *Crisis* 93, No. 10 (December 1986):20

Moore, Trudy S.

Love Can Be Lasting. *Ebony* 42, No. 2 (December 1986):123

Moore, Yvette

Automotive Luxury. *Black Enterprise* 17, No. 4 (November 1986):31

On Freedom's Road Again. *Black Enterprise* 16, No. 11 (June 1986):50

Moore-Gilbert, Bart (editor)

Literature and Imperialism. Reviewed by Robert D. Hamner. *Research in African Literatures* 17, No. 1 (Spring 1986): 162–165

Moran, Dale

How to Begin the Job-Search Process in Your Chosen Field. *Black Collegian* 17, No. 2 (November/December 1986):39–43

Which Career Is Right for You? *Black Collegian* 17, No. 1 (September/October 1986):90–98

Morehouse College (Atlanta, Georgia)

Cheikh Anta Diop's First Visit to the United States. Lawrence Edward Carter, Sr. *Journal of African Civilizations* 8, No. 1 (June 1986):307–314

Morgan, Debra Jean

Leaving the Nest. Poem. *Essence* 17, No. 1 (May 1986):164

Morgenstern, Dan, and others (editors)

Annual Review of Jazz Studies. Book review. Lewis Porter. *Black Perspective in Music* 14, No. 2 (Spring 1986):195–196

Mörner, Magnus

Adventurers and Proletarians: The Story of Migrants in Latin America. Book review. Frances Webber. *Race and Class* 28, No. 2 (August 1986):103–105

Morocco—Oral Literature

The House of Si Abd Allah: The Oral History of a Moroccan Family. Henry Munson, Jr., editor and translator. Reviewed by James A. Miller. *Research in African Literatures* 17, No. 4 (Winter 1986): 582–584

Morris, Delores (about)

After-School Specialist: Former Teacher Knows Her ABCs. Janine C. McAdams. *Essence* 17, No. 7 (November 1986):119

Morris, Steveland

See Wonder, Stevie

Morrison, Toni—Criticism and Interpretation

Ancient Properties in the New World: The Paradox of the "Other" in Toni Morrison's *Tar Baby*. Angelita Reyes. *Black Scholar* 17, No. 2 (March-April 1986):19–25

Clothes and Closure in Three Novels by Black Women. Mary Jane Lupton. *Black American Literature Forum* 20, No. 4 (Winter 1986):409–421

Intimations of Matriarchal Age: Notes on the Mythical Eva in Toni Morrison's *Sula*. Janice M. Sokoloff. *Journal of Black Studies* 16, No. 4 (June 1986):429–434

The Quest for Wholeness in Toni Morrison's *Tar Baby*. James Coleman. *Black American Literature Forum* 20, Nos. 1–2 (Spring/Summer 1986):63–73

Toni Morrison's World of Topsy-Turvydom: A Methodological Explication of New Black Literary Criticism. Clenora Hudson-Withers. *Western Journal of Black Studies* 10, No. 3 (Fall 1986):132–136

Morrison, Trudi (about)

The Lady in Charge: Trudi Morrison Runs Day-to-Day Operations of U.S. Senate. D. Michael Cheers. *Ebony* 41, No. 12 (October 1986):117

Morrison, Walter W.

Earl B. Dickerson: An Appreciation. *Crisis* 93, No. 8 (October 1986):37

Morse, Roberta N.

Black Students in Higher Education. Book review. *Journal of Negro Education* 55, No. 1 (Winter 1986):118–120

Mortages—Default

Rights of a Tenant When the Landlord Defaults on the Mortgage. Anna E. Blackburne. *Howard Law Journal* 29, No. 1 (1986):27–39

Mortgages

Mortgage Money for Minorities. Solomon J. Herbert. *Black Enterprise* 17, No. 1 (August 1986):19

Refinancing Your Mortgage. *Black Enterprise* 17, No. 4 (November 1986):40

Morticians

See Undertakers and Undertaking

Mortimer, Mildred

Dialectique de la ville de la campagne chez Gabrielle Roy et chez Mongo Beti. Book review. *Research in African Literatures* 17, No. 4 (Winter 1986): 572–574

Moser, Gerald

Literature Africana Literature Necessaria, II—Moçambique, Cabo Verde, Guiné-Bissau, Sao Tomé e Principe. Book review. *Research in African Literatures* 17, No. 1 (Spring 1986):144–145

Moses, Knolly

Melvin Van Peebles's Bold New Money Play. Interview. *Essence* 17, No. 2 (June 1986):12

Moses, Yolanda T. (joint author)

See Kinley, Barbara

Moss, Ambler H., Jr.

Panama Odyssey. Book review. *Caribbean Review* 15, No. 1 (Winter 1986):43–44

Moss, Thylias

More Lessons from a Mirror. Poem. *Callaloo* 9, No. 1 (Winter 1986):106

A Reconsideration of the Blackbird. Poem. *Callaloo* 9, No. 1 (Winter 1986):107

The Road to Todos Santos Is Closed. Poem. *Callaloo* 9, No. 1 (Winter 1986):101

Timex Remembered. Poem. *Callaloo* 9, No. 1 (Winter 1986):104–105

To Eliminate Vagueness. Poem. *Callaloo* 9, No. 1 (Winter 1986):102–103

Mothers

Alabama Super Mom Rears Officers, Gentlemen and Scholars. *Ebony* 41, No. 6 (April 1986):101

Save the Mothers. Maya Angelou. *Ebony* 41, No. 10 (August 1986):38

Mothers in Literature

Rousseau's Julie; Or, the Maternal Odyssey. Notes. Ruth Ohayon. *CLA Journal* 30, No. 1 (September 1986):69–82

Motivation

The Future of the Black Community: Human Capital, Family Aspirations, and Individual Motivation. Clifton R. Wharton, Jr. *Review of Black Political Economy* 14, No. 4 (Spring 1986):9–16

Motown

Dreamgirls: My Life as a Supreme. By Mary Wilson. Reviewed by Norman Riley. *Crisis* 93, No. 10 (December 1986):9

Motown Sound. Norman Riley. *Crisis* 93, No. 7 (August/September 1986):9

The Motown Story. By Don Waller. Reviewed by Doris E. McGinty. *Black Perspective in Music* 14, No. 3 (Fall 1986):310–311

Where Did Our Love Go? The Rise and Fall of the Motown Sound. By Nelson George. Reviewed by Tonya Bolden Davis. *Black Enterprise* 16, No. 11 (June 1986):35–37

Mottley, Elton Elombe

When Banja Play, Bajan Come. Poem. Illustrated. *International Review of African American Art* 7, No. 1 (1986):32–40

Moynihan, Daniel Patrick

Family and Nation. Book review. Tonya Bolden Davis. *Black Enterprise* 17, No. 3 (October 1986):17

Mozambique—History

A Comparative Study of Zambia and Mozambique: Africanization, Professionalization, and Bureaucracy in the African Postcolonial State. Mokubung O. Nkomo. *Journal of Black Studies* 16, No. 3 (March 1986):319–342

Mozambique—Literature

Sobre Literatura Moçambicana. By Orlando Mendes. Reviewed by Russell G. Hamilton. *Research in African Literatures* 17, No. 3 (Fall 1986): 422–425

Mphahlele, Es'kia

Bury Me at the Marketplace: Selected Letters of Es'kia Mphahlele, 1943–1980. N. Chabani Manganyi, editor. Reviewed by Brian Worsfold. *Research in African Literatures* 17, No. 3 (Fall 1986): 395–398

Muffett, David J. M.

Leo Wiener—A Plea for Re-Examination. Notes. *Journal of African Civilizations* 8, No. 2 (December 1986):188–196

Muffler, John P.

Education and the Separate But Equal Doctrine. *Black Scholar* 17, No. 3 (May-June 1986):35–41

Mugen, Donna

Center of Attraction. *Black Enterprise* 16, No. 8 (March 1986):17

Mugo, E. N.

Kikuyu People: A Brief Outline of their Customs and Traditions. Reviewed by Simon Gikandi. *Research in African Literatures* 17, No. 2 (Summer 1986): 299–301

Muhammad, Elijah (about)

From Black Muslims to Muslims. By Clifton E. Marsh. Reviewed by Sulayman S. Nyang. *Phylon* 47, No. 2 (June 1986):169–170

Mulatto, American

Nella Larsen's Use of the Near-White Female in *Quicksand*, and *Passing*. Vashti Crutcher Lewis. *Western Journal of Black Studies* 10, No. 3 (Fall 1986):137–142

Mullard, Chris

Race, Power and Resistance. Book review. Ahmed Gurnah. *Race and Class* 28, No. 1 (Summer 1986):99–103

Mullen, Harryette

Fable. Poem. *Callaloo* 9, No. 1 (Winter 1986):108

Unspoken. Poem. *Callaloo* 9, No. 2 (Spring 1986):345–346

Muller, C. H. (editor)

Explorations in the Novel: A Student's Guide to Setworks at South African Universities. Reviewed by Martin Trump. *Research in African Literatures* 17, No. 3 (Fall 1986): 419–421

Munford, Clarence J.

Slavery in the French Caribbean, 1625–1715: A Marxist Analysis. *Journal of Black Studies* 17, No. 1 (September 1986):49–69

Mungazi, Dickson A.

Application of Memmi's Theory of the Colonizer and the Colonized to the Conflicts in Zimbabwe. *Journal of Negro Education* 55, No.4 (Fall 1986):518–534

Municipal Government

Municipal Management. Kenneth Maurice Jones. *Black Enterprise* 16, No. 10 (May 1986):20

Munson, Henry Jr. (editor)

The House of Si Abd Allah: The Oral History of a Moroccan Family. Reviewed by James A. Miller. *Research in African Literatures* 17, No. 4 (Winter 1986): 582–584

Murder

Drinking, Homicide, and the Black Male. Lawrence E. Gary. *Journal of Black Studies* 17, No. 1 (September 1986):15–31

Murphy, Donna M.

Educational Disadvantagement: Associated Factors, Current Interventions, and Implications. *Journal of Negro Education* 55, No.4 (Fall 1986):495–507

Murphy, William P.

The Language of Secrecy. Book review. *Research in African Literatures* 17, No. 2 (Summer 1986): 296–298

Murray, Graham

The Worst of Times: An Oral History of the Great Depression in Britain. Book review. *Race and Class* 27, No. 4 (Spring 1986):103–104

Murray, Nancy

Anti-Racists and Other Demons: The Press and Ideology in Thatcher's Britain. *Race and Class* 27, No. 3 (Winter 1986):1–19

Government and Politics in Africa. Book review. *Race and Class* 27, No. 4 (Spring 1986):107–108

Labor of Love, Labor of Sorrow: Black Women, Work, and the Family from Slavery to the Present. Book review. *Race and Class* 28, No. 2 (August 1986):96–97

On Living in an Old Country: The National Past in Contemporary Britain. Book review. *Race and Class* 28, No. 1 (Summer 1986):93–95

Reporting the "riots." *Race and Class* 27, No. 3 (Winter 1986):86–90

Muse, Daphne

Junius Over Far. Book review. *Interracial Books for Children Bulletin* 17, Nos. 3–4 (1986):34

Music

A *Crisis* Report on Music. Norman Riley. *Crisis* 93, No. 1 (January 1986):17

Motown Sound. Norman Riley. *Crisis* 93, No. 7 (August/September 1986):9

The Rolling Stones. Norman Riley. *Crisis* 93, No. 6 (June/July 1986):14

See also Minstrels

Music, Afro-American

The Study of Music as a Symbol of Culture: The Afro-American and Euro-American Perspectives. Robert W. Stephens. *Western Journal of Black Studies* 10, No. 4 (Winter 1986):180–184

The Symposium on Black-American Music: Some Comments. Willis Patterson. *Black Perspective in Music* 14, No. 1 (Winter 1986):4–6

Music, Caribbean

Steel Artistry in Trinidad. Constance M. Green. *Black Enterprise* 17, No. 3 (October 1986):119

Music, Popular—Trinidad

Street Life: Afro-American Culture in Urban Trinidad. By Michael Lieber. Reviewed by Keith Q. Warner. *CLA Journal* 29, No. 4 (June 1986):493–496

Music—Bibliographies

Bibliography of Black Music. Volume 4: Theory, Education, and Related Studies. By Dominique-René de Lerma. Reviewed by Doris E. McGinty. *Black Perspective in Music* 14, No. 2 (Spring 1986):186–187

A Bibliography of Jazz and Blues Biographical Literature. Gary Carner. *Black American Literature Forum* 20, Nos. 1–2 (Spring/Summer 1986):161–202

Books on Black Music by Black Authors: A Bibliography. Samuel A. Floyd, Jr. *Black Perspective in Music* 14, No. 3 (Fall 1986):215–232

New Books. Terry Kroger (compiler). *Black Perspective in Music* 14, No. 2 (Spring 1986):181–184

New Books. Terry Kroger (compiler). *Black Perspective in Music* 14, No. 3 (Fall 1986):303–305

Music—Compilations

New Music. Josephine Wright (compiler). *Black Perspective in Music* 14, No. 2 (Spring 1986):196–200

Popular Music, 1920–1979; A Revised Cumulation. Edited by Nat Shapiro and Bruce Pollack. Reviewed by Doris E. McGinty. *Black Perspective in Music* 14, No. 3 (Fall 1986):311–312

Music—Dissertations and Theses

Master's Theses in Progress in Selected Colleges and Universities. Mac A. Stewart. *Negro Educational Review* 37, Nos. 3–4 (July-October 1986):103, 115

Music—Gospel

Black Gospel. An Illustrated History of the Gospel Sound. By Viv Broughton. Book review. André Prévos. *Black Perspective in Music* 14, No. 2 (Spring 1986):191–192

Black Gospel Music and Black Theology. Notes. Louis-Charles Harvey. *Journal of Religious Thought* 43, No. 2 (Fall-Winter 1986–87):19–37

Music in the Churches of Black Americans: A Critical Statement. Wendell Whalum. *Black Perspective in Music* 14, No. 1 (Winter 1986):13–20

Sallie Martin: At 90, the "Mother of Gospel" Is Being Hailed from Coast to Coast. *Ebony* 41, No. 5 (March 1986):76

Music—History

The Music of Black Americans: A History. By Eileen Southern. Reviewed by Doris E. McGinty. *Black Perspective in Music* 14, No. 2 (Spring 1986):185–186

Musicians

Art Blakey: The Big Beat! David H. Rosenthal. *Black Perspective in Music* 14, No. 3 (Fall 1986):267–289

Conversation with Israel Anyahuru. Joshua Uzoigwe. *Black Perspective in Music* 14, No. 2 (Spring 1986):126–142

Dizzy Gillespie: He Just Keeps Bopping Along. Marilyn Marshall. *Ebony* 41, No. 11 (September 1986):50

Ebony Interview with Prince. *Ebony* 41, No. 9 (July 1986):29

Kashif. Norman Riley. *Crisis* 93, No. 5 (May 1986):10–39

A Musical Entrepreneur. Ken Smikle. *Black Enterprise* 16, No. 7 (February 1986):30

On the Road with B. B. King: After 38 Years, the Legendary Monarch of the Blues Is Still a Roadrunning Troubadour. Walter Leavy. *Ebony* 41, No. 8 (June 1986):141

The Secret Dreams of Stevie Wonder. *Ebony* 42, No. 2 (December 1986):152

Wind and Thunder. *Western Journal of Black Studies* 10, No. 4 (Winter 1986):193–194

    See also Composers

    See also Singers

Music—Jazz

Dizzy Gillespie: He Just Keeps Bopping Along. Marilyn Marshall. *Ebony* 41, No. 11 (September 1986):50

Howard University Jazz Ensemble. Henry Duvall. *About Time* 14, No. 12 (December 1986):27–28

The Influence of Black Vaudeville on Early Jazz. William Howland Kenney III. *Black Perspective in Music* 14, No. 3 (Fall 1986):233–248

Jazz: America's Classical Music. William Taylor. *Black Perspective in Music* 14, No. 1 (Winter 1986):21–25

The Jazzman's Verbal Usage. Neil Leonard. *Black American Literature Forum* 20, Nos. 1–2 (Spring/Summer 1986):151–160

Jazz Styles: History and Analysis. By Mark C. Gridley. Reviewed by George L. Starks, Jr. *Black Perspective in Music* 14, No. 2 (Spring 1986):188–189

Jouer le jeu. L'improviste II. By Jacques Reda. Reviewed by André Prévos. *Black Perspective in Music* 14, No. 2 (Spring 1986):190–191

A Moment's Notice: Portraits of American Jazz Musicians. By Carol Friedman and Gary Giddins. Reviewed by George L. Starks, Jr. *Black Perspective in Music* 14, No. 3 (Fall 1986):312–313

Perri's Smoldering Harmony Ignites Jazz Chart. Gerrie Summers. *Essence* 17, No. 5 (September 1986):29

Preservation Hall Jazz Band. Joan Marie Allen. *About Time* 14, No. 12 (December 1986):26–27

Rhythm-A-Ning: Jazz Tradition and Innovation in the 80's. By Gary Giddins. Reviewed by George L. Starks, Jr. *Black Perspective in Music* 14, No. 2 (Spring 1986):187

Tradition afrikanischer Blasorchester und Entstehung des Jazz. By Alfons Michael Dauer. Reviewed by Lewis Porter. *Black Perspective in Music* 14, No. 3 (Fall 1986):314–316

Up Swings Jazz. Martin Johnson. *Essence* 17, No. 6 (October 1986):36

Why We Must Preserve Our Jazz Heritage. Wynton Marsalis. *Ebony* 41, No. 4 (February 1986):131

Music—Jazz—Bibliographies

Annual Review of Jazz Studies. Edited by Dan Morgenstern and others. Reviewed by Lewis Porter. *Black Perspective in Music* 14, No. 2 (Spring 1986):195–196

Music—Opera

Black Divas. Rosalyn Story. *Essence* 17, No. 2 (June 1986):36

Music—Operetta

In Retrospect: Will Garland and the Negro Operetta Company. Rainer E. Lotz. *Black Perspective in Music* 14, No. 3 (Fall 1986):290–303

Music—Ragtime

Ragtime: Its History, Composers, and Music. Edited by John Edward Hass. Reviewed by George L. Starks, Jr. *Black Perspective in Music* 14, No. 3 (Fall 1986):313–314

Music—Religious Aspects

Saving the Day: The Recordings of Reverend Sutton E. Griggs. Steven C. Tracy. *Phylon* 47, No. 2 (June 1986):159–166

Music—Rhythm and Blues

Black Music Critics and the Classic Blues Singers. Phillip McGuire. *Black Perspective in Music* 14, No. 2 (Spring 1986):103–125

Blues et gospels. By Marguerite Yourcenar. Reviewed by André Prévos. *Black Perspective in Music* 14, No. 2 (Spring 1986):192

Le Blues authentique. Son histoire et ses thèmes. By Robert Springer. Reviewed by André Prévos. *Black Perspective in Music* 14, No. 2 (Spring 1986):189–190

On the Road with B. B. King: After 38 Years, the Legendary Monarch of the Blues Is Still a Roadrunning Troubadour. Walter Leavy. *Ebony* 41, No. 8 (June 1986):141

Music—Rock

Where Did Our Love Go? The Rise and Fall of the Motown Sound. By Nelson George. Reviewed by Tonya Bolden Davis. *Black Enterprise* 16, No. 11 (June 1986):35–37

Music—West Africa

Musicmakers of West Africa. By John Collins. Reviewed by Jacqueline Cogdell DjeDje. *Black Perspective in Music* 14, No. 3 (Fall 1986):308–309

Muslims

From Black Muslims to Muslims. By Clifton E. Marsh. Reviewed by Sulayman S. Nyang. *Phylon* 47, No. 2 (June 1986):169–170

Mustazzi, Leonard

"To Hear New Utterance Flow": Language Before the Fall in *Paradise Lost*. Notes. *CLA Journal* 30, No. 2 (December 1986):184–209

Myers, Samuel L. (Jr.)

Black Unemployment and Its Link to Crime. *Urban League Review* 10, No. 1 (Summer 1986):98–105

Myers, Samuel L. (Jr.) (joint author)

See Darity, William (Jr.)

Myers, Woodrow (about)

The Good Doctor and His Diet: Indiana Health Commissioner Woodrow Myers, M. D., Sets Mark by Losing 201 Pounds. Frank White III. *Ebony* 41, No. 8 (June 1986):271

Myth in Literature

Images et mythes d'Haiti. By Daniel-Henry Pageaux. Reviewed by Clarisse Zimra. *Research in African Literatures* 17, No. 4 (Winter 1986): 591–593

Myth, Metaphor, and Syntax in Soyinka's Poetry. Notes. James Booth. *Research in African Literatures* 17, No. 1 (Spring 1986): 53–72

Soyinka as a Literary Critic. Notes. Obiajuru Maduakor. *Research in African Literatures* 17, No. 1 (Spring 1986): 1–38

NAACP

See National Association for the Advancement of Colored People

Nadeski, Karen

Black Journals of the United States. Book review. *Western Journal of Black Studies* 10, No. 2 (Summer 1986):102

Naisbitt, John

Careers 1990: The Changing Workplace. Kuumba Kazi-Ferrouillet. *Black Collegian* 17, No. 1 (September/October 1986):81–87

Nalty, Bernard C.

Strength for the Fight: A History of Blacks in the Military. Book review. William Leyden. *Negro Educational Review* 37, Nos. 3–4 (July-October 1986):155–156

Names, Personal

So the Name Has Been Changed: Celebrities Have Various Reasons for Adopting New and Sometimes Strange Monikers. *Ebony* 41, No. 6 (April 1986):46

Namibia—Politics and Government

Namibia: Africa's Last Colony. Reviewed by Roland S. Jefferson. *Black Scholar* 17, No. 1 (January-February 1986):46–47

Nanry, Charles (joint editor)

See Morgenstern, Dan

Natambu, Kofi (editor)

Nostalgia for the Present: An Anthology of Writings. Book review. Barbara Harlow. *Black American Literature Forum* 20, No. 3 (Fall 1986):317–326

National Association for the Advancement of Colored People

Dearborn Boycott. Margo Walker. *Black Enterprise* 17, No. 1 (August 1986):12

The NAACP and the American Occupation of Haiti. Leon D. Pamphile. *Phylon* 47, No. 1 (March 1986):91–100

The NAACP and South Africa. *Crisis* 93, No. 9 (November 1986):35–39

National Association of Black Manufacturers

Parren Mitchell's Sixteen Years: A Legislative Legacy. David C. Ruffin. *Black Enterprise* 16, No. 11 (June 1986):59–60

National Association of Market Developers

A Meeting of Marketers. Solomon J. Herbert. *Black Enterprise* 17, No. 2 (September 1986):18

National Bankers Association

NBA Protests Treasury's Banking Policy. David C. Ruffin. *Black Enterprise* 17, No. 1 (August 1986):17

NBA Sets Strategies. Joyce Davis Adams. *Black Enterprise* 16, No. 6 (January 1986):23

National Coalition of Black Meeting Planners

Meeting Planners. Solomon J. Herbert. *Black Enterprise* 17, No. 1 (August 1986):14

National Council of Negro Women

Dr. Dorothy Irene Height: Motivating the Strengths of Black Women. Adolph Dupree. *About Time* 14, No. 6 (June 1986):8–23

National Black Family Celebration. Marsha Jones. *About Time* 14, No. 10 (October 1986):23

National Economic Association—Westerfield Award

Statement on Dr. Clifton R. Wharton, Jr.—Recipient of the Samuel Z. Westerfield Award. Bernard E. Anderson. *Review of Black Political Economy* 14, No. 4 (Spring 1986):5–7

National Education Association

Testing Teachers: An Overview of NEA's Position, Policy, and Involvement. Mary Hatwood Futrell and Sharon P. Robinson. *Journal of Negro Education* 55, No.3 (Summer 1986):397–404

National Forum for Black Public Administrators

NFBPA Holds Conference. Jacqueline Moore. *Black Enterprise* 16, No. 12 (July 1986):16

National Medical Association

Breakthroughs Are Her Business: Edith Irby. Charles Whitaker. *Ebony* 41, No. 8 (June 1986):90

National Rainbow Coalition

The Rainbow Convention. Gwen McKinney. *Black Enterprise* 17, No. 1 (August 1986):12

National Technical Association

The National Technical Association: Sixty Years Young. V. Phillip Manuel. *Black Collegian* 17, No. 2 (November/December 1986):38

National Urban Coalition

Nonprofits Going It Alone. Gwen McKinney. *Black Enterprise* 16, No. 11 (June 1986):272–274

National Women's History Project

Honoring Women's History. *Interracial Books for Children Bulletin* 17, No. 1 (1986):3–5

Nation of Islam

See Black Muslims

Nationwide Securities Corporation

Brokers Go for Growth. Ken Smikle. *Black Enterprise* 16, No. 10 (May 1986):18

Natural Disasters

Nature Strikes at Colombia. Bernard Diederich. *Caribbean Review* 15, No. 1 (Winter 1986):15

Nazareth, Peter

East African Literature: An Anthology. Book review. *Research in African Literatures* 17, No. 1 (Spring 1986): 140–142

Ndebele, Njabulo

Fools and Other Stories. Book review. Gerald D. Kendrick. *Black Scholar* 17, No. 4 (July-August 1986):57–58

Ndong, Norbert

Kamerunische Marchen: Text und Kontext in ethnosoziologischer und psychologischer Sicht. Reviewed by Tunde Okanlawon. *Research in African Literatures* 17, No. 2 (Summer 1986): 294

Neal, Brenda D.

Make Your Money Grow with Investments. *Black Enterprise* 16, No. 7 (February 1986):43

Negro Ensemble Company

Jonah and the Wonderdog. Theater review. Cecilia Loving-Sloane. *Crisis* 93, No. 6 (June/July 1986):10–11

Negro Labor Victory Committee

Let Us Do Our Part: The New York City Based Negro Labor Victory Committee, 1941–1945. C. Alvin Hughes. *Afro-Americans in New York Life and History* 10, No.1 (January 1986):19–29

Negro Operetta Company

In Retrospect: Will Garland and the Negro Operetta Company. Rainer E. Lotz. *Black Perspective in Music* 14, No. 3 (Fall 1986):290–303

Nelson, Jill

Armageddon Is Now. *Essence* 17, No. 2 (July 1986):80

Black Dollars: Taking Control. *Essence* 17, No. 5 (September 1986):65

Nelson, Jill, and Davis, George

Come out with Your Hands Up: How Black Men and Women Really Feel about Each Other. *Essence* 17, No. 2 (July 1986):54

Nelson, Maudene

The Anticancer Diet. *Essence* 17, No. 2 (June 1986):66

Nelson, Raymond

Melvin B. Tolson 1898–1966: Plain Talk and Poetic Prophecy. Book review. *Callaloo* 9, No. 1 (Winter 1986):270–272

Nelson, Sandra

Fire. Poem. *Black American Literature Forum* 20, No. 3 (Fall 1986):315

The Mate. Poem. *Black American Literature Forum* 20, No. 3 (Fall 1986):316

Ngara, Emmanuel

Teaching Literature in Africa: Principles and Techniques. Reviewed by Florence Stratton. *Research in African Literatures* 17, No. 3 (Fall 1986): 451–453

Ngate, Jonathan

Propos sur la littérature negro-africaine. Book review. *Research in African Literatures* 17, No. 4 (Winter 1986): 565–566

Reading Warner-Vieyra's *Juletane*. *Callaloo* 9, No. 4 (Fall 1986):553–564

Ngema, Mbongeni

Asinamali: Addressing the South African Struggle. Theater review. Marsha Jones. *About Time* 14, No. 9 (September 1986):11

Ngugi wa Thiong'o

The Writer in a Neocolonial State. *Black Scholar* 17, No. 4 (July-August 1986):2–10

Nicaragua

Nicaragua. Directed by Marc Karlin. Reviewed by John Bevan. *Race and Class* 27, No. 3 (Winter 1986):99–102

Nicaragua—History

An Interview with Hugo Spadafora Four Months before His Death. Interview. Beatrix Parga de Bayon. *Caribbean Review* 15, No. 1 (Winter 1986):24–25 +

Nicaragua—Politics and Government

Nicaragua under Siege. Marlene Dixon and Susanne Jonas, editors. Reviewed by John A. Booth. *Caribbean Review* 15, No. 2 (Spring 1986):47

Revolutionary Comics: Political Humor from Nicaragua. Roger Sanchez Flores. *Caribbean Review* 15, No. 1 (Winter 1986):16–17

Ritual, Paradox and Death in Managua: Internacionalistas in Nicaragua. Alfred Padula. *Caribbean Review* 15, No. 1 (Winter 1986):18–19

Nicaragua—Race Relations

From Nationalism to Autonomy: The Ethnic Question in the Nicaraguan Revolution. Alison Rooper and Hazel Smith. *Race and Class* 27, No. 4 (Spring 1986):1–20

Nicaragua—Revolution

Fire from the Mountain: The Making of a Sandinista. By Omar Cabezas. Reviewed by David E. Lewis. *Black Scholar* 17, No. 1 (January-February 1986):49

Nicaragua: Revolution in the Family. By Shirley Christian. Reviewed by Saul Landau. *Race and Class* 27, No. 3 (Winter 1986):95–99

Nichols, Grace

Holding My Beads. Poem. *Essence* 17, No. 2 (June 1986):113

Nichols, Joan Kane

All But the Right Folks. Book review. Kate Shackford. *Interracial Books for Children Bulletin* 17, No. 2 (1986):14–15

Nichols, Lee

African Writers at the Microphone. Reviewed by Alex Tetteh-Lartey. *Research in African Literatures* 17, No. 1 (Spring 1986): 153–155

Nieto, Sonia

Annotated Bibliography. *Interracial Books for Children Bulletin* 17, Nos. 3–4 (1986):29–30

Equity in Education: The Case for Bilingual Education. *Interracial Books for Children Bulletin* 17, Nos. 3–4 (1986):4–8

Guidelines for Evaluating Bilingual Classrooms. *Interracial Books for Children Bulletin* 17, Nos. 3–4 (1986):26–28

Organizational Resources. *Interracial Books for Children Bulletin* 17, Nos. 3–4 (1986):31–32

Past Accomplishments, Current Needs: La Lucha Continúa. *Interracial Books for Children Bulletin* 17, No. 2 (1986):6–8

Nigeria—Children

Concepts of the Child in Some Nigerian Cultures. O. L. Okanlawon. *Journal of Black Psychology* 12, No. 2 (February 1986):61–70

Nigeria—Education

An Analysis of University of Ibadan Undergraduates' Attitudes toward Issues Incidental to the Yoruba Culture. Adedeji Awoniyi. *Negro Educational Review* 37, No. 2 (April 1986):62–70

The Relative Contribution of the Extended Family System to Schooling in Nigeria. E. E. Ezewu. *Journal of Negro Education* 55, No.2 (Spring 1986):222–228

Nigeria—History

Nigeria and Its Invaders 1851–1920. By J. U. J. Asiegbu. Reviewed by Lai Olurode. *Journal of Black Studies* 16, No. 4 (June 1986):457–460

Nigeria—Literature

Igbo Language and Culture II. F. C. Ogbalu and E. N. Emenanjo, editors. Reviewed by Kalu Ogbaa. *Research in African Literatures* 17, No. 2 (Summer 1986): 291–293

J. P. Clark. By Robert M. Wren. Reviewed by Thomas R. Knipp. *Research in African Literatures* 17, No. 2 (Summer 1986): 278–281

Uwa ndi Igbo: Journal of Igbo Life and Culture I. Chieka Ifemesia, editor. Reviewed by Don Burgess. *Research in African Literatures* 17, No. 2 (Summer 1986): 288–291

Nigeria—Novel

Class vs. Sex: The Problem of Values in the Modern Nigerian Novel. Rhonda Cobham-Sander. *Black Scholar* 17, No. 4 (July-August 1986):17–27

Nigeria—Theater

Creative Historiography and Critical Determinism in Nigerian Theater. References. Oyekan Owomoyela. *Research in African Literatures* 17, No. 2 (Summer 1986): 234–251

Nile Valley Conference

Cheikh Anta Diop in America: An Overview. Notes. Larry Williams. *Journal of African Civilizations* 8, No. 1 (June 1986):352–358

Two Interviews with Cheikh Anta Diop. Interview. Listervelt Middleton and Nile Valley Executive Committee. *Journal of African Civilizations* 8, No. 1 (June 1986):284–302

Nile Valley Executive Committee (joint author)

See Middleton, Listervelt

Nilotic Language

Iteso Thought Patterns in Tales. By Grace Akello. Reviewed by John Lamphear. *Research in African Literatures* 17, No. 2 (Summer 1986): 298–299

Nisbet, Anne-Marie

Le personnage féminin dans le roman maghrébin de langue française des indépendences à 1980: Representations et fonctions. Reviewed by Charlotte H. Bruner. *Research in African Literatures* 17, No. 4 (Winter 1986): 576–579

Niven, Alastair

The Commonwealth in Canada: Proceedings of the Second Triennial Conference of the Canadian Association for Commonwealth Literature and Language Studies. Book review. *Research in African Literatures* 17, No. 3 (Fall 1986): 435–439

Nix, Robert N. C. (Jr.)

Commencement Address: University of Pittsburgh School of Law, May 25, 1985. *Black Law Journal* 9, No. 3 (Winter 1986):296–299

Nizalowski, Edward

Margaret Williams and the Black Community of Owego, New York. *Afro-Americans in New York Life and History* 10, No.1 (January 1986):53–59

Nkomo, M. O.

Student Culture and Activism in Black South African Universities. Reviewed by Ernest F. Dube. *Journal of Negro Education* 55, No.2 (Spring 1986):240–244

Nkomo, Mokubung O.

A Comparative Study of Zambia and Mozambique: Africanization, Professionalization, and Bureaucracy in the African Postcolonial State. *Journal of Black Studies* 16, No. 3 (March 1986):319–342

Nkosi, Lewis

Home and Exile and Other Selections. Reviewed by James Booth. *Research in African Literatures* 17, No. 3 (Fall 1986): 398–401

Nobles, Wade W.

Africanity and the Black Family: The Development of a Theoretical Model. Book review. S. M. Khatib. *Journal of Black Psychology* 13, No. 1 (August 1986):24–26

African Psychology: Towards Its Reclamation, Reascension and Revitalization. Book review. S. M. Khatib. *Journal of Black Psychology* 13, No. 1 (August 1986):17–19

Nobles, Wade W., and Goddard, Lawford

Understanding the Black Family: A Guide for Scholarship and Research. Book review. S. M. Khatib. *Journal of Black Psychology* 13, No. 1 (August 1986):20–23

Nodal, Roberto

The Black Man in Cuban Society: From Colonial Times to the Revolution. *Journal of Black Studies* 16, No. 3 (March 1986):251–267

Noguchi, Rei R.

Linguistic Description and Literary Interpretation. Notes. *CLA Journal* 30, No. 2 (December 1986):171–183

Nohe, Lauran M. (joint author)

See Anders-Michalski, Judith

Nolt, Marilyn Peifer (joint author)

See Peifer, Jane Hoober

Nonviolence

Civil Rights Organization and the Indigenous Movement in Chapel Hill, N. C., 1960–1965. Marcellus Barksdale. *Phylon* 47, No. 1 (March 1986):29–42

Martin Luther King (Jr.) and the Paradox of Nonviolent Direct Action. James A. Colaiaco. *Phylon* 47, No. 1 (March 1986):16–28

Martin Luther King (Jr.) and the Quest for Nonviolent Social Change. Adam Fairclough. *Phylon* 47, No. 1 (March 1986):1–15

Norman, Fran

An Empty Stocking. Short Story. *About Time* 14, No. 12 (December 1986):25

Norment, Lynn

Anita Baker: Soul's New Romantic Singer. *Ebony* 42, No. 2 (December 1986):52

Big Weddings Are Back: Many Brides Follow Trend to Elaborate Ceremonies. *Ebony* 41, No. 8 (June 1986):148

Birth Control at School: Pass or Fail. *Ebony* 41, No. 12 (October 1986):37

The Color Purple. Film review. *Ebony* 41, No. 4 (February 1986):146

Debi Thomas: The Nation's No. 1 Skating Sensation. *Ebony* 41, No. 7 (May 1986):147

Kool and the Gang: Hottest Group of the '80s. *Ebony* 42, No. 1 (November 1986):70

L. Douglas Wilder: Virginia's Lieutenant Governor. *Ebony* 41, No. 6 (April 1986):67

One Church/One Child: Chicago Priest's Black Adoption Campaign Is Smash Success. *Ebony* 41, No. 5 (March 1986):68

Tensions between Black Men and Women. *Ebony* 41, No. 10 (August 1986):153

Whitney Houston: The Joys and Dangers of Sudden Success. *Ebony* 41, No. 9 (July 1986):126

Norris, William

Additional Light on S. Morgan Smith. *Black American Literature Forum* 20, Nos. 1–2 (Spring/Summer 1986):75–79

North, James

Freedom Rising. Book review. Mwizenge S. Tembo. *Black Scholar* 17, No. 1 (January-February 1986):47–48

North Africa in Literature

Through Foreign Eyes: Western Attitudes toward North Africa. Alf Andrew Heggoy, editor. Reviewed by Aouicha E. Hilliard. *Research in African Literatures* 17, No. 4 (Winter 1986): 584–587

North Carolina—Politics and Government

Effects of Multimember Districts on Black Representation in State Legislatures. Bernard Grofman and others. *Review of Black Political Economy* 14, No. 4 (Spring 1986):65–78

Notice to Quit

Notice to Quit. Alonzo L. Llorens. *Howard Law Journal* 29, No. 1 (1986):1–11

Novel, Afro-American

One Mother, Two Daughters: The Afro-American and the Afro-Caribbean Female *Bildungsroman*. Geta LeSeur. *Black Scholar* 17, No. 2 (March-April 1986):26–33

Novel—Africa

Cultural Revolution and the African Novel. Juliet I. Okonwo. *Black Scholar* 17, No. 4 (July-August 1986):11–16

Expatriate Characters in the Early African Novel. L. Losambe. *Phylon* 47, No. 2 (June 1986):148–158

Feminist Perspectives in African Fiction: Bessie Head and Buchi Emecheta. Nancy Topping Bazin. *Black Scholar* 17, No. 2 (March-April 1986):34–40

Novel—Africa—French Language

La ville dans le roman africain. By Roger Chemain. Reviewed by S. Ade Ojo. *Research in African Literatures* 17, No. 4 (Winter 1986): 574–576

Novel—Africa—History and Criticism

Explorations in the Novel: A Student's Guide to Setworks at South African Universities. C. H. Muller, editor. Reviewed by Martin Trump. *Research in African Literatures* 17, No. 3 (Fall 1986): 419–421

Ideologies of Race and Sex in Literature: Racism and Antiracism in the African Francophone Novel. Notes. E. P. Abanime. *CLA Journal* 30, No. 2 (December 1986):125–143

Novel—History and Criticism

Heroes are Grazing in My Garden. By Herbert Padilla. Reviewed by Roland E. Bush. *Caribbean Review* 15, No. 1 (Winter 1986):41

Novel—West Africa—History and Criticism

The West African Village Novel with Particular Reference to Elechi Amadi's *The Concubine*. By George Nyamndi. Reviewed by Ernest N. Emenyonu. *Research in African Literatures* 17, No. 4 (Winter 1986): 622–625

Noviello, Nicholas (joint author)

See Grofman, Bernard

Noyes, Sylvia G.

A Particular Patriotism in Jean Toomer's "York Beach." Notes. *CLA Journal* 29, No. 3 (March 1986):288–294

Nubians

Egypto-Nubian Presences in Ancient Mexico. Notes. Ivan Van Sertima. *Journal of African Civilizations* 8, No. 2 (December 1986):29–55

Nuclear Weapons

Reflections on the Geneva Summit: The Perspective of a Journalist from the Developing World. Don Rojas. *Black Scholar* 17, No. 1 (January-February 1986):26–30

Numismatics—Collectors and Collecting

Centennial Collectible. *Black Enterprise* 16, No. 11 (June 1986):52

Nunes-Garcia, Jose Mauricio (about)

The Life and Works of Nunes-Garcia. Dominique-René de Lerma. *Black Perspective in Music* 14, No. 2 (Spring 1986):93–102

Nursing

The Multidimensional Role of Nurses. Carolyne S. Blount. *About Time* 14, No. 4 (April 1986):8–26

Race and Class in Nursing Occupations. Julianne Malveaux and Susan Englander. *SAGE* 3, No. 1 (Spring 1986):41–45

Nursing—Dissertations and Theses

Master's Theses in Progress in Selected Colleges and Universities. Mac A. Stewart. *Negro Educational Review* 37, Nos. 3–4 (July-October 1986):117–18

Nutrition

The Anticancer Diet. Maudene Nelson. *Essence* 17, No. 2 (June 1986):66

Reagan Administration Tries to Hide Success of WIC Program. William L. Clay. *About Time* 14, No. 3 (March 1986):19

Nwachukwu-Agbada, J. O. J.

A List of B.A. Degree Projects in African Literature Completed in the English Department, University of Jos, Nigeria (1979–1984). *Research in African Literatures* 17, No. 1 (Spring 1986): 127–129

Nwonga, Donatus Ibe (editor)

Critical Perspectives on Christopher Okigbo. Reviewed by Catherine Obianuju Acholonu. *Research in African Literatures* 17, No. 4 (Winter 1986): 613–614

Nyamndi, George

The West African Village Novel with Particular Reference to Elechi Amadi's *The Concubine*. Reviewed by Ernest N. Emenyonu. *Research in African Literatures* 17, No. 4 (Winter 1986): 622–625

Nyamwezi—Language and Culture

Le Roi Nyamwezi, la Droite et la Gauche: Révision Comparative des Classifications Dualistes. By Serge Tcherkezoff. Reviewed by Wyatt MacGarrey. *Research in African Literatures* 17, No. 2 (Summer 1986): 304–306

Nyang, Sulayman S.

From Black Muslims to Muslims. Book review. *Phylon* 47, No. 2 (June 1986):169–170

Oakes, J.

Keeping Track: How Schools Structure Inequality. Reviewed by Nancy L. Arnez. *Journal of Negro Education* 55, No.2 (Spring 1986):244–246

Obadele, Imari A.

The First New African States in North America. *Black Collegian* 16, No. 3 (January/February 1986):86–97

Obafemi, Olu

Theater and Society in Africa. Book review. *Research in African Literatures* 17, No. 2 (Summer 1986): 271–272

Obesity

Fat Is Back! *Ebony* 41, No. 6 (April 1986):39

Obituaries

Alexander, Ernest. *Jet* 70, No. 19 (July 28, 1986):18

Alexander, Kelly Miller (Sr.). *Jet* 69, No. 16 (December 30-January 6, 1986):23

Andrews, Scotty. *Jet* 70, No. 10 (May 26, 1986):16

Armstrong, Charles (Sr.). *Jet* 69, No. 16 (December 30-January 6, 1986):23

Arrington, Florence. *Jet* 71, No. 5 (October 20, 1986):18

Ashby, Dorothy Jeanne Thompson. *Black Perspective in Music* 14, No. 3 (Fall 1986):322

Banks, William Venoid. *Jet* 69, No. 16 (December 30-January 6, 1986):23

Bannerman, Charles. *Black Enterprise* 17, No. 2 (September 1986):20

Bannister, Frank T. *Jet* 71, No. 8 (November 10, 1986):18

Bernhardt, Clyde E. B. *Black Perspective in Music* 14, No. 3 (Fall 1986):322

Bias, Len. *Jet* 70, No. 16 (July 7, 1986):16–17

Billups, Kenneth B. *Black Perspective in Music* 14, No. 3 (Fall 1986):322

Blackwell, Harrison (Jr.). *Jet* 70, No. 25 (September 8, 1986):18

Blewett, Kenneth G. *Jet* 70, No. 19 (July 28, 1986):18

Boyd, Arthur L. *Black Perspective in Music* 14, No. 3 (Fall 1986):322–323

Brawley, James P. *Jet* 69, No. 17 (January 13, 1986):24

Braxton, Jim. *Jet* 70, No. 22 (August 18, 1986):48

Brown, Pearly. *Jet* 70, No. 19 (July 28, 1986):18

Browning, Alice. *Jet* 69, No. 16 (December 30-January 6, 1986):23

Bubbles, John W. *Jet* 70, No. 12 (June 9, 1986):13

Burge, Rosa Louise. *Black Perspective in Music* 14, No. 3 (Fall 1986):323–324

Caesar, Adolph. *Jet* 70, No. 1 (March 24, 1986):58

Cannon, George D. *Jet* 71, No. 5 (October 20, 1986):18

Carrington, Jewel Scott. *Jet* 71, No. 5 (October 20, 1986):18

Chew, Charles. *Jet* 70, No. 18 (July 21, 1986):17

Clark, Jimmy. *Jet* 69, No. 16 (December 30-January 6, 1986):23

Clarke, Kenny ("Klook"). *Jet* 69, No. 16 (December 30-January 6, 1986):23

Coleman, Joseph. *Jet* 71, No. 11 (December 1, 1986):39

Crayton, Connie Curtis ("Pee Wee"). *Black Perspective in Music* 14, No. 3 (Fall 1986):324

Scruggs, George. *Jet* 70, No. 9 (May 19, 1986):47

Shaw, Leslie N. *Jet* 69, No. 16 (December 30-January 6, 1986):24

Shaw, Patricia Walker. *Jet* 69, No. 16 (December 30-January 6, 1986):24

Shropshear, George. *Jet* 70, No. 15 (June 30, 1986):17

Shuler, James. *Jet* 70, No. 3 (April 7, 1986):52

Simpson, Jimmy Lee. *Jet* 70, No. 15 (June 30, 1986):10

Smith, Alfred E. *Jet* 70, No. 13 (June 16, 1986):18

Stewart, Paul. *Jet* 70, No. 9 (May 19, 1986):47

Stokes, Willie ("Flukey"). *Jet* 71, No. 12 (December 8, 1986):18

Stone, Richard Enoch. *Jet* 69, No. 16 (December 30-January 6, 1986):24

Sublett, John William ("Bubbles"). *Black Perspective in Music* 14, No. 3 (Fall 1986):327

Sweeney, Alfred Lloyd. *Jet* 70, No. 16 (July 7, 1986):17

Taylor, Eddie. *Jet* 69, No. 18 (January 20, 1986):17

Terrell, Saunders ("Sonny Terry"). *Black Perspective in Music* 14, No. 3 (Fall 1986):327

Terry, Betty Jean. *Jet* 70, No. 10 (May 26, 1986):16

Terry, Sonny. *Jet* 70, No. 3 (April 7, 1986):55

Thomas, Andrew L. *Jet* 69, No. 16 (December 30-January 6, 1986):24

Thomas, Joseph V. *Jet* 71, No. 5 (October 20, 1986):18

Toles, Virginia Frances. *Jet* 70, No. 6 (April 28, 1986):14

Tucker, Lorenzo. *Jet* 70, No. 26 (September 15, 1986):51

Turner, Joseph ("Big Joe"). *Black Perspective in Music* 14, No. 3 (Fall 1986):327

Turner, Joseph Vernon. *Jet* 69, No. 16 (December 30-January 6, 1986):24

Tyler, Scott W. *Jet* 69, No. 24 (March 3, 1986):4

Veeck, Bill. *Jet* 69, No. 18 (January 20, 1986):46

Wallace, Charles. *Black Enterprise* 17, No. 2 (September 1986):20

Wallace, Sippie (nee Beulah Thomas). *Black Perspective in Music* 14, No. 3 (Fall 1986):327–328

Wallace, Sippie. *Jet* 71, No. 11 (December 1, 1986):62

Washington, Elizabeth Culver. *Jet* 69, No. 18 (January 20, 1986):17

Watson, Pearl A. *Jet* 70, No. 18 (July 21, 1986):17

Wells, William ("Dicky"). *Black Perspective in Music* 14, No. 3 (Fall 1986):328–329

Williams, Charles M. ("Cootie"). *Jet* 69, No. 16 (December 30-January 6, 1986):24

Williams, Clarence ("Clancy") (Jr.). *Jet* 71, No. 4 (October 13, 1986):46

Williams, Jasper F. *Jet* 69, No. 16 (December 30-January 6, 1986):24

Williams, Ronald. *Jet* 69, No. 16 (December 30-January 6, 1986):24

Williams, Ronald. *Jet* 69, No. 17 (January 13, 1986):24

Wilson, Teddy. *Jet* 70, No. 22 (August 18, 1986):61

Wooding, Samuel. *Jet* 69, No. 16 (December 30-January 6, 1986):24

Wright, Alexander S. *Jet* 69, No. 17 (January 13, 1986):24

Yancey, Estella ("Mama"). *Jet* 70, No. 10 (May 26, 1986):16

Yancey, Estelle ("Mama"). *Black Perspective in Music* 14, No. 3 (Fall 1986):329

Yancy, Marvin. *Jet* 69, No. 16 (December 30-January 6, 1986):24

Young, James ("Trummy"). *Black Perspective in Music* 14, No. 3 (Fall 1986):329

Obsession (Psychology)

The Perils of Obsession. Enid Ann Doggett. *Essence* 17, No. 2 (June 1986):80

Occupational Training

Black Youth Unemployment: Issues and Problems. Ernest Spaights and Harold E. Dixon. *Journal of Black Studies* 16, No. 4 (June 1986):385–396

A First for Ford. Jay Koblenz. *Black Enterprise* 16, No. 12 (July 1986):16

Youth Employment and Training Programs: The YEDPA Years. Edited by Charles L. Betsey and others. Reviewed by Robert B. Hill. *Review of Black Political Economy* 15, No. 1 (Summer 1986):107–112

See also Vocational Guidance

Occupation and Race

The Corporate Pioneers. Paul Lindsay Johnson. *Crisis* 93, No. 4 (April 1986):26–30

Ochillo, Yvonne

The Race Consciousness of Alain Locke. *Phylon* 47, No. 3 (September 1986):173–181

Oda, Masayuke (about)

Masayuke Oda. Illustrated. Robert Biddle. *International Review of African American Art* 7, No. 2 (1986):52–59

Odaga, Asenath Bole

Literature for Children and Young People in Kenya. Reviewed by Nancy J. Schmidt. *Research in African Literatures* 17, No. 4 (Winter 1986): 609–610

O'Dell, Jack

The Soviet Union is an Ally for Peace. *Black Scholar* 17, No. 1 (January-February 1986):38–43

Office Equipment and Supplies

Designing the Office of the 80s. *Black Enterprise* 16, No. 6 (January 1986):61

Moving Forward in Stationery. Margo Walker. *Black Enterprise* 16, No. 11 (June 1986):66

Office of Federal Contract Compliance Programs

Notes on Implicit Contracts and the Racial Unemployment Differential. Vince Eagan. *Review of Black Political Economy* 15, No. 1 (Summer 1986):81–91

Ogbaa, Kalu

Igbo Language and Culture II. Book review. *Research in African Literatures* 17, No. 2 (Summer 1986): 291–293

Ogbalu, F. C., and Emenanjo, E. N. (editors)

Igbo Language and Culture II. Reviewed by Kalu Ogbaa. *Research in African Literatures* 17, No. 2 (Summer 1986): 291–293

Ohayon, Ruth

Rousseau's Julie; Or, the Maternal Odyssey. Notes. *CLA Journal* 30, No. 1 (September 1986):69–82

Ojaide, Tanure

Poetic Viewpoint: Okot p'Bitek and His Personae. *Callaloo* 9, No. 2 (Spring 1986):371–383

Politics in African Poetry. Book review. *Research in African Literatures* 17, No. 4 (Winter 1986): 611–613

Ojo, S. Ade

La ville dans le roman africain. Book review. *Research in African Literatures* 17, No. 4 (Winter 1986): 574–576

Ojo-Ade, Femi

René Maran, the Black Frenchman: A Bio-Critical Study. Reviewed by Chidi Ikonne. *Research in African Literatures* 17, No. 4 (Winter 1986): 603–605

Okafor, Clement Abiaziem

Oral Literature of the Maasai. Book review. *Research in African Literatures* 17, No. 2 (Summer 1986): 301–304

Okanlawon, O. L.

Concepts of the Child in Some Nigerian Cultures. *Journal of Black Psychology* 12, No. 2 (February 1986):61–70

Okanlawon, Tunde

Kamerunische Marchen: Text und Kontext in ethnosoziologischer und psychologischer Sicht. Book review. *Research in African Literatures* 17, No. 2 (Summer 1986): 294

Okigbo, Christopher (about)

Critical Perspectives on Christopher Okigbo. Donatus Ibe Nwonga, editor. Reviewed by Catherine Obianuju Acholonu. *Research in African Literatures* 17, No. 4 (Winter 1986): 613–614

Okigbo's Technique in "Distances I." Notes. Bibliography. John Haynes. *Research in African Literatures* 17, No. 1 (Spring 1986): 73–84

Okojie, Paul

The Unequal Struggle. Book review. *Race and Class* 28, No. 2 (August 1986):93–95

Okonkwo, J. I.

Contemporary African Literature. Book review. *Research in African Literatures* 17, No. 3 (Fall 1986): 445–448

Okonwo, Juliet I.

Cultural Revolution and the African Novel. *Black Scholar* 17, No. 4 (July-August 1986):11–16

Olafioye, Tayo

Politics in African Poetry. Reviewed by Tanure Ojaide. *Research in African Literatures* 17, No. 4 (Winter 1986): 611–613

Olinder, Britta (editor)

A Sense of Place: Essays in Post-Colonial Literature. Reviewed by Bernard Hickey. *Research in African Literatures* 17, No. 3 (Fall 1986): 426–430

Olion, LaDelle (joint author)

See Gillis-Olion, Marion

Oliver, Marion (about)

This Dean Means Business: Marion Oliver Wants to Show Black Students the Advantages of Career in Business. Charles Whitaker. *Ebony* 41, No. 4 (February 1986):93

Oliver, Paul

Blues off the Record. Thirty Years of Blues Commentary. Book review. Andre Prevos. *Black Perspective in Music* 14, No. 2 (Spring 1986):190

Oliver, Stephanie Stokes

Jacob Lawrence: The Man and His Art. Illustrated. *Essence* 17, No. 7 (November 1986):89

Margaret "Shug" Avery—Beyond "The Color Purple." *Essence* 17, No. 5 (September 1986):118

Olive Schreiner (about)

Olive Schreiner and After: Essays on Southern African Literature in Honor of Guy Butler. Malvern van Wyk Smith and Don Maclennan, editors. Reviewed by Dennis Walder. *Research in African Literatures* 17, No. 3 (Fall 1986): 401–404

Olmecs

Egypto-Nubian Presences in Ancient Mexico. Notes. Ivan Van Sertima. *Journal of African Civilizations* 8, No. 2 (December 1986):29–55

Olurode, Lai

Nigeria and Its Invaders 1851–1920. Book review. *Journal of Black Studies* 16, No. 4 (June 1986):457–460

Olympic Athletes

World's Fastest Mom: On the Track or in the Nursery, Evelyn Ashford Is a Winner. *Ebony* 41, No. 8 (June 1986):155

One Church/One Child Adoption Program

One Church/One Child: Chicago Priest's Black Adoption Campaign Is Smash Success. Lynn Norment. *Ebony* 41, No. 5 (March 1986):68

Operation PUSH

PUSH Eyes CBS Stations. Ken Smikle. *Black Enterprise* 16, No. 11 (June 1986):47

Oral Literature—Africa

Interdisciplinary Dimensions of African Literature. Kofi Anyidoho, Abioseh M. Porter, Daniel Racine, and Janice Spleth, editors. Reviewed by C. L. Innes. *Research in African Literatures* 17, No. 3 (Fall 1986): 449–451

Oral-Formulaic Theory and Research: An Introduction and Annotated Bibliography. By John Miles Foley. Reviewed by Dan Ben-Amos. *Research in African Literatures* 17, No. 2 (Summer 1986): 309–310

Oral Poetry from Africa. Jack Mapanje and Landeg White, editors. Reviewed by Oyekan Owomoyela. *Research in African Literatures* 17, No. 1 (Spring 1986): 137–140

Uwa ndi Igbo: Journal of Igbo Life and Culture I. Chieka Ifemesia, editor. Reviewed by Don Burgess. *Research in African Literatures* 17, No. 2 (Summer 1986): 288–291

Oral Tradition

Creative Historiography and Critical Determinism in Nigerian Theater. References. Oyekan Owomoyela. *Research in African Literatures* 17, No. 2 (Summer 1986): 234–251

Expressing a Swahili Sense of Humor: Siu Jokes. Notes. References. Carol M. Eastman. *Research in African Literatures* 17, No. 4 (Winter 1986): 474–495

The House of Si Abd Allah: The Oral History of a Moroccan Family. Henry Munson, Jr., editor and translator. Reviewed by James A. Miller. *Research in African Literatures* 17, No. 4 (Winter 1986): 582–584

The Identity of the Hero in the Liongo Epic. References. Joseph L. Mbele. *Research in African Literatures* 17, No. 4 (Winter 1986): 464–473

Iteso Thought Patterns in Tales. By Grace Akello. Reviewed by John Lamphear. *Research in African Literatures* 17, No. 2 (Summer 1986): 298–299

Kamerunische Marchen: Text und Kontext in ethnosoziologischer und psychologischer Sicht. By Norbert Ndong. Reviewed by Tunde Okanlawon. *Research in African Literatures* 17, No. 2 (Summer 1986): 294

Kibabina's "Message About Zanzibar": The Art of Swahili Poetry. References. Appendix. Jan Feidel and Ibrahim Noor Shariff. *Research in African Literatures* 17, No. 4 (Winter 1986): 496–524

Legends and History of the Luba. By Harold Womersley. Reviewed by J. Eric Lane. *Research in African Literatures* 17, No. 2 (Summer 1986): 306–308

Oral Literature of the Maasai. By Naomi Kipury. Reviewed by Clement Abiaziem Okafor. *Research in African Literatures* 17, No. 2 (Summer 1986): 301–304

Oral Tradition: The Bridge to Africa in Paule Marshall's *Praisesong for the Widow*. Ebele O. Eko. *Western Journal of Black Studies* 10, No. 3 (Fall 1986):143–147

Theater and Society in Africa. By Mineke Schipper. Reviewed by Olu Obafemi. *Research in African Literatures* 17, No. 2 (Summer 1986): 271–272

Ordway, Nicholas (joint author)

    See Hinds, Dudley S.

Organization of Black Airline Pilots

Spreading Their Wings: Black Pilots, Totaling 175, Want to Pave the Way for More. Frank White III. *Ebony* 41, No. 4 (February 1986):75

Ormerod, Beverley

An Introduction to the French Caribbean Novel. Reviewed by Suzanne Crosta. *CLA Journal* 29, No. 4 (June 1986):497–500

Ortega, Daniel (about)

Ritual, Paradox and Death in Managua: Internacionalistas in Nicaragua. Alfred Padula. *Caribbean Review* 15, No. 1 (Winter 1986):18–19

Ortega, Noel (joint author)

    See Berrian, Brenda F.

Orthopedics

Careers in Orthotics and Prosthetics. Solomon J. Herbert. *Black Collegian* 16, No. 4 (March/April 1986):94–99

Osbey, Brenda Marie

The Galvez Cut. Poem. *Callaloo* 9, No. 1 (Winter 1986):109–111

Setting Loose the Icons. Poem. *Callaloo* 9, No. 1 (Winter 1986):112–115

Osborn, Nancy M. (joint author)

See Gradwohl, David M.

Ottley, Charlotte V. M.

Personal Best: Her PR Agency Put Their Best Foot Forward. Janine C. McAdams. *Essence* 17, No. 8 (December 1986):109

Owego, New York—History

Margaret Williams and the Black Community of Owego, New York. Edward Nizalowski. *Afro-Americans in New York Life and History* 10, No.1 (January 1986):53–59

Owomoyela, Oyekan

Creative Historiography and Critical Determinism in Nigerian Theater. References. *Research in African Literatures* 17, No. 2 (Summer 1986): 234–251

Oral Poetry from Africa. Book review. *Research in African Literatures* 17, No. 1 (Spring 1986): 137–140

Owusu, Martin

Drama of the Gods: A Study of Seven African Plays. Reviewed by Mary T. David. *Research in African Literatures* 17, No. 2 (Summer 1986): 276–278

Padilla, Herbert

Heroes are Grazing in My Garden. Reviewed by Roland E. Bush. *Caribbean Review* 15, No. 1 (Winter 1986):41

Padula, Alfred

Ritual, Paradox and Death in Managua: Internacionalistas in Nicaragua. *Caribbean Review* 15, No. 1 (Winter 1986):18–19

Pageaux, Daniel-Henri

Images et mythes d'Haiti. Reviewed by Clarisse Zimra. *Research in African Literatures* 17, No. 4 (Winter 1986): 591–593

Paige, Emmett (Jr.) (about)

From High School Drop-Out to Three-Star General: Emmett Paige (Jr.) Beat the Odds and Marched All the Way to the Top. *Ebony* 41, No. 7 (May 1986):64

Palestine Liberation Organization

Prophet Without Honor? The Reverend Jesse Jackson and the Palestinian Question. Notes. David A. Coolidge (Jr.) *Journal of Religious Thought* 43, No. 2 (Fall-Winter 1986–87):51–62

Pamphile, Leon D.

The NAACP and the American Occupation of Haiti. *Phylon* 47, No. 1 (March 1986):91–100

Pan-Africanism

Eslanda Goode Robeson, Pan-Africanist. Barbara Ranby. *SAGE* 3, No. 2 (Fall 1986):22–26

Panama Canal—History

Red, White and Blue Paradise, The American Canal Zone in Panama. By Herbert and Mary Knapp. Reviewed by Neale Pearson. *Caribbean Review* 15, No. 1 (Winter 1986):26–27 +

Panama Canal Treaties, 1977

The Limits of Victory, The Ratification of the Panama Canal Treaties. By George D. Moffett III. Reviewed by Neale Pearson. *Caribbean Review* 15, No. 1 (Winter 1986):26–27 +

Panama—History

Getting to Know the General, The Story of an Involvement. By Graham Greene. Reviewed by Neale Pearson. *Caribbean Review* 15, No. 1 (Winter 1986):26–27 +

An Interview with Hugo Spadafora Four Months before His Death. Interview. Beatrix Parga de Bayon. *Caribbean Review* 15, No. 1 (Winter 1986):24–25 +

Panama, Desastre...o Democracia. By Ricardo Arias Calderon. Reviewed by Neale Pearson. *Caribbean Review* 15, No. 1 (Winter 1986):26–27 +

Panama Odyssey. By William J. Jorden. Reviewed by Ambler H. Moss, Jr. *Caribbean Review* 15, No. 1 (Winter 1986):43–44

Panama Odyssey. By William J. Jorden. Reviewed by Neale Pearson. *Caribbean Review* 15, No. 1 (Winter 1986):26–27 +

Panama—Language and Culture

The Negros Congos of Panama: Afro-Hispanic Creole Language and Culture. John M. Lipski. *Journal of Black Studies* 16, No. 4 (June 1986):409–428

Panama—Literature

What Graham Greene Didn't Tell Us: Five Accounts of the Torrijos Legacy. Book reviews. Neale Pearson. *Caribbean Review* 15, No. 1 (Winter 1986):26–27 +

Panama—Politics and Government

An Exhibition for National Peace. Sandra Serrano. *Caribbean Review* 15, No. 1 (Winter 1986):33

Searching for Pretto: Politics and Art in Panama. Sandra Serrano. *Caribbean Review* 15, No. 1 (Winter 1986):29–32 +

Pan Asian Repertory Theatre

Theatre. Cecilia Loving-Sloane. *Crisis* 93, No. 4 (April 1986):10–12

Pang, Valerie Ooka

The Happiest Ending. Book review. *Interracial Books for Children Bulletin* 17, No. 1 (1986):6–7

Toad Is the Uncle of Heaven. Book review. *Interracial Books for Children Bulletin* 17, No. 1 (1986):9

The War between the Classes. Book review. *Interracial Books for Children Bulletin* 17, Nos. 3–4 (1986):33

Pankhurst, Richard

Shakespeare in Ethiopia. Notes. *Research in African Literatures* 17, No. 2 (Summer 1986): 169–196

Panofsky, Hans E.

Littératures africaines à la Bibliotèque Nationale, 1973–1983. Book review. *Research in African Literatures* 17, No. 4 (Winter 1986): 605–606

Papa, Kelly

Saving Lives through Public Education. *About Time* 14, No. 6 (June 1986):21

Papageorgiou, Mary R. (joint editor)

See Betsey, Charles L.

Parameswaran, Ama (editor)

The Commonwealth in Canada: Proceedings of the Second Triennial Conference of the Canadian Association for Commonwealth Literature and Language Studies. Reviewed by Alastair Niven. *Research in African Literatures* 17, No. 3 (Fall 1986):435–439

Parental Leave

Proper Pay for Parents. Frederick H. Lowe. *Black Enterprise* 16, No. 12 (July 1986):14

Parental and Medical Leave Act

Parental and Medical Leave. William L. Clay. *About Time* 14, No. 4 (April 1986):19

Proper Pay for Parents. Frederick H. Lowe. *Black Enterprise* 16, No. 12 (July 1986):14

Parenting

The Beauty in Family Relationships. Marsha Jones. *About Time* 14, No. 7 (July 1986):10–13

Changes in Family Structures. Marsha Jones. *About Time* 14, No. 3 (March 1986):14–18

Education Is a Team Effort. James M. Blount. *About Time* 14, No. 11 (November 1986):4

Facing the Challenge of Raising My Black Manchild. Larry Conley. *Essence* 17, No. 7 (November 1986):116

Fathers Who Walk Away. Walter Leavy. *Ebony* 41, No. 10 (August 1986):53

Home Again. Renita Weems. *Essence* 17, No. 8 (December 1986):63

Making Parenting a Priority. Anita Johnson Sims. *About Time* 14, No. 11 (November 1986):10–13

Perceived Parental Activity of Mothers, Fathers, and Grandmothers in Three-Generational Black Families. Melvin N. Wilson. *Journal of Black Psychology* 12, No. 2 (February 1986):43–59

Save the Fathers: Black Fathers of Today Must Fight to Regain Traditional Strengths of the Past. Alvin F. Poussaint. *Ebony* 41, No. 10 (August 1986):43

Training Parents in Child Behavior-Management Skills: A Group Approach. William L. Conwill. *Journal of Negro Education* 55, No. 1 (Winter 1986):67–77

Parents of Handicapped Children

Strategies for Interacting with Black Parents of Handicapped Children. Marion Gillis-Olion and others. *Negro Educational Review* 37, No. 1 (January 1986):8–16

Parga de Bayon, Beatrix

An Interview with Hugo Spadafora Four Months before His Death. Interview. *Caribbean Review* 15, No. 1 (Winter 1986):24–25+

Paris—Bibliotèque Nationale

Littératures africaines à la Bibliotèque Nationale, 1973–1983. Paulette Lordereau, compiler. Reviewed by Hans E. Panofsky. *Research in African Literatures* 17, No. 4 (Winter 1986): 605–606

Parker, Pat

Movement in Black: The Collected Poetry of Pat Parker. Book review. Gerald Barrax. *Callaloo* 9, No. 1 (Winter 1986):259–262

Parratt v. Taylor

Parratt v. Taylor, and Liberty Interests under the Fourteenth Amendment. Francis J. D'Eramo. *Black Law Journal* 9, No. 3 (Winter 1986):312–322

Parry, Benita

Conrad and Imperialism: Ideological Boundaries and Visionary Frontiers. Reviewed by Robert D. Hamner. *Research in African Literatures* 17, No. 1 (Spring 1986): 158–162

Pastor, Robert A.

Crossing Swords: The Psychological Divide in the Caribbean Basin. *Caribbean Review* 15, No. 1 (Winter 1986):3

Patrick, James (joint author)

See Berger, Morroe

Patterson, Gregg

Bank of the Year: Banking on Boston. *Black Enterprise* 16, No. 11 (June 1986):150

Patterson, Willis

The Symposium on Black-American Music: Some Comments. *Black Perspective in Music* 14, No. 1 (Winter 1986):4–6

Payton, Shelia I.

Internship Teaches Tangibles, Intangibles of Corporate Life. *Black Collegian* 16, No. 3 (January/February 1986):126–128

Payton, Walter (about)

Ebony Visits Payton's Place. Illustrated. *Ebony* 41, No. 11 (September 1986):92

p'Bitek, Okot—Criticism and Interpretation

Poetic Viewpoint: Okot p'Bitek and His Personae. Tanure Ojaide. *Callaloo* 9, No. 2 (Spring 1986):371–383

Peace

The Soviet Union is an Ally for Peace. Jack O'Dell. *Black Scholar* 17, No. 1 (January-February 1986):38–43

Peace Movement

Black Gains Tied Directly to Pursuit of Peace. Frances M. Beal. *Black Scholar* 17, No. 1 (January-February 1986):8–11

The Historical Black Presence in the Struggle for Peace. Frances M. Beal and Ty dePass. *Black Scholar* 17, No. 1 (January-February 1986):2–7

Peace Movement, International

Jesse Jackson Takes His Peace Program to Geneva. Don Rojas. *Black Scholar* 17, No. 1 (January-February 1986):31–34

Reflections on the Geneva Summit: The Perspective of a Journalist from the Developing World. Don Rojas. *Black Scholar* 17, No. 1 (January-February 1986):26–30

Pearson, Neale

Getting to Know the General, The Story of an Involvement. Book review. *Caribbean Review* 15, No. 1 (Winter 1986):26–27+

The Limits of Victory, The Ratification of the Panama Canal Treaties. Book review. *Caribbean Review* 15, No. 1 (Winter 1986):26–27+

Panama, Desastre...o Democracia. Book review. *Caribbean Review* 15, No. 1 (Winter 1986):26–27+

Panama Odyssey. Book review. *Caribbean Review* 15, No. 1 (Winter 1986):26–27+

Red, White and Blue Paradise, The American Canal Zone in Panama. Book review. *Caribbean Review* 15, No. 1 (Winter 1986):26–27+

What Graham Greene Didn't Tell Us: Five Accounts of the Torrijos Legacy. Book reviews. *Caribbean Review* 15, No. 1 (Winter 1986):26–27+

Witness to War: An American Doctor in El Salvador. Book review. *Caribbean Review* 15, No. 2 (Spring 1986):47–48

Peavey, Fran

Heart Politics. Book review. Tracy Dalton. *Interracial Books for Children Bulletin* 17, Nos. 3–4 (1986):38

Peebles-Meyers, Marjorie (about)

Blacks Who Overcame the Odds: Barriers of Sex and Color Didn't Stop Marjorie Peebles-Meyers from Becoming a Top M.D. *Ebony* 42, No. 2 (December 1986):68

Peifer, Jane Hoober, and Nolt, Marilyn Peifer

The Good Thoughts Series. Book review. Ashley Pennington. *Interracial Books for Children Bulletin* 17, No. 2 (1986):16–17

Penney, J. C.

J. C. Penney's Leading Edge Internships. *Black Collegian* 16, No. 3 (January/February 1986):112–116

Pennington, Ashley

The Good Thoughts Series. Book review. *Interracial Books for Children Bulletin* 17, No. 2 (1986):16–17

Peoples Temple

A Sympathetic History of Jonestown: The Moore Family Involvement in Peoples Temple. By Rebecca Moore. Reviewed by Kortright Davis. *Journal of Religious Thought* 43, No. 2 (Fall-Winter 1986–87):92–93

Pepsi-Cola U. S. A.

Harvey Buys Pepsi Plant. Gordon Borrell. *Black Enterprise* 16, No. 11 (June 1986):48

Perennial Sales Company

A Perennial Favorite. Robert A. Monroe. *Crisis* 93, No. 4 (April 1986):38

Perez-Lopez, Jorge F.

Cuba as an Oil Trader: Petroleum Deals in a Falling Market. *Caribbean Review* 15, No. 2 (Spring 1986):26–29+

Perinbam, Marie

Holy Violence: The Revolutionary Thought of Frantz Fanon. Reviewed by Hal Wylie. *Research in African Literatures* 17, No. 4 (Winter 1986):597–599

Periodicals

Black Journals of the United States. By Walter C. Daniel. Reviewed by Karen Nadeski. *Western Journal of Black Studies* 10, No. 2 (Summer 1986):102

Perkins, Huel

The Symposium on Black-American Music. *Black Perspective in Music* 14, No. 1 (Winter 1986):87–88

Perkins, Walter M.

Educational Reform and Teacher Shortages: New Career Opportunities in Education. *Black Collegian* 16, No. 4 (March/April 1986):114–120

The Minority Engineering Effort: A Spectrum of Organizations with One Unified Goal. *Black Collegian* 16, No. 3 (January/February 1986):152–161

Young, Black and in Business. *Black Collegian* 16, No. 4 (March/April 1986):51–62

Perrí

Perrí's Smoldering Harmony Ignites Jazz Chart. Gerrie Summers. *Essence* 17, No. 5 (September 1986):29

Perry, Huey L., and White, Ruth B.

The Post-Civil Rights Transformation of the Relationship between Blacks and Jews in the United States. *Phylon* 47, No. 1 (March 1986):51–60

Perry, Ivory (about)

Grass Roots Activists and Social Change: The Story of Ivory Perry. George Lipsitz. *CAAS Newsletter* 9, No. 2 (1986):1

Perry, Kelvin (about)

The Power of the Press. Lloyd Gite. *Black Enterprise* 17, No. 3 (October 1986):33

Perry, Marvin E.

Flying High on Medical Tech. *Black Enterprise* 17, No. 1 (August 1986):19

Perry, William A. ("Fridge") (about)

William A. Perry: The Man behind the "Fridge." Walter Leavy. *Ebony* 41, No. 12 (October 1986):29

Personal Appearance

Beauty and Fitness: A Sound Approach. *Essence* 17, No. 2 (June 1986):70

Grooming for Success. Rosalind J. Johnson. *Black Collegian* 17, No. 1 (September/October 1986):55–56

Personnel Management

Great Expectations: How to Read Your Boss' Mind and Become a Star Performer. Constance M. Green. *Black Enterprise* 16, No. 8 (March 1986):41–42

How to Sell Your Boss on Your Ideas. Karen Brailsford. *Black Enterprise* 16, No. 11 (June 1986):284

Managing the Cuckoo's Nest. Sharon Lopez. *Black Enterprise* 17, No. 2 (September 1986):45

Managing through Tough Times. Sharon Y. Lopez. *Black Enterprise* 16, No. 6 (January 1986):57–58

Persons, Georgia A.

Public Policy and Social Change. *Urban League Review* 10, No. 2 (Winter 1986–87):6–11

Regulatory Policy and Minority Concerns: The Impact of Changes in Telecommunications Policy. *Urban League Review* 10, No. 2 (Winter 1986–87):45–63

Pete, Gregory

Crisis Interview: Rose Marie Johnson. *Crisis* 93, No. 4 (April 1986):34–37

Dr. Nathan Hare. Interview. *Crisis* 93, No. 3 (March 1986):30–46

Peters, R. H., Chevrolet

BE 100: The New Guys on the Block. Edmund Newton. *Black Enterprise* 16, No. 11 (June 1986):119

Petersen, Frank E. (about)

Lt. General Frank E. Petersen: Top Man at Quantico. *Ebony* 42, No. 2 (December 1986):140

Petroleum Industry and Trade

Cuba as an Oil Trader: Petroleum Deals in a Falling Market. Jorge F. Perez-Lopez. *Caribbean Review* 15, No. 2 (Spring 1986):26–29+

Petry, Ann (about)

A World Made Cunningly: A Closer Look at Ann Petry's Short Fiction. Notes. Gladys J. Washington. *CLA Journal* 30, No. 1 (September 1986):14–29

Pettus, Theodore (about)

Golden Nuggets. Ken Smikle. *Black Enterprise* 17, No. 3 (October 1986):26

Philadelphia—Redevelopment

Commerce and Culture. William J. Sutton. *Black Enterprise* 16, No. 11 (June 1986):48

Philanthropists

Frances Joseph-Gaudet: Black Philanthropist. Violet Harrington Bryan. *SAGE* 3, No. 1 (Spring 1986):46–49

Philippine Islands—History

The American Press and the Repairing of the Philippines. Cedric J. Robinson. *Race and Class* 28, No. 2 (August 1986):31–44

Philippine Islands—Resistance Movements

Inside the Philippine Resistance. Zoltan Grossman. *Race and Class* 28, No. 2 (August 1986):1–29

Phillips, Emerald

See Valentino

Photography

The Photographs of Richard Samuel Roberts.
Illustrated. *Callaloo* 9, No. 2 (Spring 1986):385–390

Photography—Exhibitions

Blacks in America: A Photographic Record.
Illustrated. Barbara Hall. *About Time* 14, No. 1
(January 1986):14–15

Moneta Sleet, Jr.: Pulitzer Prize Photojournalist.
Marsha Jones. *About Time* 14, No. 10 (October
1986):12–13

Photography as a Profession

Turning Fun into Fortune. *Black Enterprise* 16,
No. 7 (February 1986):79–87

Physical Anthropology

The African Presence in Ancient America:
Evidence from Physical Anthropology. Notes.
Keith M. Jordon. *Journal of African Civilizations* 8,
No. 2 (December 1986):136–151

The Beginnings of Man and Civilization. Cheikh
Anta Diop. *Journal of African Civilizations* 8, No.
1 (June 1986):322–351

Civilization or Barbarism: An Authentic
Anthropology. Excerpt. Notes. Cheikh Anta
Diop. *Journal of African Civilizations* 8, No. 1
(June 1986):161–225

Civilization or Barbarism: The Legacy of Cheikh
Anta Diop. By Cheikh Anta Diop. Reviewed by
Leonard Jeffries, Jr. *Journal of African Civilizations*
8, No. 1 (June 1986):146–160

The First Americans. Notes. Legrand H. Clegg II.
Journal of African Civilizations 8, No. 2
(December 1986):264–273

Men Out of Asia: A Review and Update of the
Gladwin Thesis. Notes. By Harold Sterling
Gladwin. Reviewed by Runoko Rashidi. *Journal of
African Civilizations* 8, No. 2 (December
1986):248–263

Origin of the Ancient Egyptians. Notes. Cheikh
Anta Diop. *Journal of African Civilizations* 8, No.
1 (June 1986):35–63

Trait-Influences in Meso-America: The
African-Asian Connection. Notes. Wayne B.
Chandler. *Journal of African Civilizations* 8, No. 2
(December 1986):274–334

Two Interviews with Cheikh Anta Diop.
Interview. Listervelt Middleton and Nile Valley
Executive Committee. *Journal of African
Civilizations* 8, No. 1 (June 1986):284–302

Physical Education—Dissertations and Theses

Master's Theses in Progress in Selected Colleges
and Universities. Mac A. Stewart. *Negro
Educational Review* 37, Nos. 3-4 (July-October
1986):100, 109

Physical Fitness

Beauty and Fitness: A Sound Approach. *Essence*
17, No. 2 (June 1986):70

Sports Shape-Up. Marjorie Whigham. *Essence* 17,
No. 2 (June 1986):56

Physicians

Blacks Who Overcame the Odds: Barriers of Sex
and Color Didn't Stop Marjorie Peebles-Meyers
from Becoming a Top M.D. *Ebony* 42, No. 2
(December 1986):68

Breakthroughs Are Her Business: Edith Irby.
Charles Whitaker. *Ebony* 41, No. 8 (June 1986):90

A Busy Night with a Big-City Doctor. Marianne
Ilaw. *Black Enterprise* 16, No. 9 (April 1986):58–60

Cook County's Top Doctor: Dr. Agnes Lattimer
Is the Only Black Woman to Head One of the
Nation's Largest Hospitals. Charles Whitaker.
Ebony 41, No. 11 (September 1986):44

Entrepreneurial Surgeon: Dr. Ernest Bates Nurses
Ailing Firm to Fiscal Health. Mark McNamara.
Ebony 41, No. 6 (April 1986):84

The Good Doctor and His Diet: Indiana Health
Commissioner Woodrow Myers, M. D., Sets
Mark by Losing 201 Pounds. Frank White III.
Ebony 41, No. 8 (June 1986):71

Where There's a Will...from Dropout to M. D.
Bebe Moore Campbell. *Essence* 17, No. 6 (October
1986):79

Pielmeier, John

Boys of Winter. Theater review. *Crisis* 93, No. 3
(March 1986):10

Pierce, H. Bruce

Blacks and Law Enforcement: Towards Police
Brutality Reduction. *Black Scholar* 17, No. 3
(May-June 1986):49–54

Pieterse, Jan Nederveen

Amerindian Resistance: The Gathering of the
Fires. *Race and Class* 27, No. 4 (Spring 1986):35–51

Pilgrim, Richard B. (joint author)

See Hall, T. William

Pilots

The First Black Blue Angel: Lt. Cmdr. Donnie
Cochran Makes Naval History as Member of
Famed Precision Flying Team. Aldore Collier.
Ebony 41, No. 8 (June 1986):27

Spreading Their Wings: Black Pilots, Totaling 175,
Want to Pave the Way for More. Frank White III.
Ebony 41, No. 4 (February 1986):75

Pinchback, P. B. J. (about)

Great Moments in Black History: The First Black
Governor. Lerone Bennett, Jr. *Ebony* 42, No. 1
(November 1986):116

Pinderhughes, Diane

The Origins of the Civil Rights Movement: Black
Communities Organizing for Change. Book
review. *CAAS Newsletter* 9, No. 2 (1986):14

Pinkney, Alphonso

The Myth of Black Progress. Book review. Hurumia Ahadi. *Black Scholar* 17, No. 2 (March-April 1986):50–51

The Myth of Black Progress. Book review. Louis Kushnick. *Race and Class* 27, No. 3 (Winter 1986):106–108

The Myth of Black Progress. Book review. Marianne Ilaw. *Black Enterprise* 16, No. 7 (February 1986):19–21

Pittsburgh—History

The *Pittsburgh Courier*, and Black Workers in 1942. Patrick S. Washburn. *Western Journal of Black Studies* 10, No. 3 (Fall 1986):109–118

Plants, Care of

The Care and Feeding of Your House Plants. *Ebony* 41, No. 11 (September 1986):60

Plays—History and Criticism

Drama of the Gods: A Study of Seven African Plays. By Martin Owusu. Reviewed by Mary T. David. *Research in African Literatures* 17, No. 2 (Summer 1986): 276–278

Playwrights

See Dramatists

Plummer, Margery

Everlasting Glow. Short story. *About Time* 14, No. 5 (May 1986):29

Podiatry

A Career for the Future: Podiatric Medicine. Calvin M. Cunningham. *Black Collegian* 16, No. 4 (March/April 1986):102–107

Poems

The Alchemist's Dilemma. Melvin Dixon. *Callaloo* 9, No. 1 (Winter 1986):31–33

For Alice Faye Jackson, from *The Vanishing Black Family in Memoriam* (January 1986). Thadious Davis. *Black American Literature Forum* 20, No. 3 (Fall 1986):301

All Singing in a Pie. Alvin Aubert. *Callaloo* 9, No. 1 (Winter 1986):9

An Always Lei of Ginger Blossoms for the First Lady of Hawai'i: Queen Lili'uokalani. June Jordan. *Callaloo* 9, No. 1 (Winter 1986):79–80

Anniversary. Rita Dove. *Callaloo* 9, No. 1 (Winter 1986):46

Ann Street. Jay Wright. *Callaloo* 9, No. 2 (Spring 1986):309

Arthritis Dance. Michael S. Harper. *Callaloo* 9, No. 1 (Winter 1986):75

Ask Winnie Mandela. Carol Anita Lewis. *Essence* 17, No. 7 (November 1986):151

At the Edge. Luke. *Callaloo* 9, No. 1 (Winter 1986):93

Aunt Sue's Stories. Langston Hughes. *Essence* 16, No. 11 (March 1986):122

Banner. Marilyn Richardson. *Callaloo* 9, No. 2 (Spring 1986):347–348

Belly Dancer. Fred L. Hord. *Black American Literature Forum* 20, No. 3 (Fall 1986):270

Berlin Is Hard on Colored Girls. Audre Lorde. *Callaloo* 9, No. 1 (Winter 1986):89

Bessie Smith. Sybil Kein. *Essence* 17, No. 2 (July 1986):121

With Bill Pickett at the 101 Ranch. Colleen J. McElroy. *Callaloo* 9, No. 1 (Winter 1986):100

Birth of a Poet. Nia Damali. *Black American Literature Forum* 20, No. 3 (Fall 1986):303–305

The Black Axe: Cleaving for Song. Fred L. Hord. *Black American Literature Forum* 20, No. 3 (Fall 1986):268–269

Black Poets and the Children of Black Poets. George K. R. Salters. *Crisis* 93, No. 2 (February 1986):62

Blue Suede Shoes. Ai. *Callaloo* 9, No. 1 (Winter 1986):1–5

Bondage (South Africa). Karen Genevieve Binns. *Essence* 17, No. 1 (May 1986):147

Bones and Drums. Ron Wellburn. *Callaloo* 9, No. 1 (Winter 1986):126

Bourgeois vs. Baptist. Diana R. Thompson. *Essence* 17, No. 1 (May 1986):93

Boy Wearing a Dead Man's Clothes. Yusef Komunyakaa. *Callaloo* 9, No. 1 (Winter 1986):81–82

Broken Friend. Lorene V. Garrett. *Black American Literature Forum* 20, No. 3 (Fall 1986):306

Cathexis. Karen Genevieve Binns. *Essence* 17, No. 1 (May 1986):147

Changes on a Lullaby. Ed Roberson. *Callaloo* 9, No. 1 (Winter 1986):118–119

Chariots. Nikky Finney. *Essence* 17, No. 4 (August 1986):144

Claiming the Body. Beverly Wiggins Wells. *Essence* 16, No. 11 (March 1986):122

Communique. Yusef Komunyakaa. *Callaloo* 9, No. 1 (Winter 1986):83–84

Company. Rita Dove. *Callaloo* 9, No. 1 (Winter 1986):50

Covenant. Terri L. Jewell. *Black American Literature Forum* 20, No. 3 (Fall 1986):259–260

Cowboy Diplomacy. D. L. Crockett-Smith. *Black Scholar* 17, No. 1 (January-February 1986):12

Cowboy Eating His Children. D. L. Crockett-Smith. *Black Scholar* 17, No. 1 (January-February 1986):12

Relationship. Sandra San Viki Chapman. *Essence* 17, No. 7 (November 1986):132

Relativity. June Jordan. *Essence* 17, No. 1 (May 1986):169

Remembering the Fort Prison, Johannesburg. Dennis Brutus. *Black Scholar* 17, No. 4 (July-August 1986):51

The Road to Todos Santos Is Closed. Thylis Moss. *Callaloo* 9, No. 1 (Winter 1986):101

Roast Possum. Rita Dove. *Callaloo* 9, No. 1 (Winter 1986):41–42

Sassafras U.S.A. Nia Damali. *Black American Literature Forum* 20, No. 3 (Fall 1986):305

Saved Africa. Chema Ude. *Essence* 17, No. 4 (August 1986):159

Sequence (Part). Dennis Brutus. *Black Scholar* 17, No. 4 (July-August 1986):51

Setting Loose the Icons. Brenda Marie Osbey. *Callaloo* 9, No. 1 (Winter 1986):112–115

She Waits. Ella Robinson. *Black Scholar* 17, No. 3 (May-June 1986):56

Sisters in Arms. Audre Lorde. *Callaloo* 9, No. 1 (Winter 1986):87–88

The Sleeping Rocks. Nathaniel Mackey. *Callaloo* 9, No. 1 (Winter 1986):94–95

Solomon's Outer Wall. Nathaniel Mackey. *Callaloo* 9, No. 1 (Winter 1986):98–99

Some Places in America Scare You More. Esther Iverem. *Black American Literature Forum* 20, No. 3 (Fall 1986):256

For South Africa. Amelia Blossom House. *Essence* 17, No. 7 (November 1986):158

Spit Mirror. November Belford. *Black American Literature Forum* 20, No. 3 (Fall 1986):264

Stories about Chrone. Luke. *Callaloo* 9, No. 1 (Winter 1986):90–92

Straw Hat. Rita Dove. *Callaloo* 9, No. 1 (Winter 1986):37

Talkin Bout Crossin Over. C. R. David. *About Time* 14, No. 2 (February 1986):24

The Teenage Strut. Maryetta Kelsick Boose. *Black American Literature Forum* 20, No. 3 (Fall 1986):309

That Day/The Sun Was Especially Hot. Primus St. John. *Callaloo* 9, No. 1 (Winter 1986):124–125

There Is a Man Moving into My Skin. Arthur Brown. *Essence* 17, No. 1 (May 1986):92

These Are Not Brushstrokes. Cyrus Cassells. *Callaloo* 9, No. 1 (Winter 1986):18–23

The Thief. Jeanne R. Towns. *Black American Literature Forum* 20, No. 3 (Fall 1986):271

Third World Plenty. C. R. David. *About Time* 14, No. 2 (February 1986):24

Through. Ella Robinson. *Black Scholar* 17, No. 3 (May-June 1986):55

The Time. Esther Iverem. *Black American Literature Forum* 20, No. 3 (Fall 1986):254–255

Timex Remembered. Thylias Moss. *Callaloo* 9, No. 1 (Winter 1986):104–105

Tlazolteotl. Jay Wright. *Callaloo* 9, No. 1 (Winter 1986):138–139

To the Cypress Again and Again. Cyrus Cassells. *Callaloo* 9, No. 1 (Winter 1986):18–23

To Eliminate Vagueness. Thylias Moss. *Callaloo* 9, No. 1 (Winter 1986):102–103

Tomorrow. E. Ethelbert Miller. *Western Journal of Black Studies* 10, No. 3 (Fall 1986):120

A Tough Driver. Ella Robinson. *Black Scholar* 17, No. 3 (May-June 1986):55

Treating My Lady Right. Dennis Rahiim Watson. *Essence* 17, No. 6 (October 1986):140

Tsunami. Esther Iverem. *Black American Literature Forum* 20, No. 3 (Fall 1986):254–256

Twenty-Six Years after Sharpeville. Andrew Salkey. *Black Scholar* 17, No. 4 (July-August 1986):50

Two Cranial Murals. Yusef Komunyakaa. *Callaloo* 9, No. 2 (Spring 1986):300

Under the Viaduct, 1932. Rita Dove. *Callaloo* 9, No. 1 (Winter 1986):38

Undying Treachery. Lorene V. Garrett. *Black American Literature Forum* 20, No. 3 (Fall 1986):306

Unnamed. June L. Collins. *Essence* 17, No. 2 (July 1986):126

Unspoken. Harryette Mullen. *Callaloo* 9, No. 2 (Spring 1986):345–346

Van der Zee Extrapolation #1. Alvin Aubert. *Callaloo* 9, No. 1 (Winter 1986):10

Variation on Gaining a Son. Rita Dove. *Callaloo* 9, No. 1 (Winter 1986):40

Waffle House Girl. Cornelius Eady. *Essence* 17, No. 1 (May 1986):93

The Way I Think It Should Be. Lenard D. Moore. *Black American Literature Forum* 20, No. 3 (Fall 1986):266

For W. C. J. B.: Died in Exile: London March 26, '86. Dennis Brutus. *Black Scholar* 17, No. 4 (July-August 1986):51

The Weather. E. Ethelbert Miller. *Western Journal of Black Studies* 10, No. 3 (Fall 1986):119

We Came to Know Each Other. Primus St. John. *Callaloo* 9, No. 1 (Winter 1986):122–123

Were Only Men Created after God's Image. Geraldine Clark Green. *About Time* 14, No. 11 (November 1986):15

We Shall Bloom Again. Julia Watson Barbour. *Essence* 16, No. 11 (March 1986):122

When Banja Play, Bajan Come. Illustrated. Elton Elombe. *International Review of African American Art* 7, No. 1 (1986):32–40

When Earth Comes to Water. Shelly L. Hall. *Callaloo* 9, No. 1 (Winter 1986):71

When I Look at Wifredo Lam's Paintings. Jayne Cortez. *Callaloo* 9, No. 1 (Winter 1986):26–27

Who Do You Say I Am? Isbella P. Matsikidze. *Black Scholar* 17, No. 4 (July-August 1986):50

Wind. Darryl Alladice. *Essence* 16, No. 11 (March 1986):110

Winter Green. Lorene V. Garrett. *Black American Literature Forum* 20, No. 3 (Fall 1986):306–307

WORK—Night Comes. Herman McKeever. *Black American Literature Forum* 20, No. 3 (Fall 1986):310

Poetry, Afro-American—History and Criticism

Apo Koinou in Audre Lorde and the Moderns. *Callaloo* 9, No. 1 (Winter 1986):193–208

Proceedings of the Symposium on Afro-American and African Poetry and the Teaching of Poetry in Schools. Reviewed by Ernest Mathabela. *Research in African Literatures* 17, No. 1 (Spring 1986): 133–137

Poetry—Africa

Politics in African Poetry. By Tayo Olafioye. Reviewed by Tanure Ojaide. *Research in African Literatures* 17, No. 4 (Winter 1986): 611–613

See also Epic Poetry

Poetry—Africa—Anthologies

Oral Poetry from Africa. Jack Mapanje and Landeg White, editors. Reviewed by Oyekan Owomoyela. *Research in African Literatures* 17, No. 1 (Spring 1986): 137–140

Poetry—Africa—History and Criticism

Proceedings of the Symposium on Afro-American and African Poetry and the Teaching of Poetry in Schools. Reviewed by Ernest Mathabela. *Research in African Literatures* 17, No. 1 (Spring 1986): 133–137

Poetry—Collections

Race and Poetry: Two Anthologies of the Twenties. Notes. Vilma R. Potter. *CLA Journal* 29, No. 3 (March 1986):276–287

Poetry—Themes, Motives

Queen Mab and *An Essay on Man*: Scientific Prophecy versus Theodicy. Notes. Dennis M. Welch. *CLA Journal* 29, No. 4 (June 1986):462–482

Poets—Africa

La nouvelle génération de poètes congolais. By Leopold-Pindy Mamonsono. Reviewed by Daniel Whitman. *Research in African Literatures* 17, No. 4 (Winter 1986): 570–572

Poinsett, Alex

Dr. Manford Byrd, Jr.: Cooling off the Hot Seat. *Ebony* 41, No. 4 (February 1986):44

How to Deal with Ten Serious Health Problems. *Ebony* 41, No. 5 (March 1986):144

How to Get More Blacks into Congress: Enforcement of Voting Rights Act Regarded as the Most Important Step. *Ebony* 41, No. 7 (May 1986):122

A "Sharpe" Change in Newark. *Ebony* 41, No. 11 (September 1986):128

Police and Community Relations

Beyond Accountability: Labour and Policing after the 1985 Rebellions. Lee Bridges. *Race and Class* 27, No. 4 (Spring 1986):78–85

Blacks and Law Enforcement: Towards Police Brutality Reduction. H. Bruce Pierce. *Black Scholar* 17, No. 3 (May-June 1986):49–54

Political Cartoons

See Caricatures and Cartoons

Political Parties

Blacks and the Democratic Party: The Dissolution of an Irreconcilable Marriage. Mfanya D. Tryman. *Black Scholar* 17, No. 6 (November-December 1986):28–32

Politics

Quest for Power. Kenneth M. Jones. *Crisis* 93, No. 2 (February 1986):29

Politics, Black

Black American Politics: From the Washington Marches to Jesse Jackson, vol. 1. By Sanford A. Wright. Reviewed by Sanford A. Wright. *Black Scholar* 17, No. 1 (January-February 1986):45–46

Religious Belief and Political Activism in Black America: An Essay. Robert Michael Franklin. *Journal of Religious Thought* 43, No. 2 (Fall-Winter 1986–87):63–72

Which Way Black America? Arthur Flowers. *Essence* 17, No. 8 (December 1986):54

Politics in Art

An Exhibition for National Peace. Sandra Serrano. *Caribbean Review* 15, No. 1 (Winter 1986):33

Revolutionary Comics: Political Humor from Nicaragua. Roger Sanchez Flores. *Caribbean Review* 15, No. 1 (Winter 1986):16–17

Searching for Pretto: Politics and Art in Panama. Sandra Serrano. *Caribbean Review* 15, No. 1 (Winter 1986):29–32 +

Politics and Government—Africa

Government and Politics in Africa. By William Tordoff. Reviewed by Nancy Murray. *Race and Class* 27, No. 4 (Spring 1986):107–108

Interviews with Cheikh Anta Diop. Interview. Carlos Moore. *Journal of African Civilizations* 8, No. 1 (June 1986):249–283

Politics and Government—Central America

Political Systems as Export Commodities: Democracy and the Role of the US in Central America. Ricardo Arias Calderon. *Caribbean Review* 15, No. 1 (Winter 1986):21–23 +

Politics and Government—Latin America

An Interview with Hugo Spadafora Four Months before His Death. Interview. Beatrix Parga de Bayon. *Caribbean Review* 15, No. 1 (Winter 1986):24–25 +

Scheming for the Poor: The Politics of Redistribution in Latin America. By William Ascher. Reviewed by John Waterbury. *Caribbean Review* 15, No. 1 (Winter 1986):42–43

Politics in Literature

Athol Fugard. By Dennis Walder. Reviewed by Stephen Gray. *Research in African Literatures* 17, No. 2 (Summer 1986): 281–284

Grenadian Party Papers: Revealing an Imaginary Document. Short Story. Jorge I. Dominguez. *Caribbean Review* 15, No. 2 (Spring 1986):16–20

Lord Greystoke and the Darkest Africa: The Politics of the Tarzan Stories. John Newsinger. *Race and Class* 28, No. 2 (August 1986):59–71

Politics in African Poetry. By Tayo Olafioye. Reviewed by Tanure Ojaide. *Research in African Literatures* 17, No. 4 (Winter 1986): 611–613

Report Redux: Thoughts on the Imaginary Document. Short Story. Nelson P. Valdes. *Caribbean Review* 15, No. 2 (Spring 1986):21–23

The Short Fiction of Nadine Gordimer. Notes. Martin Trump. *Research in African Literatures* 17, No. 3 (Fall 1986): 341–369

South African Theater: Ideology and Rebellion. Notes. Andrew Horn. *Research in African Literatures* 17, No. 2 (Summer 1986): 211–233

Theater and Cultural Struggle in South Africa. By Robert Mshengu Kavanagh. Reviewed by Ian Steadman. *Research in African Literatures* 17, No. 2 (Summer 1986): 267–271

The Truthful Lie: Essays in a Sociology of African Drama. By Biodun Jeyifo. Reviewed by Elaine Savory Fido. *Research in African Literatures* 17, No. 2 (Summer 1986): 273–275

Pollack, Bruce (joint editor)

See Shapiro, Nat

Pollution

The Politics of Pollution: Implications for the Black Community. Robert D. Bullard and Beverly Hendrix Wright. *Phylon* 47, No. 1 (March 1986):71–78

Polygamy

From Teenage Parenthood to Polygamy: Case Studies in Black Polygamous Family Formation. Joseph W. Scott. *Western Journal of Black Studies* 10, No. 4 (Winter 1986):172–179

Poor—Medical Care

Dumping Health Care for Poor Americans. David C. Ruffin. *Black Enterprise* 16, No. 9 (April 1986):29

Pope, Alexander: Criticism and Interpretation

Queen Mab and *An Essay on Man*: Scientific Prophecy versus Theodicy. Notes. Dennis M. Welch. *CLA Journal* 29, No. 4 (June 1986):462–482

Popham, W. James

Teacher Competency Testing: The Devil's Dilemma. *Journal of Negro Education* 55, No.3 (Summer 1986):379–385

Popular Culture

The Role of Criticism in Black Popular Culture. Warren C. Swindell. *Western Journal of Black Studies* 10, No. 4 (Winter 1986):185–192

Porter, Abioseh M. (joint editor)

See Anyidoho, Kofi

Porter, Andrew C., and Freeman, Donald J.

Professional Orientations: An Essential Domain for Teacher Testing. *Journal of Negro Education* 55, No.3 (Summer 1986):284–292

Porter, Lewis

Annual Review of Jazz Studies. Book review. *Black Perspective in Music* 14, No. 2 (Spring 1986):195–196

Chicago 1940–1947. Record review. *Black Perspective in Music* 14, No. 3 (Fall 1986):318–319

The Complete Blue Note Forties Ike Quebec and John Hardee. Record review. *Black Perspective in Music* 14, No. 3 (Fall 1986):319–321

The Complete Blue Note Tina Brooks. Record review. *Black Perspective in Music* 14, No. 3 (Fall 1986):319–321

The Complete Candid Charles Mingus. Record review. *Black Perspective in Music* 14, No. 3 (Fall 1986):319–321

The Complete Thelonious Monk. Record review. *Black Perspective in Music* 14, No. 3 (Fall 1986):319–321

Edmond Hall. Rompin' in '44. Record review. *Black Perspective in Music* 14, No. 3 (Fall 1986):317–318

The Horn/1944: Alternate and Incomplete Takes. Record review. *Black Perspective in Music* 14, No. 3 (Fall 1986):317–318

The Horn/1944. Record review. *Black Perspective in Music* 14, No. 3 (Fall 1986):317–318

Ida Cox. Wild Women Don't Have the Blues. Record review. *Black Perspective in Music* 14, No. 3 (Fall 1986):318–319

Lester Young. Book review. Eileen Southern. *Black Perspective in Music* 14, No. 2 (Spring 1986):194

Sidney Bechet. The Complete Blue Note Sidney Bechet. Record review. *Black Perspective in Music* 14, No. 3 (Fall 1986):319–321

Spicy Advice. Record review. *Black Perspective in Music* 14, No. 3 (Fall 1986):317–318

Tradition afrikanischer Blasorchester und Entstehung des Jazz (African Traditions of Wind Orchestras and the Origination of Jazz). Book review. *Black Perspective in Music* 14, No. 3 (Fall 1986):314–316

Wise Woman Blues. Record review. *Black Perspective in Music* 14, No. 3 (Fall 1986):318–319

Porterfield, Harry (about)

PUSH Eyes CBS Stations. Ken Smikle. *Black Enterprise* 16, No. 11 (June 1986):47

Port Royal (South Carolina) Expedition, 1861

Gideonites and Freedmen: Adult Literacy Education at Port Royal, 1862–1865. John R. Rachal. *Journal of Negro Education* 55, No.4 (Fall 1986):453–469

Postage Stamps

The World Honors Martin Luther King (Jr.) through Commemorative Stamps. *Ebony* 41, No. 3 (January 1986):82

Potter, Vilma R.

Race and Poetry: Two Anthologies of the Twenties. Notes. *CLA Journal* 29, No. 3 (March 1986):276–287

Pound, Ezra—Criticism and Interpretation

Apo Koinou in Audre Lorde and the Moderns. Amitai F. Avi-ram. *Callaloo* 9, No. 1 (Winter 1986):192–208

Poussaint, Alvin F.

Save the Fathers: Black Fathers of Today Must Fight to Regain Traditional Strengths of the Past. *Ebony* 41, No. 10 (August 1986):43

Poverty

The Black Underclass: Theory and Reality. Creigs C. Beverly and Howard J. Stanback. *Black Scholar* 17, No. 5 (September-October 1986):24–32

Distress vs. Dependency: Changing Income Support Programs. William Darity, Jr., and Samuel Myers, Jr. *Urban League Review* 10, No. 2 (Winter 1986–87):24–33

The Economic Demise of Blacks in America: A Prelude to Genocide? Sidney M. Willhelm. *Journal of Black Studies* 17, No. 2 (December 1986):201–254

The Homeless. Joan Marie Allen. *About Time* 14, No. 10 (October 1986):18–20

Legal Comments: South African Economic Conditions. Grover G. Hankins. *Crisis* 93, No. 9 (November 1986):46–48

Long-Standing Problem of Poverty Must Be Solved. *Ebony* 41, No. 10 (August 1986):144

Poverty Patterns for Black Men and Women. Judy Claude. *Black Scholar* 17, No. 5 (September-October 1986):20–23

Scheming for the Poor: The Politics of Redistribution in Latin America. By William Ascher. Reviewed by John Waterbury. *Caribbean Review* 15, No. 1 (Winter 1986):42–43

Tax Reform: A Minimalist Approach for Assisting the Low-Income. Lynn Burbridge. *Urban League Review* 10, No. 2 (Winter 1986–87):101–112

Powell, Denise

Ever Try to Be a Wonder Woman. Poem. *Essence* 17, No. 2 (June 1986):111

Powell, Richard J.

William H. Johnson's *Minde Kerteminde*. *Black American Literature Forum* 20, No. 4 (Winter 1986):393–403

Power, Economic

Black Dollars: Taking Control. Jill Nelson. *Essence* 17, No. 5 (September 1986):65

Prabhakaran, M. P.

A Tough Row to Hoe. *Crisis* 93, No. 2 (February 1986):18

Prater, Gwendolyn Spencer (joint author)

See Azevedo, Mario

Pregnancy

Racial Differentials in the Impact of Maternal Cigarette Smoking during Pregnancy on Fetal Development and Mortality: Concerns for Black Psychologists. Edward G. Singleton and others. *Journal of Black Psychology* 12, No. 2 (February 1986):71–83

See also Prenatal Care

Pregnancy—Teenagers

Black and White Children in America: Key Facts. Children's Defense Fund. Reviewed by Gayl Fowler. *Journal of Religious Thought* 43, No. 1 (Spring-Summer 1986):130

See also Adolescent Mothers

See also Birth Control

Premenstrual Syndrome

Preventing PMS. Leslie Kotin. *Essence* 17, No. 8 (December 1986):14

Prenatal Care

Ways to Protect Your Unborn Child. *Ebony* 41,
No. 9 (July 1986):64

Prescod, Colin

Walter Rodney: Poetic Tributes. Book review.
Race and Class 28, No. 2 (August 1986):105–106

Preservation Hall Jazz Band

Preservation Hall Jazz Band. Joan Marie Allen.
About Time 14, No. 12 (December 1986):26–27

Prestage, James J., and Prestage, Jewel L.

The Consent Degree as an Instrument for
Desegregation in Higher Education. *Urban League
Review* 10, No. 2 (Winter 1986–87):113–130

Prestage, Jewel L. (joint author)

See Prestage, James J.

Pretto, Rogelio (about)

An Exhibition for National Peace. Sandra Serrano.
Caribbean Review 15, No. 1 (Winter 1986):33

Searching for Pretto: Politics and Art in Panama.
Sandra Serrano. *Caribbean Review* 15, No. 1
(Winter 1986):29–32+

Preventive Medicine

Reducing Costs with Health Care. Marsha Jones.
About Time 14, No. 4 (April 1986):12–13

Prévos, André

Black Gospel. An Illustrated History of the
Gospel Sound. Book review. *Black Perspective in
Music* 14, No. 2 (Spring 1986):191–192

Blues et gospels. Book review. *Black Perspective in
Music* 14, No. 2 (Spring 1986):192

Blues off the Record. Thirty Years of Blues
Commentary. Book review. *Black Perspective in
Music* 14, No. 2 (Spring 1986):190

The Gospel Sound. Good News and Bad Times.
Book review. *Black Perspective in Music* 14, No. 2
(Spring 1986):191

Jouer le jeu. L'improviste II. Book review. *Black
Perspective in Music* 14, No. 2 (Spring
1986):190–191

Le Blues authentique. Son histoire et ses thèmes.
Book review. *Black Perspective in Music* 14, No. 2
(Spring 1986):189–190

Price-Mars, Jean

So Spoke the Uncle. Reviewed by Michel-Rolph
Trouillot. *Research in African Literatures* 17, No. 4
(Winter 1986): 596–597

Prichard, Keith (joint author)

See Smith, James H.

Prince

Ebony Interview with Prince. *Ebony* 41, No. 9
(July 1986):29

Under the Cherry Moon. Film review. *Crisis* 93,
No. 7 (August/September 1986):11

Printmakers

Bob Blackburn and the Printmaking Workshop.
Hildreth York. *Black American Literature Forum*
20, Nos. 1–2 (Spring/Summer 1986):81–95

Printmaking Workshop

Bob Blackburn and the Printmaking Workshop.
Hildreth York. *Black American Literature Forum*
20, Nos. 1–2 (Spring/Summer 1986):81–95

Professional Development Institute

Can the School System Produce Its Own Leaders?
Edwin Hamilton. *Negro Educational Review* 37,
No. 2 (April 1986):81–87

Professional Employees

Buppies. Kenneth M. Jones. *Crisis* 93, No. 4
(April 1986):16–24

Let's Hear It for Success. *Black Enterprise* 16, No.
8 (March 1986):45–53

Professional Employees—Personal Narratives

When It's More than Just a Job. Marianne Ilaw.
Black Enterprise 16, No. 10 (May 1986):54

Prom-Jackson, Sukai (joint author)

See Johnson, Sylvia T.

Proposal Writing in Business

Act I: How to Write a Business Plan. Udayan
Gupta. *Black Enterprise* 16, No. 7 (February
1986):135–138

**Protective Industrial Insurance Company of
Alabama**

Insurance Company of the Year: Premium Profits.
Nathan McCall. *Black Enterprise* 16, No. 11 (June
1986):182

Pryor, Richard (about)

Richard Pryor Changes Direction. Charles
Whitaker. *Ebony* 41, No. 9 (July 1986):132

Richard Pryor: No Laughing Matter. Interview.
Sid Cassese. *Essence* 16, No. 11 (March 1986):78

Pseudonyms

See Anonyms and Pseudonyms

Psychology, Black

The Afro-American Woman's Emerging Selves.
Alice R. Brown-Collins and Deborah R. Sussewell.
Journal of Black Psychology 13, No. 1 (August
1986):1–11

Is There an Afro-American Cognitive Style?
Barbara J. Shade. *Journal of Black Psychology* 13,
No. 1 (August 1986):13–16

Proceedings of the Seventh Conference on
Empirical Research in Black Psychology,
November 12–15, 1982. Howard P. Ramseur.
SAGE 3, No. 2 (Fall 1986):71

Psychology—Africa

African (Black) Psychology: Issues and Synthesis.
Joseph A. Baldwin. *Journal of Black Studies* 16,
No. 3 (March 1986):235–250

African Psychology: Towards Its Reclamation,
Reascension and Revitalization. By Wade W.
Nobles. Reviewed by S. M. Khatib. *Journal of
Black Psychology* 13, No. 1 (August 1986):17–19

Psychology—Dissertations and Theses

Master's Theses in Progress in Selected Colleges
and Universities. Mac A. Stewart. *Negro
Educational Review* 37, Nos. 3–4 (July-October
1986):102, 114

Public Administrators

NFBPA Holds Conference. Jacqueline Moore.
Black Enterprise 16, No. 12 (July 1986):16

Public Contracts

When Private Companies Do Public Work. Britt
Robson. *Black Enterprise* 16, No. 7 (February
1986):140–144

Public Policy

Black Public Policy. Nancy L. Arnez. *Journal of
Black Studies* 16, No. 4 (June 1986):397–408

Public Relations Firms

Personal Best: Her PR Agency Put Their Best
Foot Forward. Janine C. McAdams. *Essence* 17,
No. 8 (December 1986):109

Public Schools

How to Save Our High Schools. *Ebony* 41, No. 6
(April 1986):144

Public Schools—Administrators

Can the School System Produce Its Own Leaders?
Edwin Hamilton. *Negro Educational Review* 37,
No. 2 (April 1986):81–87

Public Schools—Athletics

Mixing Sports and School: Leo F. Miles. Henry
Duvall. *About Time* 14, No. 5 (May 1986):23–24

Ritchie Herbert: Photography Major/Hockey
Player. J. Roger Dykes. *About Time* 14, No. 5
(May 1986):24–25

Public Schools—Counselors

Educational Specialists: Addressing a Child's
Career Development. Marsha Jones. *About Time*
14, No. 11 (November 1986):18–21

Public Schools—Desegregation

A Bittersweet Victory: Public School
Desegregation in Memphis. Roger Biles. *Journal of
Negro Education* 55, No.4 (Fall 1986):470–483

Education in the Post-Integration Era. Russell
William Irvine. *Journal of Negro Education* 55,
No.4 (Fall 1986):508–517

Gleanings from the Desegregation Research. Essay
Review. Marjorie Hanson. *Journal of Negro
Education* 55, No. 1 (Winter 1986):107–115

More Busing Battles. Kenneth Maurice Jones.
Black Enterprise 16, No. 10 (May 1986):18

Urban-Suburban Interdistrict Transfer Program.
Peggy Lyons. *About Time* 14, No. 5 (May
1986):30–31

Public Schools—Discipline

School Discipline and Your Child. Janice Hayes.
Essence 17, No. 6 (October 1986):104

Public Schools—Evaluation

Guidelines for Evaluating Bilingual Classrooms.
Sonia Nieto. *Interracial Books for Children Bulletin*
17, Nos. 3–4 (1986):26–28

Public Schools—Principals

Educational Specialists: Addressing a Child's
Career Development. Marsha Jones. *About Time*
14, No. 11 (November 1986):18–21

Public Schools—School Lunches

Decimation of School Lunches. William L. Clay.
About Time 14, No. 5 (May 1986):9

Public Schools—Students

The Effect of Ridicule on the Academic
Performance of Secondary School Students.
Muyiwa Igbalajobi. *Negro Educational Review* 37,
No. 1 (January 1986):39–45

Not Your Typical Teen Mother: Chicago Honor
Student Barbara Washington Balances Books and
Her Baby. *Ebony* 41, No. 10 (August 1986):67

Public Schools—Superintendents

Dr. Manford Byrd, Jr.: Cooling off the Hot Seat.
Alex Poinsett. *Ebony* 41, No. 4 (February 1986):44

Peter McWalters: Acting Superintendent of
Rochester Schools. James M. Blount. *About Time*
14, No. 5 (May 1986):14–21

The Power of Protesting. Dan Berube. *Black
Enterprise* 17, No. 3 (October 1986):22

Quality Professionals for Quality Education.
George C. Simmons. *About Time* 14, No. 5 (May
1986):8

Public Utility Commissions—Regulatory Policy

Regulatory Policy and Minority Concerns: The
Impact of Changes in Telecommunications Policy.
Georgia A. Persons. *Urban League Review* 10, No.
2 (Winter 1986–87):45–62

Publishers and Publishing

An Annotated Bibliography of Swahili Fiction and Drama Published between 1975 and 1984. Notes. References. Elena Zubkova Bertoncini. *Research in African Literatures* 17, No. 4 (Winter 1986): 525–562

Industry Overview: Magazine Monarchs. Ken Smikle. *Black Enterprise* 16, No. 11 (June 1986):212

The Power of the Press. Lloyd Gite. *Black Enterprise* 17, No. 3 (October 1986):33

A Question of Publishers and a Question of Audience. Faith Berry. *Black Scholar* 17, No. 2 (March-April 1986):41–49

Publishers and Publishing—Africa

The Book Trade of the World, IV: Africa. Sigfred Taubert and Peter Weidhaas, editors. Reviewed by Ilse Sternberg. *Research in African Literatures* 17, No. 1 (Spring 1986): 147–149

Puerto Ricans—United States

Past Accomplishments, Current Needs: La Lucha Continúa. Sonia Nieto. *Interracial Books for Children Bulletin* 17, No. 2 (1986):6–8

Puerto Ricans and Bilingual Education. Diana Caballero. *Interracial Books for Children Bulletin* 17, Nos. 3–4 (1986):15–16

Puerto Rican Traveling Theatre

Theatre. Cecilia Loving-Sloane. *Crisis* 93, No. 4 (April 1986):10–12

Puerto Rico—Description and Travel

Vieques: Puerto Rico's Hideaway. Constance M. Green. *Black Enterprise* 16, No. 10 (May 1986):78

Pulliam, Keshia Knight (about)

Keshia Knight Pulliam: Coping with Success at Seven. Marilyn Marshall. *Ebony* 42, No. 2 (December 1986):27

Pyramids—Egypt

Pyramid—American and African: A Comparison. Notes. Beatrice Lumpkin. *Journal of African Civilizations* 8, No. 2 (December 1986):169–187

Quaye, Tayo Tekovi (about)

Tayo Tekovi Quaye's Images of Traditional African Life. Illustrated. *Black Collegian* 16, No. 4 (March/April 1986):48–49

Quebec, Ike, and Hardee, John (about)

The Complete Blue Note Forties Ike Quebec and John Hardee. Record review. Lewis Porter. *Black Perspective in Music* 14, No. 3 (Fall 1986):319–321

Race Awareness

America, Let Me In! Katherine Gale. *About Time* 14, No. 3 (March 1986):9

Ethnocentric Manifestations in Cooper's *Pioneers*, and *The Last of the Mohicans*. Chester H. Mills. *Journal of Black Studies* 16, No. 4 (June 1986):435–449

A Number of Things. Adolph Dupree. *About Time* 14, No. 3 (March 1986):8

Race Discrimination

A Black Elite. By Daniel C. Thompson. Reviewed by C. J. Wiltz. *Phylon* 47, No. 4 (December 1986):328–329

The Color of Feminism: Or Speaking the Black Woman's Tongue. Notes. Delores S. Williams. *Journal of Religious Thought* 43, No. 1 (Spring-Summer 1986):42–58

Differences in Campaign Funds: A Racial Explanation. John Theilmann and Al Wilhite. *Review of Black Political Economy* 15, No. 1 (Summer 1986):45–58

Less Than Human Nature: Biology and the New Right. Steven Rose and Hilary Rose. *Race and Class* 27, No. 3 (Winter 1986):47–66

Martin Luther King (Jr.) and the Paradox of Nonviolent Direct Action. James A. Colaiaco. *Phylon* 47, No. 1 (March 1986):16–28

Martin Luther King (Jr.) and the Quest for Nonviolent Social Change. Adam Fairclough. *Phylon* 47, No. 1 (March 1986):1–15

Political Liberalization, Black Consciousness, and Recent Afro-Brazilian Literary Production. James H. Kennedy. *Phylon* 47, No. 3 (September 1986):199–209

Reversing the Tide of Racism. Anne Braden. *Interracial Books for Children Bulletin* 17, No. 2 (1986):3–4

Race Discrimination in Literature

Lord Greystoke and the Darkest Africa: The Politics of the Tarzan Stories. John Newsinger. *Race and Class* 28, No. 2 (August 1986):59–71

Race Identity

Armageddon Is Now. Jill Nelson. *Essence* 17, No. 2 (July 1986):80

Contemporary Style or Fundamental Substance? Dale L. Sibley. *Black Collegian* 17, No. 1 (September/October 1986):58–63

Frantz Fanon and Black Consciousness in Azania (South Africa). Thomas K. Ranuga. *Phylon* 47, No. 3 (September 1986):182–191

Impact of *Roots*: Evidence from the National Survey of Black Americans. Halford H. Fairchild and others. *Journal of Black Studies* 16, No. 3 (March 1986):307–310

Just What is "Racial Pride?" Editorial. Carolyn L. Bennett. *Journal of Negro Education* 55, No. 1 (Winter 1986):1–2

Political Liberalization, Black Consciousness, and Recent Afro-Brazilian Literary Production. James H. Kennedy. *Phylon* 47, No. 3 (September 1986):199–209

The Race Consciousness of Alain Locke. Yvonne Ochillo. *Phylon* 47, No. 3 (September 1986):173–181

Racial Definition: Background for Divergence. William Javier Nelson. *Phylon* 47, No. 4 (December 1986):318–326

The Sociological Tradition of E. Franklin Frazier: Implications for Black Studies. Clovis E. Semmes. *Journal of Negro Education* 55, No.4 (Fall 1986):484–494

Who Teaches Black Theology? Notes. Rufus Burrow (Jr.) *Journal of Religious Thought* 43, No. 2 (Fall-Winter 1986–87):7–18

Race in Literature

Race and Poetry: Two Anthologies of the Twenties. Notes. Vilma R. Potter. *CLA Journal* 29, No. 3 (March 1986):276–287

Social-Scientific Perspectives on the Afro-American Arts. Rhett S. Jones. *Black American Literature Forum* 20, No. 4 (Winter 1986):443–447

Race Relations

The African-American Intellectual and the Struggle for Black Empowerment. Charles Green and Basil Wilson. *Western Journal of Black Studies* 10, No. 2 (Summer 1986):59–69

Beyond Black Power: The Contradiction between Capital and Liberty. Anthony J. Lemelle. *Western Journal of Black Studies* 10, No. 2 (Summer 1986):70–76

The Black Middle Class in America. Thomas J. Durant (Jr.) and Joyce S. Louden. *Phylon* 47, No. 4 (December 1986):253–263

Congo or Carabali? Race Relations in Socialist Cuba. Carlos Moore. *Caribbean Review* 15, No. 2 (Spring 1986):12–15+

Effects of Percent Black on Blacks' Perceptions of Relative Power and Social Distance. Arthur S. Evans, Jr., and Michael W. Giles. *Journal of Black Studies* 17, No. 1 (September 1986):3–14

Footnotes of a Culture at Risk. Norman Riley. *Crisis* 93, No. 3 (March 1986):23–46

Race, Reform and Rebellion: The Second Reconstruction in Black America. By Manning Marable. Reviewed by Earl Smith. *Phylon* 47, No. 1 (March 1986):101–103

Race Relations in Sociological Theory. By John Rex. Reviewed by Vernon J. Williams (Jr.) *Afro-Americans in New York Life and History* 10, No.1 (January 1986):74–76

Time and Assimilation Clock. Irene I. Blea. *About Time* 14, No. 1 (January 1986):22

The United States and South Africa: History, Civil Rights and the Legal and Cultural Vulnerability of Blacks. JoAnne Cornwell. *Phylon* 47, No. 4 (December 1986):285–293

What Black Americans and Africans Can Do for Each Other. *Ebony* 41, No. 6 (April 1986):155

Race Relations—Africa

Ideologies of Race and Sex in Literature: Racism and Antiracism in the African Francophone Novel. Notes. E. P. Abanime. *CLA Journal* 30, No. 2 (December 1986):125–143

Rachal, John R.

Gideonites and Freedmen: Adult Literacy Education at Port Royal, 1862–1865. *Journal of Negro Education* 55, No.4 (Fall 1986):453–469

Racine, Daniel

Léon-Gontran Dumas: L'homme et l'oeuvre. Reviewed by Martin Steins. *Research in African Literatures* 17, No. 4 (Winter 1986): 587–588

Racine, Daniel (joint editor)

See Anyidoho, Kofi

Racism

Black Marxism: The Making of the Black Radical Tradition. Cedric J. Robinson. Reviewed by V. P. Franklin. *Phylon* 47, No. 3 (September 1986):250–251

Black Theater in a "Racial Democracy": The Case of the Brazilian Black Experimental Theater. Notes. Doris J. Turner. *CLA Journal* 30, No. 1 (September 1986):30–45

Congo or Carabali? Race Relations in Socialist Cuba. Carlos Moore. *Caribbean Review* 15, No. 2 (Spring 1986):12–15+

Interview with Cheikh Anta Diop. Interview. Notes. Bibliography. Shawna Moore. *Journal of African Civilizations* 8, No. 1 (June 1986):238–248

The Ku Klux Klan: Reasons for Support or Opposition among White Respondents. Rick Seltzer and Grace M. Lopes. *Journal of Black Studies* 17, No. 1 (September 1986):91–109

NCAA Rule 48: Racism or Reform? Vernon L. Clark, Floyd Horton, and Robert L. Alford. *Journal of Negro Education* 55, No.2 (Spring 1986):162–170

Racial Prejudice in a Capitalist State: What Happened to the American Creed. Richard T. Schaefer. *Phylon* 47, No. 3 (September 1986):192–198

The United States and South Africa: History, Civil Rights and the Legal and Cultural Vulnerability of Blacks. JoAnne Cornwell. *Phylon* 47, No. 4 (December 1986):285–293

Racism in Literature

...And Ladies of the Club. By Helen Hoover Santmyer. Reviewed by Robert F. Fleissner. *CLA Journal* 29, No. 4 (June 1986):486–489

Ideologies of Race and Sex in Literature: Racism and Antiracism in the African Francophone Novel. Notes. E. P. Abanime. *CLA Journal* 30, No. 2 (December 1986):125–143

Rackow, Silvia

Making Money with a Proper Stranger. *Black Enterprise* 16, No. 8 (March 1986):60

Radio Broadcasting

Radio Buys Settle Suits. Frederick H. Lowe. *Black Enterprise* 16, No. 8 (March 1986):14

Washington's Superstation: Howard University's WHUR-FM (96.3). Henry Duvall. *About Time* 14, No. 2 (February 1986):22–23

Raison, Hawthorne

Tapping Potential: English and Language Arts for the Black Learner. Book review. *Black Scholar* 17, No. 3 (May-June 1986):60

Ramirez, Sergio

To Bury Our Fathers: A Novel of Nicaragua. Book review. Imogen Forster. *Race and Class* 27, No. 4 (Spring 1986):92–93

Ramos, Hector

Latino Caucuses in U.S. Labour Unions. *Race and Class* 27, No. 4 (Spring 1986):69–78

Rampersad, Arnold

The Harlem Renaissance: A Historical Dictionary for the Era. Book review. *Callaloo* 9, No. 4 (Fall 1986):749–750

Langston Hughes's *Fine Clothes to the Jew*. *Callaloo* 9, No. 1 (Winter 1986):144–158

The Life of Langston Hughes: Volume I: 1902–41. Book review. Joe Johnson. *Crisis* 93, No. 9 (November 1986):12–13

The Poems of Rita Dove. *Callaloo* 9, No. 1 (Winter 1986):52–60

Ramseur, Howard P.

Proceedings of the Seventh Conference on Empirical Research in Black Psychology, November 12–15, 1982. *SAGE* 3, No. 2 (Fall 1986):71

Randolph, Laura B.

The New Jayne Kennedy: Wife, Mother, Woman. *Ebony* 41, No. 5 (March 1986):132

The Other Patti LaBelle: Wife, Mother and World Class Cook. *Ebony* 41, No. 6 (April 1986):31

Ransby, Barbara

Eslanda Goode Robeson, Pan-Africanist. *SAGE* 3, No. 2 (Fall 1986):22–26

Ranuga, Thomas K.

Frantz Fanon and Black Consciousness in Azania (South Africa). *Phylon* 47, No. 3 (September 1986):182–191

Rape

Commonwealth v. Richardson: Voir Dire and the Consent Defense to an Interracial Rape in Pennsylvania—Finding Twelve Not-Too-Angry Men. James A. Buddie. *Black Law Journal* 9, No. 3 (Winter 1986):300–311

Rape Victims

Life after Rape. Lorene E. Gray. *Essence* 17, No. 5 (September 1986):68

Rashad, Ahmad (about)

Phylicia and Ahmad: Off-Camera and Personal. Patrice Miles. *Essence* 17, No. 2 (July 1986):85

Rashad, Phylicia (about)

Phylicia and Ahmad: Off-Camera and Personal. Patrice Miles. *Essence* 17, No. 2 (July 1986):85

Rashidi, Runoko

Dr. Diop on Asia: Highlights and Insights. Notes. *Journal of African Civilizations* 8, No. 1 (June 1986):127–145

Men Out of Asia: A Review and Update of the Gladwin Thesis. Notes. Book review. *Journal of African Civilizations* 8, No. 2 (December 1986):248–263

Ray, Elaine C.

How to Get Out of That Rut and Make Life an Adventure. *Essence* 16, No. 11 (March 1986):61

Rio Grand! *Essence* 16, No. 11 (March 1986):31

Ray, Elaine C. (joint author)

See McAdams, Janine C.

Reagan, Ronald—Administration

Changes in Equal Employment Enforcement: What Enforcement Statistics Tell Us. Lynn C. Burbridge. *Review of Black Political Economy* 15, No. 1 (Summer 1986):71–80

Racial Employment and Earnings Differentials: The Impact of the Reagan Administration. Charles A. Register. *Review of Black Political Economy* 15, No. 1 (Summer 1986):59–69

Reagan, Ronald—Civil Rights

The Enforcement of Civil Rights Statutes: The Reagan Administration's Record. Barbara Wolvovitz and Jules Lobel. *Black Law Journal* 9, No. 3 (Winter 1986):252–262

Reagan, Ronald—Economic Policy

Falling Behind: A Report on How Blacks Have Fared under Reagan. Center on Budget and Policy Priorities. *Journal of Black Studies* 17, No. 2 (December 1986):148–171

Real Estate Agencies

Homes on the Range. Lloyd Gite. *Black Enterprise* 16, No. 9 (April 1986):22

Real Estate Investment

Investing in Commercial Real Estate. Denise Lamaute. *Black Enterprise* 16, No. 11 (June 1986):71–72

Own a Piece of the City. Britt Robson. *Black Enterprise* 17, No. 3 (October 1986):67

Real Estate: Home, Sweet Home. Constance Mitchell. *Black Enterprise* 16, No. 11 (June 1986):290

There's No Place Like Home. Deborah W. Hairston. *Black Enterprise* 17, No. 3 (October 1986):99

Record Reviews

Aretha. By Aretha Franklin. Reviewed by Norman Riley. *Crisis* 93, No. 10 (December 1986):8–9

Chicago 1940–1947. By Lil Green. Reviewed by Lewis Porter. *Black Perspective in Music* 14, No. 3 (Fall 1986):318–319

The Complete Blue Note Forties Ike Quebec and John Hardee. By Ike Quebec and John Hardee. Reviewed by Lewis Porter. *Black Perspective in Music* 14, No. 3 (Fall 1986):319–321

The Complete Blue Note Tina Brooks. By Tina Brooks. Reviewed by Lewis Porter. *Black Perspective in Music* 14, No. 3 (Fall 1986):319–321

The Complete Candid Charles Mingus. By Charles Mingus. Reviewed by Lewis Porter. *Black Perspective in Music* 14, No. 3 (Fall 1986):319–321

The Complete Thelonious Monk. By Thelonious Monk. Reviewed by Lewis Porter. *Black Perspective in Music* 14, No. 3 (Fall 1986):319–321

Edmond Hall. Rompin' in '44. By Edmond Hall. Reviewed by Lewis Porter. *Black Perspective in Music* 14, No. 3 (Fall 1986):317–318

The Horn/1944: Alternate and Incomplete Takes. By Ben Webster. Reviewed by Lewis Porter. *Black Perspective in Music* 14, No. 3 (Fall 1986):317–318

The Horn/1944. By Ben Webster. Reviewed by Lewis Porter. *Black Perspective in Music* 14, No. 3 (Fall 1986):317–318

Ida Cox. Wild Women Don't Have the Blues. By Ida Cox. Reviewed by Lewis Porter. *Black Perspective in Music* 14, No. 3 (Fall 1986):318–319

J Mood. By Wynton Marsalis. Reviewed by Norman Riley. *Crisis* 93, No. 9 (November 1986):9

Nascence. By Donald Harrison and Terence Blanchard. Reviewed by Norman Riley. *Crisis* 93, No. 9 (November 1986):9

Royal Garden Blues. By Branford Marsalis. Reviewed by Norman Riley. *Crisis* 93, No. 9 (November 1986):9

Saving the Day: The Recordings of Reverend Sutton E. Griggs. Steven C. Tracy. *Phylon* 47, No. 2 (June 1986):159–166

Sidney Bechet. The Complete Blue Note Sidney Bechet. By Sidney Bechet. Reviewed by Lewis Porter. *Black Perspective in Music* 14, No. 3 (Fall 1986):319–321

Spicy Advice. By Bunk Johnson's Band. Reviewed by Lewis Portr. *Black Perspective in Music* 14, No. 3 (Fall 1986):317–318

Wise Woman Blues. By Dinah Washington. Reviewed by Lewis Porter. *Black Perspective in Music* 14, No. 3 (Fall 1986):318–319

Reda, Jacques

Jouer le jeu. L'improviste II. Book review. André Prévos. *Black Perspective in Music* 14, No. 2 (Spring 1986):190–191

Redevelopment

Own a Piece of the City. Britt Robson. *Black Enterprise* 17, No. 3 (October 1986):67

Redistribution of Wealth

See Income Distribution

Reed, Adolph

The Jesse Jackson Phenomenon: The Crisis of Purpose in Afro-American Politics. Book review. Shirley Washington. *Black Scholar* 17, No. 6 (November–December 1986):52–53

Reed, Gail

Low Intensity Conflict: A War for All Seasons. *Black Scholar* 17, No. 1 (January–February 1986):14–22

Reed, Ishmael (about)

A Conversation with Ishmael Reed. Interview. Nelson George. *Essence* 17, No. 2 (July 1986):38

Reed, Wornie L.

See Watson, Wilbur H.

Reed, Wornie L. (joint author)

See Watson, Wilbur H.

Refugees—Africa

African Refugees: Reflections on the African Refugee Problem. By Gaim Kibreab. Reviewed by Maurice Herson. *Race and Class* 27, No. 4 (Spring 1986):104–105

Register, Charles A.

Racial Employment and Earnings Differentials: The Impact of the Reagan Administration. *Review of Black Political Economy* 15, No. 1 (Summer 1986):59–69

Reidy, Joseph P.

Bloods: An Oral History of the Vietnam War by Black Veterans. Book review. *Afro-Americans in New York Life and History* 10, No.1 (January 1986):76–78

Reierson, Gary B. (joint author)

See Campbell, Thomas C.

Reilly, Danny (joint author)

See Gordon, Paul

Reilly, John M.

Richard Wright and the Art of Non-Fiction: Stepping Out on the Stage of the World. *Callaloo* 9, No. 3 (Summer 1986):507–520

Reist, John S. (Jr.)

Founding or Finding? A Theology for New Church Development. Notes. *Journal of Religious Thought* 43, No. 1 (Spring-Summer 1986):102–115

Religion

See also Feasts and Rituals

Religion, Afro-American

Black Gospel Music and Black Theology. Notes. Louis-Charles Harvey. *Journal of Religious Thought* 43, No. 2 (Fall-Winter 1986–87):19–37

Black Religion and Black Radicalism: An Interpretation of the Religious History of Afro-American People. By Gayraud S. Wilmore. Reviewed by Kenneth Leech. *Race and Class* 28, No. 2 (August 1986):97–99

From Sinners to Saints: The Confessions of Saint Augustine and Malcolm X. Notes. Winston A. Van Horne. *Journal of Religious Thought* 43, No. 1 (Spring-Summer 1986):76–101

Music in the Churches of Black Americans: A Critical Statement. Wendell Whalum. *Black Perspective in Music* 14, No. 1 (Winter 1986):13–20

Religious Belief and Political Activism in Black America: An Essay. Robert Michael Franklin. *Journal of Religious Thought* 43, No. 2 (Fall-Winter 1986–87):63–72

The Role of Women in the Sanctified Church. Notes. Cheryl Townsend Gilkes. *Journal of Religious Thought* 43, No. 1 (Spring-Summer 1986):24–41

The West African Zongo and the American Ghetto: Some Comparative Aspects of the Roles of Religious Institutions. Joseph A. Sarfoh. *Journal of Black Studies* 17, No. 1 (September 1986):71–84

Religion, Afro-American—Baptist

10 Super Sunday Schools in the Black Community. By Sid Smith. Reviewed by Gayl Fowler. *Journal of Religious Thought* 43, No. 2 (Fall-Winter 1986–87):93

Religion—Africa

African Religions in Western Conceptual Schemes: The Problem of Interpretation. Reviewed by C. Ejizu. *Journal of Religious Thought* 43, No. 2 (Fall-Winter 1986–87):90

Religion—Baptist

Black Baptist Women and African Mission Work, 1870–1925. Sandy D. Martin. *SAGE* 3, No. 1 (Spring 1986):16–19

"Say Africa When You Pray": The Activities of Early Black Baptist Women Missionaries among Liberian Women and Children. Sylvia M. Jacobs. *SAGE* 3, No. 2 (Fall 1986):16–21

Religion—Church Development

Founding or Finding? A Theology for New Church Development. Notes. John S. Reist (Jr.) *Journal of Religious Thought* 43, No. 1 (Spring-Summer 1986):102–115

Religion—Latin America

Fidel y la Religion: Conversaciones con Frei Betto. Interview. Reviewed by Paul E. Sigmund. *Caribbean Review* 15, No. 2 (Spring 1986):30–31

Religion and Music

Black Gospel Music and Black Theology. Notes. Louis-Charles Harvey. *Journal of Religious Thought* 43, No. 2 (Fall-Winter 1986–87):19–37

Religion—Pastors

A Pastoral Letter from John P. Carter. John P. Carter. *Journal of Religious Thought* 43, No. 1 (Spring-Summer 1986):120–127

The Professionalism of the Ministry of Women. Notes. Delores Causion Carpenter. *Journal of Religious Thought* 43, No. 1 (Spring-Summer 1986):59–75

Saving the Day: The Recordings of Reverend Sutton E. Griggs. Steven C. Tracy. *Phylon* 47, No. 2 (June 1986):159–166

Work My Soul Must Have Done: Three Generations of Black Women in Ministry. Imani-Shelia Newsome. *SAGE* 3, No. 1 (Spring 1986):50–52

Religion—Preachers

Georgia's Reverend Sheriff: Richard Lankford Finds Joy in Preaching the Gospel and Keeping the Peace. Marilyn Marshall. *Ebony* 41, No. 5 (March 1986):92

Those Preachin' Women: Sermons by Black Women Preachers. Edited by Ella Pearson Mitchell. Reviewed by Gayl Fowler. *Journal of Religious Thought* 43, No. 1 (Spring-Summer 1986):129–130

Those Preachin' Women: Sermons by Black Women Preachers. Edited by Ella Pearson Mitchell. Reviewed by Renita J. Weems. *SAGE* 3, No. 2 (Fall 1986):56–57

Twins in the Ministry: Three Sets from Atlanta. *Ebony* 41, No. 4 (February 1986):99

The Woman as Preacher. Cheryl J. Sanders. Notes. *Journal of Religious Thought* 43, No. 1 (Spring-Summer 1986):6–23

Religion—Social Aspects

Founding or Finding? A Theology for New Church Development. Notes. John S. Reist (Jr.) *Journal of Religious Thought* 43, No. 1 (Spring-Summer 1986):102–115

Religion and Social Status

Sitting Location as an Indicator of Status of Older Blacks in the Church: A Comparative Analysis of Protestants and Catholics in the Rural South. Appendix. Wilbur H. Watson. *Phylon* 47, No. 4 (December 1986):264–275

Religion—West Africa

The West African Zongo and the American Ghetto: Some Comparative Aspects of the Roles of Religious Institutions. Joseph A. Sarfoh. *Journal of Black Studies* 17, No. 1 (September 1986):71–84

Religious Education

The Black Church as an Ally in the Education of Black Children. Notes. James D. Tyms. *Journal of Religious Thought* 43, No. 2 (Fall-Winter 1986–87):73–87

The Professionalism of the Ministry of Women. Notes. Delores Causion Carpenter. *Journal of Religious Thought* 43, No. 1 (Spring-Summer 1986):59–75

Religion: An Introduction. By T. William Hall, Richard B. Pilgrim, and Ronald R. Cavanaugh. Reviewed by Kortright Davis. *Journal of Religious Thought* 43, No. 2 (Fall-Winter 1986–87):92

10 Super Sunday Schools in the Black Community. By Sid Smith. Reviewed by Gayl Fowler. *Journal of Religious Thought* 43, No. 2 (Fall-Winter 1986–87):93

Relocation (Housing)

How to Minimize Relocation Costs. Denise Lamaute. *Black Enterprise* 17, No. 1 (August 1986):21–22

Remedial Teaching

See Universities and Colleges—Remedial Teaching

Rencher, Jay (about)

The Young Tycoons. Lloyd Gite. *Black Enterprise* 16, No. 6 (January 1986):44–47

Rencher's Editorial Service

See Rencher, Jay (about)

Rental Housing

Implied Warranty of Habitability. Harry Tun. *Howard Law Journal* 29, No. 1 (1986):103–115

See also Landlord and Tenant

Rental Housing—Laws and Legislation

Special Project on Landlord-Tenant Law in the District of Columbia Court of Appeals. *Howard Law Journal* 29, No. 1 (1986):1–189

Rent Control

Rent Control. Kenneth P. McNeely. *Howard Law Journal* 29, No. 1 (1986):165–175

Repertory Dance Theater of Los Angeles

Joe Johnson and the Repertory Dance Theater of Los Angeles. L. Martina Young. *Crisis* 93, No. 6 (June/July 1986):2

Representative Government and Representation

Effects of Multimember Districts on Black Representation in State Legislatures. Bernard Grofman and others. *Review of Black Political Economy* 14, No. 4 (Spring 1986):65–78

Republican Party

Blacks and the Democratic Party: The Dissolution of an Irreconcilable Marriage. Mfanya D. Tryman. *Black Scholar* 17, No. 6 (November-December 1986):28–32

Resistance Movements

Amerindian Resistance: The Gathering of the Fires. Jan Nederveen Pieterse. *Race and Class* 27, No. 4 (Spring 1986):35–51

Notes on the Kurdish Struggle. Sinjari Hussain. *Race and Class* 27, No. 3 (Winter 1986):92–94

Restaurants

Fairy Tales Come True. Lloyd Gite. *Black Enterprise* 17, No. 3 (October 1986):24

Restaurants—London

The Traveling Life. Kris DiLorenzo. *Crisis* 93, No. 4 (April 1986):9

Retail Sales as a Profession

The Price Is Right in Sales. Errol T. Louis. *Black Enterprise* 16, No. 7 (February 1986):67–70

Retirement Income

Finding Security in Retirement. Wanda Whitmore. *Black Enterprise* 16, No. 6 (January 1986):35

Revolutionaries

Alex La Guma Revolutionary Intellectual. Daniel Garcia Santos. *Black Scholar* 17, No. 4 (July-August 1986):55–56

Angela Davis: Talking Tough. Interview. Cheryll Y. Greene. *Essence* 17, No. 4 (August 1986):62

An Interview with Hugo Spadafora Four Months before His Death. Interview. Beatrix Parga de Bayon. *Caribbean Review* 15, No. 1 (Winter 1986):24–25+

On Revolutionary Nationalism: The Legacy of Cabral. Basil Davidson. *Race and Class* 27, No. 3 (Winter 1986):21–45

Revolutionary Comics: Political Humor from Nicaragua. Roger Sanchez Flores. *Caribbean Review* 15, No. 1 (Winter 1986):16–17

Revolutionaries—Daughters—Personal Narratives

Daughters of the Revolution. *Essence* 17, No. 1 (May 1986):97

Revolutionary Movements

The Legacy of the Black Panther Party. JoNina M. Abron *Black Scholar* 17, No. 6 (November-December 1986):33–38

Revolution in Literature

Black Soul, White Artifact: Fanon's Clinical Psychology and Social Theory. By Jack McCulloch. Reviewed by Hal Wylie. *Research in African Literatures* 17, No. 4 (Winter 1986): 599–601

Holy Violence: The Revolutionary Thought of Frantz Fanon. By Marie Perinbam. Reviewed by Hal Wylie. *Research in African Literatures* 17, No. 4 (Winter 1986): 597–599

Meridian: Alice Walker's Critique of Revolution. Karen F. Stein. *Black American Literature Forum* 20, Nos. 1–2 (Spring/Summer 1986):129–141

Rex, John

Race Relations in Sociological Theory. Reviewed by Vernon J. Williams (Jr.) *Afro-Americans in New York Life and History* 10, No.1 (January 1986):74–76

Reyes, Angelita

Ancient Properties in the New World: The Paradox of the "Other" in Toni Morrison's *Tar Baby*. *Black Scholar* 17, No. 2 (March-April 1986):19–25

Rhoden, Bill

Where There's a Will: Bonnie's Story. *Essence* 17, No. 1 (May 1986):82

Rhodesia

    See Zimbabwe—History

Ricard, Alain

Come to Laugh: A Study of African Traditional Theatre in Ghana. Book review. *Research in African Literatures* 17, No. 2 (Summer 1986): 287

Rice, Herbert W.

An Incomplete Circle: Repeated Images in Part Two of *Cane*. Notes. *CLA Journal* 29, No. 4 (June 1986):442–461

Rice—Planting and Harvesting

Rice, Rice and More Rice: Ephron Lewis' Arkansas Farm Yields the Long, Medium and Short of It. *Ebony* 42, No. 2 (December 1986):100

Rich, John Martin

Neoliberalism and Black Education. *Journal of Negro Education* 55, No. 1 (Winter 1986):21–28

Richardson, Ben (about)

A Family Affair: Ben Richardson, Candidate for New York State Senate. Adolph Dupree. *About Time* 14, No. 10 (October 1986):14–17

Richardson, Bonham C.

Slave Populations of the British Caribbean 1807–1834. Book review. *Caribbean Review* 15, No. 2 (Spring 1986):46

Richardson, Marilyn

Banner. Poem. *Callaloo* 9, No. 2 (Spring 1986):347–348

Richie, Leroy C. (about)

Leroy C. Richie: Chrysler Motors' Top Lawyer. *Ebony* 42, No. 1 (November 1986):164

Richmond, Angus

Call Me Woman. Book review. *Race and Class* 27, No. 4 (Spring 1986):90–92

Richter, Barbara, and Kotze, Sandra (compilers)

A Bibliography of Criticism of Southern African Literature in English. Reviewed by G. E. Gorman. *Research in African Literatures* 17, No. 3 (Fall 1986): 419–421

Ridicule—Psychological Aspects

The Effect of Ridicule on the Academic Performance of Secondary School Students. Muyiwa Igbalajobi. *Negro Educational Review* 37, No. 1 (January 1986):39–45

Riemenschneider, Dieter (editor)

The History and Historiography of Commonwealth Literature. Reviewed by Gareth Griffiths. Book review. *Research in African Literatures* 17, No. 3 (Fall 1986): 433–435

Riley, Joan

The Unbelonging. Book review. Jenny Bourne. *Race and Class* 27, No. 3 (Winter 1986):108–109

Riley, Jocelyn

Crazy Quilt. Book review. Betty Bacon. *Interracial Books for Children Bulletin* 17, No. 1 (1986):6–7

Riley, Norman

Aretha. Record review. *Crisis* 93, No. 10 (December 1986):8–9

Attitudes of the New Black Middle-Class. *Crisis* 93, No. 10 (December 1986):14

A *Crisis* Report on Music. *Crisis* 93, No. 1 (January 1986):17

Dreamgirls: My Life as a Supreme. Book review. *Crisis* 93, No. 10 (December 1986):9

Footnotes of a Culture at Risk. *Crisis* 93, No. 3 (March 1986):23–46

Is Sports the Great Career It's Cracked Up to Be for Blacks? *Crisis* 93, No. 8 (October 1986):30–35

J Mood. Record review. *Crisis* 93, No. 9 (November 1986):9

Khashif. *Crisis* 93, No. 5 (May 1986):10–39

Motown Sound. *Crisis* 93, No. 7 (August/September 1986):9

Nascence. Record review. *Crisis* 93, No. 9 (November 1986):9

The Rolling Stones. *Crisis* 93, No. 6 (June/July 1986):14

Royal Garden Blues. Record review. *Crisis* 93, No. 9 (November 1986):9

Valentino and Calypso. *Crisis* 93, No. 2 (February 1986):14

Vanessa Rubin. *Crisis* 93, No. 8 (October 1986):10–11

The Young Lions. *Crisis* 93, No. 9 (November 1986):8–9

Riots

See Civil Disturbances

Ripley, C. Peter (editor)

The Black Abolitionists Papers. Volume I: The British Isles, 1830–1865. Reviewed by Alexa Benson Henderson. *Phylon* 47, No. 2 (June 1986):168–169

Roberson, Ed

Changes on a Lullaby. Poem. *Callaloo* 9, No. 1 (Winter 1986):118–119

The Letter of the Mathematician's Bride Afraid of War. Poem. *Callaloo* 9, No. 1 (Winter 1986):116–117

Roberts, Cheryl G. (about)

Legacy of Success: A Young Mortician Inherits Her Father's Dream. Janine C. McAdams. *Essence* 17, No. 4 (August 1986):16

Roberts, Richard Samuel (about)

The Photographs of Richard Samuel Roberts. Illustrated. *Callaloo* 9, No. 2 (Spring 1986):385–390

Roberts, Sheila

Nadine Gordimer: Politics and the Order of Art. Book review. *Research in African Literatures* 17, No. 3 (Fall 1986): 408–411

Robeson, Eslanda Goode (about)

Eslanda Goode Robeson, Pan-Africanist. Barbara Ranby. *SAGE* 3, No. 2 (Fall 1986):22–26

Robinson, Cedric J.

The American Press and the Repairing of the Philippines. *Race and Class* 28, No. 2 (August 1986):31–44

Black Marxism: The Making of the Black Radical Tradition. Reviewed by V. P. Franklin. *Phylon* 47, No. 3 (September 1986):250–251

Robinson, Ella

Dust. Poem. *Black Scholar* 17, No. 3 (May-June 1986):56

A Promised Land. Poem. *Black Scholar* 17, No. 3 (May-June 1986):56

She Waits. Poem. *Black Scholar* 17, No. 3 (May-June 1986):56

Through. Poem. *Black Scholar* 17, No. 3 (May-June 1986):55

A Tough Driver. Poem. *Black Scholar* 17, No. 3 (May-June 1986):55

Robinson, H. Carter

Which Job Offer Do I Accept? *Black Collegian* 16, No. 4 (March/April 1986):84–85

Robinson, Hugh (about)

How One Man Is Building the City of the Future. Lloyd Gite. *Black Enterprise* 17, No. 5 (December 1986):68

Robinson, Randall (about)

Randall Robinson: Interview. Frank McCoy. *Crisis* 93, No. 9 (November 1986):20

Robinson, Sharon P. (joint author)

See Futrell, Mary Hatwood

Robinson, T. J. (about)

Fairy Tales Come True. Lloyd Gite. *Black Enterprise* 17, No. 3 (October 1986):24

Robinson, Toya L.

"A" to "Z" of Job Search. *Black Collegian* 16, No. 4 (March/April 1986):82–83

Robinson, William H.

Phillis Wheatley and Her Writings. Reviewed by Paul Edwards. *Research in African Literatures* 17, No. 1 (Spring 1986): 130–133

Robinson, William L., and Spitz, Stephen L.

Affirmative Action: Evolving Case Law and Shifting Philosophy. *Urban League Review* 10, No. 2 (Winter 1986–87):84–100

Robinson Cadillac Pontiac, Inc.

Deals on Wheels. Ann Kimbrough. *Black Enterprise* 16, No. 9 (April 1986):25

Robson, Britt

Own a Piece of the City. *Black Enterprise* 17, No. 3 (October 1986):67

When Private Companies Do Public Work. *Black Enterprise* 16, No. 7 (February 1986):140–144

Rousseau, Jean Jacques—Criticism and Interpretation

Rousseau's Julie; Or, the Maternal Odyssey. Notes. Ruth Ohayon. *CLA Journal* 30, No. 1 (September 1986):69–82

Rowell, Charles H., and Chambers, Kimberly

Studies in Afro-American Literature: An Annual Annotated Bibliography, 1985. *Callaloo* 9, No. 4 (Fall 1986):583–622

Rowley, Margaret N. (joint author)

See Darby, Henry E.

Roy, Joaquin

Spain and the Loss of America. Book review. *Caribbean Review* 15, No. 2 (Spring 1986):48

Royster, Jacqueline Jones

Black Women Missionaries: A Letter from Flora Zeto Malekebu to Lucy Hale Tapley. *SAGE* 3, No. 1 (Spring 1986):58–60

Royster, Philip M.

In Search of Our Fathers' Arms: Alice Walker's Persona of the Alienated Darling. *Black American Literature Forum* 20, No. 4 (Winter 1986):347–370

Rubenstein, Roberta

Doris Lessing. Book review. *Research in African Literatures* 17, No. 3 (Fall 1986): 411–413

Rubin, Ellen (joint author)

See Froschl, Merle

Rubin, Stan Sanvel, and Ingersoll, Earl G. (editors)

A Conversation with Rita Dove. *Black American Literature Forum* 20, No. 3 (Fall 1986):227–240

Rubin, Vanessa (about)

Vanessa Rubin. Norman Riley. *Crisis* 93, No. 8 (October 1986):10–11

Ruck-a-Tuck

The Ruck-a-Tuck International. Illustrated. Wayne Willock. *International Review of African American Art* 7, No. 1 (1986):27

Ruffin, David C.

The *Black Enterprise* Annual Economic Outlook: Walking on an Economic Tightrope. *Black Enterprise* 16, No. 6 (January 1986):50–54

Deadline: Foreign Aid to the Third World. *Black Enterprise* 16, No. 12 (July 1986):19

Do Vouchers Equal Choices for the Poor? *Black Enterprise* 17, No. 2 (September 1986):25

Dumping Health Care for Poor Americans. *Black Enterprise* 16, No. 9 (April 1986):29

Government Agencies Working behind the Scenes. *Black Enterprise* 16, No. 11 (June 1986):269–270

How to Shape Policy through Lobbying. *Black Enterprise* 17, No. 5 (December 1986):33

Judging the Judges. *Black Enterprise* 16, No. 9 (April 1986):19

A Look at Tomorrow's Issues Today. *Black Enterprise* 16, No. 7 (February 1986):35

NBA Protests Treasury's Banking Policy. *Black Enterprise* 17, No. 1 (August 1986):17

New Crop of Congressional Candidates. *Black Enterprise* 16, No. 10 (May 1986):25

Parren Mitchell's Sixteen Years: A Legislative Legacy. *Black Enterprise* 16, No. 11 (June 1986):59–60

Seeking a Big Agenda for Small Business. *Black Enterprise* 17, No. 4 (November 1986):27

Shades of Gray. *Black Enterprise* 16, No. 8 (March 1986):28–33

Whole Wheat. *Black Enterprise* 17, No. 1 (August 1986):48

Ruffin, Frances E.

Yours, Mine and Ours. *Black Enterprise* 16, No. 8 (March 1986):34–36

Runcie, John

Marcus Garvey and the Harlem Renaissance. Notes. *Afro-Americans in New York Life and History* 10, No. 2 (July 1986): 7–28

Rusch, Robert D.

Jazz Talk: The Cadence Interviews. Book review. George L. Starks, Jr. *Black Perspective in Music* 14, No. 2 (Spring 1986):187–188

Russell, Charles (joint author)

See Russell, Mary

Russell, Mary, and Russell, Charles

Vol. 1: The Black Achievers Coloring Book; Vol. 2: The Black Achievers Activity Book. Book review. Emily Leinster. *Interracial Books for Children Bulletin* 17, No. 2 (1986):17

Ryder, Georgia

The Black-American Music Symposium. *Black Perspective in Music* 14, No. 1 (Winter 1986):85–86

Sade (about)

Sade: The Story behind the Exotic Singing Sensation. Walter Leavy. *Ebony* 41, No. 7 (May 1986):155

Sage, Lorna

Doris Lessing. Reviewed by Roberta Rubenstein. *Research in African Literatures* 17, No. 3 (Fall 1986): 411–413

Saghafi, Behrooz (joint author)

See Mannan, Golam

Salamanca, Ricardo Santamaria, and Lujan, Gabriel Silva

Colombia in the Eighties: A Political Regime in Transition. *Caribbean Review* 15, No. 1 (Winter 1986):12–14+

Salazar-Carrillo, Jorge

En defensa de Mexico: pensamiento economico politico. Book review. *Caribbean Review* 15, No. 2 (Spring 1986):46

Is the Cuban Economy Knowable? A National Accounting Parable. *Caribbean Review* 15, No. 2 (Spring 1986):24–25

Sales, Direct

Part-Time Payoff of Direct Sales. Elaine Gregg. *Black Enterprise* 16, No. 10 (May 1986):58

Sales, Gary A.

The Exploitation of the Black Athlete: Some Alternative Solutions. Editorial. *Journal of Negro Education* 55, No.4 (Fall 1986):439–442

Sales Personnel—Salaries, Commission, etc.

The Price Is Right in Sales. Errol T. Louis. *Black Enterprise* 16, No. 7 (February 1986):67–70

Salkey, Andrew

Twenty-Six Years after Sharpeville. Poem. *Black Scholar* 17, No. 4 (July-August 1986):50

Walter Rodney: Poetic Tributes. Book review. Colin Prescod. *Race and Class* 28, No. 2 (August 1986):105–106

Salter, Dan Giles

Partners in Craft. *Essence* 16, No. 11 (March 1986):16

Salter, Dan Giles (joint author)

See Christmas, Rachel J.

Salters, George K. R.

Black Poets and the Children of Black Poets. Poem. *Crisis* 93, No. 2 (February 1986):62

Salvation—Comparative Studies

From Sinners to Saints: The Confessions of Saint Augustine and Malcolm X. Notes. Winston A. Van Horne. *Journal of Religious Thought* 43, No. 1 (Spring-Summer 1986):76–101

Sampson, William A.

Desegregation and Racial Tolerance in Academia. *Journal of Negro Education* 55, No.2 (Spring 1986):171–184

Sanchez, Sonia

Philadelphia: Spring, 1985. Poem. *Callaloo* 9, No. 1 (Winter 1986):120–121

Sandarg, Robert

Jean Genet and the Black Panther Party. *Journal of Black Studies* 16, No. 3 (March 1986):269–282

Sanders, Charles L.

Diabetes: A Dread Disease You Might Have and Not Know It. *Ebony* 41, No. 12 (October 1986):53

Sanders, Cheryl J.

The Woman as Preacher. Notes. *Journal of Religious Thought* 43, No. 1 (Spring-Summer 1986):6–23

Sanders, Hank

Defending Voting Rights in the Alabama Black Belt. Frances M. Beal. *Black Scholar* 17, No. 3 (May-June 1986):34

Sanderson, James H. (joint author)

See Davis, Carlton G.

Sandiford, Keith A.

Paule Marshall's *Praisesong for the Widow*: The Reluctant Heiress, or Whose Life Is It Anyway? *Black American Literature Forum* 20, No. 4 (Winter 1986):371–392

Sandinistas

An Interview with Hugo Spadafora Four Months before His Death. Interview. Beatrix Parga de Bayon. *Caribbean Review* 15, No. 1 (Winter 1986):24–25+

Nicaragua under Siege. Marlene Dixon and Susanne Jonas, editors. Reviewed by John A. Booth. *Caribbean Review* 15, No. 2 (Spring 1986):47

Ritual, Paradox and Death in Managua: Internacionalistas in Nicaragua. Alfred Padula. *Caribbean Review* 15, No. 1 (Winter 1986):18–19

Santmyer, Helen Hoover

...And Ladies of the Club. Reviewed by Robert F. Fleissner. *CLA Journal* 29, No. 4 (June 1986):486–489

Santos, Daniel Garcia

Alex La Guma Revolutionary Intellectual. *Black Scholar* 17, No. 4 (July-August 1986):55–56

Sarfoh, Joseph A.

The West African Zongo and the American Ghetto: Some Comparative Aspects of the Roles of Religious Institutions. *Journal of Black Studies* 17, No. 1 (September 1986):71–84

Satterfield, James A. (about)

Quality Control over Metal. Solomon J. Herbert. *Black Enterprise* 17, No. 5 (December 1986):37

Savage, John

Dyslexia: Understanding Reading Problems. Book review. Emily Strauss Watson. *Interracial Books for Children Bulletin* 17, No. 2 (1986):15–16

SavannahCardinals

Tracey at the Bat. Timothy W. Smith. *Black Enterprise* 17, No. 2 (September 1986):52

Scanlon, Paul A. (editor)

Stories from Central and Southern Africa. Reviewed by Adrian Roscoe. *Research in African Literatures* 17, No. 3 (Fall 1986): 413–416

Schaefer, Richard T.

Racial Prejudice in a Capitalist State: What Happened to the American Creed. *Phylon* 47, No. 3 (September 1986):192–198

Schafer, Jurgen (editor)

Commonwealth Literatur. Reviewed by Willfried F. Feuser. *Research in African Literatures* 17, No. 3 (Fall 1986): 430–433

Scheven, Yvette (compiler)

Bibliographies for African Studies, 1980–1983. Reviewed by Nancy J. Schmidt. *Research in African Literatures* 17, No. 1 (Spring 1986): 145–146

Schipper, Mineke

Littérature et méthodologie. Book review. *Research in African Literatures* 17, No. 4 (Winter 1986): 566–567

Theater and Society in Africa. Reviewed by Olu Obafemi. *Research in African Literatures* 17, No. 2 (Summer 1986): 271–272

Unheard Words: Women and Literature in Africa, the Arab World, Asia, the Caribbean and Latin America. Margaret Marshment. *Race and Class* 28, No. 1 (Summer 1986):97–99

Schmidt, Nancy J.

African Literature on Film: A Preliminary Bibliography/Filmography. Notes. *Research in African Literatures* 17, No. 2 (Summer 1986): 261–266

Bibliographies for African Studies, 1980–1983. Book review. *Research in African Literatures* 17, No. 1 (Spring 1986): 145–146

Conference on the Acquisition and Bibliography of Commonwealth and Third World Literatures in English. Book review. *Research in African Literatures* 17, No. 3 (Fall 1986): 439–440

Literature for Children and Young People in Kenya. Book review. *Research in African Literatures* 17, No. 4 (Winter 1986): 609–610

Schneider, Gail

A Beginning Investigation into the Afro-American Cemeteries of Ulster County, New York. *Afro-Americans in New York Life and History* 10, No.1 (January 1986):61–70

Schocket, Sandra

Winter Hunt for a Summer Job. *Black Collegian* 17, No. 2 (November/December 1986):67–71

Scholarships

Scholarship Central: Computerized Search Firms Can Track Down Private College Dollars. Constance García-Barrio. *Essence* 17, No. 4 (August 1986):13

Schousboe, Ingvar, and Smith, William Jay (translators)

The Pact: My Friendship with Isak Dinesen. By Thorkild Bjornvig. Reviewed by Casey Bjerregaard Black. *Research in African Literatures* 17, No. 1 (Spring 1986): 155–158

Schreiner, Olive (about)

The Re-interment on Buffelskop. Guy Butler, editor. Reviewed by Cherry Clayton. *Research in African Literatures* 17, No. 3 (Fall 1986): 404–406

Schroth, Evelyn

Nadine Gordimer's "A Chip of Glass Ruby": A Commentary on Apartheid Society. *Journal of Black Studies* 17, No. 1 (September 1986):85–90

Schwartz, Albert V.

Anti-Semitism: A Modern Perspective. Book review. *Interracial Books for Children Bulletin* 17, No. 2 (1986):18–19

Rocky IV—Mindless Jingoism. Film review. *Interracial Books for Children Bulletin* 17, No. 1 (1986):11

Rose Blanche. Book review. *Interracial Books for Children Bulletin* 17, No. 2 (1986):14

Schwartz, Joel

The Consolidated Tenants League of Harlem: Black Self-Help vs. White, Liberal Intervention in Ghetto Housing, 1934–1944. *Afro-Americans in New York Life and History* 10, No.1 (January 1986):31–51

Science—Dissertations and Theses

Master's Theses in Progress in Selected Colleges and Universities. Mac A. Stewart. *Negro Educational Review* 37, Nos. 3–4 (July-October 1986):103–106, 115–117

Science Fiction

Black Women and the Science Fiction Genre. Octavia Butler. *Black Scholar* 17, No. 2 (March-April 1986):14–18

Scott, Carol R.

Catch a Rising Star: Savvy Rhode Island Talent Agent Polishes Up New Acts. *Essence* 17, No. 2 (June 1986):18

Scott, Joseph W.

From Teenage Parenthood to Polygamy: Case Studies in Black Polygamous Family Formation. *Western Journal of Black Studies* 10, No. 4 (Winter 1986):172–179

Scott, Michael (joint author)

See Benjamin, Medea

Scott, Patricia

The Afro-American in Books for Children. Book review. *Black Scholar* 17, No. 5 (September-October 1986):59

Scott, Rebecca J.

Slave Emancipation in Cuba. The Transition to Free Labor, 1866–1899. Reviewed by David Kyle. *Caribbean Review* 15, No. 2 (Spring 1986):47

Scott, Theodore and Cornelius (about)

Twins in the Ministry: Three Sets from Atlanta. *Ebony* 41, No. 4 (February 1986):99

Scraton, Phil, and Gordon, Paul

Causes for Concern: British Criminal Justice on Trial? Book review. Busi Chaane. *Race and Class* 28, No. 1 (Summer 1986):103–107

Scruggs, Charles

The Sage in Harlem: H. L. Mencken and the Black Writers of the 1920s. Book review. John Edgar Tidwell. *Black American Literature Forum* 20, No. 3 (Fall 1986):341–344

Sculptors

Elizabeth Catlett. Illustrated. Mary Jane Hewitt. *International Review of African American Art* 7, No. 2 (1986):26–33

George Smith. Illustrated. Samella Lewis. *International Review of African American Art* 7, No. 2 (1986):6–15

Interviews with Five Bajan Artists. Illustrated. *International Review of African American Art* 7, No. 1 (1986):45–55

Maren Hassinger. Illustrated. Watson Hines. *International Review of African American Art* 7, No. 2 (1986):60–63

Masayuke Oda. Illustrated. Robert Biddle. *International Review of African American Art* 7, No. 2 (1986):52–59

Mel Edwards. Illustrated. Watson Hines. *International Review of African American Art* 7, No. 2 (1986):34–51

Richard Hunt. Illustrated. Samella Lewis. *International Review of African American Art* 7, No. 2 (1986):16–21

Seale, Doris

The Ceremony of Innocence. Book review. *Interracial Books for Children Bulletin* 17, No. 1 (1986):6

Song of the Seven Herbs. Book review. *Interracial Books for Children Bulletin* 17, No. 1 (1986):9

Who Speaks for Wolf. Book review. *Interracial Books for Children Bulletin* 17, Nos. 3–4 (1986):36

Searle, Chris

Cuba's Nicolás Guillén: Poetry and Ideology. Book review. *Race and Class* 28, No. 1 (Summer 1986):107–108

Spanning Two Languages: The Legacy of Isaac and Joseph. *Race and Class* 28, No. 1 (Summer 1986):29–42

Seay, Keith A. (about)

Savings and Loan of the Year: The Rebirth of Berkley Savings. Gordon Borell. *Black Enterprise* 16, No. 11 (June 1986):166

Sebestyen, Ouida

On Fire. Book review. Rudine Sims. *Interracial Books for Children Bulletin* 17, Nos. 3–4 (1986):34–35

Seck, Essie Tramel

The Impact of Unemployment on the Social Well-Being of the Black Family. *Urban League Review* 10, No. 1 (Summer 1986):87–97

Segregation

The Influence of Race on Rezoning Decisions: Equality of Treatment in Black and White Census Tracts, 1955–1980. Dudley S. Hinds and Nicholas Ordway. *Review of Black Political Economy* 14, No. 4 (Spring 1986):51–63

Segregation in Education

The Education of Black Children and Youths: A Framework for Excellence. By Samuel L. Banks. Reviewed by Sandra Noel Smith. *Journal of Negro Education* 55, No.4 (Fall 1986):551–552

Segregation in Higher Education

See Universities and Colleges—Desegregation

Seldon, David

The Teacher Rebellion. Book review. Kenneth Jennings. *Negro Educational Review* 37, Nos. 3–4 (July-October 1986):154–155

Self-Awareness

Armageddon Is Now. Jill Nelson. *Essence* 17, No. 2 (July 1986):80

Self-Care, Health

Are You Blue? How to Beat Depression. Stephanie Renfrow Hamilton. *Essence* 17, No. 6 (October 1986):66

Ensuring Our Health. Frances A. McMorris. *Essence* 17, No. 5 (September 1986):13

How to Deal with Ten Serious Health Problems. Alex Poinsett. *Ebony* 41, No. 5 (March 1986):144

Self-Control

How to Kick Your Bad Habits. Frank White III. *Ebony* 41, No. 11 (September 1986):86

Self-Employment

Characteristics of Minorities Who Are Entering Self-Employment. Timothy Bates. *Review of Black Political Economy* 15, No. 2 (Fall 1986):31–49

Self-Realization

How to Get Out of That Rut and Make Life an Adventure. Elaine C. Ray. *Essence* 16, No. 11 (March 1986):61

Sellin, Eric

Bibliographie méthodique et critique de la littérature algérienne de langue française, 1945–1977. Book review. *Research in African Literatures* 17, No. 4 (Winter 1986): 581

Seltzer, Rick, and Lopes, Grace M.

The Ku Klux Klan: Reasons for Support or Opposition among White Respondents. *Journal of Black Studies* 17, No. 1 (September 1986):91–109

Semmes, Clovis E.

The Sociological Tradition of E. Franklin Frazier: Implications for Black Studies. *Journal of Negro Education* 55, No.4 (Fall 1986):484–494

Senegal—Description and Travel

Dakar, Senegal: A City of Many Moods—from Blue to Indigo. Shelley Moore. *Black Enterprise* 16, No. 9 (April 1986):67–68

Senegal—Literature

Senegalese Literature: A Critical History. By Dorothy Blair. Reviewed by Mbye B. Cham. *Research in African Literatures* 17, No. 4 (Winter 1986): 567–569

Sensibar, Judith L.

The Origin of Faulkner's Art. Reviewed by Elizabeth J. Higgins. *CLA Journal* 29, No. 4 (June 1986):490–492

Sermons

Horace Bushnell: Sermons. Edited by Conrad Cherry. Reviewed by Kortright Davis. *Journal of Religious Thought* 43, No. 2 (Fall-Winter 1986–87):91–92

Those Preachin' Women: Sermons by Black Women Preachers. Edited by Ella Pearson Mitchell. Reviewed by Gayl Fowler. *Journal of Religious Thought* 43, No. 1 (Spring-Summer 1986):129–130

The Woman as Preacher. Cheryl J. Sanders. Notes. *Journal of Religious Thought* 43, No. 1 (Spring-Summer 1986):6–23

Serrano, Sandra

An Exhibition for National Peace. *Caribbean Review* 15, No. 1 (Winter 1986):33

Searching for Pretto: Politics and Art in Panama. *Caribbean Review* 15, No. 1 (Winter 1986):29–32+

Serwatka, Thomas, and others

Black Students in Special Education: Issues and Implications for Community Involvement. *Negro Educational Review* 37, No. 1 (January 1986):17–26

Set-Off and Counterclaim

A Tenant's Right to Counterclaim for a Period Predating Landlord's Claim. Angela J. Moffitt. *Howard Law Journal* 29, No. 1 (1986):41–61

Settlement Houses

See Social Settlements

Sex Discrimination

The Color of Feminism: Or Speaking the Black Woman's Tongue. Notes. Delores S. Williams. *Journal of Religious Thought* 43, No. 1 (Spring-Summer 1986):42–58

Sexism in Literature

Ideologies of Race and Sex in Literature: Racism and Antiracism in the African Francophone Novel. Notes. E. P. Abanime. *CLA Journal* 30, No. 2 (December 1986):125–143

Sex and Literature

"My Love is Black as Yours is Fair":Premarital Love and Sexuality in the Antebellum Slave Narrative. *Phylon* 47, No. 3 (September 1986):238–247

Sex Roles

The Black Male in Jeopardy. Kenneth M. Jones. *Crisis* 93, No. 3 (March 1986):17–44

The Black Man in Cuban Society: From Colonial Times to the Revolution. *Journal of Black Studies* 16, No. 3 (March 1986):251–267

Conceptual and Logical Issues in Theory and Research Related to Black Masculinity. Clyde W. Franklin II. *Western Journal of Black Studies* 10, No. 4 (Winter 1986):161–166

A Conflict of Reasons and Remedies. David Hatchett. *Crisis* 93, No. 3 (March 1986):36–47

The Destruction of the Young Black Male: The Impact of Popular Culture and Organized Sports. John C. Gaston. *Journal of Black Studies* 16, No. 4 (June 1986):369–384

Dr. Nathan Hare. Gregory Pete. *Crisis* 93, No. 3 (March 1986):30–46

The Necessary Bitch. Judy Simmons. *Essence* 17, No. 5 (September 1986):73

See also Love

Sex Roles in Marriage

Racial and Gender Perceptions of Marriage Role at a Predominantly Black University. Odell Uzzell. *Western Journal of Black Studies* 10, No. 4 (Winter 1986):167–171

Sex Roles—Stereotypes

Myth of the Black Male Shortage. Ronald E. Hall. *Black Collegian* 17, No. 2 (November/December 1986):16–18

Sexual Behavior

Games Lovers Play. Bebe Moore Campbell. *Essence* 17, No. 2 (July 1986):60

Tensions between Black Men and Women. Lynn Norment. *Ebony* 41, No. 10 (August 1986):153

What Do Men Want in Bed? Ron Harris. *Essence* 17, No. 7 (November 1986):59

Sexual Disorders

Your Man's Sexual Health. Reginald D. Ware. *Essence* 17, No. 7 (November 1986):16

Shackford, Kate

All But the Right Folks. Book review. *Interracial Books for Children Bulletin* 17, No. 2 (1986):14–15

Shade, Barbara J.

Is There an Afro-American Cognitive Style? *Journal of Black Psychology* 13, No. 1 (August 1986):13–16

Shaik, Fatima

Queen of Arts. *Essence* 17, No. 2 (July 1986):15

Shakespeare, William (about)

Shakespeare in Ethiopia. Notes. Richard Pankhurst. *Research in African Literatures* 17, No. 2 (Summer 1986): 169–196

Shakespeare in Sable: A History of Black Shakespearean Actors. By Errol Hill. Reviewed by Ruth Cowhig. *Research in African Literatures* 17, No. 2 (Summer 1986): 284–287

Shange, Ntozake

A Daughter's Geography. Reviewed by Beth Brown. *CLA Journal* 29, No. 3 (March 1986):378–380

Shanker, Albert

The Making of a Profession. *Journal of Negro Education* 55, No.3 (Summer 1986):405–421

Shannon, Magdaline (translator)

See Price-Mars, Jean

Shapiro, Nat, and Pollack, Bruce (editors)

Popular Music, 1920–1979; A Revised Cumulation. Book review. Doris E. McGinty. *Black Perspective in Music* 14, No. 3 (Fall 1986):311–312

Shariff, Ibrahim Noor (joint author)

See Feidel, Jan

Sharma, Sarla

Assessment Strategies for Minority Groups. *Journal of Black Studies* 17, No. 1 (September 1986):111–124

Shattuck, J. D.

Making It Happen in Corporate America: Mobil and the Council on Career Development for Minorities, Inc. Work Together. *Black Collegian* 16, No. 4 (March/April 1986):86–87

Sheen and Shine, Inc.

Providing a Healthier Workplace: Sheen and Shine, Inc. Marsha Jones. *About Time* 14, No. 8 (August 1986):28–29

Sheffey, Ruthe T.

In Memoriam: A Tribute to Professor Robert A. Smith. *CLA Journal* 29, No. 4 (June 1986):483–485

Shelley, Percy Bysshe—Criticism and Interpretation

Hawthorne's Beatrice Rappaccini: Unlocking her Paradoxical Nature with a Shelleyean Key. Notes. Martin F. Kearney. *CLA Journal* 29, No. 3 (March 1986):309–317

Queen Mab and *An Essay on Man*: Scientific Prophecy versus Theodicy. Notes. Dennis M. Welch. *CLA Journal* 29, No. 4 (June 1986):462–482

Sheriffs—Georgia

Georgia's Reverend Sheriff: Richard Lankford Finds Joy in Preaching the Gospel and Keeping the Peace. Marilyn Marshall. *Ebony* 41, No. 5 (March 1986):92

Sherlock, Angela

Ayahs, Lascars and Princes: Indians in Britain 1700–1947. Book review. *Race and Class* 28, No. 2 (August 1986):106–107

Shervington, Sharon

Illiterate America. Book review. *Black Enterprise* 17, No. 2 (September 1986):15

Memos That Do the Job. *Black Enterprise* 16, No. 11 (June 1986):278

Two Business Achievers Die. *Black Enterprise* 17, No. 2 (September 1986):20

Shipping Industry

Guestworkers of the Sea: Racism in British Shipping. Paul Gordon and Danny Reilly. *Race and Class* 28, No. 2 (August 1986):73–82

Shiver, Jube

Child's Play. *Black Enterprise* 17, No. 1 (August 1986):30

Simpson, Janice C.

Loving a Troubled Man. *Essence* 17, No. 6 (October 1986):75

Simpson-Kirkland, Delores (joint author)

See Smith, James H.

Sims, Anita Johnson

The Best "Deal" in Town: Bob Johnson Chevrolet. *About Time* 14, No. 8 (August 1986):24–26

Making Parenting a Priority. *About Time* 14, No. 11 (November 1986):10–13

The Professional in Management: Cleve L. Killingsworth. *About Time* 14, No. 12 (December 1986):11–12

WXXI-TV, Channel 21: Serving a Public and Educational Programming Mission. *About Time* 14, No. 9 (September 1986):12–13

Sims, Rudine

On Fire. Book review. *Interracial Books for Children Bulletin* 17, Nos. 3–4 (1986):34–35

Sims-Wood, Janet

Black Women as Workers: A Selected Listing of Master's Theses and Doctoral Dissertations. *SAGE* 3, No. 1 (Spring 1986):64–66

Singers

Anita Baker: Soul's New Romantic Singer. Lynn Norment. *Ebony* 42, No. 2 (December 1986):52

Black Divas. Rosalyn Story. *Essence* 17, No. 2 (June 1986):36

Black Music Critics and the Classic Blues Singers. Phillip McGuire. *Black Perspective in Music* 14, No. 2 (Spring 1986):103–125

DO-BE-DO-WOW! Jazz's Grand Divas. Alexis De Veaux. *Essence* 17, No. 6 (October 1986):54

Doug E. Fresh: "The Show" Must Go On. Charles E. Rogers. *Black Collegian* 16, No. 4 (March/April 1986):42–46

Janet: Hit Album Takes Another Jackson to the Top. Aldore Collier. *Ebony* 41, No. 11 (September 1986):29

Melba Moore. Charles E. Rogers. *Black Collegian* 17, No. 2 (November/December 1986):45–47

Nona Hendryx Turns on "the Heat." Charles E. Rogers. *Black Collegian* 16, No. 3 (January/February 1986):59–62

The Other Patti LaBelle: Wife, Mother and World Class Cook. Laura B. Randolph. *Ebony* 41, No. 6 (April 1986):31

Sade: The Story behind the Exotic Singing Sensation. Walter Leavy. *Ebony* 41, No. 7 (May 1986):155

Sallie Martin: At 90, the "Mother of Gospel" Is Being Hailed from Coast to Coast. *Ebony* 41, No. 5 (March 1986):76

Tina Turner: The Shocking Story of a Battered Wife Who Escaped to Fame and Fortune. *Ebony* 42, No. 1 (November 1986):31

Vanessa Rubin. Norman Riley. *Crisis* 93, No. 8 (October 1986):10–11

Where the Money Goes. Steven Ivory. *Crisis* 93, No. 5 (May 1986):28–33

Whitney Houston: The Joys and Dangers of Sudden Success. Lynn Norment. *Ebony* 41, No. 9 (July 1986):126

The Young Lions. Norman Riley. *Crisis* 93, No. 9 (November 1986):8–9

Singing Groups

The Fat Boys Enjoy a Banquet of Rap and Roles. Eric Copage. *Essence* 17, No. 2 (July 1986):34

Kool and the Gang: Hottest Group of the '80s. Lynn Norment. *Ebony* 42, No. 1 (November 1986):70

New Edition: Teen Idols of the Music World Wow Fans with Soulful Young Sound and Fancy Steps. Aldore Collier. *Ebony* 41, No. 8 (June 1986):58

Perri's Smoldering Harmony Ignites Jazz Chart. Gerrie Summers. *Essence* 17, No. 5 (September 1986):29

The Real Story behind the Real Dreamgirls: Mary Wilson Tells of the Triumphs and Tribulations of the Famed Supremes. *Ebony* 41, No. 12 (October 1986):44

Single Men

How Black Women Can Deal with the Black Male Shortage. *Ebony* 41, No. 7 (May 1986):29

Single-Parent Families

The Black Female Single-Parent Family Condition. Eleanor J. Smith and Paul M. Smith, Jr. *Journal of Black Studies* 17, No. 1 (September 1986):125–134

Changes in Family Structures. Marsha Jones. *About Time* 14, No. 3 (March 1986):14–18

Parents of Special Commitment: Single Mothers, Single Fathers and Relatives Face a Unique Challenge. Frank White III. *Ebony* 41, No. 10 (August 1986):88

Singleton, Edward G., and others

Racial Differentials in the Impact of Maternal Cigarette Smoking during Pregnancy on Fetal Development and Mortality: Concerns for Black Psychologists. *Journal of Black Psychology* 12, No. 2 (February 1986):71–83

Sisterhood in Support of Sisters in South Africa (SISA)

"In Memory of Our Children's Blood": Sisterhood and South African Women. Gloria I. Joseph and Audre Lorde. *SAGE* 3, No. 2 (Fall 1986):40–43

Siu—Folktales

Expressing a Swahili Sense of Humor: Siu Jokes. Notes. References. Carol M. Eastman. *Research in African Literatures* 17, No. 4 (Winter 1986): 474–495

Sivanandan, A.

Britain's Gulags. *Race and Class* 27, No. 3 (Winter 1986):81–85

The Struggle for Black Arts in Britain. *Race and Class* 28, No. 1 (Summer 1986):76–79

Skaters

Debi Thomas: The Nation's No. 1 Skating Sensation. Lynn Norment. *Ebony* 41, No. 7 (May 1986):147

Debi Thomas—World Figure Skating Champion. Tricia Duncan-Hall. *Black Collegian* 17, No. 1 (September/October 1986):49–52

Of Scholarship and Ice: Debi Thomas. Adolph Dupree. *About Time* 14, No. 4 (April 1986):14

With Style and Grace. Bryan Burwell. *Black Enterprise* 16, No. 11 (June 1986):52

Skiers

Bonnie St. John: A Profile in Beauty, Brains, and Courage. Aldore Collier. *Ebony* 42, No. 1 (November 1986):134

Where There's a Will: Bonnie's Story. Bill Rhoden. *Essence* 17, No. 1 (May 1986):82

Slavery

Free Coloreds in the Slave Societies of St. Kitts and Grenada, 1763–1833. By Edward L. Cox. Reviewed by Keith C. Simmonds. *Phylon* 47, No. 4 (December 1986):327–328

Goree. Shelley Moore. *Crisis* 93, No. 6 (June/July 1986):18

Slavery in the French Caribbean, 1625–1715: A Marxist Analysis. Clarence J. Munford. *Journal of Black Studies* 17, No. 1 (September 1986):49–69

Slavery—Africa

Slavery in Dutch South Africa. By Nigel Worden. Reviewed by Ken Jordaan. *Race and Class* 27, No. 3 (Winter 1986):104–105

Women and Slavery in the African Diaspora: A Cross-Cultural Approach to Historical Analysis. Rosalyn Terborg-Penn. *SAGE* 3, No. 2 (Fall 1986):11–15

Slavery—Anti-Slavery Movements

The Black Abolitionists Papers. Volume I: The British Isles, 1830–1865. C. Peter Ripley, editor. Reviewed by Alexa Benson Henderson. *Phylon* 47, No. 2 (June 1986):168–169

Slavery in the Courtroom: An Annotated Bibliography of American Cases. By Paul Finkelman. Reviewed by Mary Frances Berry. *Afro-Americans in New York Life and History* 10, No. 2 (July 1986): 65

Slavery—Emancipation

Slave Emancipation in Cuba. The Transition to Free Labor, 1866–1899. By Rebecca J. Scott. Reviewed by David Kyle. *Caribbean Review* 15, No. 2 (Spring 1986):47

Slavery—Narratives

"My Love is Black as Yours is Fair":Premarital Love and Sexuality in the Antebellum Slave Narrative. *Phylon* 47, No. 3 (September 1986):238–247

Slave Populations of the British Caribbean 1807–1834. By B. W. Higman. Reviewed by Bonham C. Richardson. *Caribbean Review* 15, No. 2 (Spring 1986):46

The Slave's Narrative. Edited by Charles T. Davis and Henry Louis Gates. Reviewed by William L. Andrews. *Black American Literature Forum* 20, Nos. 1–2 (Spring/Summer 1986):203–207

Sleet, Moneta (Jr.) (about)

Moneta Sleet, Jr.: Pulitzer Prize Photojournalist. Marsha Jones. *About Time* 14, No. 10 (October 1986):12–13

Slim-Safe Bahamian Diet

Diet Right! Bahamian Style. Janine C. McAdams. *Essence* 17, No. 4 (August 1986):124

Smikle, Ken

Brokers Go for Growth. *Black Enterprise* 16, No. 10 (May 1986):18

Bruce: The Boss. *Black Enterprise* 17, No. 2 (September 1986):36

Cashing in on Coke. *Black Enterprise* 16, No. 8 (March 1986):13

Child Care by Cassette. *Black Enterprise* 16, No. 8 (March 1986):16

Golden Nuggets. *Black Enterprise* 17, No. 3 (October 1986):26

Industry Overview: Magazine Monarchs. *Black Enterprise* 16, No. 11 (June 1986):212

Inside Hollywood. *Black Enterprise* 17, No. 5 (December 1986):48

Marketing Colleges. *Black Enterprise* 17, No. 4 (November 1986):24

A Musical Entrepreneur. *Black Enterprise* 16, No. 7 (February 1986):30

PUSH Eyes CBS Stations. *Black Enterprise* 16, No. 11 (June 1986):47

In Support of Black Media. *Black Enterprise* 17, No. 5 (December 1986):25

Smikle, Ken, and Ilaw, Marianne

Longing for Longevity. *Black Enterprise* 17, No. 4 (November 1986):52

Smith, Earl

Race, Reform and Rebellion: The Second Reconstruction in Black America. Book review. *Phylon* 47, No. 1 (March 1986):101–103

A Social History of 20th Century Urban Riots. Book review. *Phylon* 47, No. 1 (March 1986):101–103

Smith, E. D.

Barbados: From Sea to Shining...Ocean. *Black Enterprise* 16, No. 10 (May 1986):84

Jamaica: Homespun Charm, Quiet Elegance and Joyful Sounds. *Black Enterprise* 16, No. 10 (May 1986):76

The New Entrepreneur: Catering Magician. *Black Enterprise* 16, No. 11 (June 1986):301

St. Kitts and Nevis: The Life of the Landed Gentry. *Black Enterprise* 16, No. 10 (May 1986):74

Smith, Eleanor

When and Where I Enter: The Impact of Black Women on Race and Sex in America. Book review. *Western Journal of Black Studies* 10, No. 1 (Spring 1986):45–46

Smith, Eleanor J., and Smith, Paul M. (Jr.)

The Black Female Single-Parent Family Condition. *Journal of Black Studies* 17, No. 1 (September 1986):125–134

Smith, Gary

A Hamlet Rives Us: The Sonnets of Melvin B. Tolson. Notes. *CLA Journal* 29, No. 3 (March 1986):261–275

Songs for My Fathers. Book review. Gerald Barrax. *Callaloo* 9, No. 1 (Winter 1986):255–259

Smith, George (about)

George Smith. Illustrated. Samella Lewis. *International Review of African American Art* 7, No. 2 (1986):6–15

Smith, Hazel (joint author)

See Rooper, Alison

Smith, James H., and others

The Five Most Important Problems Confronting Black Students Today. *Negro Educational Review* 37, No. 2 (April 1986):52–61

Smith, Malvern van Wyk, and Maclennan, Don (editors)

Olive Schreiner and After: Essays on Southern African Literature in Honor of Guy Butler. Reviewed by Dennis Walder. *Research in African Literatures* 17, No. 3 (Fall 1986): 401–404

Smith, Paul M. (Jr.) (joint author)

See Smith, Eleanor J.

Smith, Robert P. (Jr.)

Rereading *Banjo*: Claude McKay and the French Connection. Notes. *CLA Journal* 30, No. 1 (September 1986):46–58

Smith, Robert P. (Jr.) (joint author)

See Hudson, Robert J.

Smith, Sandra Noel

The Education of Black Children and Youths: A Framework for Excellence. Book review. *Journal of Negro Education* 55, No.4 (Fall 1986):551–552

Smith, Sid

10 Super Sunday Schools in the Black Community. Reviewed by Gayl Fowler. *Journal of Religious Thought* 43, No. 2 (Fall-Winter 1986–87):93

Smith, S. Morgan (about)

Additional Light on S. Morgan Smith. William Norris. *Black American Literature Forum* 20, Nos. 1–2 (Spring/Summer 1986):75–79

Smith, Timothy W.

Tracey at the Bat. *Black Enterprise* 17, No. 2 (September 1986):52

Smith, Vernon

Cream of Vegetables. *Black Enterprise* 17, No. 2 (September 1986):18

Smith, Wayman F. (III) (about)

Corporate Profile: Success among the Suds. Joyce Davis Adams. *Black Enterprise* 16, No. 11 (June 1986):242

Smith, William Jay (joint translator)

See Schousboe, Ingvar

Smith, Willy Demarcell and Beasley, Robert R.

In Pursuit of Full Employment. Editorial. *Urban League Review* 10, No. 1 (Summer 1986):3–4

Smoking

Racial Differentials in the Impact of Maternal Cigarette Smoking during Pregnancy on Fetal Development and Mortality: Concerns for Black Psychologists. Edward G. Singleton and others. *Journal of Black Psychology* 12, No. 2 (February 1986):71–83

Snorgrass, J. William

The Black Press and Political Alliances: The Turning Point, 1928. *Western Journal of Black Studies* 10, No. 3 (Fall 1986):103–108

Social Action

Grass Roots Activists and Social Change: The Story of Ivory Perry. George Lipsitz. *CAAS Newsletter* 9, No. 2 (1986):1

How to Make Your Power Felt. *Ebony* 41, No. 4 (February 1986):87

Martin Luther King (Jr.) and the Paradox of Nonviolent Direct Action. James A. Colaiaco. *Phylon* 47, No. 1 (March 1986):16–28

Martin Luther King (Jr.) and the Quest for Nonviolent Social Change. Adam Fairclough. *Phylon* 47, No. 1 (March 1986):1–15

Part of a Whole: The Independence of the Civil Rights Movement and Other Social Movements. Judith Rollins. *Phylon* 47, No. 1 (March 1986):61–70

Public Policy and Social Change. Georgia A. Persons. *Urban League Review* 10, No. 2 (Winter 1986–87):6–11

See also Industry—Social Aspects

Social Classes

A Black Elite. By Daniel C. Thompson. Reviewed by C. J. Wiltz. *Phylon* 47, No. 4 (December 1986):328–329

The Black Middle Class in America. Thomas J. Durant (Jr.) and Joyce S. Louden. *Phylon* 47, No. 4 (December 1986):253–263

The Black Underclass: Theory and Reality. Creigs C. Beverly and Howard J. Stanback. *Black Scholar* 17, No. 5 (September-October 1986):24–32

From Working Class to Middle Class: Ideology and Socialization. Luke Tripp. *Negro Educational Review* 37, Nos. 3–4 (July-October 1986):144–153

A Review of Urban Life in Kingston, Jamaica. By Diane J. Austin. Reviewed by Bernard D. Headley. *Caribbean Review* 15, No. 1 (Winter 1986):42

Social Classes in Literature

Class vs. Sex: The Problem of Values in the Modern Nigerian Novel. Rhonda Cobham-Sander. *Black Scholar* 17, No. 4 (July-August 1986):17–27

Social Darwinism

Neo-Conservatives as Social Darwinists: Implications for Higher Education. Peter Sola, Joseph DeVitis, and John R. Danley. *Journal of Negro Education* 55, No. 1 (Winter 1986):3–20

Social Ethics

Buppies. Kenneth M. Jones. *Crisis* 93, No. 4 (April 1986):16–24

Social Ethics and the Black Family. Maulana Karenga. *Black Scholar* 17, No. 5 (September-October 1986):41–54

Social Mobility

A Longitudinal Analysis of Variations in Mobility Goals across Race-Sex Groups. Marvin P. Dawkins. *Western Journal of Black Studies* 10, No. 1 (Spring 1986):34–43

Social Policy

A Brief Prescription for a Proactive Socioeconomic Agenda. Douglas G. Glasgow. *Urban League Review* 10, No. 2 (Winter 1986–87):3–5

Health Policy and the Black Aged. Nelson McGhee, Jr., and others. *Urban League Review* 10, No. 2 (Winter 1986–87):63–71

Public Policy and Social Change. Georgia A. Persons. *Urban League Review* 10, No. 2 (Winter 1986–87):6–11

Voting Rights, Government Responsibility, and Conservative Ideology. Alex Willingham. *Urban League Review* 10, No. 2 (Winter 1986–87):12–23

See also Economic Policy

Social Responsibility

From Working Class to Middle Class: Ideology and Socialization. Luke Tripp. *Negro Educational Review* 37, Nos. 3–4 (July-October 1986):144–153

Which Way Black America? Arthur Flowers. *Essence* 17, No. 8 (December 1986):54

Social Sciences—Dissertations and Theses

Master's Theses in Progress in Selected Colleges and Universities. Mac A. Stewart. *Negro Educational Review* 37, Nos. 3–4 (July-October 1986):101, 109–112

Social Settlements

Phyllis Wheatley House: A History of the Minneapolis Black Settlement House, 1924 to 1940. Howard Jacob Karger. *Phylon* 47, No. 1 (March 1986):79–90

Social Status

Racial Definition: Background for Divergence. William Javier Nelson. *Phylon* 47, No. 4 (December 1986):318–326

Sitting Location as an Indicator of Status of Older Blacks in the Church: A Comparative Analysis of Protestants and Catholics in the Rural South. Appendix. Wilbur H. Watson. *Phylon* 47, No. 4 (December 1986):264–275

Sociobiology

Less Than Human Nature: Biology and the New Right. Steven Rose and Hilary Rose. *Race and Class* 27, No. 3 (Winter 1986):47–66

Sociologists

The Sociological Tradition of E. Franklin Frazier: Implications for Black Studies. Clovis E. Semmes. *Journal of Negro Education* 55, No.4 (Fall 1986):484–494

Sociology—Africa

The Truthful Lie: Essays in a Sociology of African Drama. By Biodun Jeyifo. Reviewed by Elaine Savory Fido. *Research in African Literatures* 17, No. 2 (Summer 1986): 273–275

Sociology—Study and Teaching

Black American Doctorates in Sociology: A Follow-up Study of their Social and Educational Origins. James E. Conyers. *Phylon* 47, No. 4 (December 1986):303–317

Sojo, Ana

Estado empresario y lucha politica en Costa Rica. Reviewed by Francisco A. Leguizamon. *Caribbean Review* 15, No. 2 (Spring 1986):45–46

Sokoloff, Janice M.

Intimations of Matriarchal Age: Notes on the Mythical Eva in Toni Morrison's *Sula*. *Journal of Black Studies* 16, No. 4 (June 1986):429–434

Sola, Peter Andre, and others

Neo-Conservatives as Social Darwinists: Implications for Higher Education. *Journal of Negro Education* 55, No. 1 (Winter 1986):3–20

Sola, Peter Andre (ed.)

Ethics, Education and Administrative Decisions: A Book of Readings. Reviewed by Joseph L. DeVitis. *Journal of Negro Education* 55, No.4 (Fall 1986):549–550

Sollors, Werner

Beyond Ethnicity: Consent and Descent in American Culture. Book review. Anthony Appiah. *Black American Literature Forum* 20, Nos. 1–2 (Spring/Summer 1986):209–224

Solomon, Barbara Miller

In the Company of Educated Women: A History of Women and Higher Education in America. Book review. *Journal of Negro Education* 55, No. 1 (Winter 1986):116–117

Solomon, Denzil K. (about)

Flying High on Medical Tech. Marvin E. Perry. *Black Enterprise* 17, No. 1 (August 1986):19

Sol Plaatje (about)

Sol Plaatje: South African Nationalist, 1876–1932. By Brian Willan. Reviewed by N. Chabani Manganyi. *Research in African Literatures* 17, No. 3 (Fall 1986):393–395

Solumatics

Tracking Films by Computer. Elaine Wapples. *Black Enterprise* 17, No. 2 (September 1986):27

South Africa—Economic Conditions

Legal Comments: South African Economic Conditions. Grover G. Hankins. *Crisis* 93, No. 9 (November 1986):46–48

South Africa—Education

Black Students' Perceptions of Factors Related to Academic Performance in a Rural Area of Natal Province, South Africa. Alan Simon. *Journal of Negro Education* 55, No.4 (Fall 1986):535–547

South Africa—History

Colonialism and the Novels of S. M. Coetzee. Notes. Stephen Watson. *Research in African Literatures* 17, No. 3 (Fall 1986): 370–392

The Origins of Forced Labor in the Witwatersrand. Moitsadi Moeti. *Phylon* 47, No. 4 (December 1986):276–284

Slavery in Dutch South Africa. By Nigel Worden. Reviewed by Ken Jordaan. *Race and Class* 27, No. 3 (Winter 1986):104–105

Sol Plaatje: South African Nationalist, 1876–1932. By Brian Willan. Reviewed by N. Chabani Manganyi. *Research in African Literatures* 17, No. 3 (Fall 1986): 393–395

The United States and South Africa: History, Civil Rights and the Legal and Cultural Vulnerability of Blacks. JoAnne Cornwell. *Phylon* 47, No. 4 (December 1986):285–293

South Africa—Literature

Athol Fugard. By Dennis Walder. Reviewed by Stephen Gray. *Research in African Literatures* 17, No. 2 (Summer 1986): 281–284

Frantz Fanon and Black Consciousness in Azania (South Africa). Thomas K. Ranuga. *Phylon* 47, No. 3 (September 1986):182–191

Home and Exile and Other Selections. Reviewed by James Booth. *Research in African Literatures* 17, No. 3 (Fall 1986):398–401

Olive Schreiner and After: Essays on Southern African Literature in Honor of Guy Butler. Malvern van Wyk Smith and Don Maclennan, editors. Reviewed by Dennis Walder. *Research in African Literatures* 17, No. 3 (Fall 1986):401–404

South Africa—Literature—English Language

A Bibliography of Criticism of Southern African Literature in English. Barbara Richter and Sandra Kotze, compilers. Reviewed by G. E. Gorman. *Research in African Literatures* 17, No. 3 (Fall 1986):419–421

South Africa—Literature—Journals and Diaries

The Re-interment on Buffelskop. Guy Butler, editor. Reviewed by Cherry Clayton. *Research in African Literatures* 17, No. 3 (Fall 1986):404–406

South African Censorship Board

A Guide to Political Censorship in South Africa. By Louise Silver. Reviewed by Neville Choonoo. *Research in African Literatures* 17, No. 3 (Fall 1986):416–418

South Africa—Politics

A Guide to Political Censorship in South Africa. By Louise Silver. Reviewed by Neville Choonoo. *Research in African Literatures* 17, No. 3 (Fall 1986):416–418

South Africa—Race Relations

Culture and Resistance in South Africa. Keorapetse Kgositsile. *Black Scholar* 17, No. 4 (July-August 1986):28–31

Interviews with Cheikh Anta Diop. Interview. Carlos Moore. *Journal of African Civilizations* 8, No. 1 (June 1986):249–283

Nelson Mandela: The Struggle Is My Life. By Nelson Mandela. Reviewed by Genevieve H. Wilson. *About Time* 14, No. 9 (September 1986):23–25

Some of Our Troops Are Missing: A Photo Essay on a South Africa Teach-In. Adolph Dupree. *About Time* 14, No. 5 (May 1986):18–19

The Struggle from Without: An Interview with South African Exile Tandi Gcabashe. *SAGE* 3, No. 2 (Fall 1986):48–51

Waiting: The Whites of South Africa. By Vincent Crapanzano. Reviewed by A. B. Assensoh. *Phylon* 47, No. 3 (September 1986):248

South Africa—Theater

South African Theater: Ideology and Rebellion. Notes. Andrew Horn. *Research in African Literatures* 17, No. 2 (Summer 1986): 211–233

Theater and Cultural Struggle in South Africa. By Robert Mshengu Kavanagh. Reviewed by Ian Steadman. *Research in African Literatures* 17, No. 2 (Summer 1986): 267–271

The Truthful Lie: Essays in a Sociology of African Drama. By Biodun Jeyifo. Reviewed by Elaine Savory Fido. *Research in African Literatures* 17, No. 2 (Summer 1986): 273–275

South Africa—Universities and Colleges

Explorations in the Novel: A Student's Guide to Setworks at South African Universities. C. H. Muller, editor. Reviewed by Martin Trump. *Research in African Literatures* 17, No. 3 (Fall 1986): 419–421

Student Culture and Activism in Black South African Universities. By M. O. Nkomo. Reviewed by Ernest F. Dube. *Journal of Negro Education* 55, No.2 (Spring 1986):240–244

South America—Civilization—Egyptian Influences

The Egyptian Presence in South America. Notes. R. A. Jairazbhoy. *Journal of African Civilizations* 8, No. 2 (December 1986):76–135

South Carolina—History—Civil War, 1861–1865

Gideonites and Freedmen: Adult Literacy Education at Port Royal, 1862–1865. John R. Rachal. *Journal of Negro Education* 55, No.4 (Fall 1986):453–469

Southern, Eileen

Benny Carter: A Life in American Music. Book review. *Black Perspective in Music* 14, No. 2 (Spring 1986):192–194

Lester Young. Book review. *Black Perspective in Music* 14, No. 2 (Spring 1986):194

The Music of Black Americans: A History. Book review. Doris E. McGinty. *Black Perspective in Music* 14, No. 2 (Spring 1986):185–186

Stride: The Music of Fats Waller. Book review. *Black Perspective in Music* 14, No. 2 (Spring 1986):194

Soyinka, Wole (about)

Gibb's Gibberish. Chinweizu, Onwuchekwa Jemie, and Ihechukwu Madubuike. *Research in African Literatures* 17, No. 1 (Spring 1986):48–52

"Larsony" With a Difference: An Examination of a Paragraph from *Toward the Decolonization of African Literature*. Notes. *Research in African Literatures* 17, No. 1 (Spring 1986): 39–47

Myth, Metaphor, and Syntax in Soyinka's Poetry. Notes. James Booth. *Research in African Literatures* 17, No. 1 (Spring 1986): 53–72

Soyinka as a Literary Critic. Notes. Obiajuru Maduakor. *Research in African Literatures* 17, No. 1 (Spring 1986): 1–38

The Unfolding of a Text: Soyinka's *Death and the King's Horseman*. Notes. Jasbir Jain. *Research in African Literatures* 17, No. 2 (Summer 1986): 252–260

Wole Soyinka's *The Road*. By Simon Gikandi. Reviewed by James Gibbs. *Research in African Literatures* 17, No. 4 (Winter 1986): 617–620

Soyinka, Wole—Criticism and Interpretation

Strong Breeds: Wole Soyinka and the Head of the Head of State in *A Play of Giants*. Lemuel A. Johnson. *Callaloo* 9, No. 2 (Spring 1986):354–370

Space—Employment Opportunities

Space: The Private Frontier. Edith K. Roosevelt. *Black Collegian* 16, No. 3 (January/February 1986):130–139

Spadafora, Hugo (about)

An Interview with Hugo Spadafora Four Months before His Death. Interview. Beatrix Parga de Bayon. *Caribbean Review* 15, No. 1 (Winter 1986):24–25+

Spady, James G.

The Changing Perception of C. A. Diop and His Work: The Preeminence of a Scientific Spirit. Notes. *Journal of African Civilizations* 8, No. 1 (June 1986):89–101

Spaights, Ernest, and Dixon, Harold E.

Black Youth Unemployment: Issues and Problems. *Journal of Black Studies* 16, No. 4 (June 1986):385–396

Spain—Colonies

Slave Emancipation in Cuba. The Transition to Free Labor, 1866–1899. By Rebecca J. Scott. Reviewed by David Kyle. *Caribbean Review* 15, No. 2 (Spring 1986):47

Spain and the Loss of America. By Timothy E. Anna. Reviewed by Joaquin Roy. *Caribbean Review* 15, No. 2 (Spring 1986):48

Special Education

Black Students in Special Education: Issues and Implications for Community Involvement. Thomas Serwatka and others. *Negro Educational Review* 37, No. 1 (January 1986):17–26

Speech Communication—Dissertations and Theses

Master's Theses in Progress in Selected Colleges and Universities. Mac A. Stewart. *Negro Educational Review* 37, Nos. 3–4 (July-October 1986):109

Spencer, Paula

Who Speaks for Wolf. Book review. Doris Seale. *Interracial Books for Children Bulletin* 17, Nos. 3–4 (1986):36

Spencer, Thelma L.

Teacher Education at Grambling State University: A Move Toward Excellence. *Journal of Negro Education* 55, No.3 (Summer 1986):293–303

Spiegelman, Paul J.

Remedies for Victim Group Isolation in the Work Place: Court Orders, Problem-Solving and Affirmative Action in the Post-*Stotts* Era. *Howard Law Journal* 29, No. 1 (1986):191–258

Spielberg, Steven

The Color Purple. Film review. *Interracial Books for Children Bulletin* 17, No. 2 (1986):20–21

The Color Purple. Film review. JoNina M. Abron. *Black Scholar* 17, No. 2 (March-April 1986):54

The Color Purple. Film review. Lynn Norment. *Ebony* 41, No. 4 (February 1986):146

The Color Purple. Film review. Marsha Jones. *About Time* 14, No. 1 (January 1986):18–19

Spinks, Michael (about)

Michael Spinks: The New King of the Ring. Walter Leavy. *Ebony* 41, No. 5 (March 1986):35

Spitz, Stephen L. (joint author)

See Robinson, William L.

Spleth, Janice (joint editor)

See Anyidoho, Kofi

Sports

As Gentle As the Wind: The Falcon Trap and Game Club. Adolph Dupree. *About Time* 14, No. 12 (December 1986):20–24

Springer, Robert

Le Blues authentique. Son histoire et ses thèmes. Book review. André Prévos. *Black Perspective in Music* 14, No. 2 (Spring 1986):189–190

Sprung, Barbara (joint author)

See Froschl, Merle

Squires, Gregory D.

Inequality in Metropolitan Industrial Revenue Bond Programs. *Review of Black Political Economy* 14, No. 4 (Spring 1986):37–50

S & S Numerical Control

Quality Control over Metal. Solomon J. Herbert. *Black Enterprise* 17, No. 5 (December 1986):37

Staffo, Donald F.

The Top 15—An Overview of Black College Football. *Black Collegian* 17, No. 2 (November/December 1986):29–35

Stage Management

Turning Fun into Fortune. *Black Enterprise* 16, No. 7 (February 1986):79–87

Stanback, Howard J. (joint author)

See Beverly, Creigs C.

Stanek, Lou Willett

Gleanings. Book review. Christine Jenkins. *Interracial Books for Children Bulletin* 17, No. 1 (1986):8

Staples, Robert

The Media as Opiate: Blacks in the Performing Arts. *Western Journal of Black Studies* 10, No. 1 (Spring 1986):6–11

The Political Economy of Black Family Life. *Black Scholar* 17, No. 5 (September-October 1986):2–11

Starks, George L. (Jr.)

Jazz Styles: History and Analysis. Book review. *Black Perspective in Music* 14, No. 2 (Spring 1986):188–189

Jazz Talk: The Cadence Interviews. Book review. *Black Perspective in Music* 14, No. 2 (Spring 1986):187–188

A Moment's Notice: Portraits of American Jazz Musicians. Book review. *Black Perspective in Music* 14, No. 3 (Fall 1986):312–313

Ragtime: Its History, Composers, and Music. Book review. *Black Perspective in Music* 14, No. 3 (Fall 1986):313–314

Rhythm-A-Ning: Jazz Tradition and Innovation in the 80's. Book review. *Black Perspective in Music* 14, No. 2 (Spring 1986):187

Willie and Dwike: An American Profile. Book review. *Black Perspective in Music* 14, No. 3 (Fall 1986):313

State Government

Effects of Multimember Districts on Black Representation in State Legislatures. Bernard Grofman and others. *Review of Black Political Economy* 14, No. 4 (Spring 1986):65–78

State Government—Employment Policy

Vision and Responsibility: The Role of States in Planning for Full Employment. Tom Bradley. *Urban League Review* 10, No. 1 (Summer 1986):66–70

Statues

Emancipation. Illustrated. *International Review of African American Art* 7, No. 1 (1986):42–45

Status Symbols

Status Symbols. Monique Greenwood. *Black Enterprise* 16, No. 10 (May 1986):63

Steadman, Ian

Theater and Cultural Struggle in South Africa. Book review. *Research in African Literatures* 17, No. 2 (Summer 1986): 267–271

Stein, Karen F.

Meridian: Alice Walker's Critique of Revolution. *Black American Literature Forum* 20, Nos. 1–2 (Spring/Summer 1986):129–141

Steins, Martin

Léon-Gontran Dumas: L'homme et l'oeuvre. Book review. *Research in African Literatures* 17, No. 4 (Winter 1986): 587–588

Stephens, Robert W.

The Study of Music as a Symbol of Culture: The Afro-American and Euro-American Perspectives. *Western Journal of Black Studies* 10, No. 4 (Winter 1986):180–184

Steppe-Jones, Cecilia, and others

Enhancing the Intellectual Potential of the Minority Gifted: A Shared Responsibility. *Negro Educational Review* 37, Nos. 3–4 (July-October 1986):127–129

Stereotypes (Psychology)

The Ten Biggest Myths about the Black Family. Lerone Bennett (Jr.) *Ebony* 41, No. 10 (August 1986):134

Sterling, Dorothy

We Are Your Sisters: Black Women in the Nineteenth Century. Book review. Beth Brown Utada. *Journal of Black Studies* 16, No. 4 (June 1986):453–456

Sternberg, Ilse

The Book Trade of the World, IV: Africa. Book review. *Research in African Literatures* 17, No. 1 (Spring 1986): 147–149

Stewart, James B., and Hyclak, Thomas J.

The Effects of Immigrants, Women, and Teenagers on the Relative Earnings of Black Males. *Review of Black Political Economy* 15, No. 1 (Summer 1986):92–101

Stewart, Mac A.

Master's Theses in Progress in Selected Colleges and Universities. *Negro Educational Review* 37, Nos. 3–4 (July-October 1986):92–118

Stewart, Omowale (about)

Interviews with Five Bajan Artists. Illustrated. *International Review of African American Art* 7, No. 1 (1986):45–55

Stikes, C. Scully

Black Students in Higher Education. Reviewed by Roberta Morse. *Journal of Negro Education* 55, No. 1 (Winter 1986):118–120

Stiles, Martin R.

J. Saunders Redding: Author, Scholar and Cultural Historian. *About Time* 14, No. 7 (July 1986):20–21

St. John, Bonnie (about)

Bonnie St. John: A Profile in Beauty, Brains, and Courage. Aldore Collier. *Ebony* 42, No. 1 (November 1986):134

Where There's a Will: Bonnie's Story. Bill Rhoden. *Essence* 17, No. 1 (May 1986):82

St. John, Primus

That Day/The Sun Was Especially Hot. Poem. *Callaloo* 9, No. 1 (Winter 1986):124–125

We Came to Know Each Other. Poem. *Callaloo* 9, No. 1 (Winter 1986):122–123

St. Kitts—History

Free Coloreds in the Slave Societies of St. Kitts and Grenada, 1763–1833. By Edward L. Cox. Reviewed by Keith C. Simmonds. *Phylon* 47, No. 4 (December 1986):327–328

Stockard, Russell (joint author)

See Fairchild, Halford H.

Stocks

Take Stock? Anyone Can Invest in the Stock Market. *Essence* 17, No. 6 (October 1986):116

Trading Places. Derek T. Dingle. *Black Enterprise* 17, No. 3 (October 1986):51

Winning at the Stock Options Game. Denise Lamaute. *Black Enterprise* 16, No. 12 (July 1986):23–24

Story, Rosalyn

Black Divas. *Essence* 17, No. 2 (June 1986):36

Stratton, Florence

Teaching Literature in Africa: Principles and Techniques. Book review. *Research in African Literatures* 17, No. 3 (Fall 1986): 451–453

Stredder, Kathleen (joint author)

See Ben-Tovim, Gideon

Student-Owned Business Enterprises

Dealing in Dolls. Pamela Toussaint. *Essence* 17, No. 1 (May 1986):20

Student Societies

The National Technical Association: Sixty Years Young. V. Phillip Manuel. *Black Collegian* 17, No. 2 (November/December 1986):38

See also Greek Letter Societies

Study, Method of

Making the Grade: The *Essence* Guide to College Survival. Edited by Janine C. McAdams and Elaine C. Ray. *Essence* 17, No. 4 (August 1986):67

Succeeding in College: Ten Common Mistakes to Avoid. *Black Collegian* 17, No. 1 (September/October 1986):79

Substance Abuse

Clara (Mother) Hale: Healing Baby "Junkies" with Love. Herschel Johnson. *Ebony* 41, No. 7 (May 1986):58

Drinking, Homicide, and the Black Male. Lawrence E. Gary. *Journal of Black Studies* 17, No. 1 (September 1986):15–31

How to Deal with the Cocaine Scourge: Education, Prevention and Treatment Are Keys to Controlling Deadly Drug. *Ebony* 41, No. 12 (October 1986):133

See also Addiction

Substance Abuse—Prevention

Massive Abuse of Illegal Drugs Must Be Stopped. *Ebony* 41, No. 10 (August 1986):149

Success

How to Make It in the White Corporate World. Charles Whitaker. *Ebony* 41, No. 5 (March 1986):102

Let's Hear It for Success. *Black Enterprise* 16, No. 8 (March 1986):45–53

Suicide

Black Men and Suicide. Lloyd Gite. *Essence* 17, No. 7 (November 1986):64

Sulaiman, Khalid A.

Palestine and Modern Arab Poetry. Book review. Barbara Harlow. *Race and Class* 27, No. 3 (Winter 1986):102–103

Sullivan, Leon H. (about)

The Sullivan Principles. Linn Washington. *Black Enterprise* 16, No. 6 (January 1986):23

Summers, Gerrie

Perri's Smoldering Harmony Ignites Jazz Chart. *Essence* 17, No. 5 (September 1986):29

Sunday Schools

10 Super Sunday Schools in the Black Community. By Sid Smith. Reviewed by Gayl Fowler. *Journal of Religious Thought* 43, No. 2 (Fall-Winter 1986–87):93

Sundiata, Sekou

I Want to Talk about You. Poem. *Essence* 17, No. 1 (May 1986):166

Natural Light. Poem. *Essence* 17, No. 1 (May 1986):170

Supremes

The Real Story behind the Real Dreamgirls: Mary Wilson Tells of the Triumphs and Tribulations of the Famed Supremes. *Ebony* 41, No. 12 (October 1986):44

Sussewell, Deborah R. (joint author)

See Brown-Collins, Alice R.

Sutton, William J.

Commerce and Culture. *Black Enterprise* 16, No. 11 (June 1986):48

Swahili—Literature—Bibliographies

An Annotated Bibliography of Swahili Fiction and Drama Published between 1975 and 1984. Notes. References. Elena Zubkova Bertoncini. *Research in African Literatures* 17, No. 4 (Winter 1986): 525–562

Swahili—Oral Literature

Expressing a Swahili Sense of Humor: Siu Jokes. Notes. References. Carol M. Eastman. *Research in African Literatures* 17, No. 4 (Winter 1986): 474–495

The Identity of the Hero in the Liongo Epic. References. Joseph L. Mbele. *Research in African Literatures* 17, No. 4 (Winter 1986): 464–473

Introduction: Swahili Verbal Arts. References. Carol M. Eastman. *Research in African Literatures* 17, No. 4 (Winter 1986): 459–463

Swahili—Poetry

Kibabina's "Message About Zanzibar": The Art of Swahili Poetry. References. Appendix. Jan Feidel and Ibrahim Noor Shariff. *Research in African Literatures* 17, No. 4 (Winter 1986): 496–524

Sweeney, Ronald (about)

When It's More than Just a Job. Marianne Ilaw. *Black Enterprise* 16, No. 10 (May 1986):54

Swift, John S. (Jr.)

The Move to Educational Excellence Does Not Mean a Move to Educational Equality. *Negro Educational Review* 37, Nos. 3–4 (July-October 1986):119–126

Swindell, Warren C.

The Role of Criticism in Black Popular Culture. *Western Journal of Black Studies* 10, No. 4 (Winter 1986):185–192

Symbolism in Language

The Language of Secrecy. By Beryl Bellman. Reviewed by William P. Murphy. *Research in African Literatures* 17, No. 2 (Summer 1986): 296–298

Symbolic Structures: An Exploration of the Culture of the Dowayos. By Nigel Barley. Reviewed by Wyatt MacGaffey. *Research in African Literatures* 17, No. 2 (Summer 1986): 295–296

Symbolism in Literature

Castration Symbolism in Recent Black American Fiction. Notes. Richard K. Barksdale. *CLA Journal* 29, No. 4 (June 1986):400–413

An Incomplete Circle: Repeated Images in Part Two of *Cane*. Notes. Herbert W. Rice. *CLA Journal* 29, No. 4 (June 1986):442–461

Symbolism in Music

The Study of Music as a Symbol of Culture: The Afro-American and Euro-American Perspectives. Robert W. Stephens. *Western Journal of Black Studies* 10, No. 4 (Winter 1986):180–184

Syphilis—Research

Bad Blood: The Tuskegee Syphilis Experiment. By James H. Jones. Reviewed by Ralph Watkins. *Afro-Americans in New York Life and History* 10, No.1 (January 1986):71–72

Taalamu, Chanzo

Slipping through the Cracks: The Status of Black Women. Book review. *Black Scholar* 17, No. 4 (July-August 1986):59–60

Talent Scouts

Catch a Rising Star: Savvy Rhode Island Talent Agent Polishes Up New Acts. Carol R. Scott. *Essence* 17, No. 2 (June 1986):18

Talk Shows

Oprah Winfrey: Stealing the Show. Audrey Edwards. *Essence* 17, No. 6 (October 1986):50

Riding the Ratings. Lucius Millander. *Black Enterprise* 16, No. 6 (January 1986):26

Talley, Clarence (about)

Clarence Talley: New Spiritual Art. *Black Collegian* 17, No. 1 (September/October 1986):60–61

Tate, Claudia

Black Women Writers at Work. Interviews. Reviewed by Beth Brown. *CLA Journal* 29, No. 3 (March 1986):380–383

Taubert, Sigfred, and Weidhaas, Peter (editors)

The Book Trade of the World, IV: Africa. Reviewed by Ilse Sternberg. *Research in African Literatures* 17, No. 1 (Spring 1986): 147–149

Tavernier, Bertrand

Round Midnight. Film review. Nelson George. *Essence* 17, No. 7 (November 1986):36

Taxation—Law

Tax Reform: A Minimalist Approach for Assisting the Low-Income. Lynn Burbridge. *Urban League Review* 10, No. 2 (Winter 1986–87):101–112

Tax Reform: Neither Fairness Nor Simplicity. William L. Clay. *About Time* 14, No. 10 (October 1986):21

Winning the Tax Revolution. Denise Lamaute. *Black Enterprise* 17, No. 5 (December 1986):62

Taylor, Lance

Trade and Growth: The First Annual W. Arthur Lewis Lecture. *Review of Black Political Economy* 14, No. 4 (Spring 1986):17–36

Taylor, Patricia A. (joint author)

See Gwartney-Gibbs, Patricia A.

Taylor, Peggy Ann

Educational Toys for Kids. *Essence* 17, No. 7 (November 1986):106

Saving Our Breasts. *Essence* 17, No. 2 (June 1986):62

Taylor, William

Jazz: America's Classical Music. *Black Perspective in Music* 14, No. 1 (Winter 1986):21–25

TC Catering Service

The New Entrepreneur: Catering Magician. E. D. Smith. *Black Enterprise* 16, No. 11 (June 1986):301

Tcherkezoff, Serge

Le Roi Nyamwezi, la Droite et la Gauche: Révision Comparative des Classifications Dualistes. Reviewed by Wyatt MacGarrey. *Research in African Literatures* 17, No. 2 (Summer 1986): 304–306

TEACH

See Equity and Choice Act, The

Teachers—Certification

Problems Regarding the Survival of Future Black Teachers in Education. Beverly B. Dupre. *Journal of Negro Education* 55, No. 1 (Winter 1986): 56–66

Strategies to Assure Certification and Retention of Black Teachers. Constance Carter Cooper. *Journal of Negro Education* 55, No. 1 (Winter 1986):46–55

Test Puts Arkansas Teachers' Jobs on the Line. Kenneth Maurice Jones. *Essence* 17, No. 2 (July 1986):36

Teachers—Competency Testing

The Black Educator: An Endangered Species. Beverly P. Cole. *Journal of Negro Education* 55, No.3 (Summer 1986):326–334

Do Not Buy the Conventional Wisdom: Minority Teachers Can Pass the Tests. Barbara J. Holmes. *Journal of Negro Education* 55, No.3 (Summer 1986):335–346

Excellence and Equity in Teacher Competency Testing: A Policy Perspective. Bernard R. Gifford. *Journal of Negro Education* 55, No.3 (Summer 1986):251–271

From Hurdles to Standards of Quality in Teacher Testing. Asa G. Hilliard III. *Journal of Negro Education* 55, No.3 (Summer 1986):304–315

Teacher Competency Testing: The Devil's Dilemma. W. James Popham. *Journal of Negro Education* 55, No.3 (Summer 1986):379–385

Teacher Competency Testing: Realities of Supply and Demand in This Period of Educational Reform. Gregory R. Anrig, Margaret E. Goertz, and Regina Clark McNeil. *Journal of Negro Education* 55, No.3 (Summer 1986):316–325

Teacher Testing: Adjustments for Schools, Colleges, and Departments of Education. Mary E. Dilworth. *Journal of Negro Education* 55, No.3 (Summer 1986):368–378

Teacher Testing and Assessment. Editorial. Sylvia T. Johnson. *Journal of Negro Education* 55, No.3 (Summer 1986):247–250

Testing Teacher Performance. Elaine P. Witty. *Journal of Negro Education* 55, No.3 (Summer 1986):358–367

Testing Teachers: An Overview of NEA's Position, Policy, and Involvement. Mary Hatwood Futrell and Sharon P. Robinson. *Journal of Negro Education* 55, No.3 (Summer 1986):397–404

Teachers—Competency Testing—National Examinations

The Impact of National Testing on Ethnic Minorities: With Proposed Solutions. Peter A. Garcia. *Journal of Negro Education* 55, No.3 (Summer 1986):347–357

The Making of a Profession. Albert Shanker. *Journal of Negro Education* 55, No.3 (Summer 1986):405–421

Teachers—Salaries, Pensions, Etc.

Black Teachers' Salaries and the Federal Courts Before *Brown v. Board of Education*: One Beginning for Equity. Bruce Beezer. *Journal of Negro Education* 55, No.2 (Spring 1986):200–213

Teachers—Training

The Black Educator: An Endangered Species. Beverly P. Cole. *Journal of Negro Education* 55, No.3 (Summer 1986):326–334

Increasing the Educational Opportunities of Black Students by Training Teachers in Multicultural Curriculum Development. Carl A. Grant and Gloria W. Grant. *Western Journal of Black Studies* 10, No. 1 (Spring 1986):29–33

The Memorable Teacher: Implications for Teacher Selection. Sylvia T. Johnson and Sukai Prom-Jackson. *Journal of Negro Education* 55, No.3 (Summer 1986):272–283

Professional Orientations: An Essential Domain for Teacher Testing. Andrew C. Porter and Donald J. Freeman. *Journal of Negro Education* 55, No.3 (Summer 1986):284–292

Teacher Education at Grambling State University: A Move Toward Excellence. Thelma L. Spencer. *Journal of Negro Education* 55, No.3 (Summer 1986):293–303

See also Teachers—Competency Testing

Teachers' Unions

The Teacher Rebellion. By David Seldon. Reviewed by Kenneth Jennings. *Negro Educational Review* 37, Nos. 3–4 (July-October 1986):154–155

Teaching as a Profession

The Making of a Profession. Albert Shanker. *Journal of Negro Education* 55, No.3 (Summer 1986):405–421

Technical Writing—Employment Opportunities

Careers in Technical Writing: Entering a New Era. John S. Bowie. *Black Collegian* 16, No. 3 (January/February 1986):51–54

Technology and Employment

The Impact of Cybernation Technology on Black Automotive Workers in the United States. By Samuel D. K. James. Reviewed by Julianne Malveaux. *Review of Black Political Economy* 15, No. 1 (Summer 1986):103–105

Teen-Age Marriage

From Teenage Parenthood to Polygamy: Case Studies in Black Polygamous Family Formation. Joseph W. Scott. *Western Journal of Black Studies* 10, No. 4 (Winter 1986):172–179

Teenage Pregnancy

See Adolescent Mothers

See Pregnancy—Teenagers

Telecommunications

Regulatory Policy and Minority Concerns: The Impact of Changes in Telecommunications Policy. Georgia A. Persons. *Urban League Review* 10, No. 2 (Winter 1986–87):45–63

Television Broadcasting

In Support of Black Media. Ken Smikle. *Black Enterprise* 17, No. 5 (December 1986):25

Television Broadcasting, Children's

Child's Play. Jube Shiver. *Black Enterprise* 17, No. 1 (August 1986):30

Television—Documentary Programs

Eye of the Beholder: The Africans. Adolph Dupree. *About Time* 14, No. 9 (September 1986):8–10

TV Special under Fire. *Black Enterprise* 17, No. 5 (December 1986):28

Television—Educational Broadcasting

WHMM-TV's Super Internship. Willette Coleman. *Black Collegian* 16, No. 3 (January/February 1986):118–124

WXXI-TV, Channel 21: Serving a Public and Educational Programming Mission. Anita Johnson Sims. *About Time* 14, No. 9 (September 1986):12–13

Television—History

Blacks and White T.V.: Afro-Americans in Television since 1948. By J. Fred McDonald. Reviewed by Robert L. Douglas, Sr. *Western Journal of Black Studies* 10, No. 1 (Spring 1986):44–45

Television Personalities

Fields in Bloom. Nikki Grimes. *Essence* 17, No. 4 (August 1986):84

Keshia Knight Pulliam: Coping with Success at Seven. Marilyn Marshall. *Ebony* 42, No. 2 (December 1986):27

Oprah Winfrey: Stealing the Show. Audrey Edwards. *Essence* 17, No. 6 (October 1986):50

Phylicia and Ahmad: Off-Camera and Personal. Patrice Miles. *Essence* 17, No. 2 (July 1986):85

Television—Political Influence

Jesse Jackson and Television: Black Image Presentation and Affect in the 1984 Democratic Campaign Debates. Bishetta D. Merritt. *Journal of Black Studies* 16, No. 4 (June 1986):347–367

Television Programs

227—Marla's Masterpiece. Aldore Collier. *Ebony* 42, No. 2 (December 1986):92

A Look at New TV Season. *Ebony* 41, No. 12 (October 1986):145

PBS Airs Its Series "The Africans." Armand White. *Essence* 17, No. 6 (October 1986):28

TV's Top Mom and Dad: Bill Cosby, Phylicia Ayers-Allen Are Role Model Parents on Award-Winning Television Show. Robert E. Johnson. *Ebony* 41, No. 4 (February 1986):29

Television—Psychological Aspects

Television Use and Confidence in Television by Blacks and Whites in Four Selected Years. Fred Bales. *Journal of Black Studies* 16, No. 3 (March 1986):283–291

Tembo, Mwizenge S.

Freedom Rising. Book review. *Black Scholar* 17, No. 1 (January-February 1986):47–48

Tennis Players

Zina Garrison: Aiming for the Top in Tennis. Marilyn Marshall. *Ebony* 41, No. 8 (June 1986):79

Terborg-Penn, Rosalyn

Women and Slavery in the African Diaspora: A Cross-Cultural Approach to Historical Analysis. *SAGE* 3, No. 2 (Fall 1986):11–15

Termination of Employment

See Employees, Dismissal of

Terrorism

Middle East Terrorism and the American Ideological System. Noam Chomsky. *Race and Class* 28, No. 1 (Summer 1986):1–28

Terry, Wallace

Bloods: An Oral History of the Vietnam War by Black Veterans. Reviewed by Joseph P. Reidy. *Afro-Americans in New York Life and History* 10, No.1 (January 1986):76–78

Tetteh-Lartey, Alex

African Writers at the Microphone. Book review. *Research in African Literatures* 17, No. 1 (Spring 1986): 153–155

Texas—History

Private Black Colleges in Texas: 1865–1954. By M. R. Heintze. Reviewed by Antoine Garibaldi. *Journal of Negro Education* 55, No.2 (Spring 1986):239–240

Texas Realty Ventures

Homes on the Range. Lloyd Gite. *Black Enterprise* 16, No. 9 (April 1986):22

Theater

The 1985 Audelco Awards. A. Peter Bailey. *Black Collegian* 16, No. 3 (January/February 1986):28

Black Theater. Fern Gillespie. *Crisis* 93, No. 1 (January 1986):35–46

Mumbo Jumbo Theater Company. Cecilia Loving-Sloane. *Crisis* 93, No. 8 (October 1986):13–14

Theatre. Cecilia Loving-Sloave. *Crisis* 93, No. 4 (April 1986):10–12

Theatre funding. James Luther. *Crisis* 93, No. 2 (February 1986):13

Theater, Black

Black Theater in a "Racial Democracy": The Case of the Brazilian Black Experimental Theater. Notes. Doris J. Turner. *CLA Journal* 30, No. 1 (September 1986):30–45

Black Theater Stages a Comeback. *Ebony* 42, No. 1 (November 1986):54

Theater—Africa

An Example of Syncretic Drama from Malawi: Malipenga. Notes. Christopher F. Kamlongera. *Research in African Literatures* 17, No. 2 (Summer 1986): 197–210

The Unfolding of a Text: Soyinka's *Death and the King's Horseman*. Notes. Jasbir Jain. *Research in African Literatures* 17, No. 2 (Summer 1986): 252–260

Theater—Africa—French Language

Theater and Society in Africa. By Mineke Schipper. Reviewed by Olu Obafemi. *Research in African Literatures* 17, No. 2 (Summer 1986): 271–272

Theater—Criticism and Interpretation

Drumbeats, Masks, and Metaphor: Contemporary Afro-American Theatre. By Genevieve Fabre. Reviewed by Errol Hill. *Black American Literature Forum* 20, No. 4 (Winter 1986):459–462

Theater—Dissertations and Theses

Master's Theses in Progress in Selected Colleges and Universities. Mac A. Stewart. *Negro Educational Review* 37, Nos. 3–4 (July-October 1986):109

Theater—History

Come to Laugh: A Study of African Traditional Theatre in Ghana. By Kwabena N. Bame. Reviewed by Alain Ricard. *Research in African Literatures* 17, No. 2 (Summer 1986): 287

Theater—Political Aspects

South African Theater: Ideology and Rebellion. Notes. Andrew Horn. *Research in African Literatures* 17, No. 2 (Summer 1986): 211–233

Theater Reviews

Asinamili: Addressing the South African Struggle. By Mbongeni Ngema. Reviewed by Marsha Jones. *About Time* 14, No. 9 (September 1986):11

Big Deal. By Bob Fosse. Reviewed by Charles E. Rogers. *Essence* 17, No. 1 (May 1986):44

Blood Knot. By Athol Fugard. Reviewed by Cecilia Loving-Sloane. *Crisis* 93, No. 3 (March 1986):10

Blues for a Gospel Queen. Reviewed by Cecilia Loving-Sloane. *Crisis* 93, No. 10 (December 1986):9–10

Boys of Winter. By John Pielmeier. Reviewed by Cecilia Loving-Sloane. *Crisis* 93, No. 3 (March 1986):10

Funny House of the Negro. By Adrienne Kennedy. Reviewed by Cecilia Loving-Sloane. *Crisis* 93, No. 8 (October 1986):14

Jonah and the Wonderdog. Performed by Negro Ensemble Company. Reviewed by Cecilia Loving-Sloane. *Crisis* 93, No. 6 (June/July 1986):10–11

Jonin'. By Gerard Brown. Reviewed by Cecilia Loving-Sloane. *Crisis* 93, No. 3 (March 1986):11–48

Lady Day at Emerson's Bar and Grill. Reviewed by Cecilia Loving-Sloane. *Crisis* 93, No. 10 (December 1986):9–10

The Life and Times of Malcolm X. Reviewed by Cecilia Loving-Sloane. *Crisis* 93, No. 9 (November 1986):11

Mama I Want to Sing. Vy Higginsen. Reviewed by Cecilia Loving-Sloane. *Crisis* 93, No. 8 (October 1986):12–13

Sweet Charity. Directed by Bob Fosse. Reviewed by Cecilia Loving-Sloane. *Crisis* 93, No. 7 (August/September 1986):10

Theilmann, John, and Wilhite, Al

Differences in Campaign Funds: A Racial Explanation. *Review of Black Political Economy* 15, No. 1 (Summer 1986):45–58

Theologians—United States

Horace Bushnell: Sermons. Edited by Conrad Cherry. Reviewed by Kortright Davis. *Journal of Religious Thought* 43, No. 2 (Fall-Winter 1986–87):91–92

Theology, Black

Black Gospel Music and Black Theology. Notes. Louis-Charles Harvey. *Journal of Religious Thought* 43, No. 2 (Fall-Winter 1986–87):19–37

From Sinners to Saints: The Confessions of Saint Augustine and Malcolm X. Notes. Winston A. Van Horne. *Journal of Religious Thought* 43, No. 1 (Spring-Summer 1986):76–101

Liberation Theology and Islamic Revivalism. Notes. Mohammad Yadegari. *Journal of Religious Thought* 43, No. 2 (Fall-Winter 1986–87):38–50

Religious Belief and Political Activism in Black America: An Essay. Robert Michael Franklin. *Journal of Religious Thought* 43, No. 2 (Fall-Winter 1986–87):63–72

Who Teaches Black Theology? Notes. Rufus Burrow (Jr.) *Journal of Religious Thought* 43, No. 2 (Fall-Winter 1986–87):7–18

Theology—Study and Teaching

Founding or Finding? A Theology for New Church Development. Notes. John S. Reist (Jr.) *Journal of Religious Thought* 43, No. 1 (Spring-Summer 1986):102–115

Heresy in Paradise and the Ghosts of Readers Past. Notes. Michael E. Bauman. *CLA Journal* 30, No. 1 (September 1986):59–68

The Professionalism of the Ministry of Women. Notes. Delores Causion Carpenter. *Journal of Religious Thought* 43, No. 1 (Spring-Summer 1986):59–75

Religion: An Introduction. By T. William Hall, Richard B. Pilgrim, and Ronald R. Cavanaugh. Reviewed by Kortright Davis. *Journal of Religious Thought* 43, No. 2 (Fall-Winter 1986–87):92

Who Teaches Black Theology? Notes. Rufus Burrow (Jr.) *Journal of Religious Thought* 43, No. 2 (Fall-Winter 1986–87):7–18

Therapy

Are You Blue? How to Beat Depression. Stephanie Renfrow Hamilton. *Essence* 17, No. 6 (October 1986):66

Thiong'o, Ngugi wa (about)

Critical Perspectives on Ngugi wa Thiong'o. G. D. Killam, editor. Reviewed by D. A. Maughan Brown. *Research in African Literatures* 17, No. 4 (Winter 1986): 614–617

Third World

See Developing Countries

Thomas, Debi (about)

Debi Thomas: The Nation's No. 1 Skating Sensation. Lynn Norment. *Ebony* 41, No. 7 (May 1986):147

Debi Thomas—World Figure Skating Champion. Tricia Duncan-Hall. *Black Collegian* 17, No. 1 (September/October 1986):49–52

Of Scholarship and Ice: Debi Thomas. Adolph Dupree. *About Time* 14, No. 4 (April 1986):14

With Style and Grace. Bryan Burwell. *Black Enterprise* 16, No. 11 (June 1986):52

Thomas, Maynell (about)

Inside Hollywood. Ken Smikle. *Black Enterprise* 17, No. 5 (December 1986):48

Thompson, Daniel C.

A Black Elite. Reviewed by C. J. Wiltz. *Phylon* 47, No. 4 (December 1986):328–329

Thompson, Diana R.

Bourgeois vs. Baptist. Poem. *Essence* 17, No. 1 (May 1986):93

Thompson, Gordon E.

Ambiguity in Tolson's *Harlem Gallery*. *Callaloo* 9, No. 1 (Winter 1986):159–170

Thornell, Richard P.

The Future of Affirmative Action in Higher Education. *Howard Law Journal* 29, No. 1 (1986):259–278

Tidwell, Billy J.

Disaggregating Black Unemployment. *Urban League Review* 10, No. 1 (Summer 1986):106–119

Tidwell, John Edgar

The Sage in Harlem: H. L. Mencken and the Black Writers of the 1920s. Book review. *Black American Literature Forum* 20, No. 3 (Fall 1986):341–344

Till, Emmett

Land of the Till Murder Revisited: Former *Ebony* Staffer Returns after 30 Years to Report on "The New Mississippi." Cloyte Murdock Larsson. *Ebony* 41, No. 5 (March 1986):53

Time Management

Ten Time-Management Tips. Diane Cole. *Essence* 17, No. 5 (September 1986):130

Timor, East—Resistance Movements

The Struggle in East Timor: An Interview with José Ramos Horta. *Race and Class* 28, No. 1 (Summer 1986):86–90

Tinker, Jack

Preparing for Medical School One Step at a Time. *Black Collegian* 16, No. 4 (March/April 1986):108–112

T. J.'s Gingerbread House

Fairy Tales Come True. Lloyd Gite. *Black Enterprise* 17, No. 3 (October 1986):24

Tobago—Description and Travel

Tobago: A Veritable Enchanted Isle. Misani Gayle. *Black Enterprise* 16, No. 10 (May 1986):82

Todman, Terence A. (about)

Terence Todman: Top Diplomat Ambassador to Denmark. D. Michael Cheers. *Ebony* 41, No. 4 (February 1986):67

Tolson, Melvin B. (about)

A Hamlet Rives Us: The Sonnets of Melvin B. Tolson. Notes. Gary Smith. *CLA Journal* 29, No. 3 (March 1986):261–275

Tolson, Melvin B.—Criticism and Interpretation

Ambiguity in Tolson's *Harlem Gallery*. Gordon E. Thompson. *Callaloo* 9, No. 1 (Winter 1986):159–170

Toomer, Jean—Criticism and Interpretation

An Incomplete Circle: Repeated Images in Part Two of *Cane*. Notes. Herbert W. Rice. *CLA Journal* 29, No. 4 (June 1986):442–461

A Particular Patriotism in Jean Toomer's "York Beach." Notes. Sylvia G. Noyes. *CLA Journal* 29, No. 3 (March 1986):288–294

Tordoff, William

Government and Politics in Africa. Book review. Nancy Murray. *Race and Class* 27, No. 4 (Spring 1986):107–108

Torres, Arnoldo

English-Only Movement Fosters Divisiveness. *Interracial Books for Children Bulletin* 17, Nos. 3–4 (1986):18–19

Torrijos, General Omar (about)

Getting to Know the General, The Story of an Involvement. By Graham Greene. Reviewed by Neale Pearson. *Caribbean Review* 15, No. 1 (Winter 1986):26–27 +

Panama Odyssey. By William J. Jorden. Reviewed by Ambler H. Moss, Jr. *Caribbean Review* 15, No. 1 (Winter 1986):43–44

Panama Odyssey. By William J. Jorden. Reviewed by Neale Pearson. *Caribbean Review* 15, No. 1 (Winter 1986):26–27 +

Toussaint, Pamela

Dealing in Dolls. *Essence* 17, No. 1 (May 1986):20

Towns, Jeanne R.

The Morning After. Poem. *Black American Literature Forum* 20, No. 3 (Fall 1986):271–272

The Thief. Poem. *Black American Literature Forum* 20, No. 3 (Fall 1986):271

Toxic Wastes—Removal

Cleaning up in Waste Removal. Lloyd Gite. *Black Enterprise* 17, No. 3 (October 1986):33

Toy Making

Black Toy Makers Make a Play for the Market. Karen Brailsford. *Black Enterprise* 17, No. 5 (December 1986):94

Toys

See also Educational Toys

Tracy, Steven C.

Saving the Day: The Recordings of Reverend Sutton E. Griggs. *Phylon* 47, No. 2 (June 1986):159–166

Sterling A. Brown: Building the Black Aesthetic Tradition. Book review. *Callaloo* 9, No. 1 (Winter 1986):273–275

Trade and Professional Associations

Network for Newcomers. David Dent. *Black Enterprise* 16, No. 9 (April 1986):20

Trade Routes—History

Trade and Growth: The First Annual W. Arthur Lewis Lecture. Lance Taylor. *Review of Black Political Economy* 14, No. 4 (Spring 1986):17–36

TransAfrica

How to Shape Policy through Lobbying. David C. Ruffin. *Black Enterprise* 17, No. 5 (December 1986):33

Randall Robinson: Interview. Frank McCoy. *Crisis* 93, No. 9 (November 1986):20

Transportation, Automotive—Freight

Setting New Transportation Lanes: E. L. Lawson Trucking Company, Inc. Carolyne S. Blount. *About Time* 14, No. 8 (August 1986):30–31

Travel

Vacations: Great Summer Get-Aways. *Ebony* 41, No. 7 (May 1986):72

Travel, Business

Making Money with a Proper Stranger. Silvia Rackow. *Black Enterprise* 16, No. 8 (March 1986):60

Money Saved Is Money Earned. Lynette Hazelton. *Black Enterprise* 16, No. 8 (March 1986):56

On Their Own: Women Traveling Solo. Marianne Ilaw. *Black Enterprise* 16, No. 8 (March 1986):68

Putting a Lid on Corporate Travel Costs. Wanda Whitmore. *Black Enterprise* 16, No. 8 (March 1986):63

Room and Board Meeting. Tony Bolden Davis. *Black Enterprise* 16, No. 8 (March 1986):58

Trinidad—Culture and Society

Street Life: Afro-American Culture in Urban Trinidad. By Michael Lieber. Reviewed by Keith Q. Warner. *CLA Journal* 29, No. 4 (June 1986):493–496

Trinidad—Oral Literature

Kaiso! the Trinidad Calypso: A Study of the Calypso as Oral Literature. By Keith Q. Warner. Reviewed by Jacqueline Cogdell DjeDje. *Black Perspective in Music* 14, No. 3 (Fall 1986):309

Tripp, Luke

Community Leadership and Black Former Activists of the 1960s. *Western Journal of Black Studies* 10, No. 2 (Summer 1986):86–89

From Working Class to Middle Class: Ideology and Socialization. *Negro Educational Review* 37, Nos. 3–4 (July-October 1986):144–153

Trollope, Anthony—Criticism and Interpretation

That Peculiar Book: Critics, Common Readers and *The Way We Live Now*. Notes. A. Abbott Ikeler. *CLA Journal* 30, No. 2 (December 1986):219–240

Trotta, Wayne L.

Overcoming the Fear of Writing. *Black Collegian* 17, No. 1 (September/October 1986):74–78

Trouillot, Michel-Rolph

So Spoke the Uncle. Book review. *Research in African Literatures* 17, No. 4 (Winter 1986): 596–597

Trumark Inc.

The Trumark of Excellence. Trudy Gallant. *Black Enterprise* 17, No. 1 (August 1986):39

Trump, Martin

Explorations in the Novel: A Student's Guide to Setworks at South African Universities. Book review. *Research in African Literatures* 17, No. 3 (Fall 1986): 419–421

The Short Fiction of Nadine Gordimer. Notes. *Research in African Literatures* 17, No. 3 (Fall 1986): 341–369

Tryman, Mfanya D.

Blacks and the Democratic Party: The Dissolution of an Irreconcilable Marriage. *Black Scholar* 17, No. 6 (November-December 1986):28–32

Tryman, Mfanya Donald

Reversing Affirmative Action: A Theoretical Construct. *Journal of Negro Education* 55, No.2 (Spring 1986):185–199

Tucker, Martin

Joseph Conrad and Africa. Book review. *Research in African Literatures* 17, No. 3 (Fall 1986): 440–442

Tun, Harry

Implied Warranty of Habitability. *Howard Law Journal* 29, No. 1 (1986):103–115

Turkey—Emigrants

Lowest of the Low: The Turkish Worker in West Germany. Günter Wallraff. *Race and Class* 28, No. 2 (August 1986):45–58

Turner, Doris J.

Black Theater in a "Racial Democracy": The Case of the Brazilian Black Experimental Theater. Notes. *CLA Journal* 30, No. 1 (September 1986):30–45

Turner, Jan

Affirmative Action Strong despite Reagan Opposition. *About Time* 14, No. 8 (August 1986):27

Turner, Tina (about)

Tina Turner: The Shocking Story of a Battered Wife Who Escaped to Fame and Fortune. *Ebony* 42, No. 1 (November 1986):31

Turner, William H. and Cahill, Edward J.

Blacks in Appalachia. Book review. Tommy W. Rogers. *Black Scholar* 17, No. 3 (May-June 1986):58–59

Tuskegee Airmen

Tuskegee Airmen: A Continuing Legacy. Marsha Jones. *About Time* 14, No. 10 (October 1986):22

Tuskegee Syphilis Experiment

Bad Blood: The Tuskegee Syphilis Experiment. By James H. Jones. Reviewed by Ralph Watkins. *Afro-Americans in New York Life and History* 10, No.1 (January 1986):71–72

Tutu, Mpho

Daughter of Tutu Spreads Appeal to Dismantle Apartheid. Henry Duvall. *About Time* 14, No. 5 (May 1986):18–19

Twins

Twins in the Ministry: Three Sets from Atlanta. *Ebony* 41, No. 4 (February 1986):99

Tyms, James D.

The Black Church as an Ally in the Education of Black Children. Notes. *Journal of Religious Thought* 43, No. 2 (Fall-Winter 1986–87):73–87

Uchida, Yoshiko

The Happiest Ending. Book review. Valerie Ooka Pang. *Interracial Books for Children Bulletin* 17, No. 1 (1986):7

Ude, Chema

Saved Africa. Poem. *Essence* 17, No. 4 (August 1986):159

Uhrbach, Jan R.

Language and Naming in *Dream on Monkey Mountain*. *Callaloo* 9, No. 4 (Fall 1986):578–582

Undertakers and Undertaking

Legacy of Success: A Young Mortician Inherits Her Father's Dream. Janine C. McAdams. *Essence* 17, No. 4 (August 1986):16

Unemployment

Black Unemployment and Its Link to Crime. Samuel L. Myers, Jr. *Urban League Review* 10, No. 1 (Summer 1986):98–105

Disaggregating Black Unemployment. Billy J. Tidwell. *Urban League Review* 10, No. 1 (Summer 1986):106–119

Emerging Two-Tier Wage Systems: Employment Opportunity or Wage Attack? Julianne Malveaux. *Urban League Review* 10, No. 2 (Winter 1986–87):34–44

The Impact of Unemployment on the Social Well-Being of the Black Family. Essie Tramel Seck. *Urban League Review* 10, No. 1 (Summer 1986):87–97

Notes on Implicit Contracts and the Racial Unemployment Differential. Vince Eagan. *Review of Black Political Economy* 15, No. 1 (Summer 1986):81–91

See also Employment—Economic Theory

Unger, Norman O.

Kareem Abdul-Jabbar: Veteran Cage Star Starts Life Anew after Fire and Break-Up. *Ebony* 41, No. 7 (May 1986):164

Manute Bol: Tallest Man in Pro Sports Outgrows "Tall Jokes." *Ebony* 42, No. 2 (December 1986):59

Unique High-Rise Window Cleaning

A Window of Opportunity. Lloyd Gite. *Black Enterprise* 16, No. 10 (May 1986):29

United Chem-Con Corporation

BE 100: The New Guys on the Block. Edmund Newton. *Black Enterprise* 16, No. 11 (June 1986):119

United National Bank

UNB Merger Announced. Kirk Jackson. *Black Enterprise* 17, No. 5 (December 1986):26

United Nations—Officials and Employees

A Conversation with Djibril Diallo. Audrey Edwards. *Essence* 16, No. 11 (March 1986):40

United States Air Force—Employment Opportunities

Air Force Programs and Opportunities. *Black Collegian* 16, No. 4 (March/April 1986):65–69

United States Army

See also Military History

United States Army—Employment Opportunities

Army: College-Level Opportunities. *Black Collegian* 16, No. 4 (March/April 1986):70–130

United States Army—General Officers

From High School Drop-Out to Three-Star General: Emmett Paige (Jr.) Beat the Odds and Marched All the Way to the Top. *Ebony* 41, No. 7 (May 1986):64

United States—Civilization—African Influences

Black-American Heritage? By David Tuesday Adamo. Reviewed by Emma S. Etuk. *Journal of Religious Thought* 43, No. 1 (Spring-Summer 1986):128

Death Shall Not Find Us Thinking That We Die. Notes. Ivan Van Sertima. *Journal of African Civilizations* 8, No. 1 (June 1986):7–16

United States—Civil War, 1861–1865

Gideonites and Freedmen: Adult Literacy Education at Port Royal, 1862–1865. John R. Rachal. *Journal of Negro Education* 55, No.4 (Fall 1986):453–469

United States Coast Guard—Employment Opportunities

Coast Guard Offers Opportunity, Responsibility. Day M. Boswell. *Black Collegian* 16, No. 4 (March/April 1986):64–65

United States Congress

Seeking Power beyond Their Numbers. David Hatchett. *Crisis* 93, No. 7 (August/September 1986):16

See also Congressional Black Caucus

United States Constitution—Fourteenth Amendment

Parratt v. Taylor, and Liberty Interests under the Fourteenth Amendment. Francis J. D'Eramo. *Black Law Journal* 9, No. 3 (Winter 1986):312–322

United States—Economic Policies

Welfare State vs. Warfare State: The Legislative Struggle for a Full-Employment Economy. Ronald V. Dellums. *Black Scholar* 17, No. 6 (November-December 1986):38–51

United States—Economic Policy

Gramm-Rudman and the Politics of Deficit Reduction. Linda F. Williams. *Urban League Review* 10, No. 2 (Winter 1986–87):72–83

NBA Protests Treasury's Banking Policy. David C. Ruffin. *Black Enterprise* 17, No. 1 (August 1986):17

United States—Equal Rights Legislation

Education and the Separate But Equal Doctrine. John P. Muffler. *Black Scholar* 17, No. 3 (May-June 1986):35–41

Institutional Reform and the Enforcement of the Fair Housing Laws. Ron C. Claiborne. *Black Scholar* 17, No. 3 (May-June 1986):42–48

United States—Ethnic Identity

Beyond Ethnicity: Consent and Descent in American Culture. By Werner Sollors. Reviewed by Anthony Appiah. *Black American Literature Forum* 20, Nos. 1–2 (Spring/Summer 1986):209–224

Ethnicity and Race in the USA: Toward the Twenty-First Century. By Richard D. Alba. Reviewed by Mary Ellison. *Race and Class* 27, No. 3 (Winter 1986):109–110

United States—Food Aid Policy

The Politics of Neglect: The U.S. Response to
Africa's Famine. Cherri D. Waters. *Urban League
Review* 10, No. 2 (Winter 1986–87):131–148

United States—History

Issues in American History: The Worker in
America. By Jane Claypool. Reviewed by Jan M.
Goodman. *Interracial Books for Children Bulletin*
17, No. 2 (1986):13

Race, Reform and Rebellion: The Second
Reconstruction in Black America. By Manning
Marable. Reviewed by Earl Smith. *Phylon* 47, No.
1 (March 1986):101–103

Spain and the Loss of America. By Timothy E.
Anna. Reviewed by Joaquin Roy. *Caribbean
Review* 15, No. 2 (Spring 1986):48

The United States and South Africa: History,
Civil Rights and the Legal and Cultural
Vulnerability of Blacks. JoAnne Cornwell. *Phylon*
47, No. 4 (December 1986):285–293

United States—International Relations

Is There a Black Foreign Policy? David Hatchett.
Crisis 93, No. 9 (November 1986):14–19

United States—International Relations—Africa

The Politics of Neglect: The U.S. Response to
Africa's Famine. *Urban League Review* 10, No. 2
(Winter 1986–87):131

What Black Americans and Africans Can Do for
Each Other. *Ebony* 41, No. 6 (April 1986):155

United States—International Relations—Central America

Endless War: How We Got Involved in Central
America—and What Can Be Done About It. By
James Chace. Reviewed by Alexander H.
McIntire, Jr. *Caribbean Review* 15, No. 1 (Winter
1986):44

Political Systems as Export Commodities:
Democracy and the Role of the US in Central
America. Ricardo Arias Calderon. *Caribbean
Review* 15, No. 1 (Winter 1986):21–23 +

United States—International Relations—Cuba

No Free Lunch: Food and Revolution in Cuba
Today. By Medea Benjamin, Joseph Collins, and
Michael Scott. Reviewed by James E. Austin.
Caribbean Review 15, No. 2 (Spring 1986):45

United States—International Relations—Developing Countries

Deadline: Foreign Aid to the Third World. David
C. Ruffin. *Black Enterprise* 16, No. 12 (July
1986):19

United States—International Relations—Grenada

Grenadian Party Papers: Revealing an Imaginary
Document. Short Story. Jorge I. Dominguez.
Caribbean Review 15, No. 2 (Spring 1986):16–20

United States—International Relations—Haiti

The NAACP and the American Occupation of
Haiti. Leon D. Pamphile. *Phylon* 47, No. 1 (March
1986):91–100

So Spoke the Uncle. By Jean Price-Mars.
Reviewed by Michel-Rolph Trouillot. *Research in
African Literatures* 17, No. 4 (Winter 1986):
596–597

United States—International Relations—Israel

Prophet Without Honor? The Reverend Jesse
Jackson and the Palestinian Question. Notes.
David A. Coolidge (Jr.) *Journal of Religious
Thought* 43, No. 2 (Fall-Winter 1986–87):51–62

United States—International Relations—Japan

Talks Held with Japan. Gwen McKinney. *Black
Enterprise* 17, No. 5 (December 1986):30

United States—International Relations—Mexico

En defensa de Mexico: pensamiento economico
politico. By Jesus Silva Herzog. Reviewed by
Jorge Salazar-Carrillo. *Caribbean Review* 15, No. 2
(Spring 1986):46

United States—International Relations—Middle East

Middle East Terrorism and the American
Ideological System. Noam Chomsky. *Race and
Class* 28, No. 1 (Summer 1986):1–28

United States—International Relations—Nicaragua

Nicaragua under Siege. Marlene Dixon and
Susanne Jonas, editors. Reviewed by John A.
Booth. *Caribbean Review* 15, No. 2 (Spring
1986):47

United States—International Relations—Panama

Getting to Know the General, The Story of an
Involvement. By Graham Greene. Reviewed by
Neale Pearson. *Caribbean Review* 15, No. 1
(Winter 1986):26–27 +

The Limits of Victory, The Ratification of the
Panama Canal Treaties. By George D. Moffett III.
Reviewed by Neale Pearson. *Caribbean Review* 15,
No. 1 (Winter 1986):26–27 +

Panama, Desastre...o Democracia. By Ricardo
Arias Calderon. Reviewed by Neale Pearson.
Caribbean Review 15, No. 1 (Winter 1986):26–27 +

Panama Odyssey. By William J. Jorden. Reviewed
by Ambler H. Moss, Jr. *Caribbean Review* 15,
No. 1 (Winter 1986):43–44

Panama Odyssey. By William J. Jorden. Reviewed
by Neale Pearson. *Caribbean Review* 15, No. 1
(Winter 1986):26–27 +

Red, White and Blue Paradise, The American
Canal Zone in Panama. By Herbert and Mary
Knapp. Reviewed by Neale Pearson. *Caribbean
Review* 15, No. 1 (Winter 1986):26–27 +

United States—International Relations—Philippines

The American Press and the Repairing of the Philippines. Cedric J. Robinson. *Race and Class* 28, No. 2 (August 1986):31–44

United States—International Relations—South Africa

Jesse Jackson: Rebuilding Bridges to Africa. D. Michael Cheers. *Ebony* 42, No. 2 (December 1986):132

Remember Soweto. Frank Dexter Brown. *Black Enterprise* 17, No. 2 (September 1986):17

South Africa: Challenge for Our Nation. William L. Clay. *About Time* 14, No. 8 (August 1986):13

United States Foreign Policy in Southern Africa: Past and Present. Herb Boyd. *Crisis* 93, No. 9 (November 1986):26–27

United States—International Relations—U.S.S.R.

Reflections on the Geneva Summit: The Perspective of a Journalist from the Developing World. Don Rojas. *Black Scholar* 17, No. 1 (January-February 1986):26–30

United States—International Relations—West Indies

Crossing Swords: The Psychological Divide in the Caribbean Basin. Robert A. Pastor. *Caribbean Review* 15, No. 1 (Winter 1986):3

United States Marine Corps—Employment Opportunities

Marine Corps. *Black Collegian* 16, No. 4 (March/April 1986):134–135

United States Marine Corps—Officers

Lt. General Frank E. Petersen: Top Man at Quantico. *Ebony* 42, No. 2 (December 1986):140

United States Navy—Employment Opportunities

The Civilian Navy: A Diversified Employer. Winifred R. Davis. *Black Collegian* 16, No. 3 (January/February 1986):144–150

Navy: Unparalleled Opportunities. Timothy J. Christmann. *Black Collegian* 16, No. 4 (March/April 1986):130–134

United States—Presidents—Elections

Jesse Jackson and Television: Black Image Presentation and Affect in the 1984 Democratic Campaign Debates. Bishetta D. Merritt. *Journal of Black Studies* 16, No. 4 (June 1986):347–367

Watch Jesse Run and Tell Me What You See: A First Look at Student Perceptions of the Jesse Jackson Presidential Candidacy. Oscar H. Gandy, Jr., and Larry G. Coleman. *Journal of Black Studies* 16, No. 3 (March 1986):293–306

United States—Presidents—Racial Attitudes

Affirmative Action Strong despite Reagan Opposition. Jan Turner. *About Time* 14, No. 8 (August 1986):27

United States—Race Relations

Black America in the 1980s: Rhetoric vs. Reality. Alphine W. Jefferson. *Black Scholar* 17, No. 3 (May-June 1986):2–9

Desegregation and Racial Tolerance in Academia. William A. Sampson. *Journal of Negro Education* 55, No.2 (Spring 1986):171–184

The Myth of Black Progress. By Alphonso Pinkney. Reviewed by Louis Kushnick. *Race and Class* 27, No. 3 (Winter 1986):106–108

The Post-Civil Rights Transformation of the Relationship between Blacks and Jews in the United States. Huey L. Perry and Ruth B. White. *Phylon* 47, No. 1 (March 1986):51–60

Which Way Black America? Arthur Flowers. *Essence* 17, No. 8 (December 1986):54

United States—Race Relations—History

The Rhetoric of Miscegenation: Thomas Jefferson, Sally Hemings, and Their Historians. B. R. Burg. *Phylon* 47, No. 2 (June 1986):117–127

United States—Religious Life and Customs

Religious Belief and Political Activism in Black America: An Essay. Robert Michael Franklin. *Journal of Religious Thought* 43, No. 2 (Fall-Winter 1986–87):63–72

United States Senate—Officials and Employees

The Lady in Charge: Trudi Morrison Runs Day-to-Day Operations of U.S. Senate. D. Michael Cheers. *Ebony* 41, No. 12 (October 1986):117

United States Supreme Court

Appointees May Tip Scales of Justice. Diane Camper. *Black Enterprise* 17, No. 3 (October 1986):29–30

Legal Comments: United States Supreme Court. Grover G. Hankins. *Crisis* 93, No. 10 (December 1986):30

United States Supreme Court—Decisions

Affirmative Reaction. Errol T. Louis. *Black Enterprise* 17, No. 3 (October 1986):21

Universities and Colleges

Blacks in College. By J. Fleming. Reviewed by Herman Brown. *Journal of Negro Education* 55, No.2 (Spring 1986):237–239

Teacher Testing: Adjustments for Schools, Colleges, and Departments of Education. Mary E. Dilworth. *Journal of Negro Education* 55, No.3 (Summer 1986):368–378

See also Black Studies Programs

Universities and Colleges, Black

Black Student Retention at Black Colleges and Universities: Problems. Issues, and Alternatives. Marvel Lang. *Western Journal of Black Studies* 10, No. 2 (Summer 1986):48–54

Is There a Conspiracy to Take over Black Colleges? Southern States Boost White Enrollment at Black Public Schools. Charles Whitaker. *Ebony* 41, No. 12 (October 1986):83

Private Black Colleges in Texas: 1865–1954. By M. R. Heintze. Reviewed by Antoine Garibaldi. *Journal of Negro Education* 55, No.2 (Spring 1986):239–240

Universities and Colleges, Black—Finance

Marketing Colleges. Ken Smikle. *Black Enterprise* 17, No. 4 (November 1986):24

Universities and Colleges—Administration

Chief Academic Officers at Black Colleges and Universities: A Comparison by Gender. Lea E. Williams. *Journal of Negro Education* 55, No.4 (Fall 1986):443–452

Universities and Colleges—Curricula

Increasing the Educational Opportunities of Black Students by Training Teachers in Multicultural Curriculum Development. Carl A. Grant and Gloria W. Grant. *Western Journal of Black Studies* 10, No. 1 (Spring 1986):29–33

Miller Curriculum Development Process Model: A Systematic Approach to Curriculum Development in Black Studies. Howard J. Miller. *Western Journal of Black Studies* 10, No. 1 (Spring 1986):19–28

Pursuit of Excellence: A Curriculum for Black Students to Select, Prepare for and Pracetice Careers. Adolph Dupree. *About Time* 14, No. 11 (November 1986):I-XVI

Universities and Colleges—Desegregation

The Consent Decree as an Instrument for Desegregation in Higher Education. James J. Prestage and Jewel L. Prestage. *Urban League Review* 10, No. 2 (Winter 1986–87):113–130

Defining the Situation. *Negro Educational Review* 37, No. 2 (April 1986):50

Desegregation and Racial Tolerance in Academia. William A. Sampson. *Journal of Negro Education* 55, No.2 (Spring 1986):171–184

Universities and Colleges—Employees

The Future of Affirmative Action in Higher Education. Richard P. Thornell. *Howard Law Journal* 29, No. 1 (1986):259–278

Universities and Colleges—Employment Opportunities

Wanted: Top Research Scholars. *Black Collegian* 17, No. 2 (November/December 1986):79

Universities and Colleges—Faculty

Angela Davis: Talking Tough. Interview. Cheryll Y. Greene. *Essence* 17, No. 4 (August 1986):62

Universities and Colleges—Financial Aid

Directory of Minority Assistance in Education. *About Time* 14, No. 5 (May 1986):26–28

Student-Aid. Sandra Roberts Bell. *Black Enterprise* 17, No. 2 (September 1986):59

Universities and Colleges—Graduate School

Black American Doctorates in Sociology: A Follow-up Study of their Social and Educational Origins. James E. Conyers. *Phylon* 47, No. 4 (December 1986):303–317

How to Get in Graduate School. S. Brandi Barnes. *Black Collegian* 17, No. 2 (November/December 1986):74–78

The MBA is Still a Hot Item. Dianne Hayes. *Black Collegian* 17, No. 2 (November/December 1986):81–85

The Professionalism of the Ministry of Women. Notes. Delores Causion Carpenter. *Journal of Religious Thought* 43, No. 1 (Spring-Summer 1986):59–75

Universities and Colleges—Race Relations

Black and Blue on Campus. Errol T. Louis. *Essence* 17, No. 4 (August 1986):67

Universities and Colleges—Recruitment

Recruitment: A Significant and Overlooked Component of Black College Survival. Wanzo F. Hendrix and William J. Nelson. *Western Journal of Black Studies* 10, No. 2 (Summer 1986):55–58

Universities and Colleges—Remedial Teaching

Autonomy and Theoretical Orientation of Remedial and Non-Remedial College Students. James Koutrelakos. *Journal of Negro Education* 55, No. 1 (Winter 1986):29–37

A Comparison of the Academic Performance of Black and White Freshman Students on an Urban Commuter Campus. Golam Mannan, Lillian Charleston, and Behrooz Saghafi. *Journal of Negro Education* 55, No.2 (Spring 1986):155–161

Universities and Colleges—Summer School

Summer Abroad 1987: Test Your "Study Abroad" IQ. Shirley O. Henderson. *Black Collegian* 17, No. 2 (November/December 1986):59–62

Summer Study in the Caribbean. Shirley O. Henderson. *Black Collegian* 16, No. 3 (January/February 1986):108–110

University of Ibadan

An Analysis of University of Ibadan Undergraduates' Attitudes toward Issues Incidental to the Yoruba Culture. Adedeji Awoniyi. *Negro Educational Review* 37, No. 2 (April 1986):62–70

University of Pennsylvania—Wharton School

This Dean Means Business: Marion Oliver Wants to Show Black Students the Advantages of Career in Business. Charles Whitaker. *Ebony* 41, No. 4 (February 1986):93

University of Zululand

Proceedings of the Symposium on Afro-American and African Poetry and the Teaching of Poetry in Schools. Reviewed by Ernest Mathabela. *Research in African Literatures* 17, No. 1 (Spring 1986): 133–137

Upton, James

A Social History of 20th Century Urban Riots. Reviewed by Earl Smith. Phylon 47, No. 1 (March 1986):101–103

Uptown Theatre

Commerce and Culture. William J. Sutton. *Black Enterprise* 16, No. 11 (June 1986):48

Urban Economics

The Political Economy of the Urban Ghetto. By Daniel R. Fusfield and Timothy Bates. Reviewed by Barbara A. P. Jones. *Review of Black Political Economy* 14, No. 4 (Spring 1986):99–102

Urban League of Rochester

A Call to Action: Community Crusade for Learning. Joan Marie Allen. *About Time* 14, No. 11 (November 1986):22–24

Urban Renewal

Commerce and Culture. William J. Sutton. *Black Enterprise* 16, No. 11 (June 1986):48

Urban Studies—Dissertations and Theses

Master's Theses in Progress in Selected Colleges and Universities. Mac A. Stewart. *Negro Educational Review* 37, Nos. 3–4 (July-October 1986):102, 113

Ure, Jean

What If They Saw Me Now? Book review. Michael E. Grafton. *Interracial Books for Children Bulletin* 17, No. 2 (1986):17

U.S.S.R.—International Relations—Central America

Political Systems as Export Commodities: Democracy and the Role of the US in Central America. Ricardo Arias Calderon. *Caribbean Review* 15, No. 1 (Winter 1986):21–23 +

U.S.S.R.—International Relations—Cuba

Cuba as an Oil Trader: Petroleum Deals in a Falling Market. Jorge F. Perez-Lopez. *Caribbean Review* 15, No. 2 (Spring 1986):26–29 +

Is the Cuban Economy Knowable? A National Accounting Parable. Jorge Salazar-Carrillo. *Caribbean Review* 15, No. 2 (Spring 1986):24–25

U.S.S.R.—International Relations—Grenada

Grenadian Party Papers: Revealing an Imaginary Document. Short Story. Jorge I. Dominguez. *Caribbean Review* 15, No. 2 (Spring 1986):16–20

Report Redux: Thoughts on the Imaginary Document. Short Story. Nelson P. Valdes. *Caribbean Review* 15, No. 2 (Spring 1986):21–23

U.S.S.R.-International Relations—United States

The Soviet Union is an Ally for Peace. Jack O'Dell. *Black Scholar* 17, No. 1 (January-February 1986):38–43

USX Corporation—Discriminatory Policies

Steel Suits Are Settled. Frederick H. Lowe. *Black Enterprise* 17, No. 4 (November 1986):22

Utada, Beth Brown

Jelly Roll, Jabbo and Fats: Nineteen Portraits in Jazz. Book review. *Journal of Black Studies* 16, No. 4 (June 1986):451–453

One More Day's Journey. Book review. *Journal of Black Studies* 16, No. 4 (June 1986):453–456

We Are Your Sisters: Black Women in the Nineteenth Century. Book review. *Journal of Black Studies* 16, No. 4 (June 1986):453–456

Uzoigwe, Joshua

Conversation with Israel Anyahuru. *Black Perspective in Music* 14, No. 2 (Spring 1986):126–142

Uzzell, Odell

Racial and Gender Perceptions of Marriage Role at a Predominantly Black University. *Western Journal of Black Studies* 10, No. 4 (Winter 1986):167–171

Valdes, Nelson P.

Report Redux: Thoughts on the Imaginary Document. Short Story. *Caribbean Review* 15, No. 2 (Spring 1986):21–23

Valentino (about)

Valentino and Calypso. Norman Riley. *Crisis* 93, No. 2 (February 1986):14

Van Horne, Winston A.

From Sinners to Saints: The Confessions of Saint Augustine and Malcolm X. Notes. *Journal of Religious Thought* 43, No. 1 (Spring-Summer 1986):76–101

Van Peebles, Melvin

Bold Money. Book review. Denise Lamaute. *Black Enterprise* 17, No. 3 (October 1986):88

Van Peebles, Melvin (about)

Melvin Van Peebles's Bold New Money Play. Interview. Knolly Moses. *Essence* 17, No. 2 (June 1986):12

Olive Schreiner and After: Essays on Southern African Literature in Honor of Guy Butler. Book review. *Research in African Literatures* 17, No. 3 (Fall 1986): 401–404

Walker, Alice (about)

The Color Purple: Writing to Undo What Writing Has Done. Valerie Babb. *Phylon* 47, No. 2 (June 1986):107–116

Walker, Alice—Criticism and Interpretation

Clothes and Closure in Three Novels by Black Women. Mary Jane Lupton. *Black American Literature Forum* 20, No. 4 (Winter 1986):409–421

Meridian: Alice Walker's Critique of Revolution. Karen F. Stein. *Black American Literature Forum* 20, Nos. 1–2 (Spring/Summer 1986):129–141

In Search of Our Fathers' Arms: Alice Walker's Persona of the Alienated Darling. Philip M. Royster. *Black American Literature Forum* 20, No. 4 (Winter 1986):347–370

Speech, after Silence: Alice Walker's *The Third Life of Grange Copeland*. Harold Hellenbrand. *Black American Literature Forum* 20, Nos. 1–2 (Spring/Summer 1986):113–128

Walker, Alison (about)

Where There's a Will...from Dropout to M. D. Bebe Moore Campbell. *Essence* 17, No. 6 (October 1986):79

Walker, Blair

A Dream Fulfilled. *Black Enterprise* 16, No. 9 (April 1986):25

Walker, Herschel (about)

Herschel Walker: Pro Football's New Million-Dollar Man. Walter Leavy. *Ebony* 42, No. 1 (November 1986):156

Walker, Margo

The Body Politic. *Black Enterprise* 16, No. 11 (June 1986):50

Dearborn Boycott. *Black Enterprise* 17, No. 1 (August 1986):12

Management of Policy Benefits. *Black Enterprise* 16, No. 11 (June 1986):65

Moving Forward in Stationery. *Black Enterprise* 16, No. 11 (June 1986):66

Walker, Sheila S.

The Feast of Good Death: An Afro-Catholic Emancipation Celebration in Brazil. *SAGE* 3, No. 2 (Fall 1986):27–31

Walking Night Bear

Song of the Seven Herbs. Book review. Doris Seale. *Interracial Books for Children Bulletin* 17, No. 1 (1986):9

Wall, Cheryl

Passing for What? Aspects of Identity in Nella Larsen's Novels. *Black American Literature Forum* 20, Nos. 1–2 (Spring/Summer 1986):97–111

Wallace, Charles (about)

Two Business Achievers Die. Sharon Shervington. *Black Enterprise* 17, No. 2 (September 1986):20

Waller, Don

The Motown Story. Book review. Doris E. McGinty. *Black Perspective in Music* 14, No. 3 (Fall 1986):310–311

Wallerstein, Immanuel

The Politics of the World Economy. Book review. Hamza Alavi. *Race and Class* 27, No. 4 (Spring 1986):87–90

Wallraff, Günter

Lowest of the Low: The Turkish Worker in West Germany. *Race and Class* 28, No. 2 (August 1986):45–58

Walmsley, Anne

A Handbook for Teaching African Literature. Book review. *Research in African Literatures* 17, No. 1 (Spring 1986): 149–153

Wapples, Elaine

Tracking Films by Computer. *Black Enterprise* 17, No. 2 (September 1986):27

War, Limited

Low Intensity Conflict: A War for All Seasons. Gail Reed. *Black Scholar* 17, No. 1 (January-February 1986):14–22

Ward, Jerry W. (Jr.)

The Wright Critical Canon: Looking toward the Future. *Callaloo* 9, No. 3 (Summer 1986):521–528

Ward, Wendell (about)

Cashing in on Chips. Lloyd Gite. *Black Enterprise* 16, No. 12 (July 1986):14

Ware, Reginald D.

Your Man's Sexual Health. *Essence* 17, No. 7 (November 1986):16

Warfield, William

Black-American Music Symposium: The Keynote Address. *Black Perspective in Music* 14, No. 1 (Winter 1986):7–12

Warner, Keith Q.

Kaiso! the Trinidad Calypso: A Study of the Calypso as Oral Literature. Book review. Jacqueline Cogdell DjeDje. *Black Perspective in Music* 14, No. 3 (Fall 1986):309

Street Life: Afro-American Culture in Urban Trinidad. Book review. *CLA Journal* 29, No. 4 (June 1986):493–496

Warner, Malcolm-Jamal (about)

Malcolm-Jamal Warner Has His Feet on Solid Ground. Charles E. Rogers. *Black Collegian* 17, No. 1 (September/October 1986):17–23

Warner-Vieyra, Myriam—Criticism and Intepretation

Reading Warner-Vieyra's *Juletane*. Jonathan Ngate. *Callaloo* 9, No. 4 (Fall 1986):553–564

Warren, Robert Penn—Criticism and Interpretation

Brother to Dragons : The Burden of Innocence. Notes. Friedemann K. Bartsch. *CLA Journal* 29, No. 3 (March 1986):336–351

Washburn, Patrick S.

The *Pittsburgh Courier*, and Black Workers in 1942. *Western Journal of Black Studies* 10, No. 3 (Fall 1986):109–118

A Question of Sedition: The Federal Government's Investigation of the Black Press during World War II. Book review. Reggie Major. *Black Scholar* 17, No. 5 (September-October 1986):58–59

Washington, Barbara (about)

Not Your Typical Teen Mother: Chicago Honor Student Barbara Washington Balances Books and Her Baby. *Ebony* 41, No. 10 (August 1986):67

Washington, D.C.—Economic Development

Washington: District of Commerce. Patricia A. Jones. *Black Enterprise* 16, No. 11 (June 1986):253

Washington, D.C.—Statehood Question

The State of Statehood. Gwen McKinney. *Black Enterprise* 16, No. 6 (January 1986):21

Washington, Denzel (about)

Denzel. Khephra Burns. *Essence* 17, No. 7 (November 1986):54

Washington, Dinah (about)

Wise Woman Blues. Record review. Dinah Washington. *Black Perspective in Music* 14, No. 3 (Fall 1986):318–319

Washington, Earl S. (about)

Earl S. Washington: Rising in Defense. *Black Collegian* 16, No. 3 (January/February 1986):142

Washington, Gladys J.

A World Made Cunningly: A Closer Look at Ann Petry's Short Fiction. Notes. *CLA Journal* 30, No. 1 (September 1986):14–29

Washington, Harold (about)

Harold Washington and the Politics of Race in Chicago. Manning Marable. *Black Scholar* 17, No. 6 (November-December 1986):14–23

Mayor Washington's Bid for Re-Election. Abdul Alkalimat. *Black Scholar* 17, No. 6 (November-December 1986):2–13

Washington, Linn

The Sullivan Principles. *Black Enterprise* 16, No. 6 (January 1986):23

Washington, Lorice

Good Things Come to Those Who Hustle While They Wait. Poem. *Essence* 17, No. 4 (August 1986):138

Washington, Lula

Crossing the Lines. Dance review. Martha Young. *Crisis* 93, No. 7 (August/September 1986):14

Washington, Margaret Murray (about)

International Council of Women of the Darker Races: Historical Notes from Margaret Murray Washington. Eleanor Hinton Hoytt. *SAGE* 3, No. 2 (Fall 1986):54–55

Washington, Shirley

The Jesse Jackson Phenomenon: The Crisis of Purpose in Afro-American Politics. Book review. *Black Scholar* 17, No. 6 (November-December 1986):52–53

Washington, Valora (joint author)

See Cole, O. Jackson

Washington Post

Post under Protest. Gwen McKinney. *Black Enterprise* 17, No. 5 (December 1986):26

Wasserstrom, Robert

Grassroots Development in Latin America and the Caribbean: Oral Histories of Social Change. Reviewed by Linda Miller. *Caribbean Review* 15, No. 1 (Winter 1986):41–42

Waterbury, John

Scheming for the Poor: The Politics of Redistribution in Latin America. Book review. *Caribbean Review* 15, No. 1 (Winter 1986):42–43

Waters, Cherri D.

The Politics of Neglect: The U.S. Response to Africa's Famine. *Urban League Review* 10, No. 2 (Winter 1986–87):131–148

Waters, Hazel

Banana Bottom. Book review. *Race and Class* 28, No. 2 (August 1986):106–107

Watkins, Ralph

Bad Blood: The Tuskegee Syphilis Experiment. Book review. *Afro-Americans in New York Life and History* 10, No.1 (January 1986):71–72

Watson, Dennis Rahiim

Treating My Lady Right. Poem. *Essence* 17, No. 6 (October 1986):140

Watson, Emily Strauss

Dyslexia: Understanding Reading Problems. Book review. *Interracial Books for Children Bulletin* 17, No. 2 (1986):15–16

The Elephant Man. Book review. *Interracial Books for Children Bulletin* 17, Nos. 3–4 (1986):33

First Your Penny. Book review. *Interracial Books for Children Bulletin* 17, No. 2 (1986):17–18

Including All of Us: An Early Childhood Curriculum about Disability. Book review. *Interracial Books for Children Bulletin* 17, Nos. 3–4 (1986):37–38

Stay Away from Simon! Book review. *Interracial Books for Children Bulletin* 17, No. 1 (1986):9

Watson, Stephen

Colonialism and the Novels of S. M. Coetzee. Notes. *Research in African Literatures* 17, No. 3 (Fall 1986): 370–392

Watson, Wilbur H.

Sitting Location as an Indicator of Status of Older Blacks in the Church: A Comparative Analysis of Protestants and Catholics in the Rural South. Appendix. *Phylon* 47, No. 4 (December 1986):264–275

Watson, Wilbur H., and others

Health Policy and the Black Aged. *Urban League Review* 10, No. 2 (Winter 1986–87):63–71

Wealth

Investing and Wealth Accumulation. Andrew F. Brimmer. *Black Enterprise* 17, No. 3 (October 1986):37

Wealth Redistribution

See Income Distribution

Weathers, Diane

Black Singles Face to Face. *Essence* 17, No. 8 (December 1986):58

Weaver, Mike (about)

The Weaver Triplets: Following in the Footsteps of Big Brother Mike. Aldore Collier. *Ebony* 41, No. 9 (July 1986):48

Weaver Triplets

See Weaver, Mike

Webber, Frances

Adventurers and Proletarians: The Story of Migrants in Latin America. Book review. *Race and Class* 28, No. 2 (August 1986):103–105

Webster, Ben (about)

The Horn/1944: Alternate and Incomplete Takes. Record review. Lewis Porter. *Black Perspective in Music* 14, No. 3 (Fall 1986):317–318

The Horn/1944. Record review. Lewis Porter. *Black Perspective in Music* 14, No. 3 (Fall 1986):317–318

Weddings

Big Weddings Are Back: Many Brides Follow Trend to Elaborate Ceremonies. *Ebony* 41, No. 8 (June 1986):148

Weems, Renita

Home Again. *Essence* 17, No. 8 (December 1986):63

Weems, Renita J.

Those Preachin' Women: Sermons by Black Women Preachers. Book review. *SAGE* 3, No. 2 (Fall 1986):56–57

Wei, Deborah

The Asian-American Success Myth. *Interracial Books for Children Bulletin* 17, Nos. 3–4 (1986):16–17

Weidhaas, Peter (joint editor)

See Taubert, Sigfred

Weight Loss

Diet Right! Bahamian Style. Janine C. McAdams. *Essence* 17, No. 4 (August 1986):124

Florida Man Sheds 197 Pounds to Become Body-Building Champ. *Ebony* 42, No. 2 (December 1986):86

The Good Doctor and His Diet: Indiana Health Commissioner Woodrow Myers, M. D., Sets Mark by Losing 201 Pounds. Frank White III. *Ebony* 41, No. 8 (June 1986):271

Life-Long Battle of the Bulge. *Ebony* 41, No. 6 (April 1986):52

Losing Weight Together: North Carolinians Shed Total of 211 Pounds. *Ebony* 42, No. 1 (November 1986):142

Weighing Less and Enjoying Life More. *Ebony* 41, No. 4 (February 1986):53

Weixlmann, Joe

The Way We Were, the Way We Are, the Way We Hope to Be. *Black American Literature Forum* 20, Nos. 1–2 (Spring/Summer 1986):3–7

Welburn, Craig (about)

A Day in the Life of a Franchise Owner. Marianne Ilaw. *Black Enterprise* 16, No. 7 (February 1986):128–132

Welch, Dennis M.

Queen Mab and *An Essay on Man*: Scientific Prophecy versus Theodicy. Notes. *CLA Journal* 29, No. 4 (June 1986):462–482

Weldon, Fay

Letters to Alice: On First Reading Jane Austen. Reviewed by Louis D. Mitchell. *CLA Journal* 30, No. 1 (September 1986):104–106

Welfare Dependency

Distress vs. Dependency: Changing Income Support Programs. William Darity, Jr., and Samuel Myers, Jr. *Urban League Review* 10, No. 2 (Winter 1986–87):24–33

Welfare Reform

Distress vs. Dependency: Changing Income Support Programs. William Darity, Jr., and Samuel Myers, Jr. *Urban League Review* 10, No. 2 (Winter 1986–87):24–33

Seeking Realistic Solutions to Welfare. Margaret Simms. *Black Enterprise* 17, No. 1 (August 1986):25

Wellburn, Ron

Bones and Drums. Poem. *Callaloo* 9, No. 1 (Winter 1986):126

Wells, Beverly Wiggins

Claiming the Body. Poem. *Essence* 16, No. 11 (March 1986):122

Wesley, Valerie Wilson

No-Name Baby. Short story. *Essence* 17, No. 1 (May 1986):138

West Africa—History

Mandinga Voyages across the Atlantic. Notes. Harold G. Lawrence. *Journal of African Civilizations* 8, No. 2 (December 1986):202–247

West Africa in Literature

The West African Village Novel with Particular Reference to Elechi Amadi's *The Concubine*. By George Nyamndi. Reviewed by Ernest N. Emenyonu. *Research in African Literatures* 17, No. 4 (Winter 1986): 622–625

West Germany—Migrant Labor

Lowest of the Low: The Turkish Worker in West Germany. Günter Wallraff. *Race and Class* 28, No. 2 (August 1986):45–58

West Indians—Festivals

Monarchial Liberty and Republican Slavery: West Indies Emancipation Celebrations in Upstate New York and Canada West. John R. McKivigan and Jason H. Silverman. *Afro-Americans in New York Life and History* 10, No.1 (January 1986):7–18

West Indians—United States

The West Indian Influence: Caribbean Blacks Enrich Life in the U.S. with Their Artistry, Industry, Intellect and Flair. Charles Whitaker. *Ebony* 41, No. 7 (May 1986):135

West Indies—Description and Travel

Aruba: Taking It "Poko Poko." Misani Gayle. *Black Enterprise* 16, No. 10 (May 1986):72

St. Kitts and Nevis: The Life of the Landed Gentry. E. D. Smith. *Black Enterprise* 16, No. 10 (May 1986):74

St. Lucia: Communing with Nature. Sharon Y. Lopez. *Black Enterprise* 16, No. 10 (May 1986):70

West Indies—Economic Development

Crossing Swords: The Psychological Divide in the Caribbean Basin. Robert A. Pastor. *Caribbean Review* 15, No. 1 (Winter 1986):3

West Indies—Economic History

The Caribbean. Kenneth M. Jones. *Crisis* 93, No. 6 (June/July 1986):22–27

West Indies—History

Slavery in the French Caribbean, 1625–1715: A Marxist Analysis. Clarence J. Munford. *Journal of Black Studies* 17, No. 1 (September 1986):49–69

West Indies—Literature

One Mother, Two Daughters: The Afro-American and the Afro-Caribbean Female *Bildungsroman*. Geta LeSeur. *Black Scholar* 17, No. 2 (March-April 1986):26–33

West Indies—Literature—Bibliographies

Studies in Caribbean and South American Literature: An Annual Annotated Bibliography, 1985. Brenda F. Berrian and others. *Callaloo* 9, No. 4 (Fall 1986):623–672

West Indies—Literature—French Language

Aimé Césaire's Lesson about Decolonization in *La Tragédie de Roi Christophe*. Notes. Hunt Hawkins. *CLA Journal* 30, No. 2 (December 1986):144–153

Léon-Gontran Dumas: L'homme et l'oeuvre. By Daniel Racine. Reviewed by Martin Steins. *Research in African Literatures* 17, No. 4 (Winter 1986): 587–588

Soleil éclate. Jacqueline Leiner, editor. Reviewed by Bernard Aresu. *Research in African Literatures* 17, No. 4 (Winter 1986): 588–591

West Indies—Novel—French Language

An Introduction to the French Caribbean Novel. By Beverley Ormerod. Reviewed by Suzanne Crosta. *CLA Journal* 29, No. 4 (June 1986):497–500

West Indies—Slavery

Free Coloreds in the Slave Societies of St. Kitts and Grenada, 1763–1833. By Edward L. Cox. Reviewed by Keith C. Simmonds. *Phylon* 47, No. 4 (December 1986):327–328

Monarchial Liberty and Republican Slavery: West Indies Emancipation Celebrations in Upstate New York and Canada West. John R. McKivigan and Jason H. Silverman. *Afro-Americans in New York Life and History* 10, No.1 (January 1986):7–18

Slave Populations of the British Caribbean 1807–1834. By B. W. Higman. Reviewed by Bonham C. Richardson. *Caribbean Review* 15, No. 2 (Spring 1986):46

West Indies—Travel

The Divi Hotels: Hospitality with That Caribbean Touch. Kuumba Kazi-Ferrouillet. *Black Collegian* 17, No. 1 (September/October 1986):144–146

Summer Study in the Caribbean. Shirley O. Henderson. *Black Collegian* 16, No. 3 (January/February 1986):108–110

Whalum, Wendell

Music in the Churches of Black Americans: A Critical Statement. *Black Perspective in Music* 14, No. 1 (Winter 1986):13–20

Wharton, Clifton R. (Jr.)

The Future of the Black Community: Human Capital, Family Aspirations, and Individual Motivation. *Review of Black Political Economy* 14, No. 4 (Spring 1986):9–16

Wharton, Clifton R. (Jr.) (about)

Statement on Dr. Clifton R. Wharton, Jr.—Recipient of the Samuel Z. Westerfield Award. Bernard E. Anderson. *Review of Black Political Economy* 14, No. 4 (Spring 1986):5–7

Wheat, Alan (about)

Whole Wheat. David C. Ruffin. *Black Enterprise* 17, No. 1 (August 1986):48

Wheatley, Phillis (about)

Phillis Wheatley and Her Writings. By William H. Robinson. Reviewed by Paul Edwards. *Research in African Literatures* 17, No. 1 (Spring 1986): 130–133

Wheeler, David M.

John Dennis and the Religious Sublime. Notes. *CLA Journal* 30, No. 2 (December 1986):210–218

Whigham, Marjorie

Sports Shape-Up. *Essence* 17, No. 2 (June 1986):56

Whitaker, Charles

Breakthroughs Are Her Business: Edith Irby. *Ebony* 41, No. 8 (June 1986):90

Cook County's Top Doctor: Dr. Agnes Lattimer Is the Only Black Woman to Head One of the Nation's Largest Hospitals. *Ebony* 41, No. 11 (September 1986):44

Harvey Gantt: The First Black Mayor of Charlotte, N.C., Is Proving to Be the Most Popular Mayor as Well. *Ebony* 41, No. 6 (April 1986):92

How to Make It in the White Corporate World. *Ebony* 41, No. 5 (March 1986):102

Is There a Conspiracy to Take over Black Colleges? Southern States Boost White Enrollment at Black Public Schools. *Ebony* 41, No. 12 (October 1986):83

Richard Pryor Changes Direction. *Ebony* 41, No. 9 (July 1986):132

This Dean Means Business: Marion Oliver Wants to Show Black Students the Advantages of Career in Business. *Ebony* 41, No. 4 (February 1986):93

W. E. B. Du Bois: A Final Resting Place for an Afro-American Giant. *Ebony* 42, No. 1 (November 1986):172

The West Indian Influence: Caribbean Blacks Enrich Life in the U.S. with Their Artistry, Industry, Intellect and Flair. *Ebony* 41, No. 7 (May 1986):135

White, Alvin Ellsworth (about)

A Tradition of Black Journalism. Lawrence D. Hogan. *About Time* 14, No. 2 (February 1986):11–13

White, Armand

PBS Airs Its Series "The Africans." *Essence* 17, No. 6 (October 1986):28

White, Frank (III)

The 25 Most Promising Careers for Blacks. *Ebony* 41, No. 12 (October 1986):67

Black Engineering Schools: The Big Six. *Ebony* 41, No. 7 (May 1986):96

Gambling Addicts: How to Tell if You Are Hooked. *Ebony* 41, No. 5 (March 1986):108

The Good Doctor and His Diet: Indiana Health Commissioner Woodrow Myers, M. D., Sets Mark by Losing 201 Pounds. *Ebony* 41, No. 8 (June 1986):71

How to Kick Your Bad Habits. *Ebony* 41, No. 11 (September 1986):86

Parents of Special Commitment: Single Mothers, Single Fathers and Relatives Face a Unique Challenge. *Ebony* 41, No. 10 (August 1986):88

Spreading Their Wings: Black Pilots, Totaling 175, Want to Pave the Way for More. *Ebony* 41, No. 4 (February 1986):75

White, George

Shifting Gears. *Black Enterprise* 17, No. 4 (November 1986):76

White, Landeg (joint editor)

See Mapanje, Jack, editor

White, Paulette Childress

The Watermelon Dress: Portrait of a Woman. Book review. Gerald Barrax. *Callaloo* 9, No. 1 (Winter 1986):265–269

White, Ruth B. (joint author)

See Perry, Huey L.

White House Conference on Small Business

Seeking a Big Agenda for Small Business. David C. Ruffin. *Black Enterprise* 17, No. 4 (November 1986):27

Whitman, Alden

American Reformers. Book review. Howard N. Meyer. *Interracial Books for Children Bulletin* 17, No. 1 (1986):10

Whitman, Daniel

La nouvelle génération de poètes congolais. Book review. *Research in African Literatures* 17, No. 4 (Winter 1986): 570–572

Whitmore, Wanda

Finding Security in Retirement. *Black Enterprise* 16, No. 6 (January 1986):35

Putting a Lid on Corporate Travel Costs. *Black Enterprise* 16, No. 8 (March 1986):63

Tax Tips for the Entrepreneur. *Black Enterprise* 16, No. 8 (March 1986):63

Wickham, Dewayne

Gray Tours South Africa. *Black Enterprise* 16, No. 9 (April 1986):20

Wickham, Dewayne (joint author)

See Dingle, Derek T.

WIC Program

Reagan Administration Tries to Hide Success of WIC Program. William L. Clay. *About Time* 14, No. 3 (March 1986):19

Wideman, John Edgar

Brothers and Keepers. Book review. Joe Johnson. *Crisis* 93, No. 3 (March 1986):14–48

Wideman, John Edgar—Criticism and Interpretation

The Shape of Memory in John Edgar Wideman's *Sent for You Yesterday.* John Bennion. *Black American Literature Forum* 20, Nos. 1–2 (Spring/Summer 1986):143–150

Widgery, David

Beating Time: Riot 'n' Race 'n' Rock 'n' Roll. Book review. Liz Fekete. *Race and Class* 28, No. 2 (August 1986):91–93

Wiener, Leo

Africa and the Discovery of America, Volume I. Reviewed by Phillips Barry. *Journal of African Civilizations* 8, No. 2 (December 1986):197–201

Wiener, Leo (about)

Leo Wiener—A Plea for Re-Examination. Notes. David J. M. Muffett. *Journal of African Civilizations* 8, No. 2 (December 1986):188–196

Wilder, Lawrence Douglas (about)

L. Douglas Wilder: Virginia's Lieutenant Governor. Lynn Norment. *Ebony* 41, No. 6 (April 1986):67

A Victory in Virginia. Kenneth Maurice Jones. *Black Enterprise* 16, No. 7 (February 1986):25

Wilhite, Al (joint author)

See Theilmann, John

Wilkins, Roy, with Mathews, Tom

Standing Fast: The Autobiography of Roy Wilkins. Book review. Donald Culverson. *Western Journal of Black Studies* 10, No. 3 (Fall 1986):159–160

Wilkinson, Jane

Tessere per un mosaico africano. Book review. *Research in African Literatures* 17, No. 3 (Fall 1986): 425–426

Un anglo d'Africa: Il Kenya visto dai suoi scrittori. Book review. *Research in African Literatures* 17, No. 1 (Spring 1986): 142–144

Willan, Brian

Sol Plaatje: South African Nationalist, 1876–1932. Reviewed by N. Chabani Manganyi. *Research in African Literatures* 17, No. 3 (Fall 1986): 393–395

Willhelm, Sidney M.

The Economic Demise of Blacks in America: A Prelude to Genocide? *Journal of Black Studies* 17, No. 2 (December 1986):201–254

Willhelm, Sidney M. (editor)

The Economic State of Black America. Editorial. *Journal of Black Studies* 17, No. 2 (December 1986):139–147

Williams, Darryl (about)

When It Has to Be There Now. *Black Enterprise* 16, No. 12 (July 1986):21

Williams, Delores S.

The Color of Feminism: Or Speaking the Black Woman's Tongue. Notes. *Journal of Religious Thought* 43, No. 1 (Spring-Summer 1986):42–58

Williams, George Washington

History of the Negro Race in America from 1619 to 1880: Negroes as Slaves, as Soldiers, as Citizens. Book review. Joe Johnson. *Crisis* 93, No. 4 (April 1986):12–14

Williams, James (about)

Mortgage Money for Minorities. Solomon J. Herbert. *Black Enterprise* 17, No. 1 (August 1986):19

Williams, John

La parole des femmes: Essais sur des romancières des Antilles de langue française. Book review. *Black Scholar* 17, No. 4 (July-August 1986):57

The Marxist Analyses of Manning Marable. Book reviews. *Phylon* 47, No. 3 (September 1986):248-250

Williams, John (translator)

Return of a Native Daughter: An Interview with Paule Marshall and Maryse Conde. *SAGE* 3, No. 2 (Fall 1986):52-53

Williams, John A.

The Use of Communications Media in Four Novels by Richard Wright. *Callaloo* 9, No. 3 (Summer 1986):529-539

Williams, Larry

Cheikh Anta Diop in America: An Overview. Notes. *Journal of African Civilizations* 8, No. 1 (June 1986):352-358

Williams, Larry (compiler)

Critical Essays on, and Publications by Cheikh Anta Diop. Bibliography. *Journal of African Civilizations* 8, No. 1 (June 1986):359-361

Williams, Lea E.

Chief Academic Officers at Black Colleges and Universities: A Comparison by Gender. *Journal of Negro Education* 55, No.4 (Fall 1986):443-452

Williams, Linda F.

Gramm-Rudman and the Politics of Deficit Reduction. *Urban League Review* 10, No. 2 (Winter 1986-87):72-83

Significant Trends in Black Voter Attitudes. *Black Scholar* 17, No. 6 (November-December 1986):24-28

Solving the Unemployment Problem: A Case for Full Employment. *Urban League Review* 10, No. 1 (Summer 1986):25-40

Williams, Margaret (about)

Margaret Williams and the Black Community of Owego, New York. Edward Nizalowski. *Afro-Americans in New York Life and History* 10, No.1 (January 1986):53-59

Williams, Monte, and McAdams, Janine C.

Avon Calling: Top Marketer Is VP of This Corporate Giant. *Essence* 17, No. 5 (September 1986):125

Williams, Paul R. (about)

Blacks Who Overcame the Odds. *Ebony* 42, No. 1 (November 1986):148

Williams, Sherley Anne

Dessa Rose. Book review. Doris Davenport. *Black American Literature Forum* 20, No. 3 (Fall 1986):335-340

Oral History Project. Poem. *Callaloo* 9, No. 1 (Winter 1986):127-129

Some Implications of Womanist Theory. *Callaloo* 9, No. 2 (Spring 1986):303-308

Williams, Sherley Anne (about)

A Conversation with Sherley Anne Williams about the Impact of Her New Novel, *Dessa Rose*. *Essence* 17, No. 8 (December 1986):31

Williams, Vernon J. (Jr.)

Race Relations in Sociological Theory. Book review. *Afro-Americans in New York Life and History* 10, No.1 (January 1986):74-76

Williams, Weldon C. (III)

Gladiator Traps: A Primer on the Representation of Black Athletes. *Black Law Journal* 9, No. 3 (Winter 1986):263-279

Williams-Myers, A. J.

The African Origin of Civilization: Myth or Reality. Notes. Book review. *Journal of African Civilizations* 8, No. 1 (June 1986):118-126

Willingham, Alex

Voting Rights, Government Responsibility, and Conservative Ideology. *Urban League Review* 10, No. 2 (Winter 1986-87):12-23

Willis, William A. (about)

Automotive Luxury. Yvette Moore. *Black Enterprise* 17, No. 4 (November 1986):31

Willock, Wayne

The Ruck-a-Tuck International. Illustrated. *International Review of African American Art* 7, No. 1 (1986):27

Wilmore, Gayraud S.

Black Religion and Black Radicalism: An Interpretation of the Religious History of Afro-American People. Book review. Kenneth Leech. *Race and Class* 28, No. 2 (August 1986):97-99

Wilson, Basil (joint author)

See Green, Charles

Wilson, Carter A.

Affirmative Action Defended: Exploding the Myths of a Slandered Policy. *Black Scholar* 17, No. 3 (May-June 1986):19-24

Wilson, Genevieve H.

Nelson Mandela: The Struggle Is My Life. Book review. *About Time* 14, No. 9 (September 1986):23–25

Wilson, Geraldine L.

African Images: A Look at Animals in Africa. Book review. *Interracial Books for Children Bulletin* 17, No. 2 (1986):13–14

Wilson, Harriet E. (about)

Our Nig; Or, Sketches from the Life of a Free Black. Henry Louis Gates, editor. Reviewed by Beth Brown. *CLA Journal* 29, No. 3 (March 1986):383–386

Wilson, Mary

Dreamgirls: My Life as a Supreme. Book review. Norman Riley. *Crisis* 93, No. 10 (December 1986):9

"My Life as a Supreme." *Essence* 17, No. 8 (December 1986):80

Wilson, Mary (about)

The Real Story behind the Real Dreamgirls: Mary Wilson Tells of the Triumphs and Tribulations of the Famed Supremes. *Ebony* 41, No. 12 (October 1986):44

Wilson, Melvin N.

Perceived Parental Activity of Mothers, Fathers, and Grandmothers in Three-Generational Black Families. *Journal of Black Psychology* 12, No. 2 (February 1986):43–59

Wilson, Olly

The Black-American Composer and the Orchestra in the Twentieth Century. *Black Perspective in Music* 14, No. 1 (Winter 1986):26–34

Wiltz, C. J.

A Black Elite. Book review.*Phylon* 47, No. 4 (December 1986):328–329

Window Cleaning

A Window of Opportunity. Lloyd Gite. *Black Enterprise* 16, No. 10 (May 1986):29

Wind and Thunder

Wind and Thunder. *Western Journal of Black Studies* 10, No. 4 (Winter 1986):193–194

Winfrey, Oprah (about)

Oprah Winfrey: Stealing the Show. Audrey Edwards. *Essence* 17, No. 6 (October 1986):50

Riding the Ratings. Lucius Millander. *Black Enterprise* 16, No. 6 (January 1986):26

WING

See Women, Immigration and Nationality Group

Witherspoon, William R.

Martin Luther King, Jr.: The Making of a Martyr. *Black Collegian* 16, No. 3 (January/February 1986):64–78

Martin Luther King, Jr.: To the Mountaintop. Book review. Elaine Gregg. *Black Enterprise* 16, No. 6 (January 1986):18

Martin Luther King, Jr.: To the Mountaintop. Book review. Hortense D. Lloyd. *Negro Educational Review* 37, No. 1 (January 1986):46–47

Witty, Elaine P.

Testing Teacher Performance. *Journal of Negro Education* 55, No.3 (Summer 1986):358–367

Wizowaty, Suzi

Night Journey. Book review. *Interracial Books for Children Bulletin* 17, Nos. 3–4 (1986):35–36

Wolvovitz, Barbara, and Lobel, Jules

The Enforcement of Civil Rights Statutes: The Reagan Administration's Record. *Black Law Journal* 9, No. 3 (Winter 1986):252–262

Women

See also Immigration—Women

Women, Afro-American

Black Women Face the 21st Century: Major Issues and Problems. Joyce A. Ladner. *Black Scholar* 17, No. 5 (September-October 1986):12–19

Conference Keynote Address: Sisterhood and Survival. Audre Lorde. *Black Scholar* 17, No. 2 (March-April 1986):5–7

Women, Afro-American—Psychology

The Afro-American Woman's Emerging Selves. Alice R. Brown-Collins and Deborah R. Sussewell. *Journal of Black Psychology* 13, No. 1 (August 1986):1–11

Women, Immigration and Nationality Group

Worlds Apart: Women under Immigration and Nationality Law. Book review. Busi Chaane. *Race and Class* 28, No. 1 (Summer 1986):103–107

Women in the Broadcasting Industry

After-School Specialist: Former Teacher Knows Her ABCs. Janine C. McAdams. *Essence* 17, No. 7 (November 1986):119

Child's Play. Jube Shiver. *Black Enterprise* 17, No. 1 (August 1986):30

Women in Business

Black Books by Mail. Tonya Bolden Davis. *Black Enterprise* 17, No. 3 (October 1986):26

Crisis Interview: Rose Marie Johnson. *Crisis* 93, No. 4 (April 1986):34–37

Fairy Tales Come True. Lloyd Gite. *Black Enterprise* 17, No. 3 (October 1986):24

Moving Forward in Stationery. Margo Walker. *Black Enterprise* 16, No. 11 (June 1986):66

Personal Best: Her PR Agency Put Their Best Foot Forward. Janine C. McAdams. *Essence* 17, No. 8 (December 1986):109

Women—Civil Rights—India

Gandhi on Women. Madhu Kishwar. *Race and Class* 28, No. 1 (Summer 1986):43–61

Women—Civil Service

Room at the Top: The Case of District Council 37 of the American Federation of State, County and Municipal Employees in New York City. Jewel Bellush. *SAGE* 3, No. 1 (Spring 1986):35–40

Women—Economic and Social Status

The Changing Status of Women in Cameroon: An Overview. Mario Azevedo and Gwendolyn Spencer Prater. *Western Journal of Black Studies* 10, No. 4 (Winter 1986):195–204

Slipping through the Cracks: The Status of Black Women. Edited by Margaret C. Simms and Julianne M. Malveaux. Reviewed by Chanzo Taalamu. *Black Scholar* 17, No. 4 (July-August 1986):59–60

When and Where I Enter: The Impact of Black Women on Race and Sex in America. By Paula Giddings. Reviewed by Eleanor Smith. *Western Journal of Black Studies* 10, No. 1 (Spring 1986):45–46

Women and Development in Africa: A Bibliography. *SAGE* 3, No. 2 (Fall 1986):65–69

Women in Education

Chief Academic Officers at Black Colleges and Universities: A Comparison by Gender. Lea E. Williams. *Journal of Negro Education* 55, No.4 (Fall 1986):443–452

In the Company of Educated Women: A History of Women and Higher Education in America. By Barbara Miller Solomon. Reviewed by Patricia Bell-Scott. *Journal of Negro Education* 55, No. 1 (Winter 1986):116–117

Women—Employment

The Black Woman Worker: A Minority Group Perspective on Women at Work. Sharlene Hesse-Biber. *SAGE* 3, No. 1 (Spring 1986):26–34

Black Women Face the 21st Century: Major Issues and Problems. Joyce A. Ladner. *Black Scholar* 17, No. 5 (September-October 1986):12–19

Black Women Workers in the Twentieth Century. Debra Lynn Newman. *SAGE* 3, No. 1 (Spring 1986):15–15

The Effects of Immigrants, Women, and Teenagers on the Relative Earnings of Black Males. James B. Stewart and Thomas J. Hyclak. *Review of Black Political Economy* 15, No. 1 (Summer 1986):93–101

Labor of Love, Labor of Sorrow: Black Women, Work, and the Family from Slavery to the Present. Book review. *Race and Class* 28, No. 2 (August 1986):96–97

See also Wages—Women

Women—Employment—Africa

The Dilemma of the Contribution of African Women toward and the Benefits They Derive from Economic Development. Immaculate Mary Amuge. *Western Journal of Black Studies* 10, No. 4 (Winter 1986):205–210

Women—Employment—Theses and Dissertations

Black Women as Workers: A Selected Listing of Master's Theses and Doctoral Dissertations. *SAGE* 3, No. 1 (Spring 1986):64–66

Women Executives

Avon Calling: Top Marketer Is VP of This Corporate Giant. Monte Williams and Janine C. McAdams. *Essence* 17, No. 5 (September 1986):125

Inside Hollywood. Ken Smikle. *Black Enterprise* 17, No. 5 (December 1986):48

Women—Health and Hygiene

Preventing PMS. Leslie Kotin. *Essence* 17, No. 8 (December 1986):14

Women—History

Honoring Women's History. *Interracial Books for Children Bulletin* 17, No. 1 (1986):3–5

We Are Your Sisters: Black Women in the Nineteenth Century. By Dorothy Sterling. Reviewed by Beth Brown Utada. *Journal of Black Studies* 16, No. 4 (June 1986):453–456

Women in Literature

Beyond the Myth of Confrontation: A Comparative Study of African and African-American Female Protagonists. Ebele Eko. *Phylon* 47, No. 3 (September 1986):219–229

Black Women in the Fiction of James Baldwin. By Trudier Davis. Reviewed by Ketu H. Katrak. *Black American Literature Forum* 20, No. 4 (Winter 1986):449–458

Black Women Heroes: Here's Reality, Where's the Fiction? Jewelle Gomez. *Black Scholar* 17, No. 2 (March-April 1986):8–13

Changes in the Image of the African Woman: A Celebration. Ebele Eko. *Phylon* 47, No. 3 (September 1986):210–218

Class vs. Sex: The Problem of Values in the Modern Nigerian Novel. Rhonda Cobham-Sander. *Black Scholar* 17, No. 4 (July-August 1986):17–27

Images of Blacks in Plays by Black Women. Elizabeth Brown-Guillory. *Phylon* 47, No. 3 (September 1986):230–237

Nella Larsen's Use of the Near-White Female in *Quicksand*, and *Passing*. Vashti Crutcher Lewis. *Western Journal of Black Studies* 10, No. 3 (Fall 1986):137–142

Rousseau's Julie; Or, the Maternal Odyssey. Notes. Ruth Ohayon. *CLA Journal* 30, No. 1 (September 1986):69–82

Some Implications of Womanist Theory. Sherley A. Williams. *Callaloo* 9, No. 2 (Spring 1986):303–308

Women in Literature—Africa

Ngambika: Studies of Women in African Literature. Edited by Carole Boyce Davies and Anne Adams Graves. Reviewed by Iely Burkhead Mohamed. *SAGE* 3, No. 2 (Fall 1986):59–60

Women in Literature—North Africa

Le personnage féminin dans le roman maghrébin de langue française des indépendences a 1980: Representations et fonctions. By Anne-Marie Nisbet. Reviewed by Charlotte H. Bruner. *Research in African Literatures* 17, No. 4 (Winter 1986):576–579

Women as Pastors

The Professionalism of the Ministry of Women. Notes. Delores Causion Carpenter. *Journal of Religious Thought* 43, No. 1 (Spring-Summer 1986):59–75

Women—Political Activities

The Lady in Charge: Trudi Morrison Runs Day-to-Day Operations of U.S. Senate. D. Michael Cheers. *Ebony* 41, No. 12 (October 1986):117

Women as Preachers

Those Preachin' Women: Sermons by Black Women Preachers. Edited by Ella Pearson Mitchell. Reviewed by Gayl Fowler. *Journal of Religious Thought* 43, No. 1 (Spring-Summer 1986):129–130

The Woman as Preacher. Cheryl J. Sanders. Notes. *Journal of Religious Thought* 43, No. 1 (Spring-Summer 1986):6–23

Women in Religion

The Role of Women in the Sanctified Church. Notes. Cheryl Townsend Gilkes. *Journal of Religious Thought* 43, No. 1 (Spring-Summer 1986):24–41

Work My Soul Must Have Done: Three Generations of Black Women in Ministry. Imani-Shelia Newsome. *SAGE* 3, No. 1 (Spring 1986):50–52

Women's Liberation Movement

The Color of Feminism: Or Speaking the Black Woman's Tongue. Notes. Delores S. Williams. *Journal of Religious Thought* 43, No. 1 (Spring-Summer 1986):42–58

Women—Socialization

The Necessary Bitch. Judy Simmons. *Essence* 17, No. 5 (September 1986):73

Women Writers

The Black Woman Writer and the Diaspora. Gloria T. Hull. *Black Scholar* 17, No. 2 (March-April 1986):2–4

Black Women and the Science Fiction Genre. Octavia Butler. *Black Scholar* 17, No. 2 (March-April 1986):14–18

Black Women Writers at Work. Interviews. By Claudia Tate. Reviewed by Beth Brown. *CLA Journal* 29, No. 3 (March 1986):380–383

Clothes and Closure in Three Novels by Black Women. Mary Jane Lupton. *Black American Literature Forum* 20, No. 4 (Winter 1986):409–421

A Conversation with Sherley Anne Williams about the Impact of Her New Novel, *Dessa Rose*. *Essence* 17, No. 8 (December 1986):31

Feminist Perspectives in African Fiction: Bessie Head and Buchi Emecheta. Nancy Topping Bazin. *Black Scholar* 17, No. 2 (March-April 1986):34–40

An Interview with Doris Lessing. Stephen Gray. *Research in African Literatures* 17, No. 3 (Fall 1986): 329–340

Literature of the Diaspora by Women of Color. Leah Creque-Harris. *SAGE* 3, No. 2 (Fall 1986):61–64

Nadine Gordimer: Politics and the Order of Art. Reviewed by Sheila Roberts. *Research in African Literatures* 17, No. 3 (Fall 1986): 408–411

One Mother, Two Daughters: The Afro-American and the Afro-Caribbean Female *Bildungsroman*. Geta LeSeur. *Black Scholar* 17, No. 2 (March-April 1986):26–33

A Question of Publishers and a Question of Audience. Faith Berry. *Black Scholar* 17, No. 2 (March-April 1986):41–49

Unheard Words: Women and Literature in Africa, the Arab World, Asia, the Caribbean and Latin America. Edited by Mineke Schipper. Reviewed by Margaret Marshment. *Race and Class* 28, No. 1 (Summer 1986):97–99

Women Writers—Conferences

The Black Woman Writer and the Diaspora, October 27–30, 1985. Linda Susan Beard. *SAGE* 3, No. 2 (Fall 1986):70–71

Womersley, Harold

Legends and History of the Luba. Reviewed by J. Eric Lane. *Research in African Literatures* 17, No. 2 (Summer 1986): 306–308

Wonder, Stevie (about)

The Secret Dreams of Stevie Wonder. *Ebony* 42, No. 2 (December 1986):152

Wood, Carl

A Teacher's Guide to African Literature. Book review. *Research in African Literatures* 17, No. 4 (Winter 1986): 606–609

Woodpecker (about)

Interviews with Five Bajan Artists. Illustrated. *International Review of African American Art* 7, No. 1 (1986):45–55

Woods, Jeanne M.

Shattering Those Career Myths. *Black Enterprise* 16, No. 11 (June 1986):282

Winnie Mandela: Part of My Soul Went with Him. Book review. *Black Enterprise* 17, No. 5 (December 1986):19

Woolf, Arthur G.

Market Structure and Minority Presence: Black-Owned Firms in Manufacturing. *Review of Black Political Economy* 14, No. 4 (Spring 1986):79–89

Woolman, John (about)

The Brooklyn African Woolman Benevolent Society Rediscovered. Notes. Sandra Shoiock Roff. *Afro-Americans in New York Life and History* 10, No. 2 (July 1986): 55–63

Worden, Nigel

Slavery in Dutch South Africa. Book review. Ken Jordaan. *Race and Class* 27, No. 3 (Winter 1986):104–105

Workfare Programs

Emerging Two-Tier Wage Systems: Employment Opportunity or Wage Attack? Julianne Malveaux. *Urban League Review* 10, No. 2 (Winter 1986–87):34–44

World Peace Council

Black Gains Tied Directly to Pursuit of Peace. Frances M. Beal. *Black Scholar* 17, No. 1 (January-February 1986):8–11

Worlds of Curls

Beauty Secret for Success. Solomon J. Herbert. *Black Enterprise* 16, No. 12 (July 1986):21

Worsford, Brian

Bury Me at the Marketplace: Selected Letters of Es'kia Mphahlele, 1943–1980. Book review. *Research in African Literatures* 17, No. 3 (Fall 1986): 395–398

Wren, Robert M.

J. P. Clark. Reviewed by Thomas R. Knipp. *Research in African Literatures* 17, No. 2 (Summer 1986): 278–281

Wright, Beverly Hendrix (joint author)

See Bullard, Robert D.

Wright, Jay

Ann Street. Poem. *Callaloo* 9, No. 2 (Spring 1986):309

Dandelion. Poem. *Callaloo* 9, No. 2 (Spring 1986):313

Guadalajara. Poem. *Callaloo* 9, No. 1 (Winter 1986):140–141

Guadalupe—Tonantzin. Poem. *Callaloo* 9, No. 1 (Winter 1986):130–137

Orchid. Poem. *Callaloo* 9, No. 2 (Spring 1986):311–312

Passionflower. Poem. *Callaloo* 9, No. 2 (Spring 1986):310

Tlazolteotl. Poem. *Callaloo* 9, No. 1 (Winter 1986):138–139

Wright, Josephine (compiler)

New Music. *Black Perspective in Music* 14, No. 2 (Spring 1986):196–200

Wright, Patrick

On Living in an Old Country: The National Past in Contemporary Britain. Book review. Nancy Murray. *Race and Class* 28, No. 1 (Summer 1986):93–95

Wright, Richard (about)

Richard Wright and the Chicago Renaissance. Robert Bone. *Callaloo* 9, No. 3 (Summer 1986):446–468

Wright, Richard—Criticism and Interpretation

Another Look at *Lawd Today*: Richard Wright's Tricky Apprenticeship. Notes. William Burrison. *CLA Journal* 29, No. 4 (June 1986):424–441

Avenging Angels and Mute Mothers: Black Southern Women in Wright's Fictional World. Miriam DeCosta-Willis. *Callaloo* 9, No. 3 (Summer 1986):540–549

Bigger Thomas's Quest for Voice and Audience in Richard Wright's *Native Son*. James A. Miller. *Callaloo* 9, No. 3 (Summer 1986):501–506

Black Boy: A Story of Soul-Making and a Quest for the Real. *Phylon* 47, No. 2 (June 1986):117–127

The Function of Violence in Richard Wright's *Native Son*. Robert James Butler. *Black American Literature Forum* 20, Nos. 1–2 (Spring/Summer 1986):9–25

Richard Wright and the Art of Non-Fiction: Stepping Out on the Stage of the World. John M. Reilly. *Callaloo* 9, No. 3 (Summer 1986):507–520

Richard Wright's Black Boy and the Trauma of Autobiographical Rebirth. Donald B. Gibson. *Callaloo* 9, No. 3 (Summer 1986):492–498

Richard Wright: A View from the Third World. Wimal Dissanayake. *Callaloo* 9, No. 3 (Summer 1986):481–489

The Use of Communications Media in Four Novels by Richard Wright. John A. Williams. *Callaloo* 9, No. 3 (Summer 1986):529–539

Wright, Faulkner and the South: Reconstitution and Transfiguration. Thadious M. Davis. *Callaloo* 9, No. 3 (Summer 1986):469–478

The Wright Critical Canon: Looking toward the Future. Jerry W. Ward, Jr. *Callaloo* 9, No. 3 (Summer 1986):521–528

Wright, Richard—Criticism and Interpretation—Bibliographies

The Critical Reception of Richard Wright in Japan: An Annotated Bibliography. Yoshinobu Hakutani and Toru Kiuchi. *Black American Literature Forum* 20, Nos. 1–2 (Spring/Summer 1986):27–61

Wright, Richard—Symposiums

Mississippi's Native Son: An International Symposium on Richard Wright (1908–1960). *SAGE* 3, No. 1 (Spring 1986):66

Wright, Sanford A.

Black American Politics: From the Washington Marches to Jesse Jackson, vol. 1. Book review. *Black Scholar* 17, No. 1 (January-February 1986):45–46

Writers

A Conversation with Ishmael Reed. Interview. Nelson George. *Essence* 17, No. 2 (July 1986):38

An Interview with Haki Madhubuti. Donnerae MacCann. *Interracial Books for Children Bulletin* 17, No. 2 (1986):9–11

Turning Fun into Fortune. *Black Enterprise* 16, No. 7 (February 1986):79–87

Writers—Africa

African Literature Today No. 14: Insiders and Outsiders. Eldred Durosimi Jones, editor. Reviewed by Lemuel A. Johnson. *Research in African Literatures* 17, No. 3 (Fall 1986): 442–444

Contemporary African Literature. Hal Wylie, Eileen Julien, and Russell J. Linnemann, editors. Reviewed by J. I. Okonkwo. *Research in African Literatures* 17, No. 3 (Fall 1986): 445–448

Writers—Africa—Interviews

African Writers at the Microphone. By Lee Nichols. Reviewed by Alex Tetteh-Lartey. *Research in African Literatures* 17, No. 1 (Spring 1986): 153–155

Writing Skills

Memos That Do the Job. Sharon Shervington. *Black Enterprise* 16, No. 11 (June 1986):278

Overcoming the Fear of Writing. Wayne L. Trotta. *Black Collegian* 17, No. 1 (September/October 1986):74–78

WWDB-FM

Radio Buys Settle Suits. Frederick H. Lowe. *Black Enterprise* 16, No. 8 (March 1986):14

Wyatt, Bryant N.

Cooper's Leatherstocking: Romance and the Limits of Character. Notes. *CLA Journal* 29, No. 3 (March 1986):295–308

Wylie, Hal

Black Soul, White Artifact: Fanon's Clinical Psychology and Social Theory. Book review. *Research in African Literatures* 17, No. 4 (Winter 1986): 599–601

Holy Violence: The Revolutionary Thought of Frantz Fanon. Book review. *Research in African Literatures* 17, No. 4 (Winter 1986): 597–599

Wylie, Hal, and others (editors)

Contemporary African Literature. Reviewed by J. I. Okonkow. *Research in African Literatures* 17, No. 3 (Fall 1986): 445–448

Wynn, Wilhelmina R.

Pieces of Days. *Callaloo* 9, No. 2 (Spring 1986):391–403

Yadegari, Mohammad

Liberation Theology and Islamic Revivalism. Notes. *Journal of Religious Thought* 43, No. 2 (Fall-Winter 1986–87):38–50

Yancy, Dorothy Cowser

Dorothy Bolden, Organizer of Domestic Workers: She Was Born Poor but She Would Not Bow Down. *SAGE* 3, No. 1 (Spring 1986):53–55

Yeh, Lillian

Linking Our Lives: Chinese American Women of Los Angeles. Book review. *Interracial Books for Children Bulletin* 17, Nos. 3–4 (1986):34

York, Hildreth

Bob Blackburn and the Printmaking Workshop. *Black American Literature Forum* 20, Nos. 1–2 (Spring/Summer 1986):81–95

Yoruba Language and Culture

An Analysis of University of Ibadan Undergraduates' Attitudes toward Issues Incidental to the Yoruba Culture. Adedeji Awoniyi. *Negro Educational Review* 37, No. 2 (April 1986):62–70

Young, Al

Invitation. Poem. *Callaloo* 9, No. 1 (Winter 1986):142–143

Young, Ann Venture

The College Language Association: Past, Present, Future Perfect. *CLA Journal* 29, No. 4 (June 1986):391–399

Young, L. Martina

Joe Johnson and the Repertory Dance Theater of Los Angeles. *Crisis* 93, No. 6 (June/July 1986):12

Young, Martha

Crossing the Lines. Dance review. *Crisis* 93, No. 7 (August/September 1986):14

Youngblood, Shay

Livin on the Front Line. Poem. *Essence* 17, No. 1 (May 1986):93

Yourcenar, Marguerite

Blues et gospels. Book review. André Prévos. *Black Perspective in Music* 14, No. 2 (Spring 1986):192

Youth—Attitudes

Conversations with Black Youths: A Round Table. Patrice Miles. *Essence* 17, No. 1 (May 1986):72

The Future of the Black Community: Human Capital, Family Aspirations, and Individual Motivation. Clifton R. Wharton, Jr. *Review of Black Political Economy* 14, No. 4 (Spring 1986):9–16

Youth—Employment

Black Youth Unemployment: Issues and Problems. Ernest Spaights and Harold E. Dixon. *Journal of Black Studies* 16, No. 4 (June 1986):385–396

The Effects of Immigrants, Women, and Teenagers on the Relative Earnings of Black Males. James B. Stewart and Thomas J. Hyclak. *Review of Black Political Economy* 15, No. 1 (Summer 1986):93–101

Emerging Two-Tier Wage Systems: Employment Opportunity or Wage Attack? Julianne Malveaux. *Urban League Review* 10, No. 2 (Winter 1986–87):34–44

Youth Employment and Training Programs: The YEDPA Years. Edited by Charles L. Betsey and others. Reviewed by Robert B. Hill. *Review of Black Political Economy* 15, No. 1 (Summer 1986):107–112

Youths and the Changing Job Market. Bernard E. Anderson. *Black Enterprise* 16, No. 8 (March 1986):25

Youth Employment and Demonstration Projects Act

Youth Employment and Training Programs: The YEDPA Years. Edited by Charles L. Betsey and others. Reviewed by Robert B. Hill. *Review of Black Political Economy* 15, No. 1 (Summer 1986):107–112

Youth—Finance, Personal

Piggy-Bank Savvy. Linda Barbanel. *Essence* 17, No. 1 (May 1986):16

Zaimaran, M. (joint author)

See De Shields, Jimm

Zak, Frederick and Roderick (about)

Twins in the Ministry: Three Sets from Atlanta. *Ebony* 41, No. 4 (February 1986):99

Zalin, Roslyn

Hogarth's Blacks: Images of Blacks in Eighteenth Century English Art. Book review. *Race and Class* 27, No. 4 (Spring 1986):99–100

Zamani Soweto Sisters Council

"In Memory of Our Children's Blood": Sisterhood and South African Women. Gloria I. Joseph and Audre Lorde. *SAGE* 3, No. 2 (Fall 1986):40–43

Zambia—History

A Comparative Study of Zambia and Mozambique: Africanization, Professionalization, and Bureaucracy in the African Postcolonial State. Mokubung O. Nkomo. *Journal of Black Studies* 16, No. 3 (March 1986):319–342

Zambos

Social-Scientific Perspectives on the Afro-American Arts. Rhett S. Jones. *Black American Literature Forum* 20, No. 4 (Winter 1986):443–447

Zanzibar—Oral Literature

Kibabina's "Message About Zanzibar": The Art of Swahili Poetry. References. Appendix. Jan Feidel and Ibrahim Noor Shariff. *Research in African Literatures* 17, No. 4 (Winter 1986): 496–524

Zettersten, Arne (editor)

East African Literature: An Anthology. Reviewed by Peter Nazareth. *Research in African Literatures* 17, No. 1 (Spring 1986): 140–142

Zimbabwe—History

Application of Memmi's Theory of the Colonizer and the Colonized to the Conflicts in Zimbabwe. Dickson A. Mungazi. *Journal of Negro Education* 55, No.4 (Fall 1986):518–534

Zimmern, Joan Cook (joint author)

See Smith, James H.

Zimra, Clarisse

Images et mythes d'Haiti. Book review. *Research in African Literatures* 17, No. 4 (Winter 1986): 591–593

La rive noire: De Harlem à la Seine. Book review. *Research in African Literatures* 17, No. 4 (Winter 1986): 601–603

Zins, Henryk

Joseph Conrad and Africa. Reviewed by Martin Tucker. *Research in African Literatures* 17, No. 3 (Fall 1986): 440–442

Zissner, William

Willie and Dwike: An American Profile. Book review. George L. Starks, Jr. *Black Perspective in Music* 14, No. 3 (Fall 1986):313

Zollar, Ann Creighton (about)

Dr. Ann Creighton Zollar: Assessing the Urban Black Family Experience. Carolyne S. Blount. *About Time* 14, No. 3 (March 1986):10–13

Zongo

The West African Zongo and the American Ghetto: Some Comparative Aspects of the Roles of Religious Institutions. Joseph A. Sarfoh. *Journal of Black Studies* 17, No. 1 (September 1986):71–84

Zoning, Exclusionary

The Influence of Race on Rezoning Decisions: Equality of Treatment in Black and White Census Tracts, 1955–1980. Dudley S. Hinds and Nicholas Ordway. *Review of Black Political Economy* 14, No. 4 (Spring 1986):51–63